Mercedes-Benz Sprinter
Owner's Workshop Manual

Euan Doig

Models covered

(6453 - 224)

Mercedes-Benz Sprinter Van (W906 / '2nd generation')
Medium- and long-wheelbase configurations with
2.1 litre (2143cc) 4-cylinder turbo-diesel engine (OM651)

*Does NOT cover pre-July '09 models with 2148cc (OM646) engines,
3.0 litre V6 diesel engine or models with petrol engines*

*Does NOT cover automatic transmission, 4WD versions, specialist body conversions,
or new W907 / '3rd generation' range introduced June 2018*

© Haynes Publishing 2019

ABCDE
FGHIJ
KLMNO
PQRST

A book in the **Haynes Owners Workshop Manual Series**

ISBN **978 1 78521 453 0**

British Library Cataloguing in Publication Data
A catalogue record for this book is available from the British Library.

Printed in Malaysia

Haynes Publishing
Sparkford, Yeovil, Somerset BA22 7JJ, England

Haynes North America, Inc
859 Lawrence Drive, Newbury Park, California 91320, USA

*Printed using NORBRITE BOOK 48.8gsm (CODE: 40N6533) from NORPAC; procurement system certified under Sustainable Forestry Initiative
standard. Paper produced is certified to the SFI Certified Fiber Sourcing Standard (CERT - 0094271)*

Contents

LIVING WITH YOUR MERCEDES-BENZ SPRINTER

MAINTENANCE

Contents

The Mercedes-Benz Benz Sprinter was launched in the UK in May 2006. The Sprinter has always drawn favourable reviews, because it's well designed and engineered, with a first rate build quality.

All engines are developments of well-proven ones that have appeared in many other Mercedes-Benz vehicles. The engines covered in this manual are of double overhead camshaft 4-valves-per-cylinder design, mounted longitudinally ('north-south') with the transmission mounted behind the engine.

Semi-independent suspension is fitted to the front, with a transverse leaf spring inside the front subframe and dampers bolted under the front wings and a semi-floating rear axle with leaf springs and dampers.

Anti-lock brakes (ABS), power steering, central locking, electric mirrors, and airbags are available for all vehicles. As the range has developed, more equipment has been fitted as standard, with the most recent models featuring passenger and side airbags, electric front windows, traction control and cruise control.

Provided that regular servicing is carried out in accordance with the manufacturer's recommendations, the Sprinter should prove very reliable and durable. The engine compartment is well designed, and most of the items requiring frequent attention are easily accessible.

Your Mercedes-Benz Sprinter manual

The aim of this manual is to help you get the best value from your vehicle. It can do so in several ways. It can help you decide what work must be done (even should you choose to get it done by a garage). It will also provide information on routine maintenance and servicing, and give a logical course of action and diagnosis when random faults occur. However, it is hoped that you will use the manual by tackling the work yourself. On simpler jobs it may even be quicker than booking the vehicle into a garage and going there twice, to leave and collect it. Perhaps most importantly, a lot of money can be saved by avoiding the costs a garage must charge to cover its labour and overheads.

The manual has drawings and descriptions to show the function of the various components so that their layout can be understood. Tasks are described and photographed in a clear step-by-step sequence. The illustrations are numbered by the Section number and paragraph number to which they relate – if there is more than one illustration per paragraph, the sequence is denoted alphabetically.

References to the 'left' or 'right' of the vehicle are in the sense of a person in the driver's seat, facing forwards.

Acknowledgements

Thanks are due to Draper Tools Limited, who provided some of the workshop tools, and to all those people at Sparkford who helped in the production of this manual.

We take great pride in the accuracy of information given in this manual, but vehicle manufacturers make alterations and design changes during the production run of a particular vehicle of which they do not inform us. No liability can be accepted by the authors or publishers for loss, damage or injury caused by any errors in, or omissions from, the information given.

Project vehicle

The main vehicle used in the preparation of this manual, and which appears in many of the photographic sequences, was a Mercedes-Benz Sprinter 314CDi standard-wheelbase.

Working on your car can be dangerous. This page shows just some of the potential risks and hazards, with the aim of creating a safety-conscious attitude.

General hazards

Scalding

• Don't remove the radiator or expansion tank cap while the engine is hot.
• Engine oil, transmission fluid or power steering fluid may also be dangerously hot if the engine has recently been running.

Burning

• Beware of burns from the exhaust system and from any part of the engine. Brake discs and drums can also be extremely hot immediately after use.

Crushing

• When working under or near a raised vehicle, always supplement the jack with axle stands, or use drive-on ramps. *Never venture under a car which is only supported by a jack*.
• Take care if loosening or tightening high-torque nuts when the vehicle is on stands. Initial loosening and final tightening should be done with the wheels on the ground.

Fire

• Fuel is highly flammable; fuel vapour is explosive.
• Don't let fuel spill onto a hot engine.
• Do not smoke or allow naked lights (including pilot lights) anywhere near a vehicle being worked on. Also beware of creating sparks (electrically or by use of tools).
• Fuel vapour is heavier than air, so don't work on the fuel system with the vehicle over an inspection pit.
• Another cause of fire is an electrical overload or short-circuit. Take care when repairing or modifying the vehicle wiring.
• Keep a fire extinguisher handy, of a type suitable for use on fuel and electrical fires.

Electric shock

• Ignition HT and Xenon headlight voltages can be dangerous, especially to people with heart problems or a pacemaker. Don't work on or near these systems with the engine running or the ignition switched on.

• Mains voltage is also dangerous. Make sure that any mains-operated equipment is correctly earthed. Mains power points should be protected by a residual current device (RCD) circuit breaker.

Fume or gas intoxication

• Exhaust fumes are poisonous; they can contain carbon monoxide, which is rapidly fatal if inhaled. Never run the engine in a confined space such as a garage with the doors shut.
• Fuel vapour is also poisonous, as are the vapours from some cleaning solvents and paint thinners.

Poisonous or irritant substances

• Avoid skin contact with battery acid and with any fuel, fluid or lubricant, especially antifreeze, brake hydraulic fluid and Diesel fuel. Don't syphon them by mouth. If such a substance is swallowed or gets into the eyes, seek medical advice.
• Prolonged contact with used engine oil can cause skin cancer. Wear gloves or use a barrier cream if necessary. Change out of oil-soaked clothes and do not keep oily rags in your pocket.
• Air conditioning refrigerant forms a poisonous gas if exposed to a naked flame (including a cigarette). It can also cause skin burns on contact.

Asbestos

• Asbestos dust can cause cancer if inhaled or swallowed. Asbestos may be found in gaskets and in brake and clutch linings. When dealing with such components it is safest to assume that they contain asbestos.

Special hazards

Hydrofluoric acid

• This extremely corrosive acid is formed when certain types of synthetic rubber, found in some O-rings, oil seals, fuel hoses etc, are exposed to temperatures above 4000C. The rubber changes into a charred or sticky substance containing the acid. *Once formed, the acid remains dangerous for years. If it gets onto the skin, it may be necessary to amputate the limb concerned*.
• When dealing with a vehicle which has suffered a fire, or with components salvaged from such a vehicle, wear protective gloves and discard them after use.

The battery

• Batteries contain sulphuric acid, which attacks clothing, eyes and skin. Take care when topping-up or carrying the battery.
• The hydrogen gas given off by the battery is highly explosive. Never cause a spark or allow a naked light nearby. Be careful when connecting and disconnecting battery chargers or jump leads.

Air bags

• Air bags can cause injury if they go off accidentally. Take care when removing the steering wheel and trim panels. Special storage instructions may apply.

Diesel injection equipment

• Diesel injection pumps supply fuel at very high pressure. Take care when working on the fuel injectors and fuel pipes.

⚠️ *Warning: Never expose the hands, face or any other part of the body to injector spray; the fuel can penetrate the skin with potentially fatal results.*

Remember...

DO

• Do use eye protection when using power tools, and when working under the vehicle.

• Do wear gloves or use barrier cream to protect your hands when necessary.

• Do get someone to check periodically that all is well when working alone on the vehicle.

• Do keep loose clothing and long hair well out of the way of moving mechanical parts.

• Do remove rings, wristwatch etc, before working on the vehicle – especially the electrical system.

• Do ensure that any lifting or jacking equipment has a safe working load rating adequate for the job.

DON'T

• Don't attempt to lift a heavy component which may be beyond your capability – get assistance.

• Don't rush to finish a job, or take unverified short cuts.

• Don't use ill-fitting tools which may slip and cause injury.

• Don't leave tools or parts lying around where someone can trip over them. Mop up oil and fuel spills at once.

• Don't allow children or pets to play in or near a vehicle being worked on.

The following pages are intended to help in dealing with common roadside emergencies and breakdowns. You will find more detailed fault finding information at the back of the manual, and repair information in the main chapters.

If your vehicle won't start and the starter motor doesn't turn

☐ Open the bonnet and make sure that the battery terminals are clean and tight.

☐ Switch on the headlights and try to start the engine. If the headlights go very dim when you're trying to start, the battery is probably flat. Get out of trouble by jump starting (see next page) using a friend's vehicle.

If your vehicle won't start even though the starter motor turns as normal

☐ Is there fuel in the tank?

☐ Is there moisture on electrical components under the bonnet? Switch off the ignition, then wipe off any obvious dampness with a dry cloth. Spray a water-repellent aerosol product (WD-40 or equivalent) on ignition and fuel system electrical connectors like those shown in the photos.

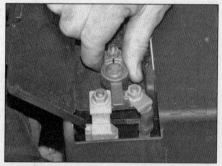

A Check the battery connections (under the passengers side footwell).

B Check the airflow meter wiring is connected securely.

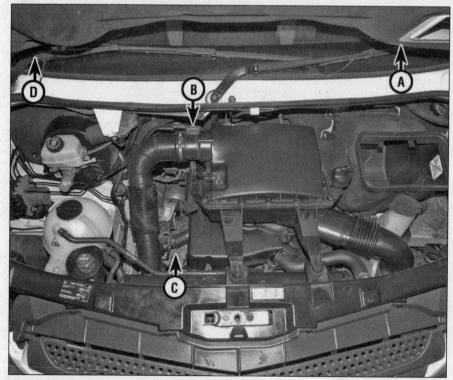

Check that electrical connections are secure (with the ignition switched off) and spray them with a water-dispersant spray like WD-40 if you suspect a problem due to damp.

C Check all the multiplugs and wiring connectors for security.

D Check that all the fuses are still in good condition and none have blown (drivers seat base fusebox shown).

Jump starting

HAYNES HINT *Jump starting will get you out of trouble, but you must correct whatever made the battery go flat in the first place. There are three possibilities:*

1 *The battery has been drained by repeated attempts to start, or by leaving the lights on.*

2 *The charging system is not working properly (alternator drivebelt slack or broken, alternator wiring fault or alternator itself faulty).*

3 *The battery itself is at fault (electrolyte low, or battery worn out).*

When jump-starting a car using a booster battery, observe the following precautions:

✔ Before connecting the booster battery, make sure that the ignition is switched off.

Caution: Remove the key in case the central locking engages when the jump leads are connected

✔ Ensure that all electrical equipment (lights, heater, wipers, etc) is switched off.

✔ Take note of any special precautions printed on the battery case.

✔ Make sure that the booster battery is the same voltage as the discharged one in the vehicle.

✔ If the battery is being jump-started from the battery in another vehicle, the two vehicles MUST NOT TOUCH each other.

✔ Make sure that the transmission is in neutral (or PARK, in the case of automatic transmission).

1 Unclip the plastic cover and connect the red jump lead to the positive (+) jump starting connection point.

2 Connect the other end of the red jump lead to the positive (+) terminal of the booster battery.

3 Connect one end of the black jump lead to the negative (-) terminal of the booster battery.

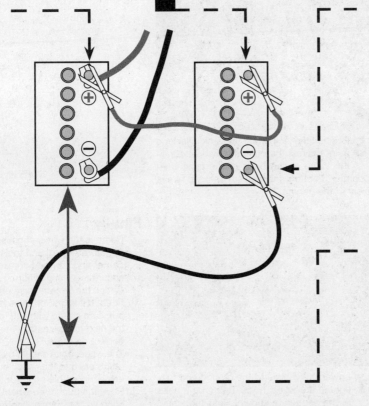

4 Connect the other end of the black jump lead negative (-) terminal to the metal connection point on the left-hand side of the engine compartment.

5 Make sure that the jump leads will not come into contact with the fan, drivebelts or other moving parts of the engine.

6 Start the engine using the booster battery and run it at idle speed. Switch on the lights, rear window demister (where fitted) and heater blower motor, then disconnect the jump leads in the reverse order of connection. Then turn off the lights, heater motor, etc.

Wheel changing

 Warning: Do not change a wheel in a situation where you risk being hit by other traffic. On busy roads, try to stop in a lay-by or a gateway. Be wary of passing traffic while changing the wheel – it is easy to become distracted by the job in hand.

Preparation

☐ When a puncture occurs, stop as soon as it is safe to do so.

☐ Park on firm level ground, if possible, and well out of the way of other traffic.

☐ Use hazard warning lights if necessary.

☐ If you have one, use a warning triangle to alert other drivers of your presence.

☐ Apply the handbrake and engage first or reverse gear.

☐ Chock the wheel diagonally opposite the one being removed – a couple of large stones will do for this.

☐ If the ground is soft, use a flat piece of wood to spread the load under the jack.

Changing the wheel

1 The jack, jack handle and wheel brace are located in a stowage compartment in the front passenger footwell. Remove the trim cover, and then undo the retaining straps to remove them from the footwell.

2 Prise up the plastic caps, then slacken the two bolts in the rear crossmember of the vehicle securing the spare wheel carrier.

3 Rotate the two bolts anti-clockwise until the spare wheel carrier can be released and the spare wheel removed.

4 Where applicable, prise off the wheel bolt plastic covers or wheel trim for access to the wheel bolts. Slacken each wheel bolt by half a turn.

5 Position the jack under the vehicle jacking point nearest the punctured wheel. Close the valve at the base of the jack, then operate the pump mechanism until the tyre is clear of the ground.

6 Undo the wheel bolts and remove the wheel. Fit the spare wheel and screw in the bolts. Lightly tighten the bolts with the wheel brace.

7 Lower the vehicle to the ground and fully tighten the wheel bolts. Tighten the bolts in the sequence shown. Refit the wheel bolt covers or wheel trims as applicable.

Finally . . .

☐ Remove the wheel chocks. Stow the punctured wheel and tools back in the carrier and stowage compartment, and secure them in position.

☐ Check the tyre pressure on the tyre just fitted. If it is low, or if you don't have a pressure gauge with you, drive slowly to the next garage and inflate the tyre to the correct pressure.

☐ The wheel bolts should be slackened and retightened to the specified torque at the earliest possible opportunity.

☐ Have the punctured wheel repaired as soon as possible, or another puncture will leave you stranded.

Identifying leaks

Puddles on the garage floor or drive, or obvious wetness under the bonnet or underneath the car, suggest a leak that needs investigating. It can sometimes be difficult to decide where the leak is coming from, especially if an engine undershield is fitted. Leaking oil or fluid can also be blown rearwards by the passage of air under the car, giving a false impression of where the problem lies.

 Warning: Most automotive oils and fluids are poisonous. Wash them off skin, and change out of contaminated clothing, without delay.

 The smell of a fluid leaking from the car may provide a clue to what's leaking. Some fluids are distinctively coloured. It may help to remove the engine undershield, clean the car carefully and to park it over some clean paper overnight as an aid to locating the source of the leak. Remember that some leaks may only occur while the engine is running.

Sump oil

Engine oil may leak from the drain plug...

Oil from filter

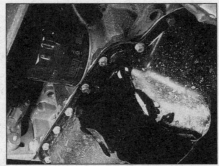

...or from the base of the oil filter.

Gearbox oil

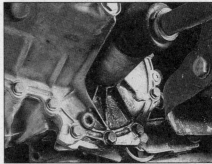

Gearbox oil can leak from the seals at the inboard ends of the driveshafts.

Antifreeze

Leaking antifreeze often leaves a crystalline deposit like this.

Brake fluid

A leak occurring at a wheel is almost certainly brake fluid.

Power steering fluid

Power steering fluid may leak from the pipe connectors on the steering rack.

Towing

When all else fails, you may find yourself having to get a tow home – or of course you may be helping somebody else. Long-distance recovery should only be done by a garage or breakdown service. For shorter distances, DIY towing using another vehicle is easy enough, but observe the following points:

☐ Use a proper tow-rope – they are not expensive. The vehicle being towed must display an ON TOW sign in its rear window.

☐ Always turn the ignition key to the 'On' position when the vehicle is being towed, so that the steering lock is released, and the direction indicator and brake lights work.

☐ Before being towed, release the handbrake and make sure the transmission is in neutral.

☐ Note that greater-than-usual pedal pressure will be required to operate the brakes, since the vacuum servo unit is only operational with the engine running.

☐ The driver of the vehicle being towed must keep the tow-rope taut at all times to avoid snatching.

☐ Make sure that both drivers know the route before setting off.

☐ Only drive at moderate speeds and keep the distance towed to a minimum. Drive smoothly and allow plenty of time for slowing down at junctions.

Introduction

There are some very simple checks which need only take a few minutes to carry out, but which could save you a lot of inconvenience and expense.

These *Weekly checks* require no great skill or special tools, and the small amount of time they take to perform could prove to be very well spent, for example:

☐ Keeping an eye on tyre condition and pressures, will not only help to stop them wearing out prematurely, but could also save your life.

☐ Many breakdowns are caused by electrical problems. Battery-related faults are particularly common, and a quick check on a regular basis will often prevent the majority of these.

☐ If your vehicle develops a brake fluid leak, the first time you might know about it is when your brakes don't work properly. Checking the level regularly will give advance warning of this kind of problem.

☐ If the oil or coolant levels run low, the cost of repairing any engine damage will be far greater than fixing the leak, for example.

Underbonnet check points

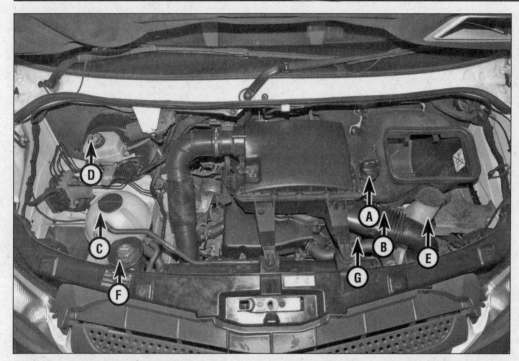

◀ **2.1 litre engine**

A *Engine oil filler cap*

B *Engine oil level dipstick*

C *Coolant reservoir*

D *Brake and clutch fluid reservoir*

E *Washer fluid reservoir*

F *AdBlue reservoir*

G *Power steering fluid reservoir*

Engine oil level

Before you start

✔ Make sure that the vehicle is on level ground.
✔ Check the oil level before the vehicle is driven, or at least 5 minutes after the engine has been switched off.

 HAYNES HINT *If the oil is checked immediately after driving the vehicle, some of the oil will remain in the upper engine components, resulting in an inaccurate reading on the dipstick.*

The correct oil

Modern engines place great demands on their oil. It is very important that the correct oil for your vehicle is used (see *Lubricants and fluids*).

Vehicle care

● If you have to add oil frequently, you should check whether you have any oil leaks. Place some clean paper under the vehicle overnight, and check for stains in the morning. If there are no leaks, then the engine may be burning oil.
● Always maintain the level between the upper and lower dipstick marks (see photo 3). If the level is too low, severe engine damage may occur. Oil seal failure may result if the engine is overfilled by adding too much oil.

1 The dipstick is brightly coloured (yellow) for easy identification. Withdraw the dipstick.

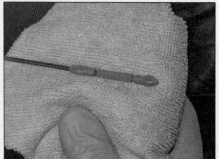

2 Using a clean rag or paper towel remove all the oil from the dipstick. Insert the clean dipstick into the tube asfar as it will go, and then withdraw it again.

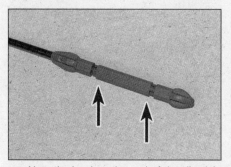

3 Note the level on the end of the dipstick, which should be between the upper (MAX) mark and the lower (MIN) mark. Approximately 1.5 litres of oil will raise the level from the lower mark to the upper mark.

4 Unscrew the oil filler cap and place some cloth rags around the filler cap aperture, then top-up the level. Add theoil slowly, checking the level on the dipstick frequently. Avoid overfilling (see *Vehicle care*).

Coolant level

 Warning: Do not attempt to remove the expansion tank pressure cap when the engine is hot, as there is a very great risk of scalding. Do not leave open containers of coolant about, as it is poisonous.

Vehicle care

● With a sealed-type cooling system, adding coolant should not be necessary on a regular basis. If frequent topping-up is required, it is likely there is a leak. Check the radiator, all hoses and joint faces for signs of staining or wetness, and rectify as necessary.

● It is important that antifreeze is used in the cooling system all year round, not just during the winter months. Don't top-up with water alone, as the antifreeze will become diluted.

1 The coolant level varies with the temperature of the engine. When the engine is cold, the coolant level should be upto the level marker (MAX) inside the filler neck of the expansion tank.

2 If topping-up is necessary, wait until the engine is cold. Slowly unscrew the cap to release any pressure present in the cooling system, and then remove the cap.

3 Add a mixture of water and the specified antifreeze (see *Lubricants and fluids*) to the expansion tank until the coolant level is up tothe (MAX) level marker. Refit the cap and tighten it securely.

Brake and clutch fluid level

Warning:
• **Brake fluid can harm your eyes and damage painted surfaces, so use extreme caution when handling and pouring it.**
• **Do not use fluid that has been standing open for some time, as** it absorbs moisture from the air, which can cause a dangerous loss of braking effectiveness.

Safety first!

● If the reservoir requires repeated topping-up this is an indication of a fluid leak somewhere in the system, which should be investigated immediately.

● If a leak is suspected, the vehicle should not be driven until the braking system has been checked. Never take any risks where brakes are concerned

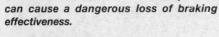

1 The MIN and MAX marks are indicated on the reservoir. The fluid level must be kept between the marks at all times.

2 If topping-up is necessary, first wipe clean the area around the filler cap to prevent dirt entering the hydraulic system. Unscrew and remove the reservoir's cap.

3 Carefully add fluid, taking care not to spill it onto the surrounding components (use a funnel). Use only the specified fluid (see *Lubricants and fluids*); mixing different types of fluid can cause damage to the system. On completion, securely refit the cap and wipe away any spilt fluid.

Power steering fluid level

✔ Park the vehicle on level ground.
✔ Set the steering wheel straight-ahead.
✔ The engine should be turned off.

Safety first!

● The need for frequent topping-up indicates a leak, which should be investigated immediately.

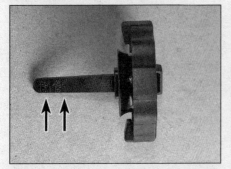

1 The fluid level should be checked when the engine is cold; the level should be up to the MAX mark on the dipstick, depending on the temperature of the liquid. MAX and MIN marks on the dipstick are given for 80°C and 20°C.

2 The reservoir is located at the front left of the engine compartment, beneath the air intake pipe.

3 If topping-up is necessary, first wipe clean the area around the filler cap to prevent dirt entering the hydraulic system. Unscrew and remove the reservoir's cap. Carefully add fluid, taking care not to spill it onto the surrounding components (use a funnel). Use only the specified fluid (see *Lubricants and fluids*). On completion, securely refit the cap and wipe away any spilt fluid.

Tyre condition and pressure

It is very important that tyres are in good condition, and at the correct pressure - having a tyre failure at any speed is highly dangerous. Tyre wear is influenced by driving style - harsh braking and acceleration, or fast cornering, will all produce more rapid tyre wear. As a general rule, the front tyres wear out faster than the rears. Interchanging the tyres from front to rear ("rotating" the tyres) may result in more even wear. However, if this is completely effective, you may have the expense of replacing all four tyres at once! Remove any nails or stones embedded in the tread before they penetrate the tyre to cause deflation. If removal of a nail does reveal that the tyre has been punctured, refit the nail so that its point of penetration is marked. Then immediately change the wheel, and have the tyre repaired by a tyre dealer.

Regularly check the tyres for damage in the form of cuts or bulges, especially in the sidewalls. Periodically remove the wheels, and clean any dirt or mud from the inside and outside surfaces. Examine the wheel rims for signs of rusting, corrosion or other damage. Light alloy wheels are easily damaged by "kerbing" whilst parking; steel wheels may also become dented or buckled. A new wheel is very often the only way to overcome severe damage.

New tyres should be balanced when they are fitted, but it may become necessary to re-balance them as they wear, or if the balance weights fitted to the wheel rim should fall off. Unbalanced tyres will wear more quickly, as will the steering and suspension components. Wheel imbalance is normally signified by vibration, particularly at a certain speed (typically around 50 mph). If this vibration is felt only through the steering, then it is likely that just the front wheels need balancing. If, however, the vibration is felt through the whole car, the rear wheels could be out of balance. Wheel balancing should be carried out by a tyre dealer or garage.

1 Tread Depth - visual check
    The original tyres have tread wear safety bands (B), which will appear when the tread depth reaches approximately 1.6 mm. The band positions are indicated by a triangular mark on the tyre sidewall (A).

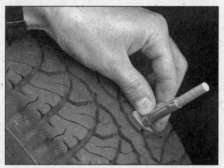

2 Tread Depth - manual check
    Alternatively, tread wear can be monitored with a simple, inexpensive device known as a tread depth indicator gauge.

3 Tyre Pressure Check
    Check the tyre pressures regularly with the tyres cold. Do not adjust the tyre pressures immediately after the vehicle has been used, or an inaccurate setting will result.

Tyre tread wear patterns

Shoulder Wear

Underinflation (wear on both sides)
Under-inflation will cause overheating of the tyre, because the tyre will flex too much, and the tread will not sit correctly on the road surface. This will cause a loss of grip and excessive wear, not to mention the danger of sudden tyre failure due to heat build-up.
Check and adjust pressures
Incorrect wheel camber (wear on one side)
Repair or renew suspension parts
Hard cornering
Reduce speed!

Centre Wear

Overinflation
Over-inflation will cause rapid wear of the centre part of the tyre tread, coupled with reduced grip, harsher ride, and the danger of shock damage occurring in the tyre casing.
Check and adjust pressures

If you sometimes have to inflate your car's tyres to the higher pressures specified for maximum load or sustained high speed, don't forget to reduce the pressures to normal afterwards.

Uneven Wear

Front tyres may wear unevenly as a result of wheel misalignment. Most tyre dealers and garages can check and adjust the wheel alignment (or "tracking") for a modest charge.
Incorrect camber or castor
Repair or renew suspension parts
Malfunctioning suspension
Repair or renew suspension parts
Unbalanced wheel
Balance tyres
Incorrect toe setting
Adjust front wheel alignment
Note: *The feathered edge of the tread which typifies toe wear is best checked by feel.*

Washer fluid level

• The windscreen washer reservoir also supplies the headlight washers.
• Screen wash additives not only keep the windscreen clean during bad weather, they also prevent the washer system freezing in cold weather – which is when you are likely to need it most. Don't top-up using plain water, as the screen wash will become diluted, and will freeze in cold weather.

Caution: On no account use engine coolant antifreeze in the screen washer system – this may damage the paintwork.

1 The screen wash fluid reservoir is located on the right-hand side (as seen from the driver's seat) of the engine compartment. Pull the filler cap to release it from the reservoir.

2 When topping-up the reservoir, a screen wash additive should be used in the quantities recommended on the bottle. On completion, securely refit the cap and wipe away any spilt fluid.

Wiper blades

• Only fit good-quality wiper blades.
• When removing an old wiper blade, note how it is fitted. Fitting new blades can be a tricky exercise, and noting how the old blade came off can save time.
• While the wiper blade is removed, take care not to knock the wiper arm from its locked position, or it could strike the glass.
• Offer the new blade into position the same way round as the old one. Ensure that it clicks home securely, otherwise it may come off in use, damaging the glass.

 HAYNES HiNT *If smearing is still a problem despite fitting new wiper blades, try cleaning the glass with neat screenwash additive or methylated spirit.*

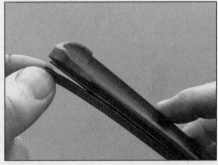

1 Check the condition of the wiper blades; if they are cracked or show any signs of deterioration, or if the glass swept area is smeared, renew them. Wiper blades should be renewed annually, regardless of their apparent condition.

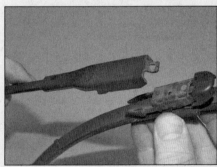

2 To remove a windscreen wiper blade, pull the arm fully away from the glass. Angle the blade slightly, then depress the two tabs before sliding the blade from place.

Battery

Caution: Before carrying out any work on the vehicle battery, read the precautions given in 'Safety first!' at the start of this manual.

✔ Make sure that the battery tray is in good condition, and that the clamp is tight. Any 'white' corrosion on the terminals or surrounding area can be removed with a solution of water and baking soda; thoroughly rinse all cleaned areas with water. Any metal parts damaged by corrosion should be covered with a zinc-based primer, then painted.

✔ If the battery is flat, and you need to jump start your vehicle, see *Roadside Repairs*.

 Battery corrosion can be kept to a minimum by applying a layer of petroleum jelly to the clamps and terminals after they are reconnected.

1 The battery is located under the passenger-side footwell.

2 Check the tightness of battery clamps to ensure good electrical connections. You should not be able to move them. Also check each cable for cracks and frayed conductors. The exterior of the battery should be inspected periodically for damage such as a cracked casing or cover.

3 If corrosion (white, fluffy deposits) is evident, remove the cables from the battery terminals, clean them with asmall wire brush, then refit them. Automotive stores sell a tool for cleaning the battery post . . .

4 . . . as well as the battery cable clamps

Bulbs and fuses

✔ Check all external lights and the horn. Refer to the appropriate Sections of Chapter 12 for details if any of the circuits are found to be inoperative.

✔ Visually check all accessible wiring connectors, harnesses and retaining clips for security, and for signs of chafing or damage.

 If you need to check your brake lights and indicators unaided, back up to a wall or garage door and operate the lights. The reflected light should show if they are working properly.

1 If a single stop-light, indicator or headlight has failed, it is likely that a bulb has blown and will need to be renewed. Refer to Chapter 12 for details. If both stop-lights have failed, it is possible that the switch has failed (see Chapter 9).

2 If more than one indicator light or headlight has failed, it is likely either that a fuse has been blown or that there is a fault in the circuit (see Chapter 12). To gain access to the fuse/relay box under the driver's seat, release the catches and the panel will be freed. The fuse locations are on the inside of the cover.

3 Additional fuses are located under the facia to the left of the glovebox. To gain access, release the catch at the top and pull the trim cover down. The fuse locations are on the inside of the cover.

Lubricants and fluids

Engine . . . . Multigrade engine oil with a viscosity suited to the ambient temperature approved in accordance with MB sheets 229.31 or 229.5. Eg. Castrol Edge 5W30

Cooling system . . . . MB 325.5 or 325.6 000 989 08 25 or 000 989 21 25 antifreeze

Manual transmission . . . . Gear oil MB 235.10 transmission oil A 001 989 84 03 09

Final drive (differential) . . . . Universal hypoid gear oil – SAE 85 W-90 or SAE 75 W-85

Power steering reservoir . . . . MB 236.3 Genuine Power Steering Fluid A000 989 10 04

Brake fluid reservoir . . . . MB 331.0 hydraulic fluid 000 989 08 07 or DOT 4 plus

Tyre pressures (cold)

Note: *The recommended tyre pressures for each vehicle are given on a sticker attached to the fusebox lid on the driver's seat base* **(see illustration)**. *The pressures given are for the original equipment tyres – the recommended pressures may vary if any other make or type of tyre is fitted; check with the tyre manufacturer or supplier for latest recommendations. Pressures are also given in the vehicle handbook.*

Chapter 1
Routine maintenance and servicing

Contents

Degrees of difficulty

| Easy, suitable for novice with little experience | Fairly easy, suitable for beginner with some experience | Fairly difficult, suitable for competent DIY mechanic | Difficult, suitable for experienced DIY mechanic 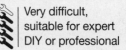 | Very difficult, suitable for expert DIY or professional |

1 Servicing specifications

Lubricants and fluids............................ Refer to *Lubricants, fluids and tyre pressures* on page 0•16

Capacities

Engine oil (including filter)...................................	11 litres
Cooling system...	9.5 litres
Fuel tank:	
Standard...	75.0 litres
Optional extra tank...................................	100.0 litres
Screen washer system....................................	6.0 litres
Rear axle	1.6 litres
Transmission:	
Code 711.651..	1.5 litres
Code 711.660..	2.0 litres

Cooling system

Antifreeze mixture:	
50% antifreeze.......................................	Protection down to -37°C
55% antifreeze.......................................	Protection down to -45°C

Note: *Refer to antifreeze manufacturer for latest recommendations*

Auxiliary belt

Auxiliary belt length	2080 mm

Braking system

Minimum brake pad lining thickness	3.0 mm
Minimum handbrake shoe lining thickness	3.0 mm

Torque wrench settings

	Nm	lbf ft
Belt tensioner guide pulley bolts	35	26
Engine oil drain plug:	30	22
Engine oil filter screw cap	25	18
Fuel filter cartridge retaining bolt	6	4
Handbrake compensator mounting bracket	25	18
Rear axle drain plug:		
Stage 1..	60	44
Stage 2..	Angle-tighten a further 90°	
Rear axle filler/level plug	100	74
Roadwheel bolts:		
Steel wheels...	240	177
Aluminium wheels.....................................	180	133
Transmission filler/level plug................................	34	25
Transmission drain plug	30	22

2 Maintenance schedule

1 The maintenance intervals in this manual are provided with the assumption that you, not the dealer, will be carrying out the work. These are the minimum maintenance intervals recommended by us for vehicles driven daily. If you wish to keep your vehicle in peak condition at all times, you may wish to perform some of these procedures more often. We encourage frequent maintenance, because it enhances the efficiency, performance and resale value of your vehicle.

2 If the vehicle is driven in dusty areas, used to tow a trailer, or driven frequently at slow speeds (idling in traffic) or on short journeys, more frequent maintenance intervals are recommended.

3 When the vehicle is new, it should be serviced by a dealer service department (or other workshop recognised by the vehicle manufacturer as providing the same standard of service) in order to preserve the warranty. The vehicle manufacturer may reject warranty claims if you are unable to prove that servicing has been carried out as and when specified, using only original equipment parts or parts certified to be of equivalent quality.

Every 250 miles or weekly
☐ Refer to Weekly checks

Every 9000 miles or 6 months, whichever occurs first
☐ Renew the engine oil and filter (Section 6)
Note: *The manufacturers recommend that the engine oil and filter are changed every 18 000 miles or 12 months if the vehicle is being operated under normal conditions. However, oil and filter changes are good for the engine and we recommend that the oil and filter are renewed more frequently, especially if the vehicle is driven in dusty areas, used to tow a trailer, or driven frequently at slow speeds (idling in traffic) or on short journeys.*

Every 18 000 miles or 12 months, whichever occurs first
In addition to the item listed in the previous service, carry out the following:
☐ Check the battery and clean the terminals (Section 7)
☐ Check the auxiliary drivebelt (Section 8)
☐ Check the electrical system (Section 9)
☐ Check under the bonnet for fluid leaks and hose condition (Section 10)
☐ Renew the fuel filter (Section 11)
☐ Check the condition of all engine compartment wiring (Section 12)
☐ Check the condition of all air conditioning system components (Section 13)
☐ Check the seat belts (Section 14)
☐ Check the antifreeze concentration (Section 15)
☐ Check the steering, suspension and roadwheels (Section 16)
☐ Check the propeller shaft and centre bearing for wear (Section 17)
☐ Check the exhaust system (Section 18)
☐ Check the underbody, and all fuel/brake lines (Section 19)
☐ Check the brake pad lining thickness (Section 20)
☐ Check the operation and adjustment of the handbrake (Section 21)
☐ Check the doors and bonnet, and lubricate their hinges and locks (Section 22)
☐ Check the security of all roadwheel bolts (Section 23)
☐ Road test (Section 24)

Every 36 000 miles or 2 years, whichever occurs first
☐ In addition to the items listed in the previous services, carry out the following:
☐ Renew the pollen filter element (Section 25)
Note: *If the vehicle is used in dusty conditions, the pollen filter should be renewed more frequently.*
☐ Renew the air filter element (Section 26)
☐ Check the transmission oil level (Section 27)
☐ Check the rear axle oil level (Section 28)
☐ Renew the brake fluid (Section 29)

Every 10 years
☐ Renew the coolant (Section 30)

3 Maintenance –
components location

Underbonnet view

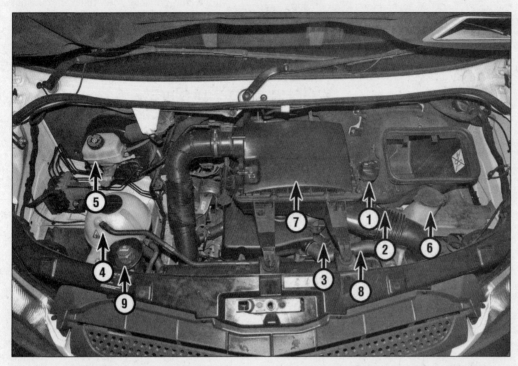

1 Engine oil filler cap
2 Engine oil dipstick (hidden behind air intake pipe)
3 Oil filter
4 Coolant expansion tank
5 Brake fluid reservoir
6 Windscreen/headlamp washer fluid reservoir
7 Air filter
8 Radiator top hose
9 AdBlue tank

Front underbody view

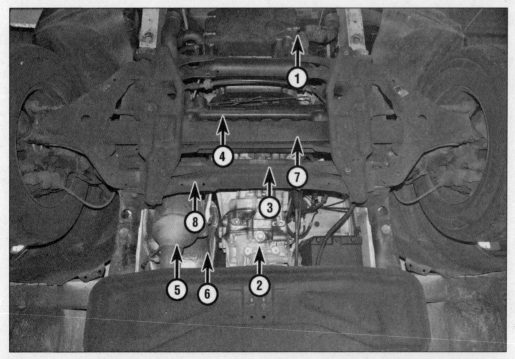

1 Engine oil drain plug
2 Transmission oil drain plug
3 Anti-roll bar
4 Power-assisted steering rack
5 Exhaust system front pipe
6 Exhaust heat shield
7 Transverse leaf spring
8 Rear mounting crossmember

Rear underbody view

1 Propeller shaft
2 Final drive unit
3 Anti-roll bar
4 Spare wheel
5 Handbrake cable
  compensating plate
  (hidden behind propeller
  shaft)
6 Suspension shock
  absorbers (dampers)
7 Handbrake cables and ABS
  wiring
8 Leaf springs

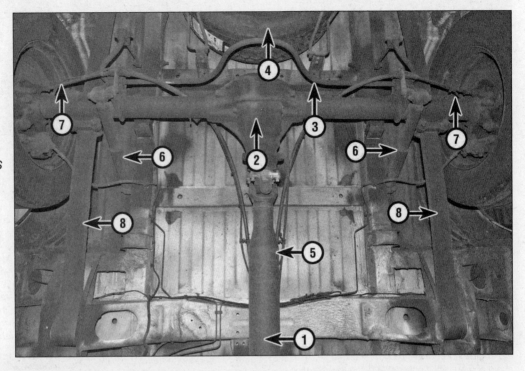

4 General Information

1 This Chapter is designed to help the home mechanic maintain his/her vehicle for safety, economy, long life and peak performance.
2 The Chapter contains a master maintenance schedule, followed by Sections dealing specifically with each task in the schedule. Visual checks, adjustments, component renewal and other helpful items are included. Refer to the accompanying illustrations of the engine compartment and the underside of the vehicle for the locations of the various components.
3 Servicing your vehicle in accordance with the mileage/time maintenance schedule and the following Sections will provide a planned maintenance programme, which should result in a long and reliable service life. This is a comprehensive plan, so maintaining some items but not others at the specified service intervals will not produce the same results.
4 As you service your vehicle, you will discover that many of the procedures can – and should – be grouped together, because of the particular procedure being performed, or because of the proximity of two otherwise unrelated components to one another. For example, if the vehicle is raised for any reason, the exhaust can be inspected at the same time as the suspension and steering components.
5 The first step in this maintenance programme

is to prepare yourself before the actual work begins. Read through all the Sections relevant to the work to be carried out, then make a list and gather all the parts and tools required. If a problem is encountered, seek advice from a parts specialist, or a dealer service department.

5 Regular maintenance

1 If, from the time the vehicle is new, the routine maintenance schedule is followed closely, and frequent checks are made of fluid levels and high-wear items, as suggested throughout this manual, the engine will be kept in relatively good running condition, and the need for additional work will be minimised.
2 It is possible that there will be times when the engine is running poorly due to the lack of regular maintenance. This is even more likely if a used vehicle, which has not received regular and frequent maintenance checks, is purchased. In such cases, additional work may need to be carried out, outside of the regular maintenance intervals.
3 If engine wear is suspected, a compression test or leakdown test (refer to Chapter 2A Section 2) will provide valuable information regarding the overall performance of the main internal components. Such a test can be used as a basis to decide on the extent of the work to be carried out. If, for example, a compression or leakdown test indicates

serious internal engine wear, conventional maintenance as described in this Chapter will not greatly improve the performance of the engine, and may prove a waste of time and money, unless extensive overhaul work is carried out first.
4 The following series of operations are those most often required to improve the performance of a generally poor-running engine:

Primary operations

a) Clean, inspect and test the battery (see 'Weekly checks' and Section 7).
b) Check all the engine related fluids (refer to 'Weekly checks').
c) Check the condition and tension of the auxiliary drivebelt (Section 8).
d) Check the condition of all hoses, and check for fluid leaks (Section 10).
e) Renew the fuel filter.
f) Check the condition of the air filter, and renew if necessary (Section 26).
5 If the above operations do not prove fully effective, carry out the following secondary operations:

Secondary operations

6 All items listed under Primary operations, plus the following:
a) Check the charging system (refer to Chapter 5).
b) Check the pre/post-heating system (refer to Chapter 5).
c) Check the fuel system and emissions control systems (refer to Chapter 4A and Chapter 4B).

6.2 The sump drain plug is located on the left-hand side of the sump

6.3a Remove the oil filler cap...

6.3b ...and withdraw the dipstick

6 Engine oil and filter renewal

1 Before starting this procedure, gather together all the necessary tools and materials. Also, make sure that you have plenty of clean rags and newspapers handy, to mop-up any spills. Ideally, the engine oil should be warm, as it will drain more easily and more built-up sludge will be removed with it. Take care not to touch the exhaust or any other hot parts of the engine when working under the vehicle. To avoid any possibility of scalding and to protect yourself from possible skin irritants and other harmful contaminants in used engine oils, it is advisable to wear gloves when carrying out this work.

2 Access to the underside of the vehicle will be greatly improved if it can be raised on a lift, driven onto ramps, or jacked up and supported on axle stands (see *Jacking and vehicle support*), but this is not vital because there is enough space beneath the van to carry out this procedure without raising the vehicle. Whichever method is chosen, make sure that the vehicle remains level, or if it is at an angle, that the drain plug is at the lowest point **(see illustration)**.

3 Open the bonnet and remove the oil filler cap, and withdraw the dipstick from the guide tube **(see illustrations)**.

4 Gently lift off the engine cover.

5 Using an oil filter cap removal tool, unscrew the cap from the oil filter **(see illustration)**. **Note:** *By removing the cap, the oil will drain from the filter housing into the sump. Remove and discard the paper filter element.*

6 Replace the oil filter element **(see illustration)** and replace the three O-rings at the same time, lubricating each with a small amount of clean oil.

7 Replace the oil filter cap, tightening to the required torque (which is printed on the cap).

8 Working under the vehicle, remove the underbody panel, then unscrew the engine oil drain plug about half a turn. Position the draining container under the drain plug, then remove the plug completely – recover the sealing washer **(see illustrations)**. **Note:** *Be aware that the engine contains a considerable amount of oil, so ensure that your container is large enough.*

> **HAYNES HINT** *As the drain plug releases from the threads, move it away sharply so the stream of oil from the sump runs into the container, not up your sleeve.*

9 Allow some time for the oil to drain, noting that it may be necessary to reposition the container as the oil flow slows to a trickle.

10 After all the oil has drained, wipe off the drain plug with a clean rag, and fit a new sealing washer. Clean the area around the drain plug opening, and refit the plug. Tighten the plug to the specified torque.

11 Remove the old oil and all tools from under the vehicle, then lower the vehicle to the ground.

12 If not already done, remove the dipstick, and then unscrew the oil filler cap from the camshaft cover. Fill the engine, using the correct grade and type of oil (see *Lubricants and fluids*). An oil can spout or funnel may help to reduce spillage. Pour in half the specified quantity of oil first, and then wait a few minutes for the oil to fall to the sump. Continue adding oil, a small quantity at a time, until the level is up to the lower mark on the dipstick. Refit the filler cap.

13 Start the engine and run it for a few minutes, then check for leaks. Note that there may be a delay of a few seconds before the oil pressure warning light goes out when the engine is first started, as the oil circulates through the engine oil galleries and the new oil filter before the pressure builds-up.

14 Switch off the engine, and wait a few

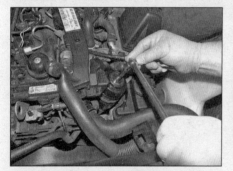

6.5 Unscrew the cap from the oil filter

6.6 Swap the element from the oil filter

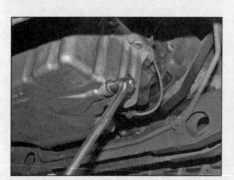

6.8a Remove the sump drain plug...

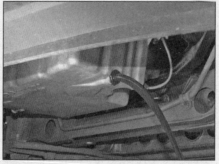

6.8b ...and drain it into a suitable container

minutes for the oil to settle in the sump once more. With the new oil circulated and the filter completely full, recheck the level on the dipstick, and add more oil as necessary.

15 Dispose of the used engine oil and filter safely, with reference to *General repair procedures* in the Reference Chapter of this manual. Do not discard the old filter with domestic household waste. The facility for waste oil disposal provided by many local council refuge tips and/or recycling centres generally has a filter receptacle alongside.

7 Battery maintenance and charging

> **Warning: Certain precautions must be followed when checking and servicing the battery. Hydrogen gas, which is highly flammable, is always present in the battery cells, so keep lighted tobacco and all other open flames and sparks away from the battery. The electrolyte inside the battery is actually dilute sulphuric acid, which will cause injury if splashed on your skin or in your eyes. It will also ruin clothes and painted surfaces.**

General

1 A routine preventive maintenance programme for the battery in your vehicle is the only way to ensure quick and reliable starts. For general maintenance, refer to *Weekly checks* at the start of this manual. Also at the front of the manual is information on jump starting. For details of removing and installing the battery, refer to Chapter 5 Section 3.

Charging

> **Warning: When batteries are being charged, hydrogen gas, which is very explosive and flammable, is produced. Do not smoke, or allow open flames, near a charging or a recently charged battery. Wear eye protection when near the battery during charging. Also, make sure the charger is unplugged before connecting or disconnecting the battery.**

2 Slow-rate charging is the best way to restore a battery that's discharged to the point where it will not start the engine. It's also a good way to maintain the battery charge in a vehicle that's only driven a few miles between starts. Maintaining the battery charge is particularly important in winter, when the battery must work harder to start the engine, and electrical accessories that drain the battery are in greater use.

3 Check the battery case for any instructions regarding charging the battery. Some maintenance-free batteries may require a particularly low charge rate or other special conditions, if they are not to be damaged.

4 It's best to use a one- or two-amp battery charger (sometimes called a 'trickle' charger). They are the safest, and put the least strain on the battery. They are also the least expensive.

8.8 Use a socket and turn the tensioner clockwise to relieve the tension

For a faster charge, you can use a higher amperage charger, but don't use one rated more than 1/10th the amp/hour rating of the battery (ie, no more than 5 amps, typically). Rapid boost charges that claim to restore the power of the battery in one to two hours are hardest on the battery, and can damage batteries not in good condition. This type of charging should only be used in emergency situations.

5 The average time necessary to charge a battery should be listed in the instructions that come with the charger. As a general rule, a trickle charger will charge a battery in 12 to 16 hours.

8 Auxiliary drivebelt check and renewal

General

1 Due to their function and construction, the belts are prone to failure after a period of time, and should be inspected periodically to prevent problems.

2 The number and type of belt used on a particular vehicle depends on the accessories fitted. Drivebelts are used to drive the coolant pump, alternator, power steering pump and air conditioning compressor.

3 The good condition and proper tension of the auxiliary drivebelts are critical to the operation of the engine. They must, therefore, be regularly inspected.

Check

4 The best way to check the condition of the belt is to remove it and inspect it out of the engine bay.

Drivebelt tension

5 The auxiliary drivebelt is tensioned by an automatic tensioner; regular checks are not required, and manual 'adjustment' is not possible.

6 If you suspect that a drivebelt is slipping and/or running slack, or that the tensioner is otherwise faulty, it must be renewed.

Drivebelt renewal

7 Remove the air filter housing as described in Chapter 4A Section 2.

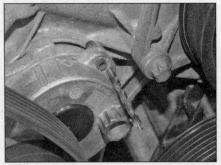

8.9 Insert metal pin to lock tensioner in position

8 Engage a 17mm bi-Hex socket with the tensioner body below the pulley, and then lever the tensioner clockwise to relieve the tension in the belt **(see illustration)**.

9 Hold the tensioner in position with the spanner/socket, and slide a 4mm pin or drill bit through the holes at the side of the tensioner to hold it in place **(see illustration)**. **Note:** *If working alone, it can be difficult to hold the tensioner in place with one hand while inserting the pin. In this instance, it can be worthwhile, moving the tensioner then holding it in place using a cable tie through the front engine lifting bracket, to give you more freedom to insert the retaining pin into the tensioner.*

10 Fit the new belt around the pulleys **(see illustration)**. Check that the belt is correctly seated on all the pulleys. Where applicable, drill bit or pin locking the tensioner.

11 Release the spanner/socket, and allow the tensioner to move into position against the belt.

9 Electrical system check

1 Check the operation of all external lights and indicators (front and rear).

2 Check for satisfactory operation of the instrument panel, its illumination and warning lights, the switches and their function lights.

3 Check the horn(s) for satisfactory operation.

4 Check all other electrical equipment for satisfactory operation.

8.10 Auxiliary drivebelt routing

11.4 Disconnect the wiring plug

11.5 Place a rag around the fuel hoses

5 Where any problems are found on cooling system components, renew the component or gasket with reference to Chapter 3.

11 Fuel filter – removal and refitting

Caution: Before starting any work on the fuel filter, wipe clean the filter assembly and the surrounding area as it is essential that no dirt or other foreign matter is allowed into the system. Place rags or similar material under the filter assembly to catch any spillages. Do not allow diesel fuel to contaminate components such as the alternator and starter motor, the coolant hoses and engine mountings, and any wiring.
Note: *Before carrying out the following procedure, read carefully the precautions given in Section 2.*

Removal

1 Disconnect the battery as described in Chapter 5 Section 3.
2 Remove the air filter housing, as described in Section 4A Section 2.
3 The fuel filter is located to the left-hand side of the cylinder head.
4 Unplug the wiring connector from the fuel filter water sensor **(see illustration)**.
5 To minimise fuel spillage, place a rag around the hoses **(see illustration)**.
6 Undo the clips and remove the fuel hoses from the filter **(see illustration)**. **Note:** *Plug the hoses to prevent contamination of the fuel system.*
7 Use pliers to open the retaining lugs and detach the drain pipe **(see illustration)**.
8 Use a screwdriver to release the retaining clips, and remove the main fuel filter from place **(see illustrations)**.

Refitting

9 Refitting is a reversal of removal, then reconnect the battery, start the engine and check around the area of the fuel filter for leaks.

11.6 Detach the fuel hoses

11.7 Open the lugs and remove the drain pipe

10 Underbonnet check for fluid leaks and hose condition

1 Visually inspect the engine joint faces, gaskets and seals for any signs of water or oil leaks. Pay particular attention to the areas around the camshaft cover, cylinder head, oil filter and sump joint faces. Bear in mind that, over a period of time, some very slight seepage from these areas is to be expected – what you are really looking for is any indication of a serious leak. Should a leak be found, renew the offending gasket or oil seal by referring to the appropriate Chapters in this manual.
2 Also check the security and condition of all engine related pipes and hoses, and all braking system pipes and hoses and fuel

lines. Ensure that all cable-ties or securing clips are in place, and in good condition. Clips that are broken or missing can lead to chafing of the hoses, pipes or wiring, which could cause more serious problems in the future.
3 Carefully check the radiator hoses and heater hoses along their entire length. Renew any hose, which is cracked, swollen or deteriorated. Cracks will show up better if the hose is squeezed. Pay close attention to the hose clips that secure the hoses to the cooling system components. Hose clips can pinch and puncture hoses, resulting in cooling system leaks. If the crimped type hose clips are used, it may be a good idea to update them with standard worm-drive clips.
4 Inspect all the cooling system components (hoses, joint faces, etc) for leaks **(see Haynes Hint)**.

12 Engine compartment wiring check

1 With the vehicle parked on level ground, apply the handbrake firmly and open the bonnet. Using an inspection light or a small electric torch, check all visible wiring within and beneath the engine compartment.
2 What you are looking for is wiring that is obviously damaged by chafing against

11.8a Release the clips...

11.8b ...and lift out the fuel filter

sharp edges, or against moving suspension/ transmission components and/or the auxiliary drivebelt, by being trapped or crushed between carelessly refitted components, or melted by being forced into contact with the hot engine castings, coolant pipes, etc. In almost all cases, damage of this sort is caused in the first instance by incorrect routing on reassembly after previous work has been carried out.

3 Depending on the extent of the problem, damaged wiring may be repaired by rejoining the break or splicing-in a new length of wire, using solder to ensure a good connection, and remaking the insulation with adhesive insulating tape or heat-shrink tubing, as appropriate. If the damage is extensive, given the implications for the vehicle's future reliability, the best long-term answer may well be to renew that entire section of the loom, however expensive this may appear.

4 When the actual damage has been repaired, ensure that the wiring loom is rerouted correctly, so that it is clear of other components, and not stretched or kinked, and is secured out of harm's way using the plastic clips, guides and ties provided.

5 Check all electrical connectors, ensuring that they are clean, securely fastened, and that each is locked by its plastic tabs or wire clip, as appropriate. If any connector shows external signs of corrosion (accumulations of white or green deposits, or streaks of 'rust'), or if any is thought to be dirty, it must be unplugged and cleaned using electrical contact cleaner. If the connector pins are severely corroded, the connector must be renewed; note that this may mean the renewal of that entire section of the loom – see your local Mercedes-Benz dealer for details.

6 If the cleaner completely removes the corrosion to leave the connector in a satisfactory condition, it would be wise to pack the connector with a suitable material, which will exclude dirt and moisture, preventing the corrosion from occurring again. A Mercedes-Benz dealer may be able to recommend a suitable product.

7 Use the same techniques to ensure that all earth points in the engine compartment provide good electrical contact through clean, metal-to-metal joints, and that all are securely fastened.

13 Air conditioning system check

1 The following maintenance checks will ensure that the air conditioner operates at peak efficiency:
a) Check the auxiliary drivebelt (see Section 8).
b) Check the system hoses for damage or leaks.
c) Inspect the condenser fins for leaves, insects and other debris. Use a clean paint brush to clean the condenser.
d) Check that the drain tube from the front

of the evaporator is clear – note that it is normal to have clear fluid (water) dripping from this while the system is in operation, to the extent that quite a large puddle can be left under the vehicle when it is parked.

2 It's a good idea to operate the system for about 30 minutes at least once a month, particularly during the winter. Long term non-use can cause hardening of the seals, and subsequent failure.

3 Because of the complexity of the air conditioning system and the special equipment necessary to service it, in-depth fault diagnosis and repairs are not included in this manual.

4 The most common cause of poor cooling is simply a low system refrigerant charge. If a noticeable drop in cool air output occurs, the following quick check will help you determine if the refrigerant level is low.

5 Warm the engine up to normal operating temperature.

6 Place the air conditioning temperature selector at the coldest setting, and put the blower at the highest setting. Open the doors – to make sure the air conditioning system doesn't cycle off as soon as it cools the passenger compartment.

7 With the compressor engaged – the clutch will make an audible click, and the centre of the clutch will rotate – feel the inlet and outlet pipes at the compressor. One side should be cold, and one hot. If there's no perceptible difference between the two pipes, there's something wrong with the compressor or the system. It might be a low charge – it might be something else. Take the vehicle to a dealer service department or an automotive air conditioning specialist.

14 Seat belt check

1 Check the seat belts for satisfactory operation and condition. Inspect the webbing for fraying and cuts. Check that they retract smoothly and without binding into their reels.
2 Check that the seat belt mounting bolts are tight, and if necessary tighten them to the specified torque wrench setting (Chapter 11).

15 Antifreeze concentration check

1 The cooling system should be filled with the recommended antifreeze and corrosion protection fluid. Over a period of time, the concentration of fluid may be reduced due to topping-up (this can be avoided by topping-up with the correct antifreeze mixture) or fluid loss. If loss of coolant has been evident, it is important to make the necessary repair before adding fresh fluid. The exact mixture of antifreeze-to-water,

which you should use, depends on the relative weather conditions. The mixture should contain at least 40% antifreeze, but not more than 70%. Consult the mixture ratio chart on the antifreeze container before adding coolant. Use antifreeze that meets the vehicle manufacturer's specifications.

2 With the engine cold, carefully remove the cap from the expansion tank. If the engine is not completely cold, place a cloth rag over the cap before removing it, and remove it slowly to allow any pressure to escape.

3 Antifreeze checkers are available from car accessory shops. Draw some coolant from the expansion tank and observe how many plastic balls are floating in the checker. Usually, 2 or 3 balls must be floating for the correct concentration of antifreeze, but follow the manufacturer's instructions.

4 If the concentration is incorrect, it will be necessary to either withdraw some coolant and add antifreeze, or alternatively drain the old coolant and add fresh coolant of the correct concentration.

16 Steering, suspension and roadwheel check

Front suspension and steering

1 Firmly apply the handbrake, and then jack up the front of the vehicle and support it securely on axle stands (see Jacking and vehicle support).

2 Visually inspect the balljoint dust covers and the steering rack-and-pinion gaiters for splits, chafing or deterioration. Any wear of these components will cause loss of lubricant, together with dirt and water entry, resulting in rapid deterioration of the balljoints or steering gear.

3 Check the power steering fluid hoses for chafing or deterioration, and the pipe and hose unions for fluid leaks. Also, check for signs of fluid leakage under pressure from the steering gear rubber gaiters, which would indicate failed fluid seals within the steering gear.

4 Grasp the roadwheel at the 12 o'clock and 6 o'clock positions, and try to rock it (see illustration). Very slight free play may be felt,

16.4 Grasp the wheel and try to rock it

17.2 Check centre bearing – arrowed

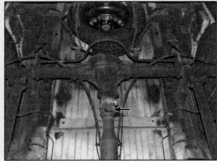

17.3 Check universal joint – arrowed

but if the movement is appreciable, further investigation is necessary to determine the source. Continue rocking the wheel while an assistant depresses the footbrake. If the movement is now eliminated or significantly reduced, it is likely that the hub bearings are at fault. If the free play is still evident with the footbrake depressed, then there is wear in the suspension joints or mountings.

5 Now grasp the wheel at the 9 o'clock and 3 o'clock positions, and try to rock it as before. Any movement felt now may again be caused by wear in the hub bearings or the steering track rod balljoints. If the outer track rod balljoint is worn, the visual movement will be obvious. If the inner joint is suspect, it can be felt by placing a hand over the rack-and-pinion rubber gaiter and gripping the track rod. If the wheel is now rocked, movement will be felt at the inner joint if wear has taken place.

6 Using a large screwdriver or flat bar, check for wear in the suspension mounting bushes by levering between the relevant suspension component and its attachment point. Some movement is to be expected, as the mountings are made of rubber, but excessive wear should be obvious. Also check the condition of any visible rubber bushes, looking for splits, cracks or contamination of the rubber.

7 With the car standing on its wheels, have an assistant turn the steering wheel back-and-forth, about an eighth of a turn each way. There should be very little, if any, lost movement between the steering wheel and roadwheels. If this is not the case, closely

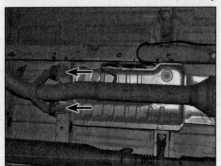

18.3 Check the exhaust rubber mountings

observe the joints and mountings previously described. In addition, check the steering column universal joints for wear, and also check the rack-and-pinion steering gear itself.

Rear suspension

8 Chock the front wheels, then jack up the rear of the vehicle and support securely on axle stands (see *Jacking and vehicle support*).
9 Working as described previously for the front suspension, check the rear hub bearings, the leaf spring mounting bushes and the shock absorber mountings for wear. Also check that the rear spring U-bolt nuts are tightened to the specified torque as given in Chapter 10.

Shock absorbers

10 Check for any signs of fluid leakage around the shock absorber body, or from the rubber gaiter around the piston rod. Should any fluid be noticed, the shock absorber is defective internally, and should be renewed. **Note:** *Shock absorbers should always be renewed in pairs on the same axle.*
11 The efficiency of the shock absorber may be checked by bouncing the vehicle at each corner. Generally speaking, the body will return to its normal position and stop after being depressed. If it rises and returns on a rebound, the shock absorber is probably suspect. Also examine the shock absorber upper and lower mountings for any signs of wear.

Roadwheels

12 Periodically remove the roadwheels, and clean any dirt or mud from the inside and outside surfaces. Examine the wheel rims for signs of rusting, corrosion or other damage. Light alloy wheels are easily damaged by 'kerbing' whilst parking, and similarly, steel wheels may become dented or buckled. Renewal of the wheel is very often the only course of remedial action possible.
13 The balance of each wheel and tyre assembly should be maintained, not only to avoid excessive tyre wear, but also to avoid wear in the steering and suspension components. Wheel imbalance is normally signified by vibration through the vehicle's

bodyshell, although in many cases it is particularly noticeable through the steering wheel. Conversely, it should be noted that wear or damage in suspension or steering components may cause excessive tyre wear. Out-of-round or out-of-true tyres, damaged wheels and wheel bearing wear/maladjustment also fall into this category. Balancing will not usually cure vibration caused by such wear.

17 Propeller shaft universal joint and centre bearing check

1 Ideally, the vehicle should be raised at the front and rear and securely supported on axle stands (see *Jacking and vehicle support*) with the rear wheels free to rotate.
2 Check around the rubber portion of the centre bearings for any signs of cracks, oil contamination or deformation of the rubber **(see illustration)**. If any of these conditions are apparent, the centre bearing(s) should be renewed as described in Chapter 8.
3 At the same time, check the condition of the universal joints by holding the propeller shaft in one hand and the transmission or rear axle flange in the other **(see illustration)**. Try to twist the two components in opposite directions and look for any movement in the universal joint spiders. Repeat this check at the centre bearing(s), and in all other areas where the individual parts of the propeller shaft or universal joints connect. If any wear is evident, refer to Chapter 8 for repair procedures. If grating or squeaking noises have been heard from below the vehicle, or if there is any sign of rust-coloured deposits around the universal joint spiders, this indicates an advanced state of wear, and should be seen to immediately.

18 Exhaust system check

1 With the engine cold, check the complete exhaust system, from its starting point at the engine to the end of the tailpipe. If necessary, raise the front and rear of the vehicle and support it on axle stands (see *Jacking and vehicle support*).
2 Check the exhaust pipes and connections for evidence of leaks, severe corrosion, and damage. Make sure that all brackets and mountings are in good condition and that all relevant nuts and bolts are tight. Leakage at any of the joints or in other parts of the system will usually show up as a black sooty stain in the vicinity of the leak.
3 Rattles and other noises can often be traced to the exhaust system, especially the brackets and rubber mountings **(see illustration)**. Try to move the pipes and silencers. If the components are able to come into contact

with the body or suspension parts, secure the system with new mountings. Otherwise separate the joints (if possible) and twist the pipes as necessary to provide additional clearance.

19 Underbody and fuel/brake line check

1 With the vehicle raised and supported on axle stands (see *Jacking and vehicle support*), thoroughly inspect the underbody and wheel arches for signs of damage and corrosion. In particular, examine the bottom of the side sills, and any concealed areas where mud can collect.
2 Where corrosion and rust is evident, press and tap firmly on the panel with a screwdriver, and check for any serious corrosion, which would necessitate repairs.
3 If the panel is not seriously corroded, clean away the rust, and apply a new coating of underseal. Refer to Chapter 11 for more details of body repairs.
4 Inspect the fuel tank and filler neck for punctures, cracks and other damage. The connection between the filler neck and tank is especially critical. Sometimes a rubber filler neck or connecting hose will leak due to loose retaining clamps or deteriorated rubber.
5 Carefully check all rubber hoses and metal fuel lines leading away from the fuel tank. Check for loose connections, deteriorated hoses, crimped lines, and other damage. Pay particular attention to the vent pipes and hoses, which often loop up around the filler neck and can become blocked or crimped. Follow the lines to the front of the vehicle, carefully inspecting them all the way. Renew damaged sections as necessary. Similarly, whilst the vehicle is raised, take the opportunity to inspect all underbody brake fluid pipes and hoses.
6 From within the engine compartment, check the security of all fuel, vacuum, power steering and brake hose attachments and pipe unions, and inspect all hoses for kinks, chafing and deterioration.

20 Brake pad wear check

1 Apply the handbrake, then jack up the front (checking front brakes) or rear (checking rear brakes) of the vehicle and support it on axle stands (see *Jacking and vehicle support*). For better access to the brake calipers, remove the roadwheels.
2 Look through the inspection window in the caliper, and check that the thickness of the friction lining material on each of the pads is not less than the recommended minimum thickness given in the Specifications **(see Haynes Hint)**.

 HAYNES HiNT *For a quick check, the thickness of the friction material of the brake pad can be measured through the aperture in the caliper body.*

3 If it is difficult to determine the exact thickness of the pad linings, or if you are at all concerned about the condition of the pads, then remove them from the calipers for further inspection (refer to Chapter 9).
4 Check the caliper on the other side of the vehicle in the same way.
5 If any one of the brake pads has worn down to, or below, the specified limit, all four pads must be renewed as a set.
6 Check the brake discs with reference to Chapter 9.
7 Before refitting the wheels, check all brake lines and flexible hoses with reference to Chapter 9. In particular, check the flexible hoses in the vicinity of the calipers, where they are subjected to most movement. Bend them between the fingers and check that this does not reveal previously hidden cracks, cuts or splits **(see illustration)**.
8 On completion, refit the roadwheels and lower the vehicle to the ground. Tighten the wheel bolts to the specified torque.

21 Handbrake operation and adjustment check

Note: *If the handbrake shoe clearance or cable-adjusting bolt requires a significant amount of adjustment, it is advisable to inspect the brake shoe lining thickness.*
1 With the vehicle on a slight slope, apply the handbrake lever, and check that it holds the vehicle stationary, then release the lever and check that there is no resistance to movement of the vehicle.
2 There are two areas of adjustment for the handbrake: the star wheel adjusters with the brake shoes, inside the rear brake disc and the adjusting bolt on the compensator unit under the centre of the vehicle. First you will need to carry out the adjustment at the brake shoes.

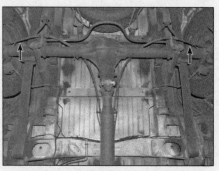
20.7 Check condition of brake hoses

3 Slacken one of the rear wheel bolts on each rear wheel, before jacking up the car.
4 Position the vehicle on level ground, and then chock the front wheels. Jack up the rear of the vehicle and securely support it on axle stands (see *Jacking and vehicle support*).
5 Firmly apply the handbrake lever, and then release it three or four times to make sure all is working, as it should. Leave the handbrake lever in the off position for the next part of the procedure.
6 Remove the two wheel bolts (one on each wheel), which had been slackened previously.
7 Turn the wheel so that access can be gained to the handbrake shoe adjuster **(see illustration)**, situated between the both handbrake shoes.
8 Using a long slim screwdriver engaged in the teeth of the adjuster, turn the adjuster until the handbrake shoes make contact and the wheel can no longer be turned **(see illustration)**. Repeat the procedure on the other rear wheel.
9 Noting the exact number of strokes required to do so, back off the brake shoe adjuster so that the rear wheel is completely free to turn. Repeat the procedure on the other rear wheel, turning the adjuster by exactly the same amount.
10 Check the operation of the handbrake by gradually applying it, and confirm that the rear wheels both start to 'drag' at the same point.
11 Further adjustment can be made at the adjustment bolt on the handbrake cable compensator unit under the centre of the vehicle.

21.7 Handbrake adjuster wheel (disc removed for clarity)

21.8 Adjusting the handbrake adjuster through the wheel bolt hole

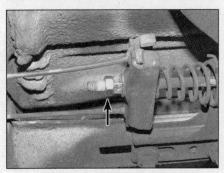

21.12a Loosen the locknut...

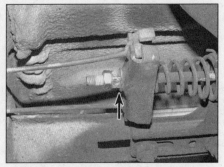

21.12b ...then slacken the cable adjuster

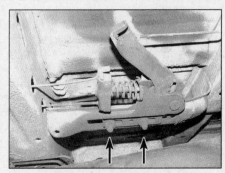

21.13 Handbrake compensator plate mounting bolts

12 From under the vehicle, locate the handbrake compensator plate and loosen the locknut **(see illustrations)** then slacken the cable adjuster nut.
13 Slacken the compensator mounting bolts **(see illustration)**.
14 Slide the mounting bracket to the rear of the vehicle.
15 Tighten the compensator mounting bracket bolts.
16 At this point apply the handbrake lever inside the passenger compartment by three notches.
17 Working back under the vehicle, tighten the cable adjuster until the rear wheels can just be turned by hand.
18 Tighten the locknut, then from inside the passenger compartment release the handbrake lever and check the wheels rotate freely.
19 On completion, lower the vehicle to the ground, refit the two wheel bolts and tighten to the specified torque.

22 Door and bonnet check and lubrication

1 Check that the doors and bonnet close securely. Check that the bonnet safety catch operates correctly. Check the operation of the door check straps.
2 Lubricate the hinges; door check straps, the striker plates and the bonnet catch sparingly with a little oil or grease.

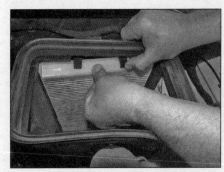

25.2a Release the securing clips...

23 Roadwheel bolt tightness check

1 Apply the handbrake, chock the wheels, and engage 1st gear.
2 Where applicable, remove the wheel bolt covers (or wheel centre cover), using the flat end of the wheel brace supplied in the tool kit.
3 Check the tightness of all wheel bolts using a torque wrench (refer to the Specifications).

24 Road test

Instruments and electrical equipment

1 Check the operation of all instruments and electrical equipment.
2 Make sure that all instruments read correctly, and switch on all electrical equipment in turn, to check that it functions properly.

Steering and suspension

3 Check for any abnormalities in the steering, suspension, handling or road 'feel'.
4 Drive the vehicle, and check that there are no unusual vibrations or noises.
5 Check that the steering feels positive, with no excessive 'sloppiness', or roughness, and check for any suspension noises when cornering and driving over bumps.

25.2b ...and remove the filter

Drivetrain

6 Check the performance of the engine, clutch, transmission and driveshafts/propeller shaft.
7 Listen for any unusual noises from the engine, clutch and transmission.
8 Make sure that the engine runs smoothly when idling, and that there is no hesitation when accelerating.
9 Check that the clutch action is smooth and progressive, that the drive is taken up smoothly, and that the pedal travel is not excessive. Also listen for any noises when the clutch pedal is depressed.
10 Check that all gears can be engaged smoothly without noise, and that the gear lever action is smooth and not abnormally vague or 'notchy'.

Braking system

11 Make sure that the vehicle does not pull to one side when braking, and that the wheels do not lock when braking hard (models with ABS).
12 Check that there is no vibration through the steering when braking.
13 Check that the handbrake operates correctly, without excessive movement of the lever, and that it holds the vehicle stationary on a slope.
14 Test the operation of the brake servo unit as follows. Depress the footbrake four or five times to exhaust the vacuum, and then start the engine. As the engine starts, there should be a noticeable 'give' in the brake pedal as vacuum builds-up. Allow the engine to run for at least two minutes, and then switch it off. If the brake pedal is now depressed again, it should be possible to detect a hiss from the servo as the pedal is depressed. After about four or five applications, no further hissing should be heard, and the pedal should feel considerably harder.

25 Pollen filter element renewal

1 The pollen filter element is located in the engine compartment, inside the heater ventilation box/housing.
2 Release the retaining clips and remove the pollen filter **(see illustrations)**.

3 Withdraw the pollen filter element, noting the position of the airflow direction arrow for refitting **(see illustration)**. Clean out any dust or dirt particles from inside the housing.

4 If carrying out a routine service, the element must be renewed regardless of its apparent condition.

5 If you are checking the element for any other reason, inspect its lower surface; if it is very dirty, renew the element. If it is only moderately dusty, it can be re-used by blowing it clean.

6 Fit the new element using a reversal of the removal procedure.

26 Air filter element renewal

1 Slacken the retaining clip and disconnect the air inlet hose from the air cleaner cover **(see illustration)**.

2 Unhook the oil filler pipe and battery positive connector from each side of the air filter housing **(see illustrations)**.

3 Unscrew the clip and remove the air exit pipe **(see illustration)**.

4 Disconnect all wiring plugs

5 Prise up the air filter housing from the two front mounting points **(see illustration)**.

6 Manoeuvre the rear of the air filter housing from the rear mounting points and remove it from the engine bay **(see illustration)**.

7 Loosen the seven captive screws around the edge of the air filter housing **(see illustration)**.

8 Lift out the element, noting its fitted position, and then clean out the housing **(see illustration)**.

9 If carrying out a routine service, the element must be renewed regardless of its apparent condition.

10 If you are checking the element for any other reason, inspect its lower surface; if it is oily or very dirty, renew the element. If it is only moderately dusty, it can be re-used by blowing it clean.

11 Fit the new element using a reversal of the removal procedure.

25.3 Note the airflow direction arrow for refitting

26.1 Disconnect the air hose from the filter housing

26.2a Unhook the oil filler pipe...

26.2b ...and the battery positive connector

26.3 Unscrew and remove the air pipe

26.5 Lift up the mounting from the two front mounts

26.6 Tug the filter housing to the right to remove it from the rear mounts

26.7 Undo the screws around the edge of the housing

26.8 Remove the filter element

27 Transmission oil level check

1 To check the oil level, raise the vehicle and support it securely on axle stands (see *Jacking and vehicle support*), making sure that the vehicle is level.
2 The filler/level plug is on the right-hand side of the transmission housing at the rear.
3 Using a suitable Allen key or socket, unscrew and remove the filler/level plug – take care, as it will probably be very tight **(see illustration)**.
4 If the oil level is correct, the oil should be up to the lower edge of the filler/level plug hole.
5 If the transmission needs topping-up, use a syringe or a plastic bottle and tube to add more lubricant of the specified type (see *Lubricants and fluids*).
6 Stop filling the transmission when the lubricant begins to run out of the hole, and then wait until the flow of oil ceases.
7 Refit the filler/level plug, and tighten it to the specified torque setting. Drive the vehicle a short distance, and then check for leaks.
8 A need for regular topping-up can only be due to a leak, which should be found and rectified without delay.

28 Rear axle oil level check

1 To check the oil level, raise the vehicle and support it securely on axle stands (see *Jacking and vehicle support*), making sure that the vehicle is level.
2 The filler/level plug is located on the differential housing cover at the rear.
3 Using a suitable Allen key or socket, unscrew and remove the filler/level plug – take care, as it will probably be very tight.
4 If the oil level is correct, the oil should be up to the lower edge of the filler/level plug hole.
5 If the axle needs topping-up, use a syringe, or a plastic bottle and tube to add more lubricant of the specified type (refer to *Lubricants and fluids*).
6 Stop filling the transmission when the

27.3 Unscrew the filler/level plug

lubricant begins to run out of the hole, and then wait until the flow of oil ceases.
7 Refit the filler/level plug, and tighten it to the specified torque.
8 A need for regular topping-up can only be due to a leak, which should be found and rectified without delay.

29 Brake fluid renewal

1 The procedure is similar to that for the bleeding of the hydraulic system as described in Chapter 9 Section 2, except that the brake fluid reservoir should be emptied by siphoning, and allowance should be made for the old fluid to be removed from the circuit when bleeding a section of the circuit.

30 Coolant renewal

 Warning: Refer to Chapter 3 and observe the warnings given. In particular, never remove the expansion tank filler cap when the engine is running, or has just been switched off, as the cooling system will be hot, and the consequent escaping steam and scalding coolant could cause serious injury. If the engine is hot, the electric cooling fan may start rotating even if the

engine is not running, so be careful to keep hands, hair and loose clothing well clear when working in the engine compartment.

 Warning: Wait until the engine is cold before starting this procedure.

Cooling system draining

1 To drain the system, remove the expansion tank filler cap.
2 If additional working clearance is required, apply the handbrake, then jack up the front of the vehicle and support it on axle stands (see *Jacking and vehicle support*).
3 Adjust the interior heater control to maximum heat output, then place a large drain tray underneath the radiator.
4 Remove the air intake hose **(see illustration)**.
5 Reach down from the engine bay and rotate the drain plug half a turn anti-clockwise to release **(see illustration)**. Allow the coolant to drain into the tray.
6 On completion, retighten the drain plug securely. Where necessary, lower the vehicle to the ground.

Cooling system flushing

7 If coolant renewal has been neglected, or if the antifreeze mixture has become diluted, then in time, the cooling system may gradually lose efficiency, as the coolant passages become restricted due to rust, scale deposits, and other sediment. The cooling system efficiency can be restored by flushing the system clean.
8 The radiator should be flushed independently of the engine, to avoid unnecessary contamination.

Radiator flushing

9 Disconnect the top and bottom hoses and any other relevant hoses from the radiator, with reference to Chapter 3.
10 Insert a garden hose into the radiator top inlet. Direct a flow of clean water through the radiator, and continue flushing until clean water emerges from the radiator bottom outlet.
11 If after a reasonable period, the water still does not run clear, the radiator can be flushed with a good proprietary cleaning agent. It is important that the manufacturer's instructions are followed carefully. If the contamination is particularly bad, remove the radiator, insert the hose in the radiator bottom outlet, and reverse-flush the radiator.

Engine flushing

12 Remove the thermostat as described in Chapter 3 then, if the radiator top hose has been disconnected from the engine, temporarily refit the thermostat housing cover and reconnect the hose.
13 With the top and bottom hoses disconnected from the radiator, insert a garden hose into the radiator top hose. Direct a clean flow of water through the engine, and continue flushing until clean water emerges from the radiator bottom hose.

30.4 Unclip and remove the air intake

30.5 Reach down and slacken the drain tap

14 On completion of flushing, refit the thermostat and reconnect the hoses with reference to Chapter 3.

Cooling system filling

15 Before attempting to fill the cooling system, make sure that all hoses and clips are in good condition, and that the clips are tight. Note that an antifreeze mixture must be used all year round, to prevent corrosion of the engine components.

16 Fill the system via the expansion tank, with the correct antifreeze mixture, until the coolant level reaches the MAX mark on the side of the expansion tank. Refit the expansion tank filler cap.

17 Start the engine and allow it to idle until it reaches normal operating temperature, then allow it to idle for a further 5 minutes.

18 Switch off the engine and allow it to cool for at least 30 minutes.

19 Remove the filler cap and top-up the coolant level to the MAX mark on the expansion tank. Refit and tighten the cap.

Antifreeze mixture

20 Mercedes-Benz state that, if the only antifreeze used is Mercedes-Benz antifreeze/inhibiter, it will last for ten years. This is subject to it being used in the recommended concentration, unmixed with any other type of antifreeze or additive, and topped-up when necessary using only that antifreeze type, mixed with clean water. If any other type of antifreeze is (or has been) added, the ten-year life period no longer applies; in this case, the system must be drained and thoroughly flushed before fresh coolant mixture is poured in.

21 If any antifreeze other than Mercedes-Benz is to be used, the coolant must be renewed at regular intervals to provide an equivalent degree of protection. The conventional recommendation is to renew the coolant every two years.

22 If the antifreeze used is to Mercedes-Benz specification, the levels of protection it affords are indicated in the Specifications Section of this Chapter. To give the recommended standard mixture ratio for this antifreeze, 40% (by volume) of antifreeze must be mixed with 60% of clean, soft water. If you are using any other type of antifreeze, follow its manufacturer's instructions to achieve the correct ratio.

23 It is best to make up slightly more than the system's specified capacity, so that a supply is available for subsequent topping-up. However, note that you are unlikely to fully drain the system at any one time (unless the engine is being completely stripped), and the capacities quoted are therefore slightly academic for routine coolant renewal.

24 Before adding antifreeze, the cooling system should be completely drained, preferably flushed, and all hoses checked for condition and security. Fresh antifreeze will rapidly find any weaknesses in the system.

25 After filling with antifreeze, a label should be attached to the expansion tank, stating the type and concentration of antifreeze used, and the date installed. Any subsequent topping-up should be made with the same type and concentration of antifreeze. If topping-up using antifreeze to Mercedes-Benz specification, note that a 50/50 mixture is permissible, purely for convenience.

Caution: Do not use engine antifreeze in the windscreen washer system, because it will damage the vehicle's paintwork. A screen wash additive should be added to the washer system in its maker's recommended quantities.

Chapter 2 Part A
Engine in-car repair procedures

Contents

Degrees of difficulty

Easy, suitable for novice with little experience	Fairly easy, suitable for beginner with some experience	Fairly difficult, suitable for competent DIY mechanic	Difficult, suitable for experienced DIY mechanic	Very difficult, suitable for expert DIY or professional

Specifications

General

Engine type.	4-cylinder in-line diesel, double overhead camshaft (DOHC)
Engine code	651.955, 651.956, 651.957
Bore	83.0 mm
Stroke	99.0 mm
Capacity	2143 cc
Emissions standard	EU5
Firing order.	1-3-4-2
Direction of crankshaft rotation	Clockwise (seen from the front of the vehicle)
Compression ratio	16.2 : 1
Compression pressures:	
New compression pressure	23.0 to 30.0 bar
Minimum compression pressure	17.0 bar (approximately)
Maximum difference between cylinders.	3.0 bar

Cylinder head bolts

Thread diameter.	M12
Length when new (from under head)	226.0 ± 0.5 mm
Maximum length.	227.5 mm

Lubrication system

Minimum system pressure at normal operating temperature:

At idle speed.	0.9 bar
At 3000 rpm	3.0 bar

Torque wrench settings

	Nm	lbf ft
Auxiliary drivebelt tensioner to major assembly carrier:		
M8	20	15
M10	45	33
Auxiliary drivebelt pulley bolts:		
M8	25	17
M10	45	33
Balancer shaft drive gear bolt:		
Stage 1	50	37
Stage 2	Angle-tighten a further 90°	
Camshaft bearing cap bolts	9	6
Camshaft sprocket bolts (left-hand thread):		
Stage 1	55	41
Stage 2	Angle-tighten a further 90°	
Connecting rod bolts*:		
Initial tightening after cracking (new rods):		
Stage 1	5	3
Stage 2	25	17
Stage 3	Angle-tighten a further 180°	
Subsequent tightening (used rods):		
Stage 1	5	3
Stage 2	25	17
Stage 3	Angle-tighten a further 90°	
Crankcase coolant drain plug	30	22
Crankshaft pulley bolts*:		
M12 x 56 mm:		
Stage 1	80	60
Stage 2	Angle-tighten a further 90°	
M12 x 129 mm:		
Stage 1	80	60
Stage 2	Angle-tighten a further 90°	
Stage 3	Angle-tighten a further 90°	
Cylinder head bolts* (see text):		
Stage 1	10	7
Stage 2	50	37
Stage 3	Angle-tighten a further 90°	
Stage 4	Angle-tighten a further 90°	
Stage 5	Angle-tighten a further 90°	
Stage 6	Angle-tighten a further 90°	
Cylinder head to timing cover M8	20	15
Cylinder head cover bolts	9	6
Engine/transmission mountings:		
Engine mounting-to-crossmember	58	43
Bracket to engine mounting	50	37
Bracket to crankcase:		
Stage 1	20	15
Stage 2	Angle-tighten a further 90°	
Rear engine support bracket to floor assembly (M10 x 22 mm)	65	48
Rear mounting to transmission	50	37
Rear mounting to support bracket	40	29
Exhaust manifold nut:		
Steel manifold	30	22
Cast manifold:		
Stage 1	15	11
Stage 2	35	26
Flywheel/driveplate bolts*:		
Stage 1	45	33
Stage 2	Angle-tighten a further 90°	
High-pressure fuel pump drive gear bolts	20	15
Intermediate gears to crankcase	80	60
Main bearing cap bolts:		
Stage 1	45	33
Stage 2	Angle-tighten a further 180°	
Major assembly carrier to crankcase:		
M6	9	6
M8	20	15
Oil filter cap	25	17

Torque wrench settings (continued)

	Nm	lbf ft
Oil filter housing:		
M6	10	7
M8	20	15
Oil level sensor	9	6
Oil pump bolts:		
M6:		
Stage 1	8	5
Stage 2	Angle-tighten a further 90°	
M8	34	25
Oil pump pick-up tube:		
Stage 1	6	4
Stage 2	Angle-tighten a further 90°	
Oil pump regulating valve	5	3
Oil spray nozzle	6	4
Oil spray nozzle control valve	20	15
Oil temperature sensor	26	19
Oil valve at crankcase	5	3
Sump drain plug	30	22
Sump:		
Upper section to crankcase:		
M6	10	7
M8	22	16
Upper section to timing cover	20	15
Lower section to upper section	10	7
Sump support to crankcase	60	44
Timing chain cover bolts	20	15
Timing chain tensioner to cylinder head	80	60
Turbocharger oil feed pipe:		
To turbocharger:		
Stage 2	9	6
Stage 2	Angle-tighten a further 90°	
Feed pipe union nut	22	16
Turbocharger oil drain pipe bolt	9	6

* Do not re-use

1 General Information

How to use this Chapter

1 This Chapter describes the repair procedures that can reasonably be carried out on the engine while it remains in the vehicle. If the engine has been removed from the vehicle and is being dismantled as described in Part B, any preliminary dismantling procedures can be ignored.

2 Note that, while it may be possible physically to overhaul items such as the piston/connecting rod assemblies while the engine is in the vehicle, such tasks are not usually carried out as separate operations. Usually, several additional procedures are required (not to mention the cleaning of components and oilways); for this reason, all such tasks are classed as major overhaul procedures, and are described in Part B of this Chapter.

3 Part B describes the removal of the engine/transmission from the vehicle, and the full overhaul procedures that can then be carried out.

Engine description

4 The engine is a 4-cylinder in-line double overhaul camshaft design, mounted in-line ('north-south') at the front of the vehicle with the transmission mounted on the rear of the engine.

5 The crankshaft is supported in five main bearing within the cast iron cylinder block. Crankshaft endfloat is controlled by thrust-washers fitted on either side of No 3 main bearing.

6 The connecting rods are attached to the crankshaft by horizontally split big-end bearings, and to the pistons by fully-floating gudgeon pins retained by circlips. The alloy pistons are fitted with three piston rings, two compression rings and one oil control ring.

7 The exhaust camshaft is driven from the crankshaft sprocket by a double-row chain, and the inlet camshaft is gear-driven from the exhaust camshaft. The camshaft also drives the fuel injection pump.

8 The camshaft is supported in bearings in the cylinder head, and actuates the valves directly, via hydraulic valve lifters.

9 The oil pump is chain-driven from the front of the crankshaft. An oil cooler is located on the oil filter housing at the left-hand front of the cylinder block.

Operations with engine in vehicle

10 The following operations can be carried out without having to remove the engine from the vehicle:

a) Removal and refitting of the cylinder head.

b) Removal and refitting of the timing chain and sprockets.
c) Removal and refitting of the camshaft.
d) Removal and refitting of the sump.
e) Removal and refitting of the big-end bearings, connecting rods, and pistons.*
f) Removal and refitting of the oil pump.
g) Renewal of the engine/transmission mountings.
h) Removal and refitting of the flywheel.

Note: * Although it is possible to remove these components with the engine in place, for reasons of access and cleanliness it is recommended that the engine be removed.

2 Compression and leakdown tests – description and interpretation

Compression test

Note: A compression tester designed for diesel engines must be used for this test.

1 When engine performance is down, a compression test can provide diagnostic clues as to the engine's condition. If the test is performed regularly, it can give warning of trouble before any other symptoms become apparent.

2 The tester is connected to an adapter, which screws into the glow plug or injector hole. On these engines, an adapter suitable

3.4 Undo the Torx bolt and pull out the camshaft position sensor

for use in the injector holes is preferable. It is unlikely to be worthwhile buying such a tester for occasional use, but it may be possible to borrow or hire one – if not, have the test performed by a garage.

3 Unless specific instructions to the contrary are supplied with the tester, observe the following points.

a) *The battery must be in a good state of charge, the air filter must be clean, and the engine should be at normal operating temperature.*

b) *All the injectors should be removed before starting the test.*

c) *The stop solenoid must be disconnected, to prevent the engine from running or fuel from being discharged.*

4 There is no need to hold the accelerator pedal down during the test, because the diesel engine air inlet is not throttled.

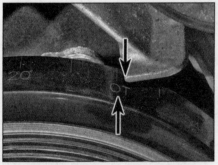

3.5a TDC (OT) mark on the crankshaft pulley/vibration damper aligned with the pointer on the crankcase

3.6a The marks on the intake bearing cap and camshaft should align...

5 Crank the engine on the starter motor. After one or two revolutions, the compression pressure should build-up to a maximum figure, and then stabilise. Record the highest reading obtained.

6 Repeat the test on the remaining cylinders, recording the pressure in each.

7 The cause of poor compression is less easy to establish on a diesel engine than on a petrol one. The effect of introducing oil into the cylinders ('wet' testing) is not conclusive, because there is a risk that the oil will sit in the swirl chamber or in the recess in the piston crown instead of passing to the rings. However, the following can be used as a rough guide to diagnosis.

8 All cylinders should produce very similar pressures; if there is a large difference, then this indicates a fault. Note that the compression should build-up quickly in a healthy engine; low compression on the first stroke, followed by gradually increasing pressure on successive strokes, indicates worn piston rings. A low compression reading on the first stroke, which does not build-up during successive strokes, indicates leaking valves or a blown head gasket (a cracked head could also be the cause). Deposits on the undersides of the valve heads can also cause low compression.

9 A low reading from two adjacent cylinders is almost certainly due to the head gasket having blown between them; the presence of coolant in the engine oil will confirm this.

10 If the compression reading is unusually high, the combustion chambers are probably

3.5b The Mercedes special tool locates over the pulley bolts

3.6b ...and the pointer with the edge of the exhaust position sensor 'window'

coated with carbon deposits. If this is the case, the cylinder head should be removed and decarbonised.

11 On completion of the test, refit the injectors or the glow plugs, and reconnect the stop solenoid.

Leakdown test

12 A leakdown test measures the rate at which compressed air fed into the cylinder is lost. It is an alternative to a compression test, and in many ways is better, since the escaping air provides easy identification of where a pressure loss is occurring (piston rings, valves or head gasket).

13 The equipment needed for leakdown testing is unlikely to be available to the home mechanic. If poor compression is suspected, have the test performed by a suitably-equipped garage.

---

3 Engine assembly/ valve timing settings – general information and usage

⚠ *Warning: When turning the engine, do not turn the engine using the camshaft sprocket bolts, and do not turn the engine backwards (ie, anti-clockwise).*

1 Top Dead Centre (TDC) is the highest point in the cylinder that each piston reaches as it travels up and down when the crankshaft turns. Each piston reaches TDC at the end of the compression stroke and again at the end of the exhaust stroke, but for valve timing TDC refers to the No 1 piston position on the compression stroke. No 1 piston is at the front end of the engine.

2 Positioning No 1 piston at TDC is an essential part of many procedures, such as timing chain removal and camshaft removal.

3 Rotate the fastener at the front anti-clockwise, then pull the cover on the top of the engine forwards to remove it.

4 Unscrew the oil filler cap, then disconnect the wiring plug, undo the retaining bolt and remove the camshaft position sensor **(see illustration)**.

5 Using a socket on the crankshaft pulley/ vibration damper hub bolt, turn the crankshaft clockwise until the 0° (OT TDC) mark on the crankshaft pulley/vibration damper is aligned with the pointer on the crankcase **(see illustration)**. Although not absolutely necessary, a special tool (No. 651 589 00 40 00) is available from Mercedes that locates over the crankshaft pulley bolts, allowing the engine to be rotated with ease **(see illustration)**.

Caution: Don't turn the crankshaft anti-clockwise as this may damage the timing chain/tensioner.

6 In this position the alignment indentations on the intake camshaft and bearing cap should align, along with the mark on the index wheel and position sensor 'window' for the exhaust camshaft **(see illustrations)**. If the marks are not aligned, rotate the crankshaft one complete revolution clockwise, and check again.

7 If necessary, the camshafts can be locked in position, although this is only necessary if the camshafts, sprockets or cylinder head are to be removed. Remove the cylinder head cover as described in Section 4, then undo the bolts and remove the camshaft bearing caps at the rear of the camshafts, adjacent to the timing chain.

8 With the camshaft aligned as previously described, it should be possible to slide the Mercedes locking tools down over the machined sections at the rear of each camshaft **(see illustration)**. **Note:** *Engines up to 31/12/11 use tool No. 651 589 01 40 00, while engines after this date use tool No. 651 589 09 40 00.*

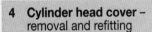

4 Cylinder head cover –
removal and refitting

Removal

1 Remove the air filter assembly and intake ducts as described in Chapter 4A Section 2.

2 Disconnect the wiring plugs from the fuel filter, fuel rail pressure sensor, etc, then release the clips and move the wiring harness duct to one side.

3 Remove the injectors as described in Chapter 4A Section 6.

4 Undo the banjo bolt, and disconnect the fuel return pipe from the fuel rail **(see illustration)**. Plug the openings to prevent contamination. Be prepared for fuel spillage. New sealing washers will be required.

5 Undo the retaining bolts around the edges and in the centre, then carefully remove the cylinder head cover. Note that the bolts are retained in the cover seal. Discard the rubber seal, a new one must be fitted.

Refitting

6 Clean the joint surfaces of the cover and cylinder head, then locate the new seal in the grooves in the cylinder head cover **(see illustration)**.

7 Position the cylinder head cover on the cylinder head, then tighten the bolts progressively to their specified torque.

8 Complete the rest of the installation by reversing the removal procedure, referring to the relevant Chapters. When all components are refitted, start the engine and check carefully around the camshaft cover for any oil leaks.

5 Crankshaft pulley –
removal and refitting

Removal

1 To gain better access, remove the fan and shroud from the rear of the radiator with reference to Chapter 3.

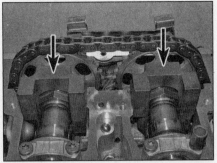

3.8 Slide the locking tools down over the flats of the camshaft flanges

2 Remove the auxiliary drivebelt as described in Chapter 1 Section 8.

3 The crankshaft must now be held stationary while the pulley bolts are loosened. The bolts are tightened to a high torque. Mercedes-Benz technicians use a tool (No. 651 589 00 40 00) that locates over 3 of the retaining bolts, allowing the crankshaft to be held, whilst the remaining bolt is slacked **(see illustration 3.5b)**. In the absence of this tool, counterhold the pulley bolts using a length of angle iron **(see illustration)**.

4 Unscrew the crankshaft pulley bolts then slide the pulley from the front of the crankshaft. Note that new bolts will be required.

Refitting

5 Wipe clean the pulley, and then slide it fully onto the crankshaft, aligning the locating dowel **(see illustration)**.

4.4 Undo the fuel return banjo bolt

5.3 Pulley can be counterheld with a length of angle-iron located between the bolt heads

6 Insert the new bolts and tighten them to the specified torque while holding the crankshaft stationary as for removal.

7 Refit the auxiliary drivebelt with reference to Chapter 1 Section 8.

8 Refit the engine undershield

6 Timing chain cover –
removal and refitting

1 As the timing chain cover is located at the rear of the engine, removal is only possible once the engine has been removed. Consequently, the procedure is described in Chapter 2B Section 9.

7 Timing chain –
inspection and renewal

Inspection

1 Remove the cylinder head cover as described in Section 4.

2 Using a socket on the crankshaft pulley/ vibration damper hub bolt, turn the engine clockwise so that the whole length of the chain can be progressively viewed at the camshaft sprocket.

3 The chain should be renewed if the sprocket is worn or if the chain is worn (indicated by excessive lateral play between the links, and excessive noise in operation). Note that the rollers on a very badly worn chain may be

4.6 Locate the new seal in the cover grooves

5.5 Align the dowel with the hole in the crankshaft

7.10 Press out one of the timing chain pins

7.11 The lubrication holes in the chain rollers must point outwards

7.12 Using the temporary link supplied in the tool kit, join the new chain to the old one

slightly grooved. To avoid future problems, if there is any doubt at all about the condition of the chain, renew it.

Renewal

Note: *This following procedure, uses a chain breaker/riveter to renew the chain without removing the timing chain cover, a second person will be required to assist fitting the timing chain. Ensure that all tools are available, as well as a new chain and new connecting link before proceeding.*

4 Two methods for chain renewal are described below. The first (recommended by Mercedes) involves splitting the original chain, joining it to the new one, then rotating the crankshaft and camshafts in unison, and 'feeding' the new chain around the various sprockets. The old chain is then removed, and the two ends of the new one joined with a 'soft' rivet link. In practice, even with an assistant, we found this method involved a considerable risk of damage due to the difficulty of rotating the shafts in unison, and maintaining chain tension. As the shafts are rotated, the chain would attempt jump teeth, and then be prone to jamming in the timing cover.

5 The second method is to remove the camshafts completely, then split the original chain, and join it to the new one. The crankshaft is then rotated, 'feeding' the chain around the fuel pump sprocket until the two ends of the new chain can be joined by a 'soft' rivet link. The camshafts are then refitted. This method eliminates any possibility

of accidental valve-to-piston contact. After careful consideration, although it involves slightly more dismantling, this is our preferred method of chain renewal.

Method 1

Note: *After-market timing chain replacement tool kits are available from various manufacturers. Try searching for AST or Laser tools.*

6 If not already done, remove the cylinder head cover as described in Section 4.

7 Using a socket on the crankshaft pulley bolt, turn the engine until the timing marks are aligned, as described in Section 7..

8 Remove the timing chain tensioner as described in Section 8.

9 Position the chain guide (supplied in the kit) on the cylinder head and secure it with 3 bolts. This will help prevent the timing chain from jumping on the sprockets. Put some clean rag into the timing chain recess to prevent anything dropping down into the engine.

10 Use the chain breaker to press out one of the timing chain pins and split the timing chain **(see illustration)**. Take care not to drop the pin.

11 Examine the new timing chain. The chain rollers may have lubrication holes on one side. These holes must point outwards – ie. when connecting the new chain to the old chain, the holes must point upwards **(see illustration)**.

12 Connect the new timing chain to the old chain using the temporary pin and spring link supplied in the tools kit **(see illustration)**. **Note:** *Make sure the new chain is connected to the old chain above the intake camshaft*

sprocket, as the engine has to be turned clockwise, in the direction of rotation to feed the chain around the sprockets.

13 With the new chain connected securely to the old chain, take a firm hold of both ends of the chain. Remove the clean rag from around the timing chain before turning the engine.

14 With the aid of an assistant, turn the engine in the direction of rotation. At the same time as turning the crankshaft, have the assistant rotate the exhaust camshaft at the same rate to maintain camshaft synchronisation, and chain tension. If the tension is not maintained, it may jam. Rotate the crankshaft/camshaft until the new chain comes all the way around to the intake camshaft sprocket. Try to keep tension on the chain as it's pulled over the intake camshaft sprocket.

15 Refit the clean rag back into the timing chain recess.

16 Remove the temporary connecting link and split the old timing chain from the new timing chain. **Note:** *Make sure the chain is pulled tight on the left-hand side of the engine, and the right-hand side slack to allow for the fitting of the chain tensioner.*

17 Check that the TDC marks on the crankshaft pulley and timing chain cover are aligned, and the marks on the camshaft and camshaft bearing caps are still aligned correctly.

18 Fit the new timing chain link, using the timing chain riveter to connect the two ends of the chain securely. Always read the instructions that come with the chain riveter, as there are many different types available. The link pins need to be riveted securely, to prevent the chain coming apart **(see illustrations)**.

19 Remove the clean rag from the timing chain recess, and fit the timing chain tensioner, with reference to Section 8. With the tensioner now fitted, check the timing marks are still in line.

20 Rotate the engine two complete turns and check the timing marks come back in alignment. Refer to Section 7 to check timing mark alignment is correct.

21 Remove the chain guide tool from the cylinder head.

22 Refit the cylinder head cover with reference to Section 4.

7.18a Join the ends of the new chain with the 'soft' rivet link and side plate supplied...

7.18b ...then use the tool to securely spread the ends of the link

Method 2

23 Remove camshafts as described in Section 9.

24 Use the chain breaker to press out one of the timing chain pins and split the timing chain **(see illustration 7.10)**.

25 Examine the new timing chain. The chain rollers may have lubrication holes on one side. These holes must point outwards – ie. when connecting the new chain to the old chain, the holes must point upwards **(see illustration 7.11)**.

26 Connect the new timing chain to the old chain using the temporary pin and spring link supplied in the tools kit. **Note:** *As the crankshaft must be turned clockwise, ensure the new chain is connected to the old chain on the tension side (intake side).*

27 With the aid of an assistant, turn the crankshaft in the direction of rotation (clockwise). At the same time as turning the crankshaft, have the assistant maintain some tension on both ends of the chain to prevent it jamming in the timing cover as the chain is 'fed' around the fuel pump sprocket. Rotate the crankshaft until the new chain comes all the way around.

28 Remove the temporary connecting link and split the old timing chain from the new timing chain.

29 Check that the TDC marks on the crankshaft pulley and timing chain cover are aligned.

30 Fit the new timing chain link, using the timing chain riveter to connect the two ends of the chain securely. Always read the instructions that come with the chain riveter, as there are many different types available. The link pins need to be riveted securely, to prevent the chain coming apart **(see illustration 7.18a and 7.18b)**.

31 Refit the camshafts as described in Section 9.

8 Timing chain tensioner and sprockets – removal, inspection and refitting.

Timing chain tensioner

Removal

1 Set the engine to TDC on No 1 cylinder as described in Section 3.

2 Remove the air filter housing as described in Chapter 4A Section 2.

3 Undo the 3 retaining bolts and remove the headshield over the EGR pipe **(see illustration)**.

4 Undo the bolts and remove the EGR pipe **(see illustration)**. Renew the gaskets.

5 On models with stop/start function, remove the rear bolt and gently push the starter heatshield down a little to access the chain tensioner **(see illustration)**.

6 Unscrew the tensioner from the right-hand side of the timing chain cover using a 27 mm

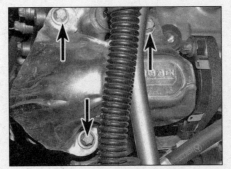

8.3 EGR pipe heatshield bolts

8.4 Remove the EGR pipe

socket or spanner **(see illustration)** – be prepared for oil spillage. Recover the sealing ring and discard; a new one will be required for refitting.

Inspection

7 Do not attempt to dismantle the tensioner assembly. If it is suspected that the tensioner is worn or faulty, the complete unit should be renewed.

Refitting

8 Compress the tensioner using hand pressure alone to expel any oil within, then locate a new sealing ring on the tensioner, then slowly screw it into position and tighten to the specified torque.

9 Refitting is the reversal of the removal procedure, referring to the relevant Chapters, where applicable. When all components are refitted, start the engine and check carefully around the tensioner for any oil leaks.

Camshaft sprockets

Removal

10 Refer to Section 3 and set the engine to TDC on No 1 cylinder. Lock the camshafts as described.

11 Use a dab of paint or a marker pen to mark the timing chain and the camshaft sprockets in relation to each other. This will help ensure that the chain is refitted correctly and the valve timing maintained.

12 Remove the timing chain tensioner as described earlier in this Section.

13 Hold the camshafts stationary using an open-ended spanner on the machined section

8.5 Undo the bolt and push the heatshield downwards slightly

of the flange at the rear, then loosen the bolts securing the sprockets to the camshafts. **Note:** *The sprocket bolts have a left-hand thread. Rotate the bolts clockwise to slacken them.*

14 At this stage the crankshaft sprocket will still be at TDC, and the crankshaft must not be turned until the camshaft sprockets have been refitted. Use a length of wire to tie the upper part of the timing chain to the cylinder head to ensure the chain remains on the fuel pump sprocket.

15 Fully unscrew the retaining bolts and remove the sprockets from the timing chain.

Inspection

16 Examine the teeth on the sprockets for wear. Each tooth forms an inverted V. If worn, the side of each tooth under tension will be slightly concave in shape when compared with the other side of the tooth (ie, the teeth will have a hooked appearance). If the teeth appear worn, the sprockets must be renewed.

Refitting

17 Ensure that the camshafts are still locked in place and that the crankshaft timing marks are still aligned, as described in Section 3. If a new sprocket is being fitted, transfer the chain alignment mark from the old sprocket to the new.

18 Engage the sprockets with the chain, aligning the marks made on the chain and sprockets before removal, then locate the sprockets on the camshaft flange.

19 Insert the sprocket retaining bolts, but only finger tighten them at this stage – the

8.6 Remove the timing chain tensioner

9.3 Paint alignment marks between the chain and sprockets

9.5b ...the last cap is marked 'K' – intake camshaft shaft, No. 5 cap

sprockets must be free to rotate independently of the camshafts. Remove the wire used to tie the chain to the cylinder head.

20 Refit the timing chain tensioner as described earlier in this Section.

21 Now tighten the camshaft sprocket retaining bolts to their specified torque. Note that the bolts have a left-hand thread.

22 Check that the crankshaft pulley mark is still aligned with the crankcase pointer, then remove the camshaft locking tools, refit the bearing caps and tighten the bolts to the specified torque.

23 Using a socket on the crankshaft pulley/vibration damper hub bolts, turn the crankshaft through two complete revolutions, and check that the crankshaft and camshaft timing marks are still aligned with No 1 piston at TDC, as described in Section 3.

24 Refit the cylinder head cover as described in Section 4.

9.15 Lubricate the bearing locations and rocker arms

9.5a No.1 exhaust cap is marked 'A' – as is the cylinder head...

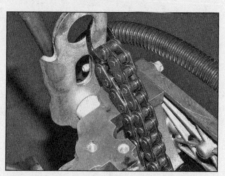

9.8 Secure the chain from slipping down the cover

Fuel pump sprocket

25 Removal of the fuel pump drive gear/sprocket is only possible once the engine has been removed. Refer to Chapter 2B.

---

9 Camshafts, rocker arms and hydraulic tappets – removal, inspection and refitting

---

Camshafts

Removal

1 Set the engine at TDC on No. 1 cylinder as described in Section 3.

2 Remove the cylinder head cover as described in Section 4.

3 Using permanent marker or paint, make alignment marks between the timing chain and the camshaft sprockets to aid refitting **(see illustration)**.

9.17 Position the lobes of No.1 cylinder camshaft as shown

4 Remove the chain tensioner as described in Section 8.

5 The camshaft bearing caps are marked A to K, starting at the No. 1 (front) cap on the exhaust side. The cylinder head is also marked to indicate the positions of the caps **(see illustrations)**. Check the bearing caps to ensure that marks are present, and if necessary make suitable marks using quick-drying paint.

6 The camshaft bearing cap bolts must now be slackened evenly, half-a-turn at a time.

⚠️ *Warning: It is absolutely essential to release the camshaft bearing caps evenly, and gradually, because the camshafts are very sensitive to fracturing.*

7 With the bolts removed, lift off the bearing caps, keeping them in order. Note that the bearing caps locate on dowels – if they are stuck, tap them gently using a soft-faced mallet.

8 Lift the camshafts from place, unhooking the sprockets from the timing chain as they are removed. Take precautions to prevent the chain from slipping down the cover – secure it using cable ties etc **(see illustration)**.

9 If required, unscrew the bolts and remove the sprockets from the camshafts.

Caution: The camshaft sprockets bolts have a left-hand thread! Rotate the bolts clockwise to remove them.

Inspection

10 Thoroughly clean the camshafts and the housing/caps.

11 Examine the camshaft journals and cam lobes for any sign of scoring, wear grooves or pitting, and if apparent, renew the relevant camshaft. Any damage of this nature may be attributable to a blocked oil passage in the cylinder head, and careful examination should be carried out to determine the cause.

12 Examine the bearing surfaces in the camshaft housing and bearing caps for excessive wear and scoring. If evident, renew the components together with the camshafts.

Refitting

13 If removed, locate the sprockets on the camshafts, and finger tighten the retaining bolts. It must be just possible to rotate the sprockets independently of the camshafts.

14 Ensure the crankshaft is still positioned at TDC on No.1 cylinder as described in Section 3.

15 Lubricate the camshaft journals and the bearing locations in the camshaft housing/caps with clean engine oil **(see illustration)**. Also lubricate the rocker arms.

16 Hook the intake camshaft sprocket into the timing chain, aligning the previously made marks, where applicable.

17 Position the intake camshaft in the housing with the top of the camshaft lobes of No. 1 cylinder (at the front of the engine – **not** the timing chain end) facing approximately upwards **(see illustration)**.

18 Refit the intake camshaft bearing caps

to their original positions, then insert the retaining bolts, and tighten them gradually, evenly, half-a-turn at a time to their specified torque.

Caution: It's essential that the camshafts are installed with as little stress as possible on their structure. They are fragile and are easily fractured.

19 If the position of the camshaft is correct, with the No.1 cylinder camshaft lobes pointing approximately upwards, the tip of the machined section on the camshaft flange should align with the mark on the No.5 bearing cap (adjacent to the timing chain) **(see illustration)**. If necessary, use an open-ended spanner on the machined section, and rotate the camshaft slightly until the tip aligns with the mark.

20 Fit the exhaust camshaft using the exact same procedure. The camshaft lobes above No.1 cylinder should be pointing upwards, and slightly towards each other **(see illustration)**.

21 Refit the timing chain tensioner as described in Section 8.

22 Check the crankshaft pulley TDC mark is still aligned with the pointer on the crankcase, and the tip of the hexagonal sections on the camshafts are still aligned with the marks on the No.5 bearing caps **(see illustration)**.

23 Temporarily refit the cylinder head cover, and check the intake and exhaust camshaft alignment marks are correct as described in Section 4.

24 Remove the cylinder head cover, and lock the camshafts in place as described in Section. If the locking tools are not available, prevent the camshafts from rotating using an open-ended spanner on their hexagonal sections, then tighten the sprocket retaining bolts to their specified torque. **Note:** *The sprocket bolts have a left-hand thread! Rotate them anti-clockwise to tighten.*

25 Once again, check the crankshaft and camshaft are still aligned as described in Section 3.

26 With the alignment correct, refit the cylinder head cover as described in Section 4.

Rocker arms and hydraulic tappets

Removal

27 Remove the camshafts as described earlier in this Section.

28 Obtain a container with 16 compartments and number the compartments to indicate the location of the rocker arms and hydraulic tappets. Lift each rocker arm and hydraulic tappet in turn and store them in the container **(see illustrations)**.

Inspection

29 The operation of the removed hydraulic tappets can be checked as follows.

a) Press down firmly on the top of each tappet, using hand pressure alone – don't use any tools as the surface of the tappets is easily damaged.

b) It should not be possible to compress the tappet using normal hand pressure, and only slightly using strong hand pressure.

c) Repeat the operation for all the tappets in turn.

d) If any one tappet can be depressed more easily than the others, renew it.

30 Check the hydraulic tappets and the bores in the cylinder head for wear and scoring. If any serious damage or wear is evident, the cylinder head and tappets must be renewed.

31 Examine the rocker arms for wear or damage. Note that the rocker arms will probably wear at the same rate as the surface of the camshaft lobes. If the rockers are worn, the camshafts are probably worn too.

Refitting

32 Lubricate the hydraulic tappet bores in the cylinder head with clean engine oil, then locate each hydraulic tappet in its original position **(see illustration)**.

33 The remainder of refitting is a reversal of removal.

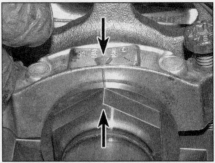

9.19 The mark on the bearing cap must align with the tip of the machined section of the flange

10 Cylinder head –
removal, inspection and refitting

Note: *New cylinder head bolts may be required – see text.*

Removal

1 Ensure that the engine is cold before attempting to remove the cylinder head.

2 Apply the parking brake, then jack up the front of the vehicle and support it on axle stands (see see *Jacking and vehicle support*).

3 Disconnect the battery negative lead as described in Chapter 5 Section 3.

4 Raise the bonnet to the fully open position.

5 Drain the engine oil and coolant as

9.20 The lobes above No.1 cylinder should be positioned as shown

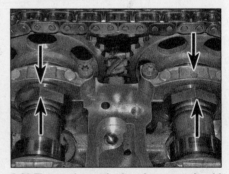

9.22 The marks on the bearing caps should align with the tips of the camshaft flanges

9.28a Remove each rocker arm

9.28b Using a magnet to lift out the hydraulic tappets

9.32 Refit the hydraulic tappets to their original locations

10.7a Remove the air filter housing front bracket...

10.7b ...and rear bracket

10.8 Move the rear lifting eye bracket to one side

10.9 Turbocharger-to-manifold bolts

described in Chapter 1 Section 6 and Chapter 1 Section 30.

6 Remove the air filter housing as described in Chapter 4A Section 2.

7 Unclip the wiring loom, undo the bolts and remove the air filter brackets from the cylinder head **(see illustrations)**. Disconnect and unclip the wiring plug, then move the rear bracket to one side, along with the particulate pressure sensor.

8 Detach the rear lifting eye bracket from the cylinder head, and move it to one side along with the oil level dipstick tube **(see illustration)**.

9 Undo the bolts securing the turbocharger to the exhaust manifold **(see illustration)**. Note that new bolts will be required.

10 Unscrew the upstream temperature sensor from the exhaust manifold **(see illustration)**.

11 With reference to Chapter 1 Section 11, remove the fuel filter assembly.

12 Disconnect the glow plug output stage wiring plug and unclip the wiring harness **(see illustration)**.

13 Disconnect the remaining output stage wiring plug, undo the 2 bolts and remove the unit **(see illustration)**.

14 LIft the clip and slide the coolant pump vacuum switch from the output stage bracket.

15 Disconnect the earth lead, undo the mounting bolts and move the glow plug output stage bracket to one side **(see illustrations)**.

16 Remove the EGR valve as described in Chapter 4B Section 2.

17 Note their fitted positions, disconnect the various wiring plugs, undo the retaining bolt and move the wiring harness and guide on the top of the engine to one side.

18 Undo the retaining bolts and remove the EGR cooler mounting bracket **(see illustration)**.

19 Undo the bolt and move the fuel pipes to one side **(see illustration)**.

20 Remove the thermostat as described in Chapter 3 Section 4.

10.10 Use a second spanner to counterhold the union

10.12 Disconnect the output stage wiring plug

10.13 Glow plug output stage retaining bolts

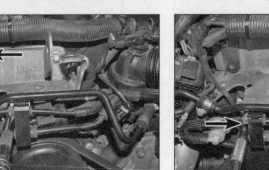

10.15a Disconnect the earth lead...

10.15b ...and undo the mounting bolts

10.18 Remove the EGR cooler bracket

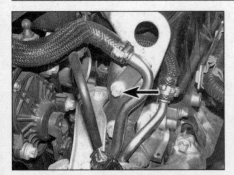

10.19 Fuel pipes bracket bolt

10.24a Coolant housing-to-cylinder head bolts

10.24b Support bracket bolts

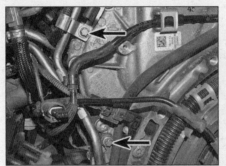

10.25 Fuel pipe retaining bolts

10.27 Pressure switch retaining bolt

21 Release the clamp and disconnect the coolant hose from the fuel filter housing.

22 Undo the union nuts and remove the high-pressure fuel pipe between the pump and fuel (common) rail. Note that new high-pressure fuel pipes will be needed upon reassembly.

23 Remove the camshafts, rocker arms and hydraulic tappets as described in Section 9.

24 Undo the 2 bolts securing the coolant housing to the rear of the cylinder head, and the 2 bolts securing the support bracket (see illustrations).

25 Disconnect the wiring plug, undo the 2 bolts and move the fuel pipe assembly to one side (see illustration).

26 Undo the bolts and remove the left-hand lifting eye from the cylinder head.

27 Undo the bolt securing the fuel pressure switch to the intake manifold (see illustration).

28 Undo the 3 bolts securing the cylinder head to the timing chain cover (see illustrations).

29 Make a final check to ensure that all relevant hoses and wires have been disconnected from the cylinder head.

30 Progressively loosen the cylinder head bolts, working in the reverse order to the tightening sequence (see illustration 10.49). Remove all cylinder head bolts.

31 Release the cylinder head from the cylinder block and locating dowels by rocking it. Do not prise between the mating faces of the cylinder head and block, as this may damage the gasket faces.

32 With the aid of an assistant, carefully lift the cylinder head, complete with exhaust manifold, from the block, and manoeuvre it out from the engine compartment.

33 Recover the cylinder head gasket.

34 Secure the timing chain to the tensioner rail using a cable tie or similar.

35 If necessary, remove the exhaust manifold from the cylinder head.

Inspection

36 Refer to Section 10 for details of the cylinder head dismantling and reassembly.

37 The mating faces of the cylinder head and block must be perfectly clean before refitting the head. Use a scraper to remove all traces of gasket and carbon, and also clean the tops of the pistons. Take particular care with the cylinder head, as the metal is easily damaged. Also make sure that debris is not allowed to enter the oil and water passages. Using adhesive tape and paper, seal the water, oil and bolt holes in the cylinder block. To prevent carbon entering the gap between the pistons and bores, smear a little grease in the gap. After cleaning each piston, rotate the crankshaft so that the piston moves down the bore, and then wipe out the grease and carbon with a cloth rag.

38 Check the block and head for nicks, deep scratches and other damage. If very slight, they may be removed from the cylinder block carefully with a file. More serious damage may be repaired by machining, but this is a specialist job.

39 If warpage of the cylinder head is suspected, use a straight-edge to check it for distortion, with reference to Section 10.

40 Clean out the bolt holes in the block using a pipe cleaner or thin rag and a screwdriver. Make sure that all oil and water is removed, otherwise there is a possibility of the block being cracked by hydraulic pressure when the bolts are tightened.

41 Examine the bolt threads and the threads in the cylinder block for damage. If necessary, use the correct size tap to chase out the threads in the block.

42 The manufacturers recommend that the cylinder head bolts are measured, to determine whether renewal is necessary; however, some owners may wish to renew all the bolts as a matter of course.

43 Measure the length of each bolt from the

10.28a Undo the bolt in the left-hand rear corner...

10.28b ...and the bolts in the timing chain tunnel

10.43 Measure from the base of bolt head to the end of the shank

10.45 Apply a thin bead of sealant to the cylinder head-to-timing cover joints

10.46 Position the gasket over the location dowels

10.48 Lubricate the underside of the bolt heads and the threads

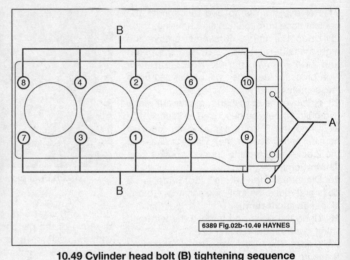

10.49 Cylinder head bolt (B) tightening sequence

A   Bolts securing the cylinder head to the timing chain cover

base of the head to the end of the shank **(see illustration)**. If the bolt length is greater than the maximum specified, the bolts should be renewed.

44 Reassemble the cylinder head with reference to Section 10. Where applicable, refit the exhaust manifold together with a new gasket.

Refitting

45 Apply a little silicone sealant (Loctite 5970) to the joints between the cylinder head and the timing cover **(see illustration)**.

46 Locate the new cylinder head gasket on

11.7 Renew the oil level dipstick guide tube O-ring seal

the block, making sure that it is the correct way up and positioned over the location dowels **(see illustration)**.

47 With the aid of an assistant, lower the cylinder head carefully onto the block.

48 Oil the threads and the cylinder head contact faces of the cylinder head bolts, then insert them and screw them into the cylinder block by hand **(see illustration)**. Ensure that the bolts are fitted to their correct locations as noted on removal.

49 Tighten the cylinder head bolts in the order shown **(see illustration)**, and in the stages given in the Specifications – ie, tighten all bolts to the Stage 1 torque, then tighten all bolts to the Stage 2 torque, and so on.

50 Tighten the 3 bolts securing the timing chain cover to the cylinder head at the front of the engine.

51 The remainder of refitting is a reversal of removal, noting the following points:

a) *Refill the cooling system and refill the engine with oil as described in Chapter 1.*

b) *Reconnect the battery negative lead as described in Chapter 5 Section 3.*

c) *When all components have been refitted, start the engine and check carefully around the engine for any oil or coolant leaks.*

11 Sump – removal and refitting

Removal

Note: *A suitable hoist and lifting tackle will be required for this operation. To carry out this procedure, the front suspension crossmember will need to be lowered, to allow enough room for the sump to be removed. A new sump gasket will be required on refitting.*

1 Remove the engine cover as described in Section 4.

2 Remove the flywheel/driveplate as described in Section 13.

3 Drain the engine oil as described in Chapter 1 Section 6. On completion, renew the sealing washer, then refit the drain plug and tighten to the specified torque.

4 Attach a suitable hoist to the engine and take the weight of the engine.

5 Unscrew the bolts from the bottom of the engine mountings at each side of the engine.

6 Lower the front suspension crossmember with reference to Chapter 10 Section 7.

7 Undo the retaining bolts and remove the engine oil level dipstick guide tube **(see illustration)**. Renew the O-ring seal.

11.9 Don't overlook the bolt in the centre of the sump lower section

11.10 Remove the timing cover-to-sump bolts

8 Disconnect the oil sensor wiring plug.
9 Undo the retaining bolts and remove the lower section of the sump **(see illustration)**. Renew the sump seal.
10 Remove the bolts securing the upper section of the sump to the timing cover **(see illustration)**.
11 Undo the bolts securing the upper section of the sump to the crankcase, then screw-in four M8 mm bolts into the 'feedthrough' holes and gradually force the sump from the crankcase **(see illustrations)**. Be sure to screw-in the bolts evenly and gradually. Do not drive a screwdriver between the sump and crankcase as this may damage the mating surfaces.
12 Undo the bolts and remove the oil pump pick-up tube **(see illustration)**. Renew the O-ring seal.

Refitting

13 Thoroughly clean the mating surfaces of the sump and cylinder block, then refit the oil pick-up tube with a new O-ring seal, and tighten the bolts to the specified torque **(see illustration)**.
14 Apply a 2.0 mm continuous bead of silicone sealant (MB recommend Loctite 5970)

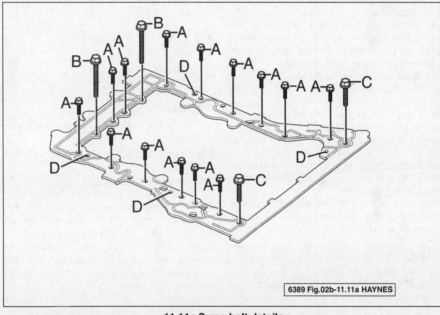

6389 Fig.02b-11.11a HAYNES

11.11a Sump bolt details

A M6 x 16 mm
B M6 x 65 mm

C M8 x 45 mm
D Screw 'feedthroughs'

11.11b Screw-in 8 mm bolts to gently force the sump from the crankcase

11.12 Oil pick-up tube bolts

11.13 Renew the pick-up tube O-ring seal

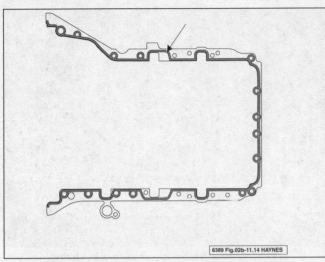

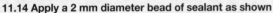

11.14 Apply a 2 mm diameter bead of sealant as shown

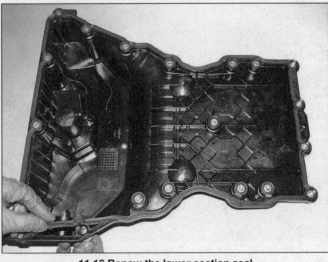

11.16 Renew the lower section seal

to the upper section of the sump as shown **(see illustration)**.

15 Manoeuvre the upper section of the sump into position, then insert the retaining bolts **(see illustration 11.11a)**, and gradually tighten them to the specified torque. Note that the bolts must be tightened within 7 minutes of the sealant being applied, or it will begin to harden.

16 Place the new seal onto the lower section of the sump, then manoeuvre it into position, inset the retaining bolts and tighten them to the specified torque **(see illustration)**.

17 Complete the rest of the installation by reversing the removal procedure, referring to the relevant Chapters.

18 When all components are refitted, start the engine and check carefully around the sump for any oil leaks.

12 Oil pump –
removal, inspection and refitting

1 Removal of the oil pump is only possible once the timing cover has been removed. Removal of this cover is only possible with the engine removed.

2 Consequently, oil pump removal, inspection

and refitting is described in Chapter 2B Section 11.

13 Flywheel/driveplate –
removal, inspection and refitting

Removal

1 Remove the manual transmission (Chapter 7 Section 5).

2 Remove the clutch as described in Chapter 6 Section 5.

3 Undo the retaining bolt and withdraw the crankshaft position sensor **(see illustration)**.

4 The flywheel/driveplate must be held stationary while the mounting bolts are loosened. To do this, counterhold the crankshaft using a socket on the crank pulley bolts, or refit a few of the clutch pressure plate bolts, and counterhold the flywheel/driveplate with a suitable bar.

5 Unscrew the mounting bolts, then lift the flywheel/driveplate from the rear of the crankshaft **(see illustrations)**. Note that the location dowel ensures the flywheel/driveplate can only be fitted in one position. Discard the flywheel bolts, new ones must be fitted.

Inspection

6 If the flywheel-to-clutch mating surface is deeply scored, cracked or otherwise damaged, then the flywheel must be renewed, unless it is possible to have it surface ground. Seek the advice of a Mercedes-Benz dealer or engine reconditioning specialist.

7 If the ring gear is badly worn or has missing teeth, then it must be renewed. This job is best left to a Mercedes-Benz dealer or engine reconditioning specialist.

8 On vehicles with dual mass flywheels, check the rotational and lateral movement as follows.

9 In order to check the rotational movement, lock the flywheel in place as previously described. Rotate the flywheel secondary element (drive surface) by hand anti-clockwise, mark its position in relation to the primary flywheel element (bolted to the crankshaft), then rotate it by hand clockwise and mark its position. Bear in mind, that the free rotational movement is being measured here – do not use excessive force to rotate the secondary element. Mark the limits of the rotational movement in relation to the number of flywheel starter ring gear teeth **(see illustrations)**.

10 If the number of starter ring gear teeth

13.3 Remove the crankshaft position sensor

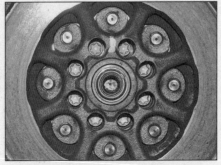

13.5a Unscrew the flywheel/driveplate bolts

13.5b Note the locating dowel and hole

travelled by the flywheel secondary element exceeds 8 (flywheel manufacturer SACHS or LUK), the flywheel may need replacing.

11 In order to check the lateral movement of the flywheel, attach a length of steel strip to the flywheel secondary element (drive surface), and mount a DTI gauge so that it measures in-line with the transmission mounting flange holes **(see illustration)**. Pull the steel strip away from the flywheel, zero the DTI gauge, then push the strip towards the flywheel and read off the measurement. The maximum permissible amount of lateral movement specified by Mercedes-Benz is 2.5 mm (flywheel manufacturer LUK), or 10.0 mm (flywheel manufacturer SACHS). If the dimension measured exceeds this, the flywheel may need replacing.

12 Check the condition of the spigot bearing in the centre of the flywheel or in the end of the crankshaft, and renew if necessary **(see illustration)**.

13 It is recommended that the flywheel/driveplate securing bolts are renewed whenever removed. **Note:** *On vehicles equipped with an LUK dual mass flywheel, a centrifugal-force pendulum is incorporated into the design to further increase the damping capacity at low engine speeds, and prolong service life. A characteristic of this design is that when operated/shaken by hand, the flywheel will emit a pronounced rattle. This is not a fault, and is not grounds for replacement.*

Refitting

14 Commence refitting by cleaning the mating faces of the crankshaft and flywheel/driveplate.

15 Make sure that the location dowel is in position in the end of the crankshaft.

16 Locate the flywheel/driveplate onto the crankshaft, then insert the new mounting bolts and hand-tighten them.

17 Lock the flywheel/driveplate using the method employed during removal, then tighten the securing bolts progressively in a diagonal sequence to the specified torque.

18 The remainder of refitting is a reversal of removal.

13.9a Turn the flywheel secondary element anti-clockwise and mark the limit of its travel on the starter ring gear teeth...

13.9b ...then turn the secondary element clockwise, and mark its travel limit again

13.11 Attach a length of steel strip to the flywheel secondary element (drive surface)

13.12 The spigot bearing is in the centre of the flywheel

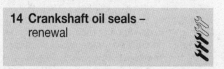

14 Crankshaft oil seals – renewal

Front oil seal

1 Remove the crankshaft pulley/vibration damper and inspect it as described in Section 5.

2 Measure and note the fitted depth of the oil seal in the crankcase **(see illustration)**.

3 Prise the oil seal from the cover using a hooked instrument. Alternatively, drill a small hole in the oil seal, and use a self-tapping screw and a pair of pliers to remove it **(see illustrations)**.

Caution: Take great care not to damage the crankshaft surface.

4 Clean the seal location in the crankcase, and also clean the oil seal contact surface on the crankshaft.

5 Press the new seal into the crankcase (open end first) to the previously-noted depth, using a suitable tube or socket. Do not apply any lubricant to the seal or the crankshaft. Generic insertion tools are available that locate over the end of the crankshaft. The seal is then located over the tool, and slid squarely into place.

6 Refit the crankshaft pulley/vibration damper as described in Section 5.

Rear oil seal

7 Remove the flywheel/driveplate as described in Section 13.

8 Prise the oil seal from the cover using a screwdriver/hooked instrument **(see illustration)**.

14.2 Note the fitted depth of the seal

14.3a Carefully drill a small hole...

14.3b ...screw in a self-tapping screw, and pull out the seal

14.8 Take care not to damage the crankshaft surface when removing the seal

14.10 The insertion tool fits inside the seal, over the end of the crankshaft

14.11 The seal must be flush with the timing cover

9 Clean the seal location in the crankcase, and also clean the oil seal contact surface on the crankshaft. The new seal must be installed without lubricant.

10 Fit the new oil seal housing over the crankshaft and into the timing cover. Generic insertion tools are available, that located over the end of the crankshaft. The seal is then located over the tool, and slid squarely into place **(see illustration)**.

11 The seal must be fitted so it's rear edge is flush with the edge of the timing cover **(see illustration)**.

12 Refit the flywheel/driveplate (Section 13).

15 Cylinder head front cover – removal and refitting

1 Disconnect the battery as described in Chapter 5 Section 3.

2 Remove the cylinder head cover as described in Section 4.

3 Remove the brake vacuum pump as described in Chapter 9 Section 13.

4 Remove the timing chain tensioner as described in Section 8.

5 Remove the fuel pre-delivery pump (depending on model), as described in Chapter 4A.

6 Undo the retaining bolts from cover on the front of the cylinder head.

7 Using a screwdriver release the locking

ratchet in the upper timing chain slide rail, and then withdraw the cover from the front of the cylinder head.

16 Engine/transmission mountings – inspection and renewal

Inspection

1 Three engine/transmission mountings are used, one on either side of the engine, and one under the rear of the transmission.

2 For improved access, raise the front of the vehicle and support it securely on axle stands, as described in *Jacking and vehicle support*.

3 Check the condition of the mounting rubber to see if it is cracked, hardened or separated from the metal at any point. Renew the mounting if any such damage or deterioration is evident.

4 Check that all the mounting bolts are securely tightened.

5 Using a large screwdriver or metal bar, check for wear in the mounting by carefully levering against it to check for free play. Where this is not possible, enlist the aid of an assistant to move the engine/transmission back-and-forth, or from side-to-side, while you observe the mounting. If excessive free play is found, check first that the fasteners are correctly secured, and then renew any worn components as required.

Renewal

Front engine mountings

6 Support the engine, either using a hoist and lifting tackle connected to the engine lifting brackets, or by positioning a jack and interposed block of wood under the sump. Ensure that the engine is adequately supported before proceeding.

7 Depending on which engine mounting requires removal, it may be necessary to remove the air filter housing and washer fluid reservoir to make access easier. See the relevant Chapters to remove any other components.

8 Unscrew and remove the engine mounting upper bolt. Depending on model, disconnect the earth cable from the engine mounting **(see illustrations)**.

9 If working on the right-hand engine mounting, below the exhaust manifold/turbo, remove the heat shield.

10 Working under the vehicle, ndo the engine mounting lower nuts **(see illustration)**.

11 Raise the engine as necessary, taking care not to stretch any hoses or wiring, and remove the mounting. If necessary, unbolt the mounting bracket from the side of the cylinder block **(see illustrations)**.

12 Refitting is a reversal of removal, and tighten the mounting bolts to the specified torque.

Rear engine/transmission mounting

13 Raise the front of the vehicle and support

16.8a Upper mounting bolt (note earth cable) – left-hand mounting

16.8b Upper mounting bolt – right-hand mounting

16.10 Engine mounting lower retaining nuts

it securely on axle stands (see *Jacking and vehicle support*).

14 Support the transmission using a jack and interposed block of wood.

15 Unbolt the mounting bracket from the underbody, then unscrew the bolts securing the mounting rubber to the rear of the transmission. Lower the bracket together with the mounting from the underbody **(see illustrations)**.

16 The mounting rubber can then be unbolted from the top of the mounting bracket.

17 Refitting is a reversal of removal.

16.11a Engine mounting bracket – right-hand side

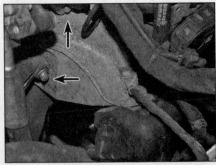

16.11b Engine mounting bracket – left-hand side

16.15a Unscrew the rear mounting bolts...

16.15b ...then undo the mounting bracket bolts

Chapter 2 Part B
Engine removal and engine overhaul procedures

Contents

Degrees of difficulty

Easy, suitable for novice with little experience	Fairly easy, suitable for beginner with some experience	Fairly difficult, suitable for competent DIY mechanic	Difficult, suitable for experienced DIY mechanic	Very difficult, suitable for expert DIY or professional

Specifications

Cylinder head
Maximum gasket face distortion: . . . . 0.08 mm
Cylinder head height . . . . 126.85 mm to 127.15 mm
Wear limit after machining . . . . 126.65 mm

Valves
Valve stem diameter. . . . . 6.960 mm to 6.975 mm
   Intake . . . . 6.960 mm to 6.975 mm
   Exhaust. . . . . 6.955 mm to 6.970 mm
Valve seat angle . . . . 45°

Pistons
Piston protrusion . . . . 0.38 mm to 0.62 mm

Piston rings
End gaps:
   Top compression ring. . . . . 0.22 to 0.37 mm
   Second compression ring. . . . . 0.80 to 1.00 mm
   Oil control ring . . . . 0.20 to 0.40 mm
Clearance in grooves:
   Top compression ring. . . . . 0.12 to 0.16 mm
   Second compression ring. . . . . 0.05 to 0.09 mm
   Oil control ring . . . . 0.03 to 0.07 mm

Big-end bearing cap bolts
Maximum length. . . . . 48.0 mm

Crankshaft main bearing cap bolts
Length when new. . . . . 61.8 mm to 62.2 mm
Maximum length. . . . . 63.8 mm

Crankshaft
Endfloat . . . . 0.300 mm
Endfloat thrustwasher thicknesses . . . . 2.15, 2.20, 2.25, 2.35 and 2.40 mm
Main bearings clearance on crankshaft. . . . . 0.080 mm
Big-end bearings clearance on crankshaft . . . . 0.080 mm

Torque wrench settings
See Chapter 2A.

1 General Information

1 Included in this Chapter are details of removing the engine from the vehicle and general overhaul procedures for the cylinder head, cylinder block/crankcase and all other engine internal components.

2 The information given ranges from advice concerning preparation for an overhaul and the purchase of parts, to detailed step-by-step procedures covering removal, inspection, renovation and refitting of engine internal components.

3 After Section 5, all instructions are based on the assumption that the engine has been removed from the vehicle. For information concerning in-car engine repair, as well as the removal and refitting of those external components necessary for full overhaul, refer to Part A of this Chapter, and to Section 6. Ignore any preliminary dismantling operations described in Parts A or B that are no longer relevant once the engine has been removed from the vehicle.

2 Engine overhaul – general information

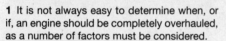

1 It is not always easy to determine when, or if, an engine should be completely overhauled, as a number of factors must be considered.

2 High mileage is not necessarily an indication that an overhaul is needed, while low mileage does not preclude the need for an overhaul. Frequency of servicing is probably the most important consideration. An engine, which has had regular and frequent oil and filter changes, as well as other required maintenance, should give many thousands of miles of reliable service. Conversely, a neglected engine may require an overhaul very early in its life.

3 Excessive oil consumption is an indication that piston rings, valve seals and/or valve guides are in need of attention. Make sure that oil leaks are not responsible before deciding that the rings and/or guides are worn. Perform a compression test, as described in Chapter 2A Section 2, to determine the likely cause of the problem.

4 Check the oil pressure with a gauge fitted in place of the oil pressure switch, and compare it with that specified in Part A. If it is extremely low, the main and big-end bearings, and/or the oil pump, are probably worn out.

5 Loss of power, rough running, knocking or metallic engine noises, excessive valve gear noise, and high fuel consumption may also point to the need for an overhaul, especially if they are all present at the same time. If a complete service does not remedy the situation, major mechanical work is the only solution.

6 A full engine overhaul involves restoring all internal parts to the specification of a new engine. During a complete overhaul, the pistons and the piston rings are renewed, and the cylinder bores are reconditioned. New main and big-end bearings are generally fitted; if necessary, the crankshaft may be reground, to compensate for wear in the journals. The valves are also serviced as well, since they are usually in less-than-perfect condition at this point. Always pay careful attention to the condition of the oil pump when overhauling the engine, and renew it if there is any doubt as to its serviceability. The end result should be an as-new engine that will give many trouble-free miles.

7 Critical cooling system components such as the hoses, thermostat and coolant pump should be renewed when an engine is overhauled. The radiator should be checked carefully, to ensure that it is not clogged or leaking.

8 Before beginning the engine overhaul, read through the entire procedure, to familiarise yourself with the scope and requirements of the job. Overhauling an engine is not difficult if you follow carefully all of the instructions, have the necessary tools and equipment, and pay close attention to all specifications. It can, however, be time-consuming. Plan on the vehicle being off the road for a minimum of two weeks, especially if parts must be taken to an engineering works for repair or reconditioning. Check on the availability of parts and make sure that any necessary special tools and equipment are obtained in advance. Most work can be done with typical hand tools, although a number of precision measuring tools are required for inspecting parts to determine if they must be renewed. Often the engineering works will handle the inspection of parts and offer advice concerning reconditioning and renewal.

9 Always wait until the engine has been completely dismantled, and until all components (especially the cylinder block/crankcase and the crankshaft) have been inspected, before deciding what service and repair operations must be performed by an engineering works. The condition of these components will be the major factor to consider when determining whether to overhaul the original engine, or to buy a reconditioned unit. Do not, therefore, purchase parts or have overhaul work done on other components until they have been thoroughly inspected. As a general rule, time is the primary cost of an overhaul, so it does not pay to fit worn or sub-standard parts.

10 As a final note, to ensure maximum life and minimum trouble from a reconditioned engine, everything must be assembled with care, in a spotlessly clean environment.

3 Engine removal – methods and precautions

1 If you have decided that the engine must be removed for overhaul or major repair work, several preliminary steps should be taken.

2 Locating a suitable place to work is extremely important. Adequate workspace, along with storage space for the vehicle, will be needed. If a workshop or garage is not available, at the very least, a flat, level, clean work surface is required.

3 Cleaning the engine compartment and engine/transmission before beginning the removal procedure will help keep tools clean and organised.

4 An engine hoist will also be necessary. Make sure the equipment is rated in excess of the weight of the engine (and transmission if both are being removed). Safety is of primary importance, considering the potential hazards involved in lifting the engine out of the vehicle.

5 If this is the first time you have removed an engine, an assistant should ideally be available. Advice and aid from someone more experienced would also be helpful. There are many instances when one person cannot simultaneously perform all of the operations required when lifting the engine out of the vehicle.

6 Plan the operation ahead of time. Before starting work, arrange for the hire of or obtain all of the tools and equipment you will need. Some of the equipment necessary to perform engine removal and installation safely and with relative ease (in addition to an engine hoist) is as follows: a heavy duty trolley jack, complete sets of spanners and sockets (see *Tools and working facilities*), wooden blocks, and plenty of rags and cleaning solvent for mopping-up spilled oil, coolant and fuel. If the hoist must be hired, make sure that you arrange for it in advance, and perform all of the operations possible without it beforehand. This will save you money and time.

7 Plan for the vehicle to be out of use for quite a while. An engineering works will be required to perform some of the work which the do-it-yourselfer cannot accomplish without special equipment. These places often have a busy schedule, so it would be a good idea to consult them before removing the engine, in order to accurately estimate the amount of time required to rebuild or repair components that may need work.

8 Always be extremely careful when removing and refitting the engine. Serious injury can result from careless actions. Plan ahead and take your time, and a job of this nature, although major, can be accomplished successfully.

9 On all models, the engine is removed by lifting the assembly out from the front of the vehicle.

4 Engine and transmission – removal, separation and refitting

Removal

1 Disconnect the battery negative lead as described in Chapter 5 Section 3.

2 Remove the air filter assembly and intake ducts as described in Chapter 4A Section 2.

4.3 Undo the mounting bolts and remove the bracket

4.8a Undo the screws for the power steering cooler pipe mounts on the right...

4.8b ...and left of the engine bay

4.9a Remove the top mounting bolts at the front wings...

4.9b ...the four front mounting bolts...

4.9c ...and the two Torx screws in each front wing

3 Unscrew the four bolts and remove the rear mounting bracket for the air filter assembly **(see illustration)**.
4 Remove the plastic trim panel from the top of the engine.
5 Remove the headlights as described in Chapter 12 Section 12.
6 Remove the radiator as described in Chapter 3 Section 3.
7 Remove the intercooler as described in Chapter 4A Section 14.
8 Remove the mounting screws for the power steering cooler pipes and manoeuvre them out of the way **(see illustrations)**.
9 Undo the front module's mounting bolts and screws **(see illustrations)**.
10 Unclip and disengage the bonnet release cable.
11 Unclip the wiring harness where applicable and manoeuvre the module from place **(see illustration)**.
12 Undo the bolts and remove the heatshield above the turbocharger.
13 Syphon out the fluid, then disconnect the hoses, undo the bolts and remove the power steering pump fluid reservoir. Release the wiring harness retaining clip where applicable.
14 Disconnect the fluid hoses from the power steering pump.
15 Raise the front of the vehicle and support it securely on axle stands (see Vehicle jacking and support 13 Section 5).
16 Drain the engine oil and coolant as described in Chapter 1 Section 6 and Chapter 1 Section 30.
17 Release the clamps and disconnect the

coolant hoses from the radiator, thermostat housing and electric circulation pump (where applicable).
18 Disconnect the hoses, undo the retaining bolt(s) and remove the coolant expansion tank

4.11 Gently pull the module forward from place

4.18b Unplug the wiring connector

(see illustrations). Disconnect the sensor wiring plug as the tank is withdrawn.
19 Release the clamps and disconnect the air ducts to and from the intercooler **(see illustration)**.

4.18a Coolant expansion tank retaining bolt

4.19 Prise out the clip and disconnect the air ducts from the intercooler

4.25 Plug the fuel supply pipes

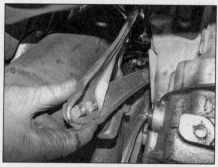

4.30 Unbolt and remove the exhaust bracket

4.34 Remove the crossmember from under the transmission

20 Remove the auxiliary drivebelt as described in Chapter 1 Section 8.

21 Disconnect the following wiring plugs, noting their locations and harness routing, and where the clips are mounted:

a) Starter motor
b) SAM unit.
c) Earth connection for fusebox on battery.
d) Pull the harness from the bulkhead.
e) Earth connection on the transmission.
f) Reversing light switch.
g) Transmission control module (TCM) – automatic transmission only.

22 Undo the bolt securing the air conditioning pipe to the oil filter housing.

23 Disconnect the heater hose at the engine compartment bulkhead.

24 Where applicable, disconnect the fluid pipes from the automatic transmission cooler. Be prepared for fluid spillage.

25 Mark the fuel supply and return pipes to aid refitting, then disconnect them **(see illustration)**. Plug the openings to prevent contamination.

26 On models with an auxiliary heating element, remove the shield, prise open the cap, and disconnect the wiring lead from the underisde of the transmission tunnel.

27 Remove the air conditioning compressor as described in Chapter 3 Section 10.

28 Undo the bolt securing the power steering pipe to the engine sump (where applicable).

29 Remove the catalytic converter or particulate filter (as applicable) as described in Chapter 4B Section 5.

30 Remove the exhaust pipe bracket from the transmission **(see illustration)**.

31 Disconnect the gear change/selector rod/cable from the transmission as described in Chapter 7 Section 3.

32 Disconnect the fluid pipe from the clutch slave cylinder as described in Chapter 6 Section 3.

33 Position a trolley jack under the rear of the transmission with a block of wood interposed at the jack head.

34 Undo the bolts and remove the crossmember from the rear of the transmission **(see illustration)**.

35 With reference to Chapter 8 Section 2, disconnect the propeller shaft from the transmission. Support the free end of the shaft to prevent damage to the joints.

36 Attach a hoist to the engine lifting eyes, and take the weight of the engine.

37 Unscrew the lower bolts from the engine front mountings.

38 With the help of an assistant, lift and tilt the engine and transmission to withdraw it from the engine compartment, taking care not to damage the surrounding components and wiring. It will be necessary to move the hoist forwards and guide the engine and transmission up through the engine compartment, taking care not to damage the surrounding components. Move the hoist forwards and lower the engine/transmission assembly to the ground.

39 To remove the transmission from the engine, refer to Chapter 7 Section 5 as necessary.

Refitting

40 Before refitting the engine and transmission, check the condition of the engine/transmission mountings. In particular, check if they are compressed, are damaged or split, or have signs of oil leakage. If necessary, renew them with reference to Chapter 2A Section 16.

41 The reconnection and refitting procedures are a reversal of removal, noting the following additional information.

a) Tighten all nuts and bolts to the specified torque wrench settings, where given.
b) Bleed the clutch hydraulic system as described in.
c) Reconnect the propeller shaft to the flange on the rear of the transmission with reference to Chapter 8 Section 2.
d) Refill the power steering fluid reservoir with fresh fluid and bleed the system as described in Chapter 10 Section 19.
e) Ensure that all wiring, hoses and brackets are positioned and routed as noted before removal.
f) On completion, refill the engine with oil as described in Chapter 1 Section 6, and refill the cooling system as described in Chapter 1 Section 30.

5 Engine overhaul – dismantling sequence

1 It is much easier to dismantle and work on the engine if it is mounted on a portable engine stand. These stands can often be hired from a tool hire shop. Before the engine is mounted on a stand, the flywheel/driveplate should be removed, so that the stand bolts can be tightened into the end of the cylinder block/crankcase.

2 If a stand is not available, it is possible to dismantle the engine with it blocked up on a sturdy workbench, or on the floor. Be extra careful not to tip or drop the engine when working without a stand.

3 If you are going to obtain a reconditioned engine, all the external components around the engine must be removed first, so that they can be transferred to the new engine (just as they will if you are doing a complete engine overhaul yourself). These components include the following.

a) Ancillary unit mounting brackets (oil filter, alternator, power steering pump, engine mountings, crankcase breather housing, etc).
b) Thermostat and housing.
c) Dipstick tube.
d) All electrical switches and sensors.
e) Inlet and exhaust manifolds.
f) Injectors and fuel pipes (Chapter 4A).

Note: When removing the external components from the engine, pay close attention to details that may be helpful or important during refitting. Note the fitted position of gaskets, seals, spacers, pins, washers, bolts, and other small items.

4 If you are obtaining a 'short' engine (which consists of the engine cylinder block/crankcase, crankshaft, pistons and connecting rods all assembled), then the cylinder head(s), sump, oil pump, and timing chain will have to be removed also.

5 If you are planning a complete overhaul, the engine can be dismantled, and the internal components removed, in the order given below, referring to Part A or B of this Chapter unless otherwise stated.

a) Inlet and exhaust manifolds (Chapter 4B).

6.4a Remove the valve cap...

6.4b ...and spring

6.5 Lift off the spring seat

b) *Timing chain, sprockets and tensioner.*
c) *Cylinder head(s).*
d) *Flywheel/driveplate.*
e) *Sump.*
f) *Oil pump.*
g) *Piston/connecting rod assemblies.*
h) *Crankshaft.*

6 Before beginning the dismantling and overhaul procedures, make sure that you have all of the correct tools necessary. Refer to *Tools and working facilities* for further information.

6.6 Remove the valves from the combustion chamber

6.7 Store the valve components in a labelled bag

6 Cylinder head – dismantling

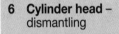

Note: *New and reconditioned cylinder heads are available from the manufacturer, and from engine overhaul specialists. Be aware that some specialist tools are required for the dismantling and inspection procedures, and new components may not be readily available. It may therefore be more practical and economical for the home mechanic to purchase a reconditioned head, rather than dismantle, inspect and recondition the original head. A valve spring compressor tool will be required for this operation.*

1 Remove the cylinder head as described in Chapter 2A Section 10.
2 Remove the exhaust manifold as described in Chapter 4B Section 3.
3 Remove the glow plugs as described in Chapter 5 Section 10.
4 Using a valve spring compressor, compress the spring on each valve in turn until the split collets can be removed. Release the compressor, and lift off the spring cap and spring **(see illustrations)**. If, when the valve spring compressor is screwed down, the spring cap refuses to free and expose the split collets, gently tap the top of the tool, directly over the spring cap, with a light hammer. This will free the retainer.
5 Using a pair of pliers or special removal tool, carefully extract the valve stem oil seal from the top of the guide, then lift off the spring seat **(see illustration)**.
6 Withdraw the valve through the combustion chamber **(see illustration)**.

7 It is essential that each valve is stored with its collets, cap, spring, and spring seat. The valves should also be kept in their correct sequence, unless they are so badly worn that they are to be renewed. If they are going to be kept and used again, place each valve assembly in a labelled polythene bag or similar small container **(see illustration)**. Label each bag No 1 inlet, No 1 exhaust, No 2 inlet, No 2 exhaust, etc, noting that No 1 valve is nearest to the timing chain end of the engine.

7 Cylinder head and valves – cleaning and inspection

1 Thorough cleaning of the cylinder head and valve components, followed by a detailed inspection, will enable you to decide how

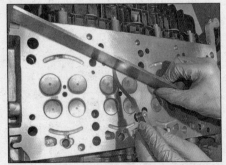

7.6 Use a straight-edge and feeler blade to check the cylinder head gasket face for distortion

much valve service work must be carried out during the engine overhaul. **Note:** *If the engine has been severely overheated, it is best to assume that the cylinder head is warped – check carefully for signs of this.*

Cleaning

2 Scrape away all traces of old gasket material from the cylinder head.
3 Scrape away the carbon from the combustion chambers and ports, then wash the cylinder head thoroughly with paraffin or a suitable solvent.
4 Scrape off any heavy carbon deposits that may have formed on the valves, then use a power-operated wire brush to remove deposits from the valve heads and stems.

Inspection

Note: *Be sure to perform all the following inspection procedures before concluding that the services of a machine shop or engine overhaul specialist are required. Make a list of all items that require attention.*

Cylinder head

5 Inspect the head very carefully for cracks, evidence of coolant leakage, and other damage. If cracks are found, a new cylinder head should be obtained.
6 Use a straight-edge and feeler blade to check that the cylinder head gasket surface is not distorted **(see illustration)**. If it is, it may be possible to have it machined, provided that the cylinder head is not reduced to less than the specified height.
7 Examine the valve seats in each of the

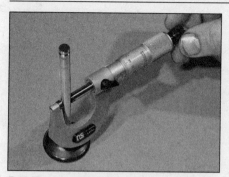

7.12 Measure the valve stem diameter with a micrometer

combustion chambers. If they are severely pitted, cracked, or burned, they will need to be renewed or recut by an engine overhaul specialist. If they are only slightly pitted, this can be removed by grinding-in the valve heads and seats with fine valve-grinding compound, as described later in this Section.

8 Check the valve guides for wear by inserting the relevant valve, and checking for side-to-side motion of the valve. A very small amount of movement is acceptable. If the movement seems excessive, remove the valve. Measure the valve stem diameter (see later in this Section), and renew the valve if it is worn. If the valve stem is not worn, the wear must be in the valve guide, and the guide must be renewed. The renewal of new valve guides should be entrusted to a Mercedes-Benz dealer or engine overhaul specialist, who will have the necessary tools available.

9 If renewing the valve guides, the valve seats should be recut or reground only after the guides have been fitted.

10 Examine the camshaft bearing surfaces in the cylinder head and the bearing caps for signs of wear or damage. If the bearings are excessively worn, consult a Mercedes-Benz dealer, or an engine overhaul specialist for further advice.

Valves

⚠️ *Warning: The exhaust valves on most petrol and diesel engines are filled with sodium to improve their heat transfer. Sodium is a highly reactive substance, and will ignite or explode spontaneously on contact with*

water (including water vapour in the air). These valves must NOT be disposed of as ordinary scrap. Seek advice from a Mercedes-Benz dealer when disposing of the valves.

11 Examine the head of each valve for pitting, burning, cracks, and general wear. Check the valve stem for scoring and wear ridges. Rotate the valve, and check for any obvious indication that it is bent. Look for pits or excessive wear on the tip of each valve stem. Renew any valve that shows any such signs of wear or damage.

12 If the valve appears satisfactory at this stage, measure the valve stem diameter at several points using a micrometer (see illustration). Any significant difference in the readings obtained indicates wear of the valve stem. Should any of these conditions be apparent, the valve(s) must be renewed.

13 If the valves are in satisfactory condition, they should be ground (lapped) into their respective seats, to ensure a smooth, gas-tight seal. If the seat is only lightly pitted, or if it has been recut, fine grinding compound should be used to produce the required finish. Coarse valve-grinding compound should not be used, unless a seat is badly burned or deeply pitted. If this is the case, the cylinder head and valves should be inspected, to decide whether seat recutting, or even the renewal of the valve or seat insert (where possible) is required.

14 Valve grinding is carried out as follows. Place the cylinder head upside-down on a bench.

15 Smear a trace of (the appropriate grade of) valve-grinding compound on the seat face, and press a suction grinding tool onto the valve head. With a semi-rotary action, grind the valve head to its seat, lifting the valve occasionally to redistribute the grinding compound. A light spring placed under the valve head will greatly ease this operation.

16 If coarse grinding compound is being used, work only until a dull, matt even surface is produced on both the valve seat and the valve, then wipe off the used compound, and repeat the process with fine compound. When a smooth unbroken ring of light grey matt finish is produced on both the valve and seat, the grinding operation is complete. Do not

grind-in the valves any further than absolutely necessary, or the seat will be prematurely sunk into the cylinder head.

17 When all the valves have been ground-in, carefully wash off all traces of grinding compound using paraffin or a suitable solvent, before reassembling the cylinder head.

Valve components

18 Examine the valve springs for signs of damage and discoloration. Compare the length of the valve springs with that of a new component, where possible, and if necessary renew the springs.

19 Stand each spring on a flat surface, and check it for squareness. If any of the springs are damaged, distorted or have lost their tension, obtain a complete new set of springs. It is normal to renew the valve springs as a matter of course if a major overhaul is being carried out.

20 Renew the valve stem oil seals regardless of their apparent condition.

Hydraulic tappets

21 Refer to Section 7 for further details.

8 Cylinder head – reassembly

1 Lubricate the stems of the valves, and insert the valves into their original locations (see illustration). If new valves are being fitted, insert them into the locations to which they have been ground.

2 Refit the spring seat.

3 Working on the first valve, dip the new valve stem seal in fresh engine oil. New seals are normally supplied with protective sleeves, which should be fitted to the tops of the valve stems to prevent the collet grooves from damaging the oil seals. If no sleeves are supplied, wind a little thin tape round the top of the valve stems to protect the seals. Carefully locate the seal over the valve and onto the guide. Take care not to damage the seal as it is passed over the valve stem. Use a suitable socket or tube to press the seal firmly onto the guide (see illustrations). Remove the sleeve from the valve stem.

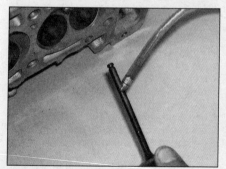

8.1 Lubricate the stems of the valves before inserting them

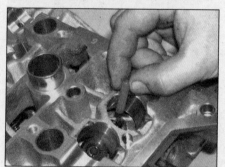

8.3a Locate the protective sleeve on the valve stem...

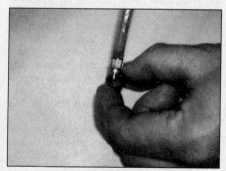

8.3b ...then oil the new valve stem seal...

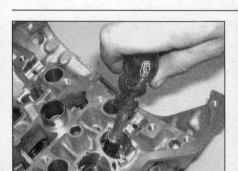

8.3c ...and press it onto the valve guide

8.5 Fit the split collets

9.3a Undo the bolts in the timing chain tunnel (camshafts removed for clarity)...

9.3b ...and the bolt in the left-hand rear corner

9.6a Timing cover bolts accessible from the rear...

4 Locate the valve spring on top of the seat, then refit the spring cap. On engines where the spring is tapered, make sure that the large diameter end of the spring locates on the seat.

5 Fit the compressor tool, then compress the valve spring and locate the split collets in the recess in the valve stem **(see illustration)**. Release the compressor, then repeat the procedure on the remaining valves.

6 With all the valves installed, support the cylinder head on blocks of wood and, using a hammer and interposed block of wood, tap the end of each valve stem to settle the components.

7 Refit the glow plugs as described in Chapter 5 Section 10.

8 Refit the exhaust manifold as described in Chapter 4B Section 3.

9 Refit the cylinder head(s) as described in Part A or Part B of this Chapter.

9 Timing cover – removal and refitting

Removal

1 Remove the flywheel/driveplate as described in Chapter 2A Section 13.

2 Remove the cylinder head cover as described in Chapter 2A Section 4.

3 Undo the 3 bolts securing the rear of the cylinder head to the timing cover **(see illustrations)**.

4 Disconnect the hose, then disconnect the wiring plug at the top of the timing cover.

5 Undo the retaining bolts and move the fuel pipe assembly to one side.

6 Unscrew the bolts and carefully prise the timing cover from place **(see illustrations)**. *Caution: Do not prise between the cylinder head and the timing cover – the mating surfaces and cylinder head gasket are easily damaged.*

Refitting

7 Clean the mating surfaces of the timing cover, cylinder head and crankcase, removing all traces of sealant, oil and dirt. Take care not to damage/scratch the sealing surfaces – use a non-abrasive cleaner, then prise the crankshaft oil seal from the cover.

8 Apply a continuous 2.0 mm bead of silicone sealant (MB recommend Loctite 5970) to the timing cover as shown **(see illustration)**. *Note: The timing cover must be refitted within 7 minutes of the sealing being applied as it will start to harden.*

9 Manoeuvre the timing cover into position,

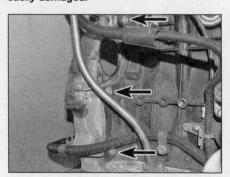

9.6b ...and right-hand side of the engine

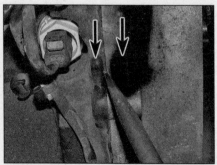

9.6c Leverage points are provided between the timing cover and crankcase

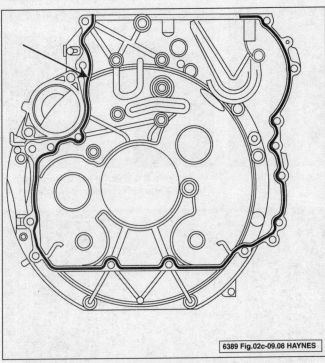

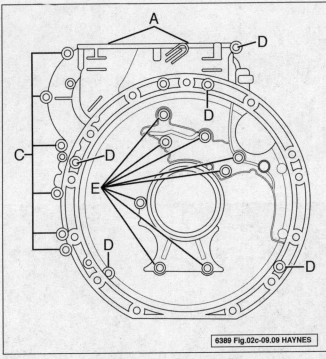

9.8 Apply a 2.0 mm bead of sealant as indicated by the thick, black line

9.9 Timing cover bolts details

A M8 x 90 mm	*D M8 x 60 mm*
C M8 x 30 mm	*E M8 x 30 mm*

then insert the retaining bolts **(see illustration)** and tighten them to the torque specified in Chapter 2A.

10 The remainder of refitting is a reversal of removal, noting the following points:

a) *Fit a new crankshaft rear oil seal as described in Chapter 2A Section 14, prior to refitting the flywheel/driveplate.*

b) *Upon completion, check for oil leaks prior to venturing onto the road.*

10.3 Make alignment marks between the gears

10.4 Undo the bolt and pull the gear from place

10.7 Slide the gear into place, aligning the marks (see text)

10.8 Use a plastic tool to move the backlash compensator element anti-clockwise slightly

10 Timing gears – removal and refitting

Intermediate gears

Removal

1 Set the engine at TDC on No.1 cylinder as described in Chapter 2A Section 3.

2 Remove the timing cover as described in Section 9.

3 Using paint or permanent marker, make alignment marks between the intermediate gears and the crankshaft gear, balance shaft gears, oil/vacuum pump and fuel pump gears **(see illustration)**.

4 Undo the retaining bolts and gently pull the gears from place **(see illustration)**.

5 Examine the gears for signs of damage, wear or deterioration, and replace if necessary.

Refitting

6 Ensure the engine is still set to TDC on No.1 cylinder.

7 Slide one of the intermediate gears into position as far as the backlash compensator element **(see illustration)**. Align the previously made marks where applicable, allowing for the marks to be slightly out (in a clockwise direction) due to the spring-loaded design of the backlash compensator element.

8 Using a plastic tool, apply slight anti-clockwise pressure to the backlash compensator element, whilst at the same time, pressing the gear into place **(see illustration)**.

10.12 The faint line on the balance shaft should align with the raised lug on the housing

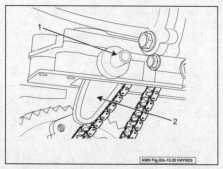

10.20 Timing chain side rail (2) and bearing pin (1)

10.21 Fuel pump drive gear retaining bolts

9 If the gear is correctly installed, there should be zero clearance between the backlash compensator element of the intermediate gear and the adjoining gears.

10 Insert the retaining bolt and tighten it to the specified torque, then repeat this procedure on the remaining intermediate gear.

11 If the basic timing position of the camshafts has been lost, set the camshaft timing as described in Chapter 2A Section 3.

12 If the basic timing position of the balancer shafts have been lost, remove the lower section of the sump and oil pick-up tube and baffle plate (see Chapter 2A Section 11), then with the engine set to TDC on No.1 cylinder (Chapter 2A Section 3), The mark on each balancer shaft must align with the corresponding marks on the housing **(see illustration)**. **Note:** *On the accompanying illustration, the mark on the shaft is shown slightly mis-aligned with the raised lug. This is because due to lighting conditions etc., it was impossible to photograph with the mark/lug accurately aligned.*

13 If the balancer shaft timing is not correct, the shaft gear retaining bolts must be slackened, and Mercedes special tool No. 651 589 02 63 00 slid into place over the corresponding sections of the shafts, locking them in the correct position (with the previously described marks aligned), whilst the gear retaining bolts are tightened to the specified torque. In the absence of these tools, we suggest that the engine is taken to a suitably equipped dealer/repairer and have them set the position of the shafts.

14 The remainder of refitting is a reversal of removal.

Fuel pump drive gear

Removal

15 Set the engine at TDC on No.1 cylinder as described in Chapter 2A Section 3.

16 Remove the timing cover as described in Section 2A Section 6.

17 Remove the sump as described in Chapter 2A Section 11.

18 Remove the timing chain tensioner as described in Chapter 2A Section 8.

19 Referring to the description earlier in this

Section, remove the intermediate drive gear between the crankshaft and the fuel pump.

20 Thread a suitable bolt into the end of the timing chain side rail bearing pin, attach a slide-hammer to the pin and pull it from place **(see illustration)**.

21 Undo the retaining bolts, detach the fuel pump drive gear from the pump shaft, and disengage it from the timing chain **(see illustration)**.

Refitting

22 Refitting is a reversal of removal.

11 Oil pump –
  removal, inspection
  and refitting

Removal

1 Set the engine at TDC on No.1 cylinder as described in Chapter 2A Section 3.

2 Remove the timing cover as described in Section 2A Section 6.

3 Remove the vacuum pump as described in Section 4.

4 Remove the lower section of the sump as described in Chapter 2A Section 11.

5 Undo the bolts and remove the oil pump pick-up tube. Renew the O-ring seal.

6 Remove the intermediate gear between the crankshaft and oil pump drive gear as described in Section 11.

7 Undo the 2 retaining bolts and withdraw the oil pump assembly from the crankcase **(see illustration)**.

Inspection

8 It would appear at the time of writing that the oil pump is only available as a complete assembly. Consequently, no dismantling of the pump is recommend. If the pump is faulty, the complete assembly may need to be replaced. Consult a Mercedes-Benz dealer or specialist.

Refitting

9 Prior to fitting the oil pump, fill it with clean engine oil.

10 Manoeuvre the pump into the crankcase, then insert the retaining bolts and tighten them to the specified torque.

11 The remainder of refitting is a reversal of removal.

**12 Piston/connecting rod
  assembly –**
  removal

1 Remove the cylinder head, flywheel/driveplate and sump as described in Chapter 2A. Where fitted, remove the oil pick-up tube and baffle plate from the base of the crankcase.

2 If there is a pronounced wear ridge at the top of any bore, it may be necessary to remove it with a scraper or ridge reamer, to avoid piston damage during removal. Such a ridge indicates excessive wear of the cylinder bore.

3 Check the connecting rods and big-end caps for identification marks. Both rods and caps should be marked with the cylinder number on the inlet manifold side of each assembly. Note that No 1 cylinder is at the front of the engine. If no marks are present, using a hammer and centre-punch, paint or similar, mark each connecting rod and big-end bearing cap with its respective cylinder number on the flat-machined surface provided – note on which side of the connecting rods the marks are made.

4 Similarly, check the piston crowns for a direction marking. An arrow on each piston crown should point towards the timing chain end of the engine. On some engines, this mark may be obscured by carbon build-up,

11.7 Oil pump retaining bolts

14.7 Piston oil spray jet

in which case the piston crown should be cleaned to check for a mark. In some cases, the direction arrow may have worn off, in which case a suitable mark should be made on the piston crown using a scriber – do not deeply score the piston crown, but ensure that the mark is easily visible.

5 Turn the crankshaft to bring piston No 1 to BDC (bottom dead centre).

6 Unscrew the bolts from No 1 piston big-end bearing cap. Take off the cap, and recover the bottom half bearing shell. If the bearing shells are to be re-used, tape the cap and the shell together.

7 Using a hammer handle, push the piston up through the bore, and remove it from the top of the cylinder block. Take care not to damage the piston cooling oil spay jets in the cylinder block as the piston/connecting rod assembly is removed. Recover the bearing shell, and tape it to the connecting rod for safekeeping.

8 Loosely refit the big-end cap to the connecting rod, and secure with the bolts – this will help to keep the components in their correct order.

9 Remove No 4 piston assembly in the same way before turning the crankshaft.

10 Turn the crankshaft as necessary to bring the remaining pistons to BDC, and remove them in the same manner.

13 Crankshaft – removal

1 Remove the sump, the timing chain cover, timing chain, crankshaft sprocket, and the

14.8 Clean damaged threads using a tap

flywheel/driveplate, as described in this Chapter.

2 Unbolt and remove the front cover from the crankshaft, then unbolt the baffle plate from the crankcase (where fitted).

3 Remove the pistons and connecting rods, as described in Section 21. If no work is to be done on the pistons and connecting rods, there is no need to remove the cylinder head, or to push the pistons out of the cylinder bores. The pistons should just be pushed far enough up the bores so that they are positioned clear of the crankshaft journals.

4 Check the crankshaft endfloat as described in Section 13, then proceed as follows.

5 Lift the crankshaft from the crankcase.

6 Recover the upper bearing shells from the cylinder block, and tape them to their respective caps for safe-keeping. Similarly, recover the upper thrustwasher halves, noting their orientation.

14 Cylinder block/crankcase – cleaning and inspection

Cleaning

1 Remove all external components, brackets and electrical switches/sensors from the block. Note the position of any mounting brackets before removal. For complete cleaning, the core plugs should ideally be removed. Drill a small hole in the plugs, and then insert a self-tapping screw into the hole. Pull out the plugs by pulling on the screw with a pair of grips, or by using a slide hammer.

2 Scrape all traces of gasket from the cylinder block/crankcase, taking care not to damage the gasket/sealing surfaces.

3 Where applicable, remove the oil gallery plugs, and use new plugs when the engine is reassembled.

4 If the castings are extremely dirty, they should be steam-cleaned.

5 After the castings have been steam-cleaned, clean all oil holes and oil galleries one more time. Flush all internal passages with warm water until the water runs clear. Dry thoroughly, and apply a light film of oil to all mating surfaces, to prevent rusting. Also oil the cylinder bores. If you have access to compressed air, use it to speed up the drying process, and to blow out all the oil holes and galleries.

 Warning: Wear eye protection when using compressed air.

6 If the castings are not very dirty, you can do an adequate cleaning job with hot (as hot as you can stand!), soapy water and a stiff brush. Take plenty of time, and do a thorough job. Regardless of the cleaning method used, be sure to clean all oil holes and galleries very thoroughly, and to dry all components well. Protect the cylinder bores as described above, to prevent rusting.

7 Where applicable, the piston oil spray jets can be removed from the cylinder block for cleaning. Renew any jets which show signs of damage. Check the oil spray hole and oil passages for blockage **(see illustration)**.

8 All threaded holes must be clean, to ensure accurate torque readings during reassembly. To clean the threads, run the correct-size tap into each of the holes to remove rust, corrosion, thread sealant or sludge, and to restore damaged threads **(see illustration)**. If possible, use compressed air to clear the holes of debris produced by this operation.

9 Ensure that all threaded holes in the cylinder block are dry.

10 After coating the mating surfaces of the new core plugs with suitable sealant, fit them to the cylinder block. Make sure that they are driven in straight and seated correctly, or leakage could result.

11 Where applicable, fit the new oil gallery plugs.

12 If the engine is not going to be reassembled right away, cover it with a large plastic bag to keep it clean; protect all mating surfaces and the cylinder bores as described above, to prevent rusting.

Inspection

13 Visually check the cylinder block/crankcase for cracks and corrosion. Look for stripped threads in the threaded holes. If there has been any history of internal water leakage, it may be worthwhile having an engine overhaul specialist check the cylinder block/crankcase with special equipment. If defects are found, have them repaired if possible, or renew the assembly.

14 Check each cylinder bore for scuffing and scoring. Check for signs of a wear ridge at the top of the cylinder, indicating that the bore is excessively worn.

15 If the cylinder walls are badly scored or scuffed, then the cylinders will have to be rebored by a suitably qualified specialist, and new oversize pistons will have to be fitted. A Mercedes-Benz dealer or engineering workshop will normally be able to supply suitable oversize pistons when carrying out the reboring work.

16 Inspect the upper surface of the cylinder block for damage. Use a straight-edge and feeler blade to check that the cylinder head gasket surface is not distorted. Note also that on in-line diesel engines, the piston protrusion must be checked whenever the cylinder head surface is machined.

17 After checking the cylinder block/crankcase, refit the items removed.

Piston protrusion

18 When inspecting the cylinder block, the piston protrusion should be checked – this is particularly important if the cylinder head face has been machined. If the piston protrusion is too great, the pistons may hit the swirl chambers when the engine is running, causing expensive damage.

19 Measure the protrusion of the piston from the sealing face of the cylinder head (a dial gauge should be used if possible). If the protrusion is greater than the specified maximum, consult a Mercedes-Benz dealer or an engine-reconditioning specialist for advice – it is likely that the cylinder block will have to be renewed.

15 Piston/connecting rod assembly – cleaning and inspection

Cleaning

1 Before the inspection process can begin, the piston/connecting rod assemblies must be cleaned, and the original piston rings removed from the pistons.

2 Carefully expand the old rings over the top of the pistons. The use of two or three old feeler blades will be helpful in preventing the rings dropping into empty grooves **(see illustration)**. Be careful not to scratch the piston with the ends of the ring. The rings are brittle, and will snap if they are spread too far. They are also very sharp – protect your hands and fingers. Note that the third ring incorporates an expander. Always remove the rings from the top of the piston. Keep each set of rings with its piston if the old rings are to be re-used. Note which way up each ring is fitted to ensure correct refitting.

3 Scrape away all traces of carbon from the top of the piston. A hand-held wire brush (or a piece of fine emery cloth) can be used, once the majority of the deposits have been scraped away.

4 Remove the carbon from the ring grooves in the piston, using an old ring. Break the ring in half to do this (be careful not to cut your fingers – piston rings are sharp). Be careful to remove only the carbon deposits – do not remove any metal, and do not nick or scratch the sides of the ring grooves.

5 Once the deposits have been removed, clean the piston/connecting rod assembly with paraffin or a suitable solvent, and dry thoroughly. Make sure that the oil return holes in the ring grooves are clear.

Inspection

6 If the pistons and cylinder bores are not damaged or worn excessively, and if the cylinder block does not need to be rebored, the original pistons can be refitted. Measure the piston diameters, and check that they are within limits for the corresponding bore diameters. If the piston-to-bore clearance is excessive, the block will have to be rebored, and new pistons and rings fitted. Normal piston wear shows up as even vertical wear on the piston thrust surfaces, and slight looseness of the top ring in its groove. New piston rings should always be used when the engine is reassembled. Note that the piston and bore size grades are stamped

on the piston crowns, and on the adjacent cylinder head mating face of the cylinder block.

7 Carefully inspect each piston for cracks around the skirt, around the gudgeon pin holes, and at the piston ring 'lands' (between the ring grooves).

8 Look for scoring and scuffing on the piston skirt, holes in the piston crown, and burned areas at the edge of the crown. If the skirt is scored or scuffed, the engine may have been suffering from overheating, and/or abnormal combustion, which caused excessively high operating temperatures. The cooling and lubrication systems should be checked thoroughly. Scorch marks on the sides of the pistons show that blow-by has occurred. A hole in the piston crown, or burned areas at the edge of the piston crown, indicates that abnormal combustion (pre-ignition, knocking or detonation) has been occurring. If any of the above problems exist, the causes must be investigated and corrected, or the damage will occur again. The causes may include a faulty fuel injector.

9 Corrosion of the piston, in the form of pitting, indicates that coolant has been leaking into the combustion chamber and/or the crankcase. Again, the cause must be corrected, or the problem may persist in the rebuilt engine.

10 New pistons can be purchased from a Mercedes-Benz dealer or motor factor.

11 Examine each connecting rod carefully for signs of damage, such as cracks around the big-end and small-end bearings. Check that the rod is not bent or distorted. Damage is highly unlikely, unless the engine has been seized or badly overheated. Detailed checking of the connecting rod assembly can only be carried out by a Mercedes-Benz dealer or engine repair specialist with the necessary equipment.

12 The gudgeon pins are of the floating type, secured in position by two circlips. The pistons and connecting rods can be separated as follows.

13 Using a small screwdriver, prise out the circlips, and push out the gudgeon pin **(see illustrations)**. Hand pressure should be sufficient to remove the pin. Identify the piston

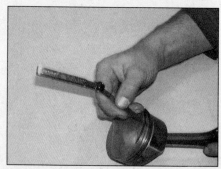

15.2 Use an old feeler gauge blade to help remove the piston rings

and rod to ensure correct reassembly. Discard the circlips – new ones must be used on refitting.

14 Examine the gudgeon pin and connecting rod small-end bearing for signs of wear or damage. It should be possible to push the gudgeon pin through the connecting rod bush by hand, without noticeable play. Wear can be cured by renewing both the pin and bush. Bush renewal, however, is a specialist job – press facilities are required, and the new bush must be reamed accurately.

15 The connecting rods themselves should not be in need of renewal, unless seizure or some other major mechanical failure has occurred. Check the alignment of the connecting rods visually, and if the rods are not straight, take them to an engine overhaul specialist for a more detailed check.

16 Examine all components, and obtain any new parts from your Mercedes-Benz dealer. If new pistons are purchased, they will be supplied complete with gudgeon pins and circlips. Circlips can also be purchased individually.

17 Position the piston in relation to the connecting rod as noted on removal.

18 Apply a smear of clean engine oil to the gudgeon pin. Slide it into the piston and through the connecting rod small-end. Check that the piston pivots freely on the rod, then secure the gudgeon pin in position with two new circlips. Ensure that each circlip is correctly located in its groove in the piston.

15.13a Prise out the circlips...

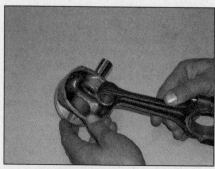

15.13b ...then press out the gudgeon pin and separate the connecting rod

16.2 Check the crankshaft end float using a dial test indicator (DTI)

16 Crankshaft – inspection

Checking crankshaft endfloat

1 If the crankshaft endfloat is to be checked, this must be done when the crankshaft is still installed in the cylinder block/crankcase, but is free to move.

2 Check the endfloat using a dial gauge in contact with the end of the crankshaft. Push the crankshaft fully one way, and then zero the gauge. Push the crankshaft fully the other way, and check the endfloat. The result can be compared with the specified amount, and will give an indication as to whether new thrustwasher halves are required **(see illustration)**. Note that all thrustwashers must be of the same thickness.

3 If a dial gauge is not available, feeler blades can be used. First push the crankshaft fully towards the flywheel/driveplate end of the engine, and then use feeler blades to measure the gap between the web of No 3 crankpin and the thrustwasher halves.

Inspection

4 Clean the crankshaft using paraffin or a suitable solvent, and dry it, preferably with compressed air if available. Be sure to clean the oil holes with a pipe cleaner or similar probe, to ensure that they are not obstructed.

5 Check the main and big-end bearing journals for uneven wear, scoring, pitting and cracking.

6 Big-end bearing wear is accompanied by distinct metallic knocking when the engine is running (particularly noticeable when the engine is pulling from low speed) and some loss of oil pressure.

7 Main bearing wear is accompanied by severe engine vibration and rumble – getting progressively worse as engine speed increases – and again by loss of oil pressure.

8 Check the bearing journal for roughness by running a finger lightly over the bearing surface. Any roughness (which will be accompanied by obvious bearing wear) indicates that the crankshaft requires regrinding (where possible) or renewal.

9 If the crankshaft has been reground, check for burrs around the crankshaft oil holes (the holes are usually chamfered, so burrs should not be a problem unless regrinding has been carried out carelessly). Remove any burrs with a fine file or scraper, and thoroughly clean the oil holes.

10 Have the crankshaft inspected and measured by a Mercedes Benz dealer or engine reconditioning specialist. They will be able to advise of any reconditioning work needed, and supply the appropriate replacement bearings etc.

17 Main and big-end bearings, and bearing cap bolts – inspection

Bearings

1 Even though the main and big-end bearings should be renewed during the engine overhaul, the old bearings should be retained for close examination, as they may reveal valuable information about the condition of the engine. The bearing shells are graded by thickness.

2 Bearing failure can occur due to lack of lubrication, the presence of dirt or other foreign particles, overloading the engine, or corrosion. Regardless of the cause of bearing failure, the cause must be corrected before the engine is reassembled to prevent it from happening again.

3 When examining the bearing shells, remove them from the cylinder block/crankcase, the connecting rods and the connecting rod big-end bearing caps. Lay them out on a clean surface in the same general position as their location in the engine. This will enable you to match any bearing problems with the corresponding crankshaft journal. Do not touch any shell's bearing surface with your fingers while checking it, or the delicate surface may be scratched.

4 Dirt and other foreign matter get into the engine in a variety of ways. It may be left in the engine during assembly, or it may pass through filters or the crankcase ventilation system. It may get into the oil, and from there into the bearings. Metal chips from machining operations and normal engine wear are often present. Abrasives are sometimes left in engine components after reconditioning, especially when parts are not thoroughly cleaned using the proper cleaning methods. Whatever the source, these foreign objects often end up embedded in the soft bearing material, and are easily recognised. Large particles will not embed in the bearing, and will score or gouge the bearing and journal. The best prevention for this cause of bearing failure is to clean all parts thoroughly, and keep everything spotlessly clean during engine assembly. Frequent and regular engine oil and filter changes are also recommended.

5 Lack of lubrication (or lubrication breakdown) has a number of interrelated causes. Excessive heat (which thins the oil), overloading (which squeezes the oil from the bearing face) and oil leakage (from excessive bearing clearances, worn oil pump or high engine speeds) all contribute to lubrication breakdown. Blocked oil passages, which may be the result of misaligned oil holes in a bearing shell, will also oil-starve a bearing, and destroy it. When lack of lubrication is the cause of bearing failure, the bearing material is wiped or extruded from the steel backing of the bearing. Temperatures may increase to the point where the steel backing turns blue from overheating.

6 Driving habits can have a definite effect on bearing life. Full-throttle, low-speed operation (labouring the engine) puts very high loads on bearings, tending to squeeze out the oil film. These loads cause the bearings to flex, which produces fine cracks in the bearing face (fatigue failure). Eventually, the bearing material will loosen in pieces, and tear away from the steel backing.

7 Short-distance driving leads to corrosion of bearings, because insufficient engine heat is produced to drive off the condensed water and corrosive gases. These products collect in the engine oil, forming acid and sludge. As the oil is carried to the engine bearings, the acid attacks and corrodes the bearing material.

8 Incorrect bearing installation during engine assembly will lead to bearing failure as well. Tight-fitting bearings leave insufficient bearing running clearance, and will result in oil starvation. Dirt or foreign particles trapped behind a bearing shell result in high spots on the bearing, which lead to failure.

9 Do not touch any shell's bearing surface with your fingers during reassembly; there is a risk of scratching the delicate surface, or of depositing particles of dirt on it.

10 As mentioned at the beginning of this Section, the bearing shells should be renewed as a matter of course during engine overhaul; to do otherwise is false economy.

Bolts

11 It's strongly recommended that the main and big-end bearing cap bolts are renewed regardless of their apparent condition.

18 Engine overhaul – reassembly sequence

1 Before reassembly begins, ensure that all new parts have been obtained, and that all necessary tools are available. Read through the entire procedure to familiarise yourself with the work involved, and to ensure that all items necessary for reassembly of the engine are at hand. In addition to all normal tools and materials, thread-locking compound will be needed. A suitable tube of liquid sealant (Loctite 5970 or equivalent) will also be required for the joint faces that are fitted without gaskets.

2 In order to save time and avoid problems, engine reassembly can be carried out in the following order, referring to Part A of this Chapter unless otherwise stated. Where applicable, use new gaskets and seals when refitting the various components.

a) *Crankshaft.*
b) *Piston/connecting rods.*
c) *Oil pump.*
d) *Sump.*
e) *Flywheel/driveplate.*
f) *Cylinder head.*
g) *Intermediate gears and timing cover.*
h) *Engine external components.*

3 At this stage, all engine components should be absolutely clean and dry, with all faults repaired. The components should be laid out (or in individual containers) on a completely clean work surface.

19 Piston rings – refitting

1 Before fitting new piston rings, the ring end gaps must be checked as follows.
2 Lay out the piston/connecting rod assemblies and the new piston ring sets, so that the ring sets will be matched with the same piston and cylinder during the end gap measurement and subsequent engine reassembly.
3 Insert the top ring into the first cylinder, and push it down the bore using the top of the piston. This will ensure that the ring remains square with the cylinder walls. Position the ring near the bottom of the cylinder bore, at the lower limit of ring travel. Note that the top and second compression rings are different. The second ring is easily identified by the step on its lower surface.
4 Measure the end gap using feeler blades.
5 Repeat the procedure with the ring at the top of the cylinder bore, at the upper limit of its travel **(see illustration)**, and compare the measurements with the figures given in the Specifications.
6 If the gap is too small (unlikely if genuine Mercedes-Benz parts are used), it must be enlarged, or the ring ends may contact each other during engine operation, causing serious damage. Ideally, new piston rings providing the correct end gap should be fitted. As a last resort, the end gap can be increased by filing the ring ends very carefully with a fine file. Mount the file in a vice equipped with soft jaws, slip the ring over the file with the ends contacting the file face, and slowly move the ring to remove material from the ends. Take care, as piston rings are sharp, and are easily broken.
7 With new piston rings, it is unlikely that the end gap will be too large. If the gaps are too large, check that you have the correct rings for your engine and for the particular cylinder bore size.
8 Repeat the checking procedure for each

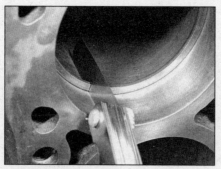

19.5 Measure the piston ring end-gaps

ring in the first cylinder, and then for the rings in the remaining cylinders. Remember to keep rings, pistons and cylinders matched up.
9 Once the ring end gaps have been checked and if necessary corrected, the rings can be fitted to the pistons.
10 Fit the piston rings using the same technique as for removal. Fit the bottom (oil control) ring first, and work up. When fitting the oil control ring, first insert the wire expander, then fit the ring with its gap positioned 180° from the protruding wire ends of the expander. Ensure that the rings are fitted the correct way up – the top surface of the rings is normally marked TOP **(see illustration)**. Arrange the gaps of the top and second compression rings 120° either side of the oil control ring gap, but make sure that none of the rings gaps are positioned over the gudgeon pin hole. **Note:** *Always follow any instructions supplied with the new piston ring sets – different manufacturers may specify different procedures. Do not mix up the top and second compression rings, as they have different cross-sections.*

20 Crankshaft – refitting

1 If the original crankshaft is in good condition and is being refitted, new main bearing shells, which are the same size as the removed shells, should be fitted.
2 If the crankshaft has been reground, undersize bearing shells must be fitted. The

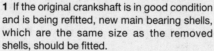

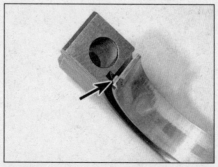

20.4 Ensure that the tab on each bearing shell engages with the notch in the cap

19.10 Fit the oil control ring expander

engine-reconditioning specialist normally supplies the appropriate shells.
3 Clean the backs of the bearing shells, and the bearing locations in both the cylinder block/crankcase and the main bearing caps.
4 Press the bearing shells into their locations, ensuring that the tab on each shell engages in the notch in the cylinder block/crankcase or bearing cap **(see illustration)**. Take care not to touch any shell's bearing surface with your fingers. If the original bearing shells are being used for the check, ensure that they are refitted in their original locations. Note that the bearings shells with oil grooves fit in the cylinder block, and the plain bearing shells fit in the bearing caps.
5 Where applicable, ensure that the oil spray jets are fitted to the cylinder block.
6 Liberally lubricate each bearing shell in the cylinder block/crankcase and cap with clean engine oil.
7 Fit the upper thrustwasher halves to the appropriate bearing location in the cylinder block as follows **(see illustration)**.
8 Ensure that any oil grooves in the thrustwasher halves face out towards the crankshaft journals.
9 The crankshaft can now be lowered into position.
10 Locate the lower bearing shells in the balance shaft housing/main bearing bridge, and lubricate them with clean engine oil.
11 Install the thrustwashers each side of the No.3 or No.4 (depending on production date) bearing position in the housing/bridge. Ensure the oil grooves in the washer point outwards towards the crankshaft collars.

20.7 Fit the upper thrustwasher halves

21.4a Insert the bearing shells in the conrod...

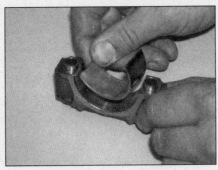

21.4b ...and big-end cap

21.5a Lubricate the pistons, rings...

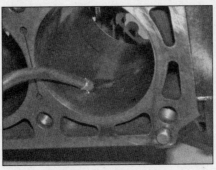

21.5b ...and cylinder bores

12 Gently lower the housing/bridge into position, then insert the retaining bolts and tighten them to the specified torque, starting at the middle and working outwards progressively.
13 The remainder of refitting is a reversal of removal.

21 Piston/connecting rod assemblies – refitting

Note: *A piston ring compressor tool will be required for this operation. Note that the following procedure assumes that the main bearing caps are in place.*

1 If the big-end journals on the crankshaft are in good condition, new big-end bearing shells, which are the same size as the removed shells, should be fitted.

2 If the crankshaft has been reground, undersize bearing shells must be fitted. The engine-reconditioning specialist normally supplies the appropriate shells.
3 Clean the backs of the bearing shells, and the bearing locations in both the connecting rod and bearing cap.
4 Press the bearing shells into their locations, ensuring that the tab on each shell engages in the notch in the connecting rod and cap **(see illustrations)**. Take care not to touch the bearing surface of the shell with your fingers.
5 Lubricate the cylinder bores, the pistons, and piston rings, then lay out each piston/connecting rod assembly in its respective position **(see illustrations)**.
6 Start with assembly No 1. Make sure that the piston rings are still spaced as described in Section 17, and then clamp them in

position with a piston ring compressor **(see illustration)**.
7 Insert the piston/connecting rod assembly into the top of cylinder No 1. Ensure that the arrow on the piston crown points towards the front of the engine, and that the identifying marks on the connecting rods and big-end caps are positioned as noted before removal. Using a block of wood or hammer handle against the piston crown, tap the assembly into the cylinder until the piston crown is flush with the top of the cylinder **(see illustration)**. Where applicable, take care not to damage the piston cooling oil spray jets as the piston/connecting rod assemblies are refitted.
8 Ensure that the bearing shell is still correctly installed. Liberally lubricate the crankpin and both bearing shells. Taking care not to mark the cylinder bores or damage the piston oil jets (where fitted), pull the piston /connecting rod assembly down the bore and onto the crankpin. Refit the big-end bearing cap **(see illustration)**. Note that the bearing shell locating tabs must abut each other. On some engines, the caps and rods are 'fractured' to ensure improved component location. Ensure the matching pair (cap and rod) are fitted together.
9 Lightly lubricate the bolt threads, then screw the big-end bearing cap bolts by hand into position in the connecting rods.
10 Progressively tighten the bolts to the specified torque and angle, observing the two tightening stages given in the Specifications. It is recommended that an angle-measuring gauge is used to angle-tighten the bolts. If a gauge is not available, use a dab of white paint to make alignment marks between the bolt and bearing cap prior to tightening; the marks can then be used to check that the bolt has been rotated sufficiently during tightening.
11 Once the bearing cap bolts have been correctly tightened, rotate the crankshaft and check that it turns freely. Some stiffness is to be expected if new components have been fitted, but there should be no signs of binding or tight spots.
12 Refit the remaining piston/connecting rod assemblies in the same way.

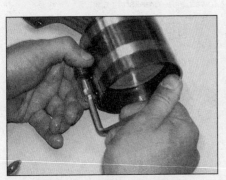

21.6 Fit a piston ring compressor

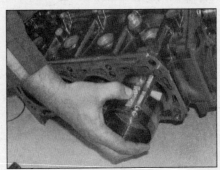

21.7 Insert the piston into the cylinder bore

21.8 Refit the big-end bearing caps

22 Engine –
initial start-up after overhaul

1 Refit the remainder of the engine components in the correct order listed in this Chapter. Refit the engine to the vehicle as described in the relevant Section of this Chapter. Double-check the engine oil and coolant levels, and make a final check that everything has been reconnected. Make sure that there are no tools or rags left in the engine compartment.

2 Reconnect the battery negative lead as described in Chapter 5 Section 3.

3 Disconnect the injector harness wiring plug at the right-hand rear of the engine compartment.

4 Turn the engine using the starter motor until the oil pressure warning lamp goes out.

5 If the lamp fails to extinguish after several seconds of cranking, check the engine oil level and oil filter security. Assuming these are correct, check the security of the oil pressure switch cabling – do not progress any further until you are satisfied that oil is being pumped around the engine at sufficient pressure.

6 Reconnect the injector wiring plug.

7 Start the engine, but be aware that as fuel system components have been disturbed, the cranking time may be a little longer than usual.

8 While the engine is idling, check for fuel, water and oil leaks. Don't be alarmed if there are some odd smells and the occasional plume of smoke as components heat up and burn off oil deposits.

9 Assuming all is well; keep the engine idling until hot water is felt circulating through the top hose.

10 After a few minutes, recheck the oil and coolant levels, and top-up as necessary.

11 There is no need to retighten the cylinder head bolts once the engine has been run following reassembly.

12 If new pistons, rings or crankshaft bearings have been fitted, the engine must be treated as new, and run-in for the first 600 miles. Do not operate the engine at full-throttle, or allow it to labour at low engine speeds in any gear. It is recommended that the engine oil and filter are changed at the end of this period.

Chapter 3
Cooling, heating and ventilation systems

Contents

Degrees of difficulty

Easy, suitable for novice with little experience	Fairly easy, suitable for beginner with some experience	Fairly difficult, suitable for competent DIY mechanic	Difficult, suitable for experienced DIY mechanic	Very difficult, suitable for expert DIY or professional

Specifications

General

System type . . . . Sealed cooling system with auxiliary belt driven coolant pump. The system also has a thermostat and a thermostatically controlled thermo-viscous cooling fan.

Pressure cap opening pressure . . . . 1.5 bar

Thermostat:
    Opening commences . . . . 80 ± 2°C
    Fully open . . . . 100°C
Coolant type . . . . See Lubricants and fluids
Cooling system total capacity . . . . See Chapter 1

Air conditioning system

Refrigerant R134a

Torque wrench settings

	Nm	lbf ft
Air conditioning compressor bolts	20	15
Air conditioning refrigerant pipes-to-compressor bolts	20	15
Alternator mounting bracket bolts	45	33
Cooling fan blades to viscous coupling	10	7
Coolant pump mounting bolts	20	15
Coolant pump pulley bolts	10	7
Cylinder block drain plug	30	22
Thermostat housing mounting bolts	10	7
Viscous fan coupling to coolant pump/bearing body	54	40

2.3 Coolant hoses with worm-drive clip

1 General information and precautions

1 The cooling system is of pressurised type, comprising a pump, an aluminium crossflow radiator, temperature-conscious thermo-viscous cooling fan, and a thermostat. Cold coolant from the radiator passes through the hose to the coolant pump, where it is pumped around the cylinder block and head passages. After cooling the cylinder bores, combustion surfaces and valve seats, the coolant reaches the underside of the thermostat, which is initially closed. The coolant passes through the heater and is returned through the cylinder block to the coolant pump.

2 When the engine is cold, the coolant circulates only through the cylinder block, cylinder head, expansion tank and heater. When the coolant reaches a predetermined temperature, the thermostat opens and the coolant passes through to the radiator. As the coolant circulates through the radiator, it is cooled by the inrush of air when the car is in forward motion. Airflow is supplemented by the action of the cooling fan as necessary. Upon reaching the bottom of the radiator, the coolant is now cooled and the cycle is repeated.

3 The coolant pump is mounted externally on the front of the engine, and is driven by the auxiliary drivebelt.

4 Coolant temperature information for the gauge mounted in the instrument panel, and for the fuel system, is provided by temperature

sensors mounted in the thermostat housing or in the cylinder head, depending on model. A coolant level switch is fitted to bottom of the radiator expansion tank.

5 The thermo-viscous cooling fan is controlled by the temperature of air behind the radiator. When the air temperature reaches a predetermined level, a bi-metallic coil opens a valve within the unit, and silicon fluid is fed through a system of vanes. Half of the vanes are driven directly by the coolant pump pulley by the auxiliary drivebelt, and the remaining half are connected to the fan blades. The vanes are arranged so that drive is transmitted to the fan blades in relation to the drag, or viscosity of the fluid, and this in turn depends on ambient temperature and engine speed. The fan is therefore only operated when required.

6 All models have a coolant expansion tank that collects the coolant, which is displaced from the system as it expands due to the rise in temperature. The displaced coolant is returned to the radiator as the system cools.

7 The vehicle interior heater operates by means of coolant from the engine cooling system. Coolant flow through the heater matrix is regulated by a valve, which is controlled by a temperature sensor in the heater unit. Temperature control is further achieved by blending cool air from outside the vehicle (or from the air conditioning system) with the warm air from the heater matrix, in the desired ratio.

8 Refer to Sections 9 and 10 for information on the air conditioning system.

⚠️ *Warning: Do not attempt to remove the pressure cap, or disturb any part of the cooling system, while the engine is hot, as there is a high risk of scalding. If the pressure cap must be removed before the engine and radiator have fully cooled (even though this is not recommended), the pressure in the cooling system must first be relieved. Cover the cap with a thick layer of cloth, to avoid scalding, and slowly unscrew the pressure cap until a hissing sound is heard (be prepared to refit the cap quickly if bubbling noises are heard and hot coolant starts to come out). When the hissing stops, indicating that the pressure has reduced, slowly unscrew the pressure cap until it can be removed; if more hissing sounds are heard, wait until they have stopped before unscrewing the cap completely. At all times, keep your face well away from the pressure cap opening, and protect your hands.*

⚠️ *Warning: Do not allow antifreeze to come into contact with your skin, or with the painted surfaces of the vehicle. Rinse off spills immediately with plenty of water. Never leave antifreeze lying around in an open container, or in a puddle in the driveway or on the garage floor. Children and pets are attracted by its sweet smell, but antifreeze can be fatal if ingested.*

⚠️ *Warning: The cooling fan could cut in even if the engine is not running (if the ignition is on). Be*

careful to keep your hands, hair, and any loose clothing well clear when working in the engine compartments.

2 Cooling system hoses – disconnection and renewal

1 The number, routing and pattern of hoses will vary according to model, but the same basic procedure applies. Before commencing work, make sure that the new hoses are to hand, along with new hose clips if needed. It is good practice to renew the hose clips at the same time as the hoses.

2 Drain the cooling system as described in Chapter 1 Section 30, saving the coolant if it is fit for re-use. Squirt a little penetrating oil onto the hose clips if they are corroded.

3 Release the hose clips from the hose concerned. The clip most commonly used on the Mercedes-Benz is a spring clip, which is released by squeezing its tags together with pliers, at the same time working the clip away from the hose stub **(see illustration)**.

4 Unclip any wires, cables or other hoses, which may be attached to the hose being removed. Make notes for reference when reassembling, if necessary.

5 Release the hose from its stubs with a twisting motion. Be careful not to damage the stubs on delicate components such as the radiator, or thermostat housings. If the hose is stuck fast, the best course is often to cut it off using a sharp knife, but again be careful not to damage the stubs.

6 Before fitting the new hose, smear the stubs with washing-up liquid or a suitable rubber lubricant to aid fitting. Do not use oil or grease, which may attack the rubber.

7 Fit the hose clips over the ends of the hose, and then fit the hose over its stubs. Work the hose into position. When satisfied, locate and tighten the hose clips.

8 Refill the cooling system as described in Chapter 1. Run the engine, and check that there are no leaks.

9 Recheck the tightness of the hose clips on any new hoses after a few hundred miles.

10 Top-up the coolant level if necessary (see *Weekly checks*).

3 Radiator – removal, inspection and refitting

Removal

1 Refer to Chapter 1 Section 30 and drain the cooling system.

2 Remove the front grille as described Chapter 11, Section 22.

3 Remove the front bumper as described in Chapter 11 Section 20.

4 Slacken the retaining clips and disconnect the top hose from the radiator and the smaller hose from the expansion tank **(see illustration)**.

3.4 Disconnect the hoses from the radiator

3.7a Undo the bolts and remove the right cover...

3.7b ...and then the left cover

3.9a Remove the three coolant hoses

3.9b The bottom hose has a sprung clip

3.10 Unscrew the small plastic panel

3.11 Remove the two bottom retaining bolts

5 Remove the cooling fan, as described in Section 5.

6 Unbolt the horn and disconnect the wiring plug.

7 Loosen the retaining bolts and remove the cover to each side of the radiator (see illustrations).

8 On fans with air-conditioning, remove the coolant hoses to the left of the radiator.

9 Undo the clips and remove the three hoses to the rear of the radiator at its right-hand edge (see illustrations).

10 Undo the retaining screw and remove the small plastic panel at the front left of the radiator (see illustration).

11 Undo the two retaining bolts at each bottom corner of the radiator (see illustration).

12 This will cause the intercooler to drop down at the same time, so it would be worth supporting it, either with cable ties or on an axle stand to protect the hoses (see illustration).

13 Undo the mounting screws for the expansion tank and AdBlue filler tube, and move out of the way (see illustration).

14 Release the mounting clips using long-nosed pliers and manoeuvre the radiator from place (see illustrations).

Inspection

15 Clear the radiator core of flies, small leaves or other debris by brushing or hosing. Check the condition of all hoses, clips, mountings and retaining spring clips, and renew as necessary.

16 Carefully examine the radiator/expansion tank for signs of leaks, corrosion of the alloy core, or damage to the plastic side, top or bottom compartments, as applicable. Should the radiator/expansion tank require attention,

3.12 Support the intercooler to protect the hoses

3.14a Unclip the radiator, push it backwards...

this work should be left to a specialist due to the nature of its construction.

Refitting

17 Refitting the radiator is the reverse

3.13 Remove the header tank and AdBlue filler

3.14b ...then lift the radiator from place

4.3 Temperature sensor and heating element wiring plugs

4.4a Disconnect the various hoses...

4.4b ...from the thermostat housing

4.5a Undo the bolts at the front...

4.5b ...and top of the thermostat housing

c) *Renew the hose O-ring seals if they show signs of deterioration.*
d) *Tighten all bolts to their specified torque wrench settings (where given).*
e) *Ensure the coolant hose clips are positioned so that they do not foul any other component, then tighten them securely.*
f) *Refill the cooling system as described in Chapter 1 Section 30.*

5 Cooling fan – removal and refitting

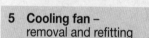

sequence to removal, noting the following points:
a) *Ensure that the lower mounting lugs properly engage with the rubber mountings, and that (where applicable) the locating studs are pressed fully home.*
b) *Make sure that the radiator retaining clips are a secure fit.*
c) *Make sure the hoses are tightened securely.*
d) *After fitting, fill the cooling system as described in Chapter 1 Section 30.*

4 Thermostat – removal, testing and refitting

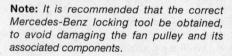

Removal

1 Drain the coolant as described in Chapter 1 Section 30.

2 Remove the air filter housing, as described in Chapter 4A Section 2.
3 Disconnect the wiring plugs from the temperature sensor and heating element at the thermostat housing **(see illustration)**.
4 Note their fitted locations, then disconnect the various coolant hoses from the thermostat housing **(see illustrations)**.
5 Undo the retaining bolts and remove the thermostat housing **(see illustrations)**. Note that no attempt must be made to remove the heating element from the housing – if defective the complete housing must be renewed.

Refitting

6 Refitting is a reversal of removal, but note the following additional points:
a) *Clean all mating surfaces thoroughly before reassembly.*
b) *Renew the thermostat housing seal/gasket regardless of condition (where applicable).*

Note: *It is recommended that the correct Mercedes-Benz locking tool be obtained, to avoid damaging the fan pulley and its associated components.*

Removal

1 Refer to Chapter 1 Section 30 and drain the cooling system.
2 Remove the front grille as described Chapter 11, Section 22.
3 Remove the front bumper as described in Chapter 11 Section 20.
4 Slacken the retaining clips and disconnect the top hose from the radiator and the smaller hose from the expansion tank **(see illustration)**.
5 Using a screwdriver, depress the tab on either side of the fan shroud to release the shroud **(see illustration)**.
6 Lift the shroud and move it towards the rear of the engine bay
7 Lift the shroud and move it towards the rear of the engine bay **(see illustration)**.

5.4 Disconnect the hoses from the radiator

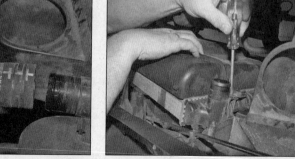

5.5 Depress the tab to release the clip

5.7 Release the shroud and move it rearwards

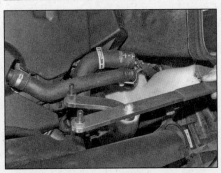

5.9 Hold the water pump pulley in place

5.10 Undo the bolt for the viscous fan clutch

5.11 Remove the fan and shroud from place at the same time

8 Place a piece of card between the fan and the radiator, to prevent radiator damage. **Note:** *Space is extremely tight in this area.*

9 Using a suitable such as a peg spanner, counterhold the water pump pulley in place **(see illustration)**.

10 Using an 8mm Allen key, loosen the bolt on the viscous fan clutch **(see illustration)**.

11 Detach the fan from its clutch and lift the fan and shroud at the same time **(see illustration)**.

Refitting

12 Refitting is a reversal of removal. Ensure that all bolts are tightened to the specified torque.

---

6 Cooling system electrical switches – removal and refitting

Coolant level sensor

1 The sensor is mounted in the bottom of the coolant expansion tank **(see illustration)**.

2 Refer to the relevant part of Chapter 1 Section 30 and partially drain the expansion tank, so that the level is below the position of the sensor.

3 Ensure that the ignition is switched off, and then unplug the wiring from the coolant level switch at the connector.

4 Turn the sensor clockwise a quarter of a turn, and pull to remove it from the expansion tank. Check the sealing ring, renew if required.

5 Refit the level sensor by following the removal procedure in reverse, noting the following points:

a) Fit a new O-ring seal to the sensor body, if required.

b) On completion, top-up the expansion tank.

Engine coolant temperature (ECT) sensor

Removal

6 The coolant temperature sensor is located in the thermostat housing, on the left-hand side of the engine, at the front**(see illustration)**.

7 Ensure that the engine is cold, then refer to Chapter 1 Section 30 and partially drain the cooling system.

8 Ensure that the ignition is switched off, and then unplug the wiring from the sensor at the connector.

9 Release the retaining clip and pull the sensor to remove it from the thermostat housing. Recover the sealing ring.

Refitting

10 Refitting is a reversal of removal, noting the following points:

a) Use a new sealing ring, where fitted.

b) On completion, top-up the cooling system as described in Chapter 1 or 'Weekly checks'.

---

7 Coolant pump – removal and refitting

Removal

1 Disconnect the battery as described in Chapter 5 Section 3.

2 Refer to Chapter 1 Section 30 and drain the cooling system.

3 Remove the cooling fan and shroud as described in Section 5.

4 Remove the auxiliary drivebelt as described in Chapter 1 Section 8.

5 Undo the bolt and remove the belt guide pulleys from above and beside the pump **(see illustrations)**.

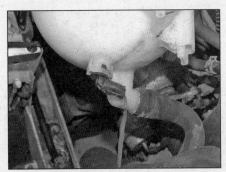

6.1 Coolant level sensor

6.6 Coolant temperature sensor

7.5a Remove the belt guide pulley beside the pump...

7.5b ...and above

7.6 Coolant pump retaining bolts

7.7 Removing the coolant pump

7.9 Fit new coolant pump gasket

6 Undo and remove the bolts securing the coolant pump **(see illustration)**.

7 Withdraw the pump, and recover the gasket **(see illustration)**. Discard the gasket, as a new one will be required when refitting.

Refitting

8 Carefully clean the coolant pump and cylinder block mating surfaces, removing all traces of the old gasket or sealant. Take care to avoid scoring the surfaces, as this will cause leakage.

9 Refit the coolant pump by following the removal procedure in reverse, noting these points:

a) *Fit a new gasket when refitting the pump (see illustration).*

b) *Refit and tension the auxiliary drivebelt with reference to Chapter 1.*

c) *On completion, refill the cooling system with reference to Chapter 1.*

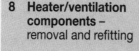

8 Heater/ventilation components – removal and refitting

1 Before working on any of the heater ventilation components, disconnect the battery as described in Chapter 5 Section 3.

Heater control panel

2 Remove the central instrument surround, as described in Chapter 11 Section 26.

3 Undo the four retaining screws and manoeuvre the heater control unit from place **(see illustration)**.

4 Noting their locations, disconnect the wiring connectors from the rear of the heater control panel **(see illustration)**.

5 Disconnect the heater control cables as they become available **(see illustrations)**.

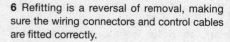
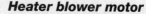

6 Refitting is a reversal of removal, making sure the wiring connectors and control cables are fitted correctly.

Heater blower motor

7 Remove the glovebox as described in Chapter 11 Section 26.

8 Move the sound-deadening material to one side and hook out of the way.

9 Disconnect the wiring connector from the heater blower motor **(see illustration)**.

10 Use a trim removal tool to raise the locating tab at the 10 o'clock position on the blower motor **(see illustration)**.

11 Rotate the blower motor anti-clockwise and remove from place **(see illustration)**.

12 Refitting is a reversal of removal, making sure that all wiring connections are securely remade. Operate the fan before refitting the glovebox to check it is fitted correctly.

8.3 Slacken the screws and remove the heater controls

8.4 Disconnect the wiring connectors

8.5a Press the clip to detach the control cable

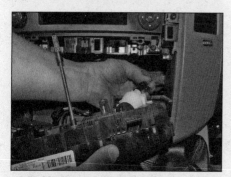

8.5b Manoeuvre the unit from the end of the cables

8.9 Disconnect the wiring connector(s)

8.10 Use a tool or screwdriver to raise the locating tab

8.11 Remove the motor from place

8.14 Unplug the blower resistor plug

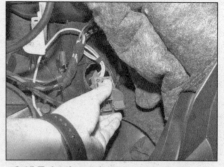

8.15 Twist the resistor anti-clockwise to remove

Blower resistor pack

13 Remove the glovebox as described in Chapter 11 Section 26.

14 Squeeze the tabs and disconnect the wiring plug for the blower resistor **(see illustration)**.

15 Rotate the blower resistor to remove **(see illustration)**.

16 Refitting is a reversal of removal

Heater housing

⚠️ *Warning: On models fitted with air conditioning, the air conditioning refrigerant MUST be discharged prior to removal – see Section 9.*

17 Remove the radio, speakers, glove compartment, instrument panel and facia trim panels, as described in Chapter 11.

18 Remove the left- and right-hand kick panels, as described in Chapter 11 Section 23.

19 Remove the facia, as described in Chapter 11 Section 26.

20 Unplug the OBD connector, as described in Chapter 12 Section 6.

21 Remove the headlining, as described in Chapter 11 Section 23.

22 Unclip the wiring from each A-pillar and across the top of the windscreen **(see illustration)**.

23 Unplug the rearmost connector from the airbag control unit **(see illustration)**.

24 Fold the sound-deadening trim up and out of the way.

25 Unplug the wiring connectors by the blower resistor **(see illustration)**.

26 Unclip the lower fusebox and manoeuvre from place **(see illustration)**.

27 Remove the gear selector from place, as described in Chapter 7 Section 2.

28 Disconnect the wiring plugs from the steering column.

29 Remove the steering column, as described in Chapter 10 Section 13.

30 Place hose clamps around each heater pipe in the engine bay **(see illustration)**.

31 Using a clip removal tool, disconnect the pipes from the firewall **(see illustration)**, and use a container to catch the small amount of coolant in the hoses.

32 On models with air conditioning, working inside the engine compartment (with the system discharged), unscrew the two nuts securing the air conditioning pipe union to the bulkhead. Separate the pipes from the evaporator and quickly seal the pipe and evaporator unions to prevent the entry of moisture into the refrigerant circuit. Discard the sealing rings, new ones must be used on refitting.

Caution: Failure to seal the refrigerant pipe unions will result in the dehydrator

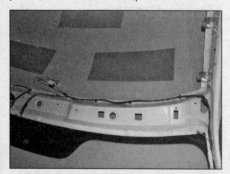

8.22 Unclip the wiring from place around the windscreen

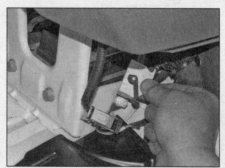

8.23 Unplug the rearmost wiring connector at the airbag control unit

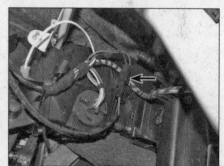

8.25 Unplug the wiring plug by the resistor

8.26 Detach the lower fusebox and move out of the way

8.30 Clamp each heater hose

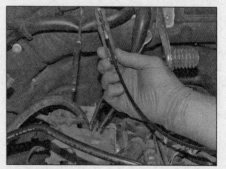

8.31 Using a clip removal tool will make undoing the heater retaining clips much easier

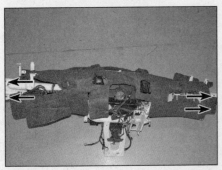

8.33 Slacken the four crossmember mounting bolts (crossmember removed for clarity)

8.34 Undo the four mounting bolts in the engine bay

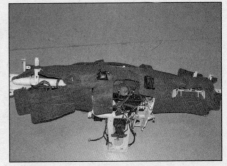

8.35 Withdraw the facia and crossmember from place

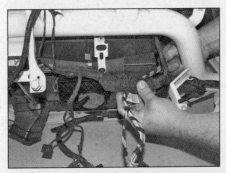

8.37 Unclip the wiring loom and disconnect the wiring plugs

8.38 Undo the three mounting nuts and two bolts

8.39 Withdraw the heater housing from the crossmember

reservoir to become saturated, necessitating its renewal.
33 Remove the four bolts at either end of the facia mounting crossmember **(see illustration)**.
34 Working inside the engine compartment, slacken the four crossmember mounting bolts **(see illustration)**.
35 With the help of an assistant, remove the crossmember and heater unit as one item **(see illustration)**.

36 Remove the heater blower unit, as described earlier in this Section.
37 Unclip the wiring loom from the heater housing and disconnect the wiring connectors, noting their fitted positions for refitting **(see illustration)**.
38 Undo the three retaining nuts and two bolts from the heater housing **(see illustration)**.
39 With all the fixings removed, withdraw the heater housing from the crossmember **(see illustration)**.
40 Refitting is a reversal of removal, making sure that all connections are securely remade.

Heater matrix

41 Remove the heater housing, as described previously in this Section.
42 Gently prise off the foam surround from the ends of the heater pipes **(see illustration)**.
43 Slacken the screw for the heater pipes retaining bracket on the side of the heater housing **(see illustration)**.
44 Using a screwdriver release the tabs on each side of the heater matrix **(see illustration)**.
45 The heater matrix can now be withdrawn from the heater housing **(see illustration)**.
Note: *On models with air conditioning, the evaporator can also be removed at this point.*
46 Refitting is a reversal of removal, noting the following points:
a) *On completion, refill the cooling system as described in Chapter 1 Section 30.*
b) *Run the engine and check the heater operation. It is not unknown for a heater*

8.42 Ease off the foam surround

8.43 Loosen the mounting screws

8.44 Release the tabs holding the matrix

8.45 Withdraw the heater matrix

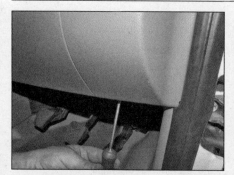

8.48 Slacken the screw to release the panel

8.49 Undo the screw for the vent panel

8.50 Undo the bottom screw from the vent panel

8.53 Remove the screws and manoeuvre the vent from place

8.58a Unclip the outer cable from the retaining clip

8.58b Releasing the outer cable from the heater valve

not to work initially, due to the formation of an airlock (especially when a new heater matrix has been fitted).

Facia air vents

Outermost dashboard vents

47 Unclip the panel from the A-pillar as described in Chapter 11 Section 23.
48 Remove the screw and lower dashboard panel **(see illustration)**.
49 Remove the screw from the top of the vent **(see illustration)**.
50 Remove the screws from the bottom of the vent panel **(see illustration)**.
51 Remove the vent from place.

Driver's-side central vent

52 Remove the instrument panel surround, as described in Chapter 11 Section 26.
53 Undo the two screws and remove the vent panel from place **(see illustration)**.
54 Refitting is a reversal of removal.

Passenger side central vent

55 Follow the same procedure as for the driver's-side vent.

Heater control cables

56 Depending on model, there are a number of control cables fitted to the heater housing behind the facia panel. To access these, remove the relevant panels as described in Chapter 11.
57 Remove the heater control panel, as described previously (paragraphs 2 to 6).
58 Release the securing clip holding the outer cable to the housing, and then disconnect the

inner cable from the relevant control lever **(see illustrations)**. Withdraw the cable from behind the facia, noting its fitted position (and colour).
59 Refitting is a reversal of removal.

9 Air conditioning system –
general information
and precautions

1 An air conditioning system is fitted as standard equipment on later high specification models, and was available as an optional extra on some lower specification models. In conjunction with the heater, the system enables any reasonable air temperature to be achieved inside the vehicle, it also reduces the humidity of the incoming air, aiding demisting even when cooling is not required.
2 The refrigeration circuit of the air conditioning system functions in a similar way to a domestic refrigerator. A compressor, belt-driven from the crankshaft pulley, draws refrigerant in its gaseous state from an evaporator. The refrigerant heats up as a result of being compressed, but is then passed through a condenser (mounted in front of the engine radiator) where it loses heat and enters its liquid state. After dehydration, the refrigerant is passed through an evaporator (mounted inside the heater housing) where it is allowed to expand and reverts to being gas. This change of state has the effect of absorbing heat from the air passing over the evaporator fins, reducing its temperature. This

cool air is mixed with warm air from the heater unit to achieve the desired cabin temperature. The refrigerant is directed back to the compressor and the cycle is then repeated.
3 Various subsidiary controls and sensors protect the system against excessive temperature and pressures. Additionally, engine idle speed is increased when the system is in use to compensate for the additional load imposed by the compressor. Electronic sensors detect the rotational speed differential between the engine and the compressor – if this becomes too great (due to a malfunctioning compressor), the compressor clutch is disengaged, to preserve the drivebelt.
4 The air conditioning electronic control system can only be tested using dedicated equipment. For this reason, it is recommended that problems with the operation of the air conditioning system be referred to a Mercedes-Benz dealer for diagnosis.

⚠ *Warning: The refrigeration circuit contains pressurised liquid refrigerant. The refrigerant is potentially dangerous, and should only be handled by qualified persons. Refrigerant that is allowed to come into contact with the skin will cause severe frostbite. It is not itself poisonous, but in the presence of a naked flame (including inhalation through a lighted cigarette), it forms a poisonous gas. Uncontrolled discharging of the refrigerant is dangerous and is also extremely damaging to the environment. For these reasons,*

disconnection of any part of the system without specialised knowledge and equipment is not recommended.
• Do not allow refrigerant lines to be exposed to temperatures in excess of 110°C, for example during welding or paint-drying operations.
• Do not operate the air conditioning system if it is known to be short of refrigerant, or component damage may result.

10 Air conditioning system components – removal and refitting

⚠️ Warning: Refer to the previous Section before proceeding. Before carrying out any of the procedures detailed below, the air conditioning system MUST be professionally discharged by a garage or air conditioning specialist.

Note: The car may be driven once the system has been discharged, but the air conditioning system should NOT be switched on, as this will cause damage to the compressor. The safest option is to have the system discharged where the car is to be worked on, and not move the car until the system has been recharged. With air conditioning becoming an increasingly common fitment, mobile air conditioning specialists are becoming more widespread.

Evaporator

1 The evaporator is situated inside the heater housing behind the facia panel along side the heater matrix. To remove the evaporator, follow the procedures as described for removing the heater matrix in Section 8 of this Chapter.

Receiver/drier

2 The receiver/drier stores refrigerant and removes moisture from the system. When any major air conditioning component (compressor, condenser or evaporator) is renewed, or the system has been apart and exposed to air for any length of time, the receiver/drier must be renewed. This is to ensure correct functioning of the air conditioning system.
3 Gloves must be worn when disconnecting the refrigerant lines, even though the system

will have been discharged at this point (refer to the warning at the start of this Section). Where applicable, recover the O-ring seals – new ones must be used when refitting. Cover the pipe ends, to prevent the entry of foreign matter.
4 Open the bonnet and disconnect the wiring connector from the top of the receiver/dryer.
5 With the system discharged, undo the two retaining screws and disconnect the refrigerant lines from the receiver/drier. Plug the end of the lines to prevent the ingress of dirt and moisture.
6 Slacken the clamp screw on the mounting bracket and withdraw the receiver/drier out from the engine compartment.
7 Refitting is a reversal of removal, noting the following points:
a) Use new O-ring seals when reconnecting the refrigerant lines, and tighten the unions securely.
b) Lubricate the O-ring seals with clean refrigerant oil.
c) If the receiver/drier is being renewed, add 20 cc of clean refrigerant oil to the new receiver/drier. This will maintain the correct oil level in the system after the repairs are completed.
d) Have the system professionally recharged before attempting to use it.

Condenser

8 Follow the procedures for removing the radiator, as described in Section 3.
9 Gloves must be worn when disconnecting the refrigerant lines, even though the system will have been discharged at this point (refer to the warning at the start of this Section).
10 Unscrew the unions on the two pipes at the side of the condenser, and disconnect them. Recover the O-ring seals – new ones must be used when refitting. Cover the pipe ends to prevent the entry of foreign matter.
11 Carefully lift the condenser out of its lower mountings and remove it from the car, taking care not to damage the fins or pipework.
12 Refitting is a reversal of removal, noting the following points:
a) Use new O-ring seals when reconnecting the refrigerant lines, and tighten the unions securely.
b) Lubricate the O-ring seals with clean refrigerant oil.
c) Renew the receiver/drier, see paragraph 2 in this Section.

d) Have the system professionally recharged before attempting to use it.

Compressor

13 Disconnect the battery negative cable and position it away from the terminal.
14 Apply the handbrake, then jack up the front of the vehicle and support it on axle stands as described in Jacking and vehicle support). Where fitted, remove the plastic shield from under the engine.
15 Remove the auxiliary drivebelt as described in the relevant part of Chapter 1.
16 Undo the retaining bolt and disconnect the refrigerant line bracket from the transmission housing.
17 Support the compressor (it is a heavy unit) and remove the mounting bolts. Depending on the exact type of compressor, and on the engine to which it is fitted, there will be either three or four mounting bolts. Lift the compressor and move it forward to access the refrigerant lines and wiring connector.
18 If the compressor is being removed as part of another procedure (such as engine removal), it is sufficient to remove the mounting bolts and tie the compressor up to one side without disconnecting the refrigerant lines. If the compressor is being removed completely, proceed as follows.
19 Gloves must be worn when disconnecting the refrigerant lines, even though the system will have been discharged at this point (refer to the warning at the start of this Section). Unscrew the unions on the two pipes on the compressor, and disconnect them. Recover the O-ring seals – new ones must be used when refitting.
20 Disconnect the wiring plug from the top of the compressor.
21 It is advisable to cover the openings on the compressor while it is removed, to reduce oil loss and to prevent foreign matter from entering.
22 Refitting is a reversal of removal, noting the following points:
a) Use new O-ring seals when reconnecting the refrigerant lines, and tighten the unions securely.
b) Tighten the mounting bolts securely.
c) Renew the receiver/drier, see paragraph 2 in this Section.
d) Have the system professionally recharged before attempting to use it.

Chapter 4 Part A
Fuel system

Contents

Degrees of difficulty

Easy, suitable for novice with little experience		Fairly easy, suitable for beginner with some experience		Fairly difficult, suitable for competent DIY mechanic		Difficult, suitable for experienced DIY mechanic		Very difficult, suitable for expert DIY or professional	

Specifications

General

System type	Direct injection common rail with high-pressure delivery pump and Electronic Diesel Control
Fuel injection pump pressure.	up to 1600 bar
Turbocharger type	Variable vane geometry

Torque wrench settings

	Nm	lb ft
Camshaft position sensor	8	6
Common rail:		
Mounting bolts	14	10
Fuel return banjo bolt	20	15
Crankshaft position sensor	8	6
Engine oil level dipstick guide tube	10	7
Exhaust manifold-to-cylinder head *	30	22
Fuel injector clamp bolts*:		
Stage 1	7	5
Stage 2	Angle-tighten a further 90°	
Stage 3	Angle-tighten a further 90°	
Fuel injection pump	15	10
Fuel tank level sensor/pump cover retaining rings.	80	60
Fuel tank retaining strap bolts	56	41
Fuel temperature sensor	23	17
Intake manifold	16	11
High-pressure fuel pipe unions:		
Stage 1	7	5
Stage 2	33	25
Knock sensor	20	15
Rear crossmember-to-body	25	18
Steering shaft-to-pinion pinch bolt nut *	24	18
Throttle body bolts	10	7
Turbocharger-to-exhaust manifold:		
Stage 1	20	15
Stage 2	Angle-tighten a further 90°	
Turbocharger oil feed banjo bolt-to-turbocharger	18	14
Turbocharger oil return.	10	7
Turbocharger support bracket:		
To-turbocharger	30	22
To-cylinder block	20	15

* Use new nuts/bolts

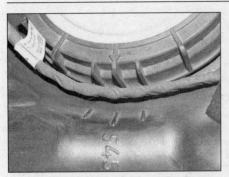

3.5 Alignment marks for sender unit locking ring

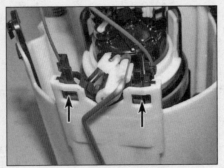

3.6a Unclip the sender...

1 General information and precautions

General information

1 Fuel is drawn from a tank under the rear of the vehicle, by a tank-mounted pump, through the pipework, and through fuel filter/water separator/heater into the high-pressure injection pump. The high-pressure injection pump is driven by timing chain end of the inlet camshaft, and supplies very high pressure fuel to the common fuel rail, which is connected to each individual injector. The injectors are operated by solenoids controlled by the ECM, based on information supplied by various sensors. The multi-hole injectors are capable of multiple pre-, and post-injections per stroke. The engine ECM also controls the pre-heating side of the system – refer to Chapter 5B for more details.

2 The EDC (electronic diesel control) system fitted, incorporates a 'drive by wire' system, where the traditional accelerator cable is replaced by an accelerator pedal position sensor. The position and rate-of-change of the accelerator pedal is reported by the position sensor to the ECM, which then adjusts the fuel injectors to deliver the required amount of fuel, and optimum combustion efficiency.

3 Fuel level in the tank is determined by a level sensor in the in-tank pump module.

4 The exhaust system incorporates a turbocharger, EGR and on some models, a diesel particulate filter. Further detail of the emission control systems can be found in Chapter 4B.

Precautions

5 When working on diesel fuel system components, scrupulous cleanliness must be observed, and care must be taken not to introduce any foreign matter into fuel lines or components.

6 After carrying out any work involving disconnection of fuel lines, it is advisable to check the connections for leaks; pressurise the system by cranking the engine several times.

7 Electronic control units are very sensitive components, and certain precautions must be taken to avoid damage to these units as follows.

8 When carrying out welding operations on the vehicle using electric welding equipment, the battery and alternator should be disconnected.

9 Although the underbonnet-mounted modules will tolerate normal underbonnet conditions, they can be adversely affected by excess heat or moisture. If using welding equipment or pressure-washing equipment in the vicinity of an electronic module, take care not to direct heat, or jets of water or steam, at the module. If this cannot be avoided, remove the module from the vehicle, and protect its wiring plug with a plastic bag.

10 Before disconnecting any wiring, or removing components, always ensure that the ignition is switched off.

11 Do not attempt to improvise ECM fault diagnosis procedures using a test lamp or multi-meter, as irreparable damage could be caused to the module.

12 After working on fuel injection/engine management system components, ensure that all wiring is correctly reconnected before reconnecting the battery or switching on the ignition.

2 Air cleaner assembly – removal and refitting

Removal

1 Remove the air filter housing as described in Chapter 1 Section 26.

Refitting

2 Refitting is a reversal of removal.

3 Fuel gauge/pump sender unit – removal and refitting

⚠ *Warning: Observe the precautions in this Section before working on any component in the fuel system.*

Removal

1 Disconnect the battery as described in Chapter 5 Section 3.

2 Remove the fuel tank as described in Section 4.

3 If not already done, disconnect the fuel gauge wiring from the sender unit, and then release the retaining clips and disconnect the fuel lines, noting which way around they are fitted. **Note:** *Depending on model, there maybe a different number of fuel lines and wiring connectors*.

4 The retaining rings must now be loosened and removed. To do this, Mercedes-Benz technicians use a special tool which engages with the outer part of the ring. Ideally, this tool should be obtained, however it should be possible to fabricate a homemade version.

5 Make note of the markings on the locking ring and fuel tank to aid refitting **(see illustration)**, with the ring removed, carefully withdraw the sender unit from the fuel tank. Recover the sealing gaskets, taking care not to damage the fuel sender unit. **Note:** *If the sender unit is going to be removed from the tank for any length of time, it is worth screwing the retaining ring back on to the neck because the tank could gradually distort, making it difficult to refit the ring*.

6 If required, the sender unit can be separated from the assembly, release the retaining clips and slide the unit out from the housing, then disconnect the small wires, noting their fitted positions **(see illustrations)**.

7 Connect a hand-held multi-meter to the centre two terminals in the sender/pump unit socket. With the float arm at its lower stop

3.6b ...and disconnect the wiring plug

3.7a Meter should read around 160 ohms with the float at its lower position

position (tank empty) the resistance should be approx 160 ohms. With the float arm at its upper stop position (tank full) the resistance should be approximately 50 ohms **(see illustrations)**.

Refitting

8 Refitting is a reversal of removal, but always renew the sender unit sealing gaskets, and tighten the retaining rings to the specified torque. Making sure that the marks noted on removal are aligned.

3.7b Meter should read around 50 ohms with the float at its highest position

4.6 Slacken the screws and take away the panel

4 Fuel tank – removal and refitting

1 Observe the precautions in Section 1 before working on any component in the fuel system.

Removal

2 The fuel tank must be emptied before the operation can be started. This is best achieved by waiting until the tank is almost empty through the course of normal driving.
3 Park the vehicle on a level surface and chock the rear roadwheels. Raise the front of the vehicle, support it securely on axle stands as described in *Jacking and vehicle support*.

⚠️ **Warning: The use of an inspection pit is not advised; fuel vapours are heavier than air and can quickly**

build-up on the floor of the pit, causing a potential hazard.
4 Disconnect the battery as described in Chapter 5 Section 3.
5 Remove the fuel flap as described in Chapter 11 Section 13.
6 Undo the four retaining screws and remove the panelling around the fuel filler neck **(see illustration)**.
7 Undo the filler neck screw and remove **(see illustration)**.
8 Working under the vehicle, prise out the seal around the filler neck **(see illustration)**.
9 Disconnect the fuel tank wiring plug by the filler neck **(see illustration)**.

10 Disconnect the fuel tank underbody wiring plug **(see illustration)**.
11 Using a small screwdriver, prise up the retaining clips and disconnect the fuel lines **(see illustration)**.
12 Slacken the securing nuts on the straps that support the fuel tank, but do not remove completely at this point **(see illustration)**. These are prone to corrosion, so use a wire brush and some penetrating oil to release the retaining nuts.
13 Support the fuel tank and remove the support straps.
14 Lower the tank. If your vehicle has a bleed line above the tank, disconnect it when it becomes available.

4.7 Slacken and remove the filler neck screw

4.8 Remove the filler neck seal

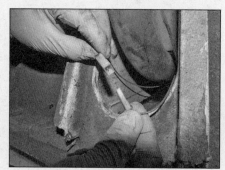

4.9 Unplug the wiring connector

4.10 Unplug the underbody wiring connector

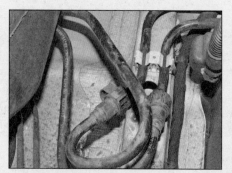

4.11 Separate the fuel lines from the tank

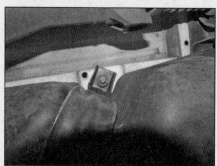

4.12 Loosen the bolts for the retaining straps

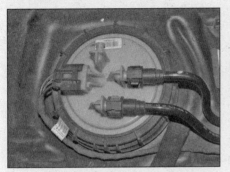

4.15a Disconnect the fuel hoses...

4.15b ...and unplug the connector

5.3 Unplug the wiring connector under the tank

5.4 Disconnect the feed line

15 Disconnect the fuel hoses and wiring plug **(see illustrations)**, then remove the fuel tank from the vehicle.

16 If required, remove the fuel gauge/pump sender unit as described in Section 3.

17 Swill the tank out with clean fuel. If the tank shows signs of leakage, it should be renewed.

⚠️ *Warning: Do not attempt to repair the tank yourself by welding, soldering or brazing. The tank will contain an explosive mixture of air and fuel vapour, even when emptied of liquid fuel.*

Refitting

18 Refitting is a reversal of removal, tightening all fixings to the correct torque, where specified.

5 Ad Blue tank –
removal and refitting

Removal

1 Remove the front bumper as described in Chapter 11 Section 20.
2 Drain the AdBlue tank.
3 Disconnect the wiring plug from the delivery unit on the bottom of the tank **(see illustration)**.
4 Disconnect the feed pipe from the delivery unit **(see illustration)**.
5 Use a suitable plug to block the feed line, to prevent contamination.
6 Undo the three mounting screws to remove the pump from place **(see illustration)**.
7 Working under the vehicle, remove two of the three mounting bolts.
8 Remove the mounting bolt from the front crossmember **(see illustration)**.

Refitting

9 Refitting is reversal of removal.

6 Fuel injectors –
removal and refitting

⚠️ *Warning: Exercise extreme caution when working on the fuel injectors. Never expose the hands or any part of the body to injector spray, as the high working pressure can cause the fuel to penetrate the skin, with possibly fatal results. You are strongly advised to have any work which involves testing the injectors under pressure carried out by a dealer or fuel injection specialist. Refer to the precautions given in Section 1 of this Chapter before proceeding.*

Note: *Take care not to allow dirt into the fuel rail, injectors or fuel pipes during this procedure. Keep the fuel pipes and injectors identified for position to ensure correct refitting. As the fuel pipes are removed, plug the ends of the pipes, injectors and fuel rail to prevent dirt ingress.*

Removal

1 Remove the air filter housing, as described in Section 2.
2 Disconnect the fuel return hoses from the top of the injectors **(see illustration)**. Be prepared for fuel spillage. Plug the openings to prevent contamination. **Note:** *When the white marking on the return fitting is visible, the connection is locked. If the marking is not visible, the connection is not secure.*
3 Undo the union nuts and remove the

5.6 Undo the three screws to remove the pump

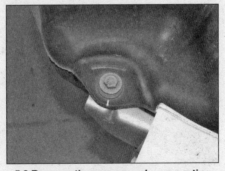

5.8 Remove the crossmember mounting bolt

6.2 Pull up the collar to cover the 'white' mark, and disconnect the hoses

6.3 Remove the pipes between the common rail and the injectors

6.4 Slide out the clip and disconnect the wiring plug

6.5 Injector clamp retaining bolt

6.6 Withdraw the injector and clamp from the cylinder head

high-pressure fuel injection pipes between the common fuel rail and the injectors **(see illustration)**. Note that Mercedes insist that new pipes are fitted. Plug all openings as they become accessible.

4 Release the clips and disconnect the wiring plugs from each injector **(see illustration)**. Unclip the harness guide and move it to one side.

5 Slacken and remove the injector clamp retaining bolts from each injector **(see illustration)**. Discard the bolts, as new ones will be required when refitting.

6 Withdraw the injectors and clamps from the cylinder head. If necessary, use a slide hammer/ puller to withdraw the injectors, making sure it is in the vertical position **(see illustration)**. Recover the sealing rings/washers and discard. New ones must be used for refitting. **Note:** *If the injectors are to be refitted, it's essential that they're refitted to their original locations. Mark the injectors with permanent marker (or similar) to indicate the cylinder number.*

Caution: If a impact extractor (slide hammer) is used to release the injectors, damage to the injectors is likely, and replacements will be required.

Refitting

7 Thoroughly clean the injectors and their locating holes in the cylinder head. Use a bottle brush (or similar) and and vacuum cleaner to remove all traces of carbon/debris from the area.

8 Renew the sealing washers at the base of each injector **(see illustration)**.

9 Apply special grease (Mercedes No. A 001 898 42 51 10) to the injector bodies to prevent them seizing in place.

10 Make a note of any numbers on the injectors **(see illustration)**. If new injectors are being fitted, a control unit adaption must be carried out using Mercedes-Benz diagnostic equipment (or equivalent). These numbers will be needed during the adaption process.

11 Fit the injectors in to the holes in the cylinder heads. If the original injectors are being refitted, they must be fitted into their original locations. Note that the retaining brackets must be fitted at the same time as the injectors are inserted.

12 Fit the new high-pressure fuel pipes, and tighten the unions to their specified torque. The pipes must be installed 'without tension'.

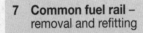

6.8 Renew the injector sealing washers

13 Insert the injector retaining bolts and tighten them to the specified torque.

14 The remainder of refitting is a reversal of removal, noting the following points:

a) Tighten all fasteners to their specified torque where given.

b) Lubricate the return (leak-off) pipe rubber seals prior to refitting.

c) If new injectors have been fitted, carry out the control unit adaption using Mercedes-Benz diagnostic equipment (or similar). Entrust this task to a dealer or suitably equipped specialist.

7 Common fuel rail – removal and refitting

Removal

1 Remove the air cleaner assembly, as described in Section 2.

7.3 Remove the pipes between the common rail and the injectors

6.10 Make a note of the injector numbers

2 Disconnect the wiring plugs from the fuel filter, fuel rail pressure sensor, fuel quantity control valve, etc, then release the clips and move the wiring harness duct to one side.

3 Undo the union nuts and remove the high-pressure fuel injection pipes between the common fuel rail and the injectors **(see illustration)**. Take care not to bend or squeeze the pipes. Plug all openings as they become accessible. Mark the pipes with paint (or similar) to indicate their fitted positions.

4 Undo the banjo bolt, and disconnect the fuel return pipe from the fuel rail **(see illustration)**. Plug the openings to prevent contamination. Be prepared for fuel spillage. New sealing washers will be required.

5 Slacken the common rail mounting bolts, then undo the union securing the high-pressure pipe from the pump to the rail, and remove the pipe support brackets.

6 Completely remove the mounting bolts, and withdraw the common rail.

7.4 Fuel return pipe banjo bolt

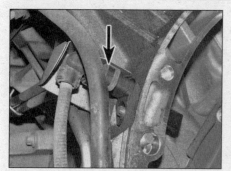

8.5 Crankshaft position sensor wiring plug

8.12 Slide out the locking catch and disconnect the mass air flow sensor wiring plug

8.16 Charge air temperature sensor

Refitting

7 Refitting is a reversal of removal, noting the following points:

a) *Examine the condition of the rigid, high-pressure fuel pipes. If they show any sign of wear or damage, particularly at the tapered seats at each end, renew them. It may be prudent to renew them regardless of condition.*

b) *Tighten all fasteners to their specified torque where given.*

c) *Check the fuel system for leaks prior to refitting the engine cover.*

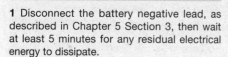

8 Engine management control system components – removal and refitting

1 Disconnect the battery negative lead, as described in Chapter 5 Section 3, then wait at least 5 minutes for any residual electrical energy to dissipate.

Crankshaft sensor

2 Remove the air cleaner assembly, as described in Section 2.

3 Raise the front of the vehicle and support it securely on axle stands (see Vehicle jacking and support 13 Section 5).

4 The sensor is fitted to the left-hand side of the cylinder block, adjacent to the transmission bell housing. Where fitted, undo the bolt and remove the sensor heatshield.

5 Disconnect the sensor wiring plug (**see illustration**).

6 Undo the retaining bolt and withdraw the sensor.

7 Refitting is a reversal of removal, tightening the sensor retaining bolt to the specified torque.

Coolant temperature sensor

8 Removal of the sensor is described in Chapter 2B.

Accelerator pedal position sensor

9 The sensor is integral with the accelerator pedal assembly, see Section 9.

Mass airflow/ Intake air temperature sensor

10 Remove the air cleaner assembly, as described in Section 2.

11 Slacken the clamps and remove the air intake hose from the front of the air filter housing.

12 Disconnect the wiring plug from the mass air flow sensor (**see illustration**).

13 Undo the screws and remove the outlet duct from the housing. Note that the mass airflow sensor and the integral air intake temperature sensor can only be replaced complete with the air outlet ducting.

14 Refitting is a reversal of removal.

Stop-light switch

15 The engine control module receives a signal from the stop-light switch which indicates when the brakes are being applied. Stop-light switch removal and refitting details can be found in Chapter 9 Section 11.

Charge air temperature sensor

16 The charge air temperature sensor is located in the charge air duct adjacent to the air conditioning compressor at the front, left-hand side of the engine (**see illustration**).

17 Disconnect the wiring plug, then squeeze together the side of the retaining clips and pull the sensor from the duct. Renew the O-ring seal.

18 Refitting is a reversal of removal.

Camshaft position sensor

19 Remove the air filter housing as described in Section 2.

20 Disconnect the camshaft position sensor wiring plug (**see illustration**).

21 Undo the retaining bolt and withdrawn the sensor from place. Renew the sensor sealing ring.

22 Refitting is a reversal of removal, tightening the sensor retaining bolt to the specified torque.

23 Refit the engine top cover.

Knock sensor

24 Two knock sensors are fitted to these engines. Both on the left-hand side of the cylinder block, below the intake manifold.

25 To remove the sensor for cylinders 1 and 2, remove the EGR cooler as described in Chapter 4B Section 2. There's no need to disconnect the coolant hoses from the cooler, simply move it to one side.

26 To remove the sensor for cylinders 3 and 4, remove the EGR valve as described in Chapter 4B Section 2.

27 Disconnect the wiring plug, then undo the bolt and remove the sensor (**see illustration**).

28 Refitting is a reversal of removal. It's essential that the sensor retaining bolt is tightened to the specified torque.

Fuel pump control unit

Note: *If the control unit is to be renewed, prior to removal, Mercedes-Benz diagnostic equipment (or equivalent) must be connected*

8.20 Camshaft position sensor

8.27 Knock sensors (cylinder head removed for clarity)

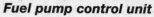

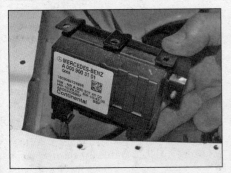

8.30 Fuel pump control unit

9.1 Pedal assembly retaining nuts

10.2 Unclip the coolant hose

to the diagnostic plug and the stored data in the control unit retrieved. This information is essential for correctly programming the replacement control unit. Entrust this task to a Mercedes dealer or suitably equipped specialist.

29 Remove the driver's seat cushion as described in Chapter 11 Section 24.

30 Disconnect the wiring plugs and remove the control unit **(see illustration)**.

31 Refitting is a reversal of removal.

9 Accelerator pedal – removal and refitting

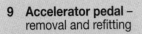

Removal

1 Undo the 2 retaining nuts, disconnect the wiring plug and remove the pedal **(see illustration)**. No dismantling of the pedal assembly is recommended.

Refitting

2 Refitting is a reversal of removal.

10 Throttle body – removal and refitting

Removal

1 Remove the air filter assembly as described in Section 2.

2 Unhook the coolant hose from the holder **(see illustration)**.

3 Mark their fitted positions, then disconnect the various hoses from the vacuum reservoir **(see illustration)**.

4 Undo the retaining bolts and remove the vacuum reservoir **(see illustration)**.

5 Undo the mounting bolts, swivel the EGR cooler upwards and place to one side with the coolant hoses still attached.

6 Undo the bolts and remove the EGR pipe to the intake manifold. New seals will be required.

7 Disconnect the wiring plug, detach the various brackets, then undo the bolts and remove the mixing chamber **(see illustrations)**.

10.3 Disconnect the vacuum hoses

10.4 Vacuum reservoir retaining bolts

8 Disconnect the throttle valve wiring plug, and remove the throttle body **(see illustrations)**. Renew the seal.

Refitting

9 Refitting is a reversal of removal, tightening the fasteners to their specified torque where given.

10.7a Throttle body-to-mixing chamber bolts (3 arrowed – 1 hidden), and lower mounting bolt

10.7b Mixing chamber-to-manifold bolts

10.8a Slide out the locking clip and disconnect the wiring plug

10.8b Renew the throttle body seal

11.8 Charge air duct retaining bolt

11.10 Squeeze together the clips each side and disconnect the vacuum hose

11.12 Pump-to-fuel rail upper union and clamp bolt

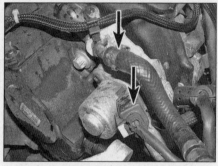

11.13 Fuel supply hose and quantity valve wiring plug

11 Fuel injection pump – removal and refitting

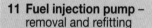

> ⚠️ **Warning: Observe the precautions in 'Safety first!' before working on any component in the fuel system.**

Removal

1 Remove the air filter assembly, as described in Section 2.

2 Raise the vehicle and support it securely on axle stands (see *Jacking and vehicle support*).

3 Remove the throttle body as described in Section 10.

4 Undo the 2 bolts and move the wiring harness bracket above the left-hand engine mounting to one side.

5 Undo the 2 bolts and remove the mounting plate for the mixing chamber.

6 Release the clamps and remove the charge air hose from the intercooler to the duct alongside the left-hand side of the engine.

7 Disconnect the wiring plug from the air temperature sensor on the charge air duct.

8 Undo the retaining bolt at the front, then carefully manoeuvre the charge air duct rearwards from place **(see illustration)**.

9 Disconnect the wiring plugs from the fuel quantity control valve and the fuel temperature sensor.

10 Disconnect the vacuum pipe from the vacuum pump **(see illustration)**.

11 Undo the bolts securing the high-pressure fuel pipe support bracket.

12 Using a second spanner to counterhold, undo the union nuts securing the high-pressure fuel pipe to the pump and fuel rail **(see illustration)**. Be prepared for fuel spillage. Plug the openings as they become accessible.

13 Disconnect the remaining fuel hose from the pump **(see illustration)**. Plug the openings to prevent contamination. Be prepared for fuel spillage.

14 Undo the 3 retaining bolts, unhook the wiring harness from the EGR pipe bracket, and detach the high-pressure pump **(see illustrations)**. Note that the retaining bolts and the O-ring seal must be renewed.

15 With the exception of drive gear removal, Mercedes Benz insist that no further dismantling of the pump is to be carried out. If a fault is suspected, have the pump inspected by a Mercedes Benz dealer or specialist.

Refitting

16 Refitting is a reversal of removal, noting the following points:

a) *Ensure the mating surfaces of the pump and cylinder head are clean.*

b) *Apply a little clean engine oil to the new pump O-ring seal prior to refitting.*

c) *All high-pressure fuel pipes must be fitted 'without tension'.*

d) *Tighten all fasteners to their specified torque, where given.*

e) *Upon completion, switch the ignition on for at least 15 seconds to circulate fuel through the pump. Failure to do so may damage the pump.*

12 Electronic control module (ECM) – removal and refitting

Removal

Caution: Electronic Control Modules (ECMs) contain components that are sensitive to the levels of static electricity generated by a person during normal activity. Once the multiway harness connectors has been unplugged, the exposed ECM connector pins can freely conduct stray static electricity to these components, damaging or even destroying them – the damage will be invisible and may not manifest itself immediately. Expensive repairs can be avoided by observing the following basic handling rules:

• *Handle a disconnected ECM by its case only; do not allow fingers or tools to come into contact with the pins.*

• *When carrying an ECM, earth yourself from time to time by touching a metal object such as an unpainted water pipe, this will discharge any potentially damaging static that may have built-up.*

• *Do not leave the ECM unplugged from its connector for any longer than is absolutely necessary.*

1 The electronic control module (ECM) is located in the left-hand side of the engine compartment **(see illustration)**. First, make sure that the ignition is switched off, and the earth lead is disconnected from the battery negative terminal.

11.14a Fuel pump lower retaining bolt...

11.14b ...and upper retaining bolts (one hidden)

12.1 The ECM is on the left-hand side of the engine bay

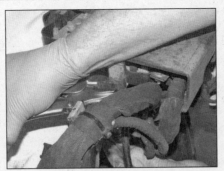

12.2 Remove the two shear bolts

12.3 Pull the body control module out

2 The ECM cover is held on by shear bolts, which can be removed using mole grips or pliers **(see illustration)**.

3 Unclip the ECM and lift it from place **(see illustration)**.

4 Take careful note of all the wiring connections, then unplug.

Refitting

8 Refitting is a reversal of removal.

---

13 Inlet manifold –
removal and refitting

Intake manifold

1 Disconnect the battery negative lead as described in Chapter 5 Section 3.

2 Remove the plastic cover from the top of the engine.

3 Drain the cooling system as described in Chapter 1 Section 30.

4 Remove the fuel filter as described in Chapter 1 Section 11.

5 Remove the EGR valve as described in Chapter 4B Section 2.

6 At the rear, left-hand corner of the engine, undo the bolts securing the fuel supply and return pipes bracket, and move it to one side **(see illustration)**.

7 Disconnect the coolant hose from the outlet **(see illustration)**.

8 Unclip the fuel hose, then undo the bolts and remove the fuel filter housing. A new seal will be required.

9 Undo the clamp bolts, then undo the unions and remove the high-pressure fuel pipe between the fuel rail and the pump. Plug the openings to prevent contamination.

10 Slacken the securing bolts and remove the dipstick tube and bracket.

11 Make a final check to ensure all wiring/hoses that may impede manifold removal have been disconnected.

12 Gradually, evenly, undo the captive retaining bolts and lift the intake manifold from place. Renew the manifold seal.

13 Refitting is a reversal of removal, noting the following points:

a) *Tighten all fasteners to their specified torque, where given.*

b) *Top up the cooling system as described in Chapter 1 Section 30.*

c) *Check for leaks before refitting the engine cover/undershield.*

13.6 Fuel pipes bracket bolts

---

14 Intercooler –
removal, inspection and refitting

Note: *The intercooler is located at the front end of the vehicle, below the radiator.*

Removal

1 Remove the radiator as described in Chapter 3 Section 3.

2 Slacken the retaining clips and disconnect the air hoses from each side of the intercooler **(see illustrations)** then manoeuvre from place. It is possible to use screwdrivers to release the clips, but specialist tools make the job much easier. **Note:** *Plug the ends of the hoses to prevent contamination.*

Inspection

3 Clear the intercooler core of flies, small

13.7 Disconnect the coolant hose above the intake manifold

14.2a Disconnect the air hoses...

14.2b ...from each side of the intercooler

14.2c A specialist tool can make releasing the clips much easier

leaves or other debris by brushing or hosing. Check the condition of all hoses, clips, mountings and retaining spring clips, and renew as necessary.

4 Carefully examine the intercooler for signs of cracks, splits, corrosion of the alloy core, or damage to the plastic side sections. Should the intercooler require attention, this work should be left to a specialist due to the nature of its construction.

Refitting

5 Refitting the intercooler is the reverse sequence to removal, noting the following points:

a) *Ensure that the mounting bolts are secure.*

b) *Make sure that the intercooler hose clips are a secure fit.*

15 Idle speed and fault diagnosis

1 Experienced home mechanics equipped with an accurate tachometer suitable for Diesel engines can check the engine idle speed, although the vehicle must be taken to a suitably equipped Mercedes-Benz dealer or fuel injection specialist for any other assessment. Neither the air/fuel mixture nor the engine idle speed are manually adjustable.

2 A diagnostic socket, located under the passenger side facia panel, next to the bonnet release lever, is incorporated in the engine management system wiring harness, to which dedicated electronic test equipment can be connected. The test equipment is capable of 'interrogating' the engine management system ECM electronically and accessing its internal fault log. In this manner, faults can be pinpointed quickly and simply, even if their occurrence is intermittent. Testing all the system components individually in an attempt to locate the fault by elimination is a time consuming operation that is unlikely to be fruitful (particularly if the fault occurs dynamically), and also carries high risk of damage to the ECM's internal components.

Chapter 4 Part B
Emission control and exhaust systems

Contents

Degrees of difficulty

Easy, suitable for novice with little experience	Fairly easy, suitable for beginner with some experience	Fairly difficult, suitable for competent DIY mechanic 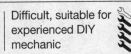	Difficult, suitable for experienced DIY mechanic	Very difficult, suitable for expert DIY or professional

Specifications

General

Emissions level	EU5

Torque wrench settings

	Nm	lbf ft
EGR cooler:		
M6	10	7
M8	20	15
EGR valve	10	7
Exhaust manifold to cylinder head	30	22
Exhaust manifold to front pipe	23	17
Lambda (oxygen) sensor	50	37
Turbocharger hose clips	3	2
Turbocharger to exhaust manifold	30	22
Turbocharger to front exhaust pipe	23	17

1 General information

1 All diesel engine models are also designed to meet strict emission requirements. All models are fitted with a crankcase emission control system, a catalytic converter/particulate filter, and an exhaust gas recirculation (EGR) system.

2 The emission control systems function as follows.

Crankcase emission control

3 To reduce the emission of unburned hydrocarbons from the crankcase into the atmosphere, the engine is sealed and the blow-by gases and oil vapour are drawn from inside the crankcase, through a wire mesh oil separator, into the intake tract to be burned by the engine during normal combustion.

Exhaust emission control

4 To minimise the level of exhaust pollutants released into the atmosphere, all models are fitted with a catalytic converter and a diesel particulate filter incorporated into the front section of the exhaust pipe.

5 The catalytic converter consists of a canister containing a fine mesh impregnated with a catalyst material, over which the hot exhaust gases pass. The catalyst speeds up the oxidation of harmful carbon monoxide, unburned hydrocarbons and soot, effectively reducing the quantity of harmful products released into the atmosphere via the exhaust gases.

Particulate filter

6 This device is designed to trap carbon particulates produced by the combustion process. The particle filter is fitted downstream of the catalytic converter. In order to prevent the filter blocking, pressure and temperature sensors are fitted to the filter. Under the normal, high-speed driving conditions, the soot particles are burnt off in the filter by the high temperature of the exhaust gases. However, where the driving conditions are such that the exhaust gases are not sufficiently high, the engine management system injects fuel into the cylinders after the point of combustion. These are called post-injections, and raise the temperature of the exhaust gases, causing the soot particles in the filter to be burnt off.

7 On some models, an additive known as Adblue is added to the fuel to help clean the particulate filter. For more information concerning Adblue, consult your vehicle handbook or Mercedes Dealer.

Exhaust gas recirculation (EGR) system

8 This system is designed to recirculate small quantities of exhaust gas into the intake tract, and therefore into the combustion process. This process reduces the level of unburnt hydrocarbons present in the exhaust gas before it reaches the catalytic converter. The system is controlled by the engine management system ECM, using the information from its various sensors, via the EGR valve which is fitted to the metal pipe connecting the intake and exhaust manifolds. On all models, the exhaust gasses are cooled prior to entering the intake manifold by passing through a cooler mounted on the side of the EGR valve. Engine coolant circulates through the cooler.

2.10 Disconnect the hoses from the vacuum reservoir

2.11 Vacuum reservoir bolts

2.12 Detach the drain hose from the EGR cooler

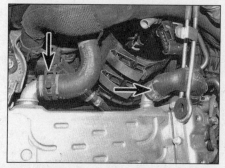

2.13 Release the clips and disconnect the hoses

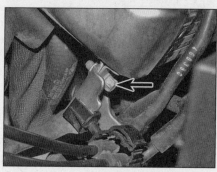

2.14a Remove the front, lower bolt...

2.14b ...followed by the 3 upper, and 3 lower bolts at the rear

2 Engine emission control systems – testing and component renewal

Crankcase emission control

Testing

1 The components of this system require no attention other than to check that the hose(s) are clear and undamaged at regular intervals.

2 If the system is thought to be faulty, renew the crankcase pressure limiting valve as follows.

Oil separator

3 The oil separator is incorporated into the cylinder head cover. Removal of the cover is described in Chapter 2A Section 4.

4 Refitting is a reversal of removal. Tighten the retaining bolts securely.

Exhaust emission control

Testing

5 The performance of the catalytic converter or diesel particulate filter can be checked only by using Mercedes Benz diagnostic equipment (or equivalent). Entrust this task to a dealer or suitable equipped specialist.

6 Before assuming that the catalytic converter/particulate filter is faulty, it is worth checking whether the problem is not due to a faulty injector(s). Refer to your Mercedes Benz dealer for further information.

Catalytic converter and particulate filter – renewal

7 Refer to Section 5 for removal and refitting details.

Exhaust gas recirculation (EGR) system

Testing

8 Comprehensive testing of the system can only be carried out using specialist electronic equipment which is connected to the injection system diagnostic wiring connector (see Chapter 12 Section 6).

EGR cooler – renewal

9 Drain the coolant as described in Chapter 1 Section 30.

10 Disconnect the various vacuum hoses from the vacuum reservoir (see illustration).

11 Undo the bolts and remove the vacuum reservoir (see illustration).

12 Unclip the fuel drain hose from the EGR cooler (see illustration).

13 Apply clamps to the EGR cooler hoses, then disconnect the hoses (see illustration).

14 Undo the retaining bolts, and remove the EGR cooler (see illustrations). Renew the gasket.

15 Refitting is a reversal of removal.

Exhaust gas recirculation (EGR) valve – renewal

16 Remove the EGR cooler as described earlier in this Section.

17 Undo the bolt that retains the fuel pipe bracket (see illustration).

18 Undo the bolts and remove the EGR pipe between the mixing chamber and the EGR valve (see illustration). Renew the gaskets.

19 Disconnect the wiring plug for the

2.17 Remove the fuel pipe bracket to access the EGR pipe bolts

2.18 Remove the pipe between the mixing chamber and EGR valve

pressure sensor on the mixing chamber **(see illustration)**.

20 Undo the 10 retaining bolts and remove the mixing chamber **(see illustration)**.

21 Disconnect the vacuum solenoid wiring plug, then undo the 5 bolts securing the fuel supply and return pipes bracket **(see illustration)**.

22 Slacken the upper bolt, undo the lower bolt and remove the shield over the fuel supply pipe.

23 Release the clamp, then disconnect the fuel supply hose from the high-pressure pump and move it one side. Be prepared for fuel spillage.

24 Prise the wiring harness clips from place, then undo the 4 bolts and move the wiring harness bracket to one side.

25 Disconnect the EGR valve wiring plug and vacuum hose.

26 Undo the 4 retaining bolts and remove the EGR valve **(see illustration)**. Renew the seal/gasket.

27 Refitting is a reversal of removal.

1 Remove the turbocharger as described in Section 4.

2 Unscrew the mounting bolts and remove the heat shield above the manifold **(see illustration)**.

3 Using two spanners, loosen and remove the exhaust manifold temperature sensor **(see illustration)**.

4 Slacken the four retaining nuts (three visible from the front and one hidden behind) and remove the bracket supporting the particulate filter sensor **(see illustration)**.

5 Undo the retaining bolts (two above and one below) and remove the EGR pipe shield **(see illustration)**.

6 Unscrew the retaining studs and remove the exhaust manifold. Renew the manifold gasket **(see illustration)**.

7 Ensure the manifold and cylinder head mating surfaces are clean, then check the condition/security of the mounting studs. Renew as necessary.

8 Refit the manifold and tighten the new retaining nuts to the specified torque.

9 Refit the turbocharger as described in Section 4.

2.19 Unplug the pressure sensor

2.20 Mixing chamber retaining bolts

2.21 Fuel pipe bracket retaining bolts

2.26 EGR valve lower retaining bolts

3.2 Undo and remove heat shield

3.3 Slacken and remove the temperature sensor

3.4 Remove the EGR support bracket

3.5 Slacken the bolts and remove the shield

3.6 Undo the studs to remove the manifold

4.3a Disconnect the vacuum hoses...

4.3b ...from the actuators...

4.3c ...and the housing

4 Turbocharger – removal and refitting

Removal

1 The turbocharger's internal components rotate at very high speed and as such are very sensitive to contamination; a great deal of damage can be caused by small particles of dirt, particularly if they strike the delicate turbine blades. Refer to the Caution and Warning notes given below before working on or removing the turbocharger unit.

Caution: Thoroughly clean the area around all oil pipe unions before disconnecting them, to prevent the ingress of dirt. Store dismantled components in a sealed container to prevent contamination. Cover the turbocharger air inlet ducts to prevent
debris entering and clean using lint-free cloths only.

⚠️ **Warning: Do not run the engine with the turbocharger air inlet hose disconnected, since the depression at the inlet can build up very suddenly if the engine speed is raised, and there is the risk of foreign objects being sucked in and then ejected at very high speed.**

2 Remove the air cleaner assembly as described in Section 4A Section 2.

3 Disconnect the vacuum hoses from the boost pressure control flap actuators and housing **(see illustrations)**.

4 Raise the front of the vehicle and support it securely on axle stands (see *Jacking and vehicle support*).

5 Remove the alternator as described in Chapter 5 Section 5.

6 Working underneath the vehicle, undo the bolts and remove the bracket above the
alternator location, then disconnect the wiring plug **(see illustration)**.

7 Working underneath the vehicle, undo the bolts and remove the turbocharger oil return pipes assembly **(see illustration)**. Renew the seals.

8 Slacken the retaining bolt and remove the bracket to the exhaust particulate filter **(see illustration)**.

9 Undo the retaining bolts and remove the turbocharger front support bracket **(see illustration)**.

10 Reaching up from below, slacken the retaining bolt and remove the upper rear mounting bolt.

11 Undo the bolts securing the exhaust manifold heat shield **(see illustration)**.

12 Undo the bolts securing the exhaust manifold to the turbocharger assembly **(see illustration)**. Note that new bolts will be required.

4.6 Remove the bracket above the alternator location

4.7 Oil return pipe bolts

4.8 Remove the bracket at the particulate filter

4.9 Remove the front support bracket

4.11 Remove the exhaust heat shield

4.12 Slacken bolts and remove exhaust clamp

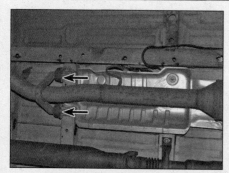

5.2 Exhaust rubber mountings

5.6 Remove the upper heat shield

5.7 Undo the retaining clamp

13 Manoeuvre the turbocharger upwards from place. Renew the gasket between the exhaust manifold and turbocharger.

14 No further dismantling of the turbocharger assembly is recommended.

Refitting

15 The remainder of refitting is a reversal of removal, noting the following points:

a) Tighten all fasteners to their specified torque where given.

b) Renew all seals disturbed during the removal procedure.

c) We consider it prudent to change the engine oil and filter following turbocharger renewal.

d) Ensure the charge air ducts are clean and free from debris prior to refitting.

e) Check for correct operation and fluid leaks.

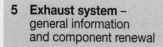

5 Exhaust system –
general information
and component renewal

General information

1 Depending on model, the exhaust system is made up of an exhaust manifold, a catalytic converter, front silencer, a front pipe and a rear tailpipe incorporating one or two silencers.

2 The exhaust system is suspended along its entire length by rubber mountings **(see illustration)** which are secured to the underside of the vehicle. The downpipe is secured to the transmission by means of a mounting bracket attached to the side of the transmission housing.

3 The catalytic converter (where fitted) is part of the front pipe and attached to the exhaust manifold either by a flange joint or by a joint and sealing ring secured by a clamp.

Removal

4 Each exhaust section can be removed individually or, alternatively, the complete system can be removed as a unit.

5 Before removing any part of the system, first jack up the front or rear of the vehicle, as applicable, and support it on axle stands (see *Jacking and vehicle support*). Alternatively (or if the complete exhaust system is being removed) position the vehicle over an inspection pit or on ramps.

Front pipe/silencer/catalytic converter

6 Open the bonnet and undo the retaining bolts and remove the heat shield from above the exhaust manifold **(see illustration)**.

7 Remove the clamp securing the front pipe/silencer to the exhaust manifold **(see illustration)**. Recover the sealing gasket.

8 Working under the vehicle, remove the clamp securing the front pipe to the middle section.

9 Unbolt the front pipe from the bracket on the rear of the transmission, and then withdraw the pipe/silencer from under the vehicle.

Middle and rear pipes/silencers

10 Unscrew the retaining bolts/nuts from the securing clamps and separate the front and rear sections of the exhaust system.

11 Support the rear pipe and silencers, and then release the rubber mountings. Lower the exhaust and remove it from under the vehicle.

Complete system

12 Unscrew and remove the clamp bolts securing the catalytic converter/front pipe to the exhaust manifold/turbocharger, separate and, where necessary, recover the gasket.

13 Release the rubber mounting along the length of the exhaust, and then unbolt the mounting bracket from the transmission.

14 With the help of an assistant, support the rear of the exhaust system, then unhook the rubber mountings and lower the system to the floor. Slide the system forwards from over the rear axle and withdraw it from under the vehicle.

Refitting

15 Each section is refitted by a reverse of the removal sequence, noting the following points.

a) Ensure that all traces of corrosion have been removed from the flanges and renew all necessary gaskets.

b) Inspect the rubber mountings for signs of damage or deterioration and renew as necessary.

c) Renew the sealing rings/gaskets between the front pipe/front silencer and catalytic converter.

d) Make sure all mounting brackets are refitted securely.

e) Prior to tightening the exhaust system joints, ensure that all rubber mountings are correctly located and that there is adequate clearance between the exhaust system and vehicle under-body.

6 Catalytic converters –
general information
and precautions

1 The catalytic converter is a reliable and simple device, with no moving parts and as such requires no maintenance. There are, however, some facts of which an owner should be aware if the converter is to function properly for its full service life.

a) DO NOT use fuel or engine oil additives – these may contain substances harmful to the catalytic converter.

b) DO NOT continue to use the car if the engine burns oil to the extent of leaving a visible trail of blue smoke.

c) Remember that the catalytic converter operates at very high temperatures. DO NOT, therefore, park the car in dry undergrowth, over long grass or piles of dead leaves after a long run.

d) Remember that the catalytic converter is FRAGILE – do not strike it with tools during servicing work.

e) The catalytic converter, used on a well-maintained and well-driven car, should last for between 50 000 and 100 000 miles – if the converter is no longer effective it must be renewed.

Notes

Chapter 5
Starting and charging systems

Contents

Degrees of difficulty

Easy, suitable for novice with little experience	Fairly easy, suitable for beginner with some experience	Fairly difficult, suitable for competent DIY mechanic 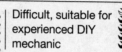	Difficult, suitable for experienced DIY mechanic	Very difficult, suitable for expert DIY or professional

Specifications

General

Electrical system type .... 12 volt negative earth

Battery

Charge condition:
Poor	12.5 volts
Normal	12.6 volts
Good	12.7 volts

Glow plugs

Nominal operating voltage	11.5 V
Electrical resistance	0.75 to 1.5 ohms (approximately at operating temperature)
Current consumption	14 to 16 amps (per glow plug, after approximately 8 seconds of operation)
Post-heating	180 seconds up to maximum coolant temperature of 40°C

Torque wrench settings

	Nm	lbf ft
Alternator mounting bolts	20	15
Glow plugs	18	14
Glow plug wiring terminal	4	3
Starter motor main cable nut	14	10
Starter motor mounting bolts	40	30

1 General information, precautions and battery disconnection

General information

1 The engine electrical system consists mainly of the charging and starting systems. Because of their engine-related functions, these components are covered separately from the body electrical devices such as the lights, instruments, etc (which are covered in Chapter 12).

2 The electrical system is of 12-volt negative earth type.

3 The battery may be of the low maintenance or maintenance-free (sealed for life) type and is charged by the alternator, which is belt-driven from the crankshaft pulley.

4 The starter motor is of pre-engaged type incorporating an integral solenoid. On starting, the solenoid moves the drive pinion into engagement with the flywheel ring gear before the starter motor is energised. Once the engine has started, a one-way clutch prevents the motor armature being driven by the engine until the pinion disengages from the flywheel.

5 To assist cold starting, models are fitted with a preheating system, which comprises four glow plugs (one per cylinder), a glow plug control unit, a facia-mounted warning lamp, a coolant temperature sensor and the associated electrical wiring.

6 The glow plugs are miniature electric heating elements, encapsulated in a metal case with a probe at one end and electrical connection at the other. Each combustion chamber has one glow plug threaded into it. When the glow plug is energised, it heats up rapidly causing the temperature of the air charge drawn into each of the combustion chambers to rise. The glow plug probe is positioned directly in line with the incoming spray of fuel from the injectors. Hence the fuel passing over the glow plug probe is also heated, allowing its optimum combustion temperature to be achieved more readily. In addition, small particles of the fuel passing over the glow plugs are ignited and this helps to trigger the combustion process.

7 The duration of the preheating period is governed by the glow plug control unit, which is fitted to the left-hand inner wing panel, below the battery tray. This device monitors the temperature of the engine coolant via a sensor threaded into the cylinder head and then alters the preheating time (the length for which the glow plugs are supplied with current) to suit the conditions.

8 A facia-mounted warning lamp informs the driver that preheating is taking place. The lamp extinguishes when sufficient preheating has taken place to allow the engine to be started, but power will still be supplied to the glow plugs for a further period until the engine is started. If no attempt is made to start the engine, the power supply to the glow plugs is switched off to prevent battery drain and glow plug burnout. Note that the warning lamp will also illuminate during normal driving if a preheating system malfunction occurs. The system employs post-heating (after-heating), which operates as follows. After the engine has been started, the glow plugs continue to operate for a further period of time as given in this Chapter's Specifications. This helps to improve fuel combustion whilst the engine is warming-up, resulting in quieter, smoother running and reduced exhaust emissions. The duration of the post-heating period is dependent on the coolant temperature.

Precautions

9 Further details of the various systems are given in the relevant Sections of this Chapter. While some repair procedures are given, the usual course of action is to renew the component concerned.

10 It is necessary to take extra care when working on the electrical system to avoid damage to semi-conductor devices (diodes and transistors), and to avoid the risk of personal injury. In addition to the precautions given in *Safety first!* at the beginning of this manual, observe the following when working on the system:

• *Always remove rings, watches, etc, before working on the electrical system. Even with the battery disconnected, capacitive discharge could occur if a component's live terminal is earthed through a metal object. This could cause a shock or nasty burn.*

• *Do not reverse the battery connections. Components such as the alternator, electronic control units, or any other components having semi-conductor circuitry could be irreparably damaged.*

• *If the engine is being started using jump leads and a slave battery, connect the batteries positive-to-positive and negative-to-negative (see Jump starting). This also applies when connecting a battery charger but in this case both of the battery terminals should first be disconnected.*

• *Never disconnect the battery terminals, the alternator, any electrical wiring or any test instruments when the engine is running.*

• *Do not allow the engine to turn the alternator when the alternator is not connected.*

• *Never test for alternator output by flashing the output lead to earth.*

• *Never use an ohmmeter of the type incorporating a hand-cranked generator for circuit or continuity testing.*

• *Always ensure that the battery negative lead is disconnected when working on the electrical system.*

• *Before using electric arc welding equipment on the car, disconnect the battery, alternator and components such as the engine control module (ECM) to protect them from the risk of damage.*

Battery disconnection

11 The radio/CD unit fitted as standard equipment by Mercedes-Benz is equipped with a built-in security code to deter thieves. If the power source to the unit is cut, the anti-theft system will activate. Even if the power source is immediately reconnected, the radio/CD unit will not function until the correct security code has been entered. Therefore, if you do not know the correct security code for the radio/CD unit, do not disconnect the battery negative terminal of the battery or remove the radio/CD unit from the vehicle. Refer to your Mercedes-Benz dealer for further information on whether the unit fitted to your vehicle has a security code.

12 Refer to the precautions listed in *Disconnecting the battery* in the Reference Chapter.

---

2 Battery –
testing and charging

Testing

Standard and low maintenance battery

1 If the vehicle covers a small annual mileage, it is worthwhile checking the specific gravity of the electrolyte every three months to determine the state of charge of the battery. Use a hydrometer to make the check and compare the results with the following table. The temperatures quoted in the table are ambient (air) temperatures. Note that the specific gravity readings assume an electrolyte temperature of 15°C. For every 10°C below 15°C subtract 0.007. For every 10°C above 15°C add 0.007.

	Ambient temperature – 25°C	
	Above	Below
Fully-charged	1.210 to 1.230	1.270 to 1.290
70% charged	1.170 to 1.190	1.230 to 1.250
Discharged	1.050 to 1.070	1.110 to 1.130

2 If the battery condition is suspect, first check the specific gravity of electrolyte in each cell. A variation of 0.040 or more between any cells indicates loss of electrolyte or deterioration of the internal plates.

3 If the specific gravity variation is 0.040 or more, the battery should be renewed. If the cell variation is satisfactory but the battery is discharged, it should be charged as described later in this Section.

Maintenance-free battery

4 Where a 'sealed for life' maintenance-free battery is fitted, topping-up and testing of the electrolyte in each cell is not possible. The condition of the battery can therefore only be tested using a battery condition indicator or a voltmeter.

5 Certain models may be fitted with a maintenance-free battery with a built-in charge condition indicator. The indicator is located in the top of the battery casing, and indicates the condition of the battery from its colour. If the indicator shows green, then the battery is in a good state of charge. If the indicator turns darker, eventually to black, then the battery requires charging, as described later in this Section. If the indicator shows clear/yellow, then the electrolyte level in the battery is too low to allow further use, and the battery should be renewed. Do not attempt to charge, load or jump-start a battery when the indicator shows clear/yellow.

All battery types

6 If testing the battery using a voltmeter, connect the voltmeter across the battery and compare the result with those given in the Specifications under 'charge condition'. The test is only accurate if the battery has not been subjected to any kind of charge for the previous six hours. If this is not the case, switch on the headlights for 30 seconds, then wait four to five minutes before testing the battery after switching off the headlights. All other electrical circuits must be switched off, so check that the doors are fully shut when making the test.

7 If the voltage reading is less than 12.2 volts, then the battery is discharged, whilst a reading of 12.2 to 12.4 volts indicates a partially discharged condition.

8 If the battery is to be charged, remove it from the vehicle and charge it as described later in this Section.

Charging

Note: *The following is intended as a guide only. Always refer to the manufacturer's recommendations (often printed on a label attached to the battery) before charging a battery.*

Standard and low maintenance battery

9 Charge the battery at a rate equivalent to 10% of the battery capacity (eg, for a 46 Ah battery charge at 4.6 A) and continue to charge the battery at this rate until no further rise in specific gravity is noted over a four hour period.

10 Alternatively, a trickle charger charging at the rate of 1.5 amps can safely be used overnight.

11 Specially rapid 'boost' charges, which are claimed to restore the power of the battery in 1 to 2 hours are not recommended, as they can cause serious damage to the battery plates through overheating.

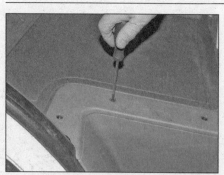

3.2 Undo the 3 screws and remove the step trim

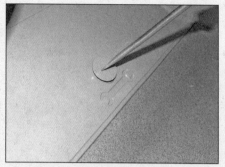

3.3a Undo the screw and remove the footwell panel...

3.3b ...and the footwell mat

12 While charging the battery, note that the temperature of the electrolyte should never exceed 38ºC.

Maintenance-free battery

13 This battery type takes considerably longer to fully recharge than the standard type, the time taken being dependent on the extent of discharge, but it will take anything up to three days.

14 A constant voltage type charger is required, to be set, when connected, to 13.9 to 14.9 volts with a charger current below 25 amps. Using this method, the battery should be usable within three hours, giving a voltage reading of 12.5 volts, but this is for a partially discharged battery and, as mentioned, full charging can take considerably longer.

15 If the battery is to be charged from a fully discharged state (condition reading less than 12.2 volts), have it recharged by your dealer or local automotive electrician, as the charge rate is higher and constant supervision during charging is necessary.

3 Battery – removal and refitting

Note: *Refer to 'Disconnecting the battery' in the Reference Chapter before proceeding.*

Removal

1 The battery is located beneath the passenger's footwell.

2 Undo the three retaining screws and remove the step trim **(see illustration)**.
3 Undo the screw holding the footwell panel, and remove, along with the footwell mat **(see illustrations)**.
4 Loosen the four retaining screws and remove the battery cover **(see illustration)**.
5 Loosen the clamp bolt and disconnect the battery negative cable from the terminal **(see illustration)**.
6 Loosen the clamp bolt and disconnect the battery positive cable from the terminal **(see illustration)**.
7 Remove the clamp securing the battery.
8 The battery can now be lifted out from the passenger compartment.

Refitting

9 Refitting is a reversal of removal, but smear petroleum jelly on the terminals after reconnecting the leads to reduce corrosion, and always reconnect the positive lead(s) first, followed by the negative lead(s). Tighten the battery clamp plate bolt securely.

4 Alternator/charging system – testing

Note: *Refer to the precautions given in 'Safety first!' and in Section 1 of this Chapter before starting work.*

1 If the ignition warning light fails to illuminate when the ignition is switched on, first check the alternator wiring connections for security.

If satisfactory, check that the warning light bulb has not blown, and that the bulb holder is secure in its location in the instrument panel. If the light still fails to illuminate, check the continuity of the warning light feed wire from the alternator to the bulb holder. If all is satisfactory, the alternator is at fault and should be renewed or taken to an auto-electrician for testing and repair.

2 If the ignition warning light illuminates when the engine is running, stop the engine and check that the drivebelt is intact and that the alternator connections are secure. If all is so far satisfactory, check the alternator brushes and slip-rings as described in Section. If the fault persists, the alternator should be renewed, or taken to an auto-electrician for testing and repair.

3 If the alternator output is suspect even though the warning light functions correctly, the regulated voltage may be checked as follows.

4 Connect a voltmeter across the battery terminals, and start the engine.

5 Increase the engine speed until the voltmeter reading remains steady. The reading should be approximately 12 to 13 volts, and no more than 14 volts.

6 Switch on as many electrical accessories (eg, the headlights and heater blower) as possible, and check that the alternator maintains the regulated voltage at around 13 to 14 volts.

7 If the regulated voltage is not as stated, the fault may be due to worn brushes, weak brush springs, a faulty voltage regulator, a

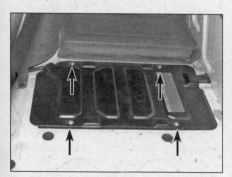

3.4 Loosen screws and remove the battery cover

3.5 Slacken the clamp to disconnect the negative terminal

3.6 Unclip the plastic cover above the battery positive (+) lead clamp and terminal

5.5 Remove the intercooler hose

5.6a Remove the plastic cap, undo the nut securing the battery positive lead...

5.6b ...and disconnect the wiring plugs from the alternator

faulty diode, a severed phase winding, or worn or damaged slip-rings. The brushes and slip-rings may be checked. The alternator should be renewed or taken to an auto-electrician for testing and repair.

5 Alternator – removal and refitting

Removal

1 The alternator is bolted to the right-hand side of the engine block and is driven by the auxiliary belt.
2 Disconnect the battery as described in Section 3.
3 Apply the handbrake, then jack up the front of the vehicle and support it on axle stands, as described in *Jacking and vehicle support*.

4 Detach the auxiliary drivebelt as described in Chapter 1 Section 8.
5 Unfasten the clips and remove the right-hand intercooler hose **(see illustration)**.
6 Prise off the protective cap (where fitted) and unscrew the nut securing the battery positive lead to the alternator terminal **(see illustrations)**. Position the lead to one side.
7 Undo the three mounting bolts and remove the small support bracket above the alternator **(see illustration)**.
8 Unscrew and remove the alternator mounting bolts **(see illustrations)**.
9 Then lower the alternator from place **(see illustration)**.

Refitting

10 Refitting is a reversal of removal. Refit the auxiliary drivebelt as described in Chapter 1 Section 8.

6 Starting system – testing

Note: *Refer to the precautions given in 'Safety first!' and in Section 1 of this Chapter before starting work.*

1 If the starter motor fails to operate during the normal starting procedure, the possible causes are as follows:
a) *The engine immobiliser is faulty.*
b) *The battery is faulty.*
c) *The electrical connections between the switch, solenoid, battery and starter motor are somewhere failing to pass the necessary current from the battery through the starter to earth.*
d) *The solenoid is faulty.*
e) *The starter motor is mechanically or electrically defective.*

2 To check the battery, switch on the headlights. If they dim after a few seconds, this indicates that the battery is discharged – recharge (see Section 3) or renew the battery. If the headlights glow brightly, operate the starter switch while watching the headlights. If they dim, then this indicates that current is reaching the starter motor, therefore the fault must lie in the starter motor. If the lights continue to glow brightly (and no clicking sound can be heard from the starter motor solenoid), this indicates that there is a fault in the circuit or solenoid – see the following paragraphs. If the starter motor turns slowly when operated, but the battery is in good condition, then this indicates either that the starter motor is faulty, or there is considerable resistance somewhere in the circuit.

3 If a fault in the circuit is suspected, disconnect the battery leads (including the earth connection to the body), the starter/solenoid wiring and the engine/transmission earth strap. Thoroughly clean the connections, and reconnect the leads and wiring. Use a voltmeter or test light to check that full battery voltage is available at the battery positive lead connection to the solenoid. Smear petroleum jelly around the battery terminals to prevent corrosion – corroded connections are among the most frequent causes of electrical system faults.

5.7 Remove the bracket above the alternator

5.8a Undo the three upper mounting bolts...

5.8b ...then the two lower mounting bolts

5.9 Remove the alternator downwards

7.4 Slacken the bolts and remove the bracket

7.6 Slacken the bolts and remove the bracket

7.8 Remove the heatshield above the starter

4 If the battery and all connections are in good condition, check the circuit by disconnecting the ignition switch supply wire from the solenoid terminal. Connect a voltmeter or test lamp between the wire end and a good earth (such as the battery negative terminal), and check that the wire is live when the ignition switch is turned to the 'start' position. If it is, then the circuit is sound – if not the circuit wiring can be checked as described in Chapter 12.

5 The solenoid contacts can be checked by connecting a voltmeter or test light between the battery positive feed connection on the starter side of the solenoid and earth. When the ignition switch is turned to the 'start' position, there should be a reading or lighted bulb, as applicable. If there is no reading or lighted bulb, the solenoid is faulty.

6 If the circuit and solenoid are proved sound, the fault must lie in the starter motor. In this event, it may be possible to have the starter motor overhauled by a specialist, but check on the cost of spares before proceeding, as it may prove more economical to obtain a new or exchange motor.

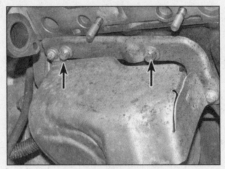

7.9 Undo the retaining bolts and remove the heat shield bracket

7.10 Undo the nut, disconnect the wiring to the starter motor solenoid

Access is extremely limited. A universal joint may be required.

9 Undo the retaining bolts and remove the support bracket for the heatshield **(see illustration)**.

10 Disconnect the wiring from the starter motor **(see illustration)**.

11 Undo the mounting bolts and lower the starter motor from place. Note that we found it easier to unscrew the upper mounting bolt using a series of extension rods, working over the top of the transmission.

Refitting

12 Refitting is a reversal of removal tightening the mounting bolts to the specified torque. Ensure all wiring is correctly routed and its retaining nuts are securely tightened.

8 Starter motor – overhaul

1 If the starter motor is thought to be defective, it should be removed from the vehicle and taken to an auto-electrician for assessment. In the majority of cases, new starter motor brushes can be fitted at a reasonable cost. However, check the cost of repairs first as it may prove more economical to purchase a new or exchange motor.

9 Glow plug control unit – removal and refitting

Removal

1 The control unit is located on the top front edge of the engine.

2 Remove the battery as described in Section 3.

3 Disconnect the wiring plugs from the control unit and move them to one side **(see illustration)**.

4 Undo the retaining bolts/nuts and withdraw the control unit from the engine compartment.

Refitting

5 Refitting is a reversal of removal.

7 Starter motor – removal and refitting

Removal

1 The starter motor is fitted to the right-hand side of the cylinder block.

2 Disconnect the battery negative lead as described in Section 3.

3 Remove the air intake pipe, as described in Chapter 4A Section 2.

4 Remove the support bracket **(see illustration)**.

5 Raise the front of the vehicle and support it securely on axle stands (see *Jacking and vehicle support*).

6 Working under the vehicle, undo the four retaining bolts and remove the support bracket **(see illustration)**.

7 Lower the vehicle to the ground.

8 Undo the bolts and remove the heat shield over the starter motor **(see illustration)**. **Note:**

9.3 Disconnect the wiring plugs from the control unit

10.4 Release the various clips and move the harness duct to one side

10.5 The glow plugs are located beneath the common fuel rail

10.6 Unscrew the glow plugs to remove (fuel filter housing removed for clarity)

10 Glow plugs – removal, inspection and refitting

Removal

Caution: The glow plugs are very delicate, and easily damaged – handle with care.

Note: *Some deep sockets do not have the required width to clear the collar around the top of the glow plug. Take care to use a socket that does clear the collar. Due to the extremely congested area around the glow plugs, we recommend that you use Mercedes tools 001589800900 and 611589003700 for this task.*

1 Disconnect the battery negative lead as described in Section 3.

2 Remove the plastic cover on the top of the engine.

3 Remove the fuel filter as described in Chapter 1 Section 11. There's no need to disconnect the hoses from the filter – place the filter to one side.

4 Disconnect the wiring plugs from the fuel filter, fuel rail pressure sensor, etc, then release the clips and move the wiring harness duct to one side **(see illustration)**.

5 Squeeze together the sides using long-nosed pliers, and disconnect the glow plug wiring connectors **(see illustration)**.

6 Clean the area around the glow plugs to prevent contamination, then using a deep socket, unscrew and remove them **(see illustration)**.

7 If the torque required to remove a glow plug exceeds 25 Nm, Mercedes recommends bringing the engine up to operating temperature and trying again. Bear in mind that if the hexagonal section of the plug breaks off, the plug will then need to be drilled out, which may involve cylinder head removal.

Inspection

8 Inspect the glow plugs for signs of damage. Burnt or eroded glow plug tips can be caused by a bad injector spray pattern. Have the injectors checked if this sort of damage is found.

Caution: The glow plugs may be damaged if battery voltage (12v) is applied to them.

Refitting

9 Thoroughly clean the glow plugs, and the glow plug seating areas in the cylinder head.

10 Apply a thin smear of anti-seize compound to the glow plug threads, then refit the glow plug and tighten it to the specified torque.

11 Reconnect the wiring to the glow plug. The connectors are a push-fit.

12 The remainder of refitting is a reversal of removal.

Chapter 6
Clutch

Contents

Degrees of difficulty

Easy, suitable for novice with little experience	Fairly easy, suitable for beginner with some experience	Fairly difficult, suitable for competent DIY mechanic 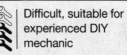	Difficult, suitable for experienced DIY mechanic	Very difficult, suitable for expert DIY or professional

Specifications

General

Type	Self-adjusting, single dry plate with diaphragm spring, hydraulically-operated
Friction plate:	
Diameter	240 or 260 mm
Lining thickness:	
New (approximate)	3.6 to 4.0 mm
Service limit	2.6 to 3.0 mm

Torque wrench settings

	Nm	lbf ft
Brake servo-to-pedal pivot bolt*	20	15
Pedal assembly retaining nuts	20	15
Pressure plate retaining bolts:		
Stage 1	16	12
Stage 2	25	18
Slave cylinder mounting bolt	8	6

* Do not re-use

1 General information and precautions

1 All models are fitted with a single dry plate clutch system. The main components consist of a friction disc, pressure plate (or cover), hydraulic master cylinder and release bearing/slave cylinder.

2 The clutch pressure plate is bolted to the rear face of the flywheel, and the friction disc is located between the pressure plate and the flywheel friction surface. The friction disc is splined to the transmission input shaft and is free to slide along the splines. Friction lining material is riveted to each side of the disc, and the disc hub incorporates cushioning springs to absorb transmission shocks and ensure a smooth take-up of drive. The pressure plate incorporates an internal diaphragm spring mounted on a fulcrum ring. When the inner fingers of the spring are depressed, the outer perimeter draws the pressure plate away from the friction disc.

3 The release bearing is part of the slave cylinder and is operated by the clutch pedal, using hydraulic pressure. The pedal acts on the hydraulic master cylinder pushrod, and hydraulic pressure operates the slave cylinder, which incorporates the release bearing.

4 When the clutch pedal is depressed, the release bearing is pushed forwards, to bear against the centre of the diaphragm spring, thus pushing the centre of the diaphragm spring inwards.

5 When the clutch pedal is released, the diaphragm spring forces the pressure plate into contact with the friction linings on the friction disc, and simultaneously pushes the friction disc forwards on its splines, forcing it against the flywheel. The friction disc is now firmly sandwiched between the pressure plate and the flywheel, and drive is taken up.

6 The clutch is self-adjusting. As wear takes place on the friction disc over a period of time, the pressure plate automatically moves closer to the friction plate to compensate.

⚠ *Warning: Dust created by clutch wear and deposited on the clutch components may contain asbestos, which is a health hazard. DO NOT blow it out with compressed air, or inhale any of it. DO NOT use petrol (or petroleum-based solvents) to clean off the dust. Brake system cleaner or methylated spirit should be used to flush the dust into a suitable receptacle. After the clutch components are wiped clean with rags, dispose of the contaminated rags and cleaner in a sealed, marked container.*

⚠ *Warning: Hydraulic fluid is poisonous; wash off immediately and thoroughly in the case of skin contact, and seek immediate medical advice if any fluid is swallowed or gets into the eyes. Certain types of hydraulic fluid are inflammable, and may ignite when allowed into contact with hot components; when servicing any hydraulic system, it is safest to assume that the fluid is inflammable, and to take precautions against the risk of fire as though it is petrol that is being handled. Hydraulic fluid is also an effective paint stripper, and will attack plastics; if any is spilt, it should be washed off immediately, using copious quantities of fresh water. Finally, it is hygroscopic (it absorbs moisture from the air) – old fluid may be contaminated and unfit for further use. When topping-up or renewing the fluid, always use the recommended type, and ensure that it comes from a freshly opened, sealed container.*

2.2 Disconnect the clutch fluid supply pipe

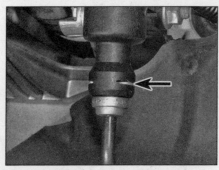

2.4 Prise out the wire clip a little

2.5 Rotate switches and remove from place

2.6 Use a punch to drive out the pin

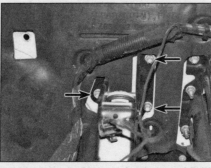

2.7 Master cylinder retaining nuts and fluid supply hose

2 Clutch master cylinder – removal and refitting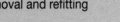

Note: *Refer to the precautions given in Section 1 regarding the use of hydraulic fluid.*

Removal

1 To reduce fluid loss, draw off as much fluid as possible from the appropriate chamber of the brake fluid reservoir, using a clean syringe, until the fluid level is below the level of the clutch master cylinder supply pipe.

2 With the fluid removed, disconnect the clutch fluid supply pipe from the reservoir **(see illustration)**.

3 With reference to Chapter 11 Section 23, remove the driver's side lower facia panel (above the pedals).

4 Prise out the wire clip a little, and disconnect the fluid pressure pipe from the clutch master cylinder **(see illustration)**. Be prepared for fluid spillage. Plug the openings to prevent contamination.

5 Turn the clutch pedal switches through 90 degrees anti-clockwise and remove from the bracket **(see illustration)**.

6 Drive out the hinge pin with a punch **(see illustration)**.

7 Undo the 3 nuts and slide the master cylinder from the pedal bracket. Manoeuvre the cylinder from place, and pull the supply hose through the bulkhead as the cylinder is withdrawn **(see illustration)**.

Refitting

8 Refitting is a reversal of removal. Bleed the clutch hydraulic system as described in Section 4.

3 Clutch slave cylinder – removal, inspection and refitting

Removal

1 Remove the transmission as described in Chapter 7 Section 5.

2 If not already disconnected, release the retaining clip from the clutch fluid hose on the transmission bellhousing, and remove the hose **(see illustration)**.

3 Undo the retaining bolts and withdraw the release bearing/slave cylinder from the transmission housing, complete with bleed screw connection **(see illustration)**.

Inspection

4 With internal cylinders, spin the release bearing, and check it for excessive roughness. If any excessive movement or roughness is evident, renew the bearing. If a new clutch has been fitted, it is wise to renew the release bearing as a matter of course.

Refitting

5 Refitting is a reversal of removal. Tighten the retaining bolts to the specified torque, and bleed the clutch hydraulic system as described in Section 4.

4 Clutch hydraulic system – bleeding

Note: *Refer to the precautions given in Section 1 regarding the use of hydraulic fluid.*

1 The correct operation of the hydraulic system is only possible after removing all air from the circuit, and this is achieved by bleeding the system.

2 During the bleeding procedure, add only clean, unused hydraulic fluid of the recommended type. Never re-use fluid that has already been bled from the system. Ensure that sufficient fluid is available before starting work.

3 If there is any possibility of incorrect fluid being already in the system, both the clutch and brake circuits must be flushed completely

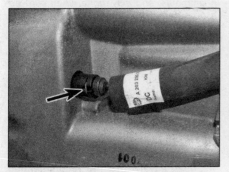

3.2 Clutch fluid pipe retaining clip

3.3 Release bearing/slave cylinder retaining bolts

with uncontaminated, correct fluid, and new seals should be fitted to the various components.

4 If hydraulic fluid has been lost from the system, or air has entered because of a leak, ensure that the fault is cured before proceeding further.

5 Apply the parking brake, then jack up the front of the vehicle and support it on axle stands (see Vehicle jacking and support 13 Section 5). Undo the fasteners and remove the transmission undershield.

6 Remove the dust cap from the slave cylinder bleed screw, and clean away any dirt.

7 Note that the brake fluid reservoir feeds both the brake and clutch hydraulic systems.

8 Mercedes-Benz recommended that pressure-bleeding equipment be used to bleed the system. Some pressure-bleeding kits are operated by the reservoir of pressurised air contained in a spare tyre; however, note that it will probably be necessary to reduce the pressure to a lower level than normal. Refer to the instructions supplied with the kit. If a pressure-bleeding kit is not available, use the normal bleeding method described for the brake hydraulic circuit in Chapter 1 Section 29.

9 By connecting a pressurised, fluid-filled container to the brake fluid reservoir, bleeding can be carried out simply by opening the bleed screw on the clutch slave cylinder, and allowing the fluid to flow out until no more air bubbles can be seen in the expelled fluid. This method has the advantage that the large reservoir of fluid provides an additional safeguard against air being drawn into the system during bleeding.

10 Collect a clean glass jar, a suitable length of plastic or rubber tubing which is a tight fit over the bleed screw, and a ring spanner to fit the screw.

11 Fit the spanner and tube to the slave cylinder bleed screw **(see illustration)**, place the other end of the tube in the jar, and pour in sufficient fluid to cover the end of the tube.

12 Connect the pressure-bleeding equipment to the brake/clutch fluid reservoir in accordance with its manufacturer's instructions.

13 Loosen the bleed screw half a turn using the spanner, and allow fluid to drain into the jar until no more air bubbles emerge.

14 When bleeding is complete, tighten the bleed screw, and disconnect the hose and the pressure bleeding equipment.

15 Wash off any spilt fluid, check once more that the bleed screw is tightened securely, and refit the dust cap.

16 Check the hydraulic fluid level in the reservoir, and top-up if necessary (see *Weekly checks*).

17 Discard any hydraulic fluid that has been bled from the system, as it will not be fit for re-use.

18 Check the feel of the clutch pedal. If it feels at all spongy, air must still be present in the system, and further bleeding is required. Failure to bleed satisfactorily after a reasonable repetition of the bleeding procedure may be due to worn master or slave cylinder seals.

19 On completion, refit the undershield and lower the vehicle to the ground.

5 Clutch assembly – removal, inspection and refitting

> ⚠️ *Warning: Dust created by clutch wear and deposited on the clutch components may contain asbestos, which is a health hazard. DO NOT blow it out with compressed air, or inhale any of it. DO NOT use petrol or petroleum-based solvents to clean off the dust. Brake system cleaner or methylated spirit should be used to flush the dust into a suitable receptacle. After the clutch components are wiped clean with rags, dispose of the contaminated rags and cleaner in a sealed, marked container.*

Removal

1 Remove the transmission as described in Chapter 7 Section 5.

2 If the original clutch is to be refitted, make alignment marks between the clutch pressure plate assembly and the flywheel, so that the clutch can be refitted in its original position.

3 Progressively unscrew the bolts securing the clutch pressure plate assembly to the flywheel, and recover the washers (where fitted) **(see illustration)**.

4.11 Prise out the rubber cap to expose the bleed screw

4 Withdraw the clutch pressure plate assembly (cover) and disc from the flywheel **(see illustrations)**. Be prepared to catch the friction disc, and note which way round the friction disc is fitted – the two sides of the disc may be marked Engine side and Transmission side, or the side with the part number on faces the flywheel. The greater projecting side of the hub faces away from the flywheel. On some models a twin-plate clutch is fitted. On these models, the friction disc hub drive gear locates in the second disc centre – it's not possible to fit this plate the wrong way around.

Inspection

Note: *Due to the amount of work involved in removing the clutch assembly, it is considered to be normal practice to replace the assembly regardless of condition.*

5 Clean the cover, disc, and flywheel. Do not inhale the dust, as it may contain asbestos, which is dangerous to health.

6 Examine the fingers of the diaphragm spring for wear or scoring. If the depth of any scoring is excessive, a new cover assembly must be fitted.

7 Examine the pressure plate for scoring, cracking and discoloration. Light scoring is acceptable, but if excessive, a new assembly must be fitted.

8 Examine the friction disc linings for wear cracking, and for contamination with oil or grease. Using vernier calipers, check the thickness of the linings and compare with the details given in the Specifications. Check the

5.3 Pressure plate retaining bolts

5.4a Note the fitted position of the clutch plate/friction disc

5.4b Twin-disc clutch friction plate and drive gear

5.12a Special tool to adjust the pressure plate...

5.12b ...which presses down on the diaphragm spring fingers

5.12c Turn the adjusting ring anti-clockwise...

5.12d ...and release the pressure on the diaphragm

5.16a Centralise the clutch plate...

5.16b ...and fit the assembly onto the flywheel

disc hub and splines for wear by temporarily fitting it on the transmission input shaft. Renew the friction disc as necessary.

9 Examine the flywheel friction surface for scoring, cracking and discoloration (caused by overheating). If excessive, it may be possible to have the flywheel machined by an engineering works, otherwise it should be renewed.

10 Ensure that all parts are clean, and free of oil or grease, before reassembling. Do not apply any lubricant to the splines of the friction disc hub. Note that a new pressure plate may be coated with protective grease. It is only permissible to clean the grease away from the friction disc lining contact area. Removal of the grease from other areas will shorten the service life of the clutch.

11 Check the spigot bearing in the end of the crankshaft or in the centre of the flywheel. Make sure that it turns smoothly and quietly. If the transmission input shaft contact face on the bearing is worn or damaged, fit a new bearing.

Refitting

12 If you are re-using the pressure plate, the adjustment ring will need to be reset. Position the pressure plate in a hydraulic press

(Mercedes technicians use a special tool) **(see illustrations)**, with a block of wood placed under the central portion of the pressure plate, directly below the diaphragm spring fingers (not on the friction face). Apply pressure to the diaphragm spring fingers until the adjusting ring is loose. While still applying pressure, use a screwdriver to rotate the adjusting ring anti-clockwise **(see illustrations)**. Hold the adjustment ring in place, and then release the pressure on the diaphragm spring fingers.

13 It is important to ensure that no oil or grease gets onto the friction disc linings, or the pressure plate and flywheel faces. It is advisable to refit the clutch assembly with clean hands, and to wipe down the pressure plate and flywheel faces with a clean rag before assembly begins.

14 Offer the disc to the flywheel, with the greater projecting side of the hub facing away from the flywheel (most friction discs will have an Engine side marking which should face the flywheel, or Gearbox side (Getriebeseite) which should face the gearbox). Hold the friction disc against the flywheel while the pressure plate assembly is offered into position, or alternatively use the centralising tool described later to hold the disc on the flywheel.

15 Fit the clutch pressure plate assembly, where applicable aligning the marks with those on the flywheel. Ensure that the pressure plate assembly locates over the dowels on the flywheel. Insert the securing bolts and washers, and tighten them finger-tight, so that the friction disc is gripped, but can still be moved. Note that new pressure plates are supplied with the adjustment ring pre-set.

16 The friction disc must now be centralised, to ensure correct alignment of the transmission input shaft with the spigot bearing in the crankshaft/flywheel **(see illustrations)**. To do this, a proprietary tool may be used, or alternatively, use a wooden mandrel made to fit inside the friction disc hub and spigot bearing. Insert the tool through the friction disc into the spigot bearing, and make sure that it is central.

17 Tighten the clutch pressure plate bolts progressively and in diagonal sequence, until the specified torque setting is achieved, and then remove the centralising tool.

18 Check the release bearing in the front of the transmission for smooth operation, and if necessary renew it with reference to Section 3.

19 Refit the transmission as described in Chapter 7 Section 5.

Chapter 7
Manual transmission

Contents

Degrees of difficulty

| Easy, suitable for novice with little experience | | Fairly easy, suitable for beginner with some experience | | Fairly difficult, suitable for competent DIY mechanic | | Difficult, suitable for experienced DIY mechanic | | Very difficult, suitable for expert DIY or professional | |

Specifications

General

Type	6 forward speeds and reverse. Synchromesh on all forward and reverse gears
Transmission codes	711.680 and 711.685

Lubrication

Transmission capacity	See Chapter 1 Section 1
Lubricant type	See *Lubricants and fluids* on page 0•16

Torque wrench settings

	Nm	lbf ft
Gearchange lever base to instrument panel support	20	14
Oil filler plug	34	25
Oil drain plug	30	22
Output shaft flange retaining bolt*	110	81
Propeller shaft intermediate bearing-to-floor retaining bolts	135	100
Propeller shaft safety bracket to floor retaining bolts	70	52
Propeller shaft-to-transmission output shaft flange bolts:*		
Stage 1	40	30
Stage 2	Angle-tighten a further 60°	
Speedo sensor to transmission housing	14	10
Transmission mounting to crossmember	58	43
Transmission to engine	38	28

* Use new nuts/bolts

1.4 Find the transmission model number on the right-hand side of the casting

2.2 Pull back the rubber gaiter

home mechanic. The bulk of the information in this Chapter is therefore devoted to removal and refitting procedures.

4 The transmission's oil capacity depends on its model number. The number will be found on the right-hand side next to the raised grid area of the casting **(see illustration)**.

1 General Information

1 A 6-speed manual transmission is bolted to the rear of the engine. Drive is transmitted from the crankshaft via the clutch to the input shaft, which has a splined extension to accept the clutch friction disc. The transmission output shaft transmits the drive via the propeller shaft to the rear differential. The input shaft runs in-line with the output shaft. The input shaft and output shaft gears are in constant mesh with the lay-shaft gear cluster. Selection of gears is by sliding synchromesh hubs, which lock the appropriate output shaft gears to the output shaft.

2 Gear selection is via a facia-mounted lever

and selector mechanism incorporating cables to the transmission. The selector mechanism causes the appropriate selector fork to move its respective synchro-sleeve along the shaft, to lock the gear pinion to the synchro-hub. Since the synchro-hubs are splined to the output shaft, this locks the pinion to the shaft, so that the drive can be transmitted. To ensure that gearchanging can be made quickly and quietly, a synchromesh system is fitted to all the gears, consisting of baulk rings and spring-loaded fingers, as well as the gear pinions and synchro-hubs. The synchromesh cones are formed on the mating faces of the baulk rings and gear pinions.

3 Because of the complexity, possible unavailability of parts and special tools necessary, internal repair procedures for the transmission are not recommended for the

2 Gear lever – removal and refitting

Removal

1 Remove the gearlever surround panel from the facia as described in Chapter 11 Section 26.
2 Disengage the rubber gaiter from the gearchange lever **(see illustration)**.
3 Unplug the wiring connector for the reversing light switch from the gearlever mounting **(see illustration)**.
4 Using pliers, slide out the retaining clip for the bottom gearshift cable mount **(see illustration)**.
5 Then prise the gearshift cables off the two balljoints **(see illustrations)**.
6 Undo the mounting bolts and detach the shift gate from the mounting bracket and remove the gearlever **(see illustrations)**.
7 Remove the second gearshift cable from its top and bottom mounts.

Refitting

8 Refitting is a reversal of removal.

2.3 Disconnect the reversing light wiring plug

2.4 Slide the cable mount from place

2.5a Prise off the top (green) gearshift cable...

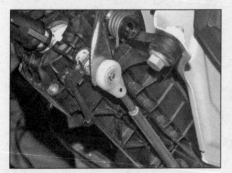

2.5b ...and the bottom (white) cable

2.6a Undo the bolts, detach the gate...

2.6b ...then remove the gearlever

3 Gear lever and cables –
removal, refitting and adjusting

Removal

1 Remove the gear lever as described in Section 2.

2 Raise the vehicle as described in *Jacking and vehicle support*.

3 Working under the vehicle, lever the cable ball sockets from the selector levers on the side of the transmission, and then remove the mounting bracket and unclip the outer cables **(see illustrations)**. Note the fitted position of the cables for refitting.

4 Working inside the vehicle, prise out the boot from the floor of the vehicle, then withdraw the cables up through the floor panel.

5 Release the cables from the gear lever assembly, as described in Section 2.

Refitting

6 Refitting is a reversal of removal, noting the following points:

a) Tighten the gear lever base retaining bolts to the specified torque.

b) Check the condition of the cables and bushes, and renew if required.

c) Make sure the cables are fitted securely and the correct way around, as noted on removal.

d) Adjust the cables as described in paragraphs 7 to 11 of this section.

Adjusting

7 From inside the vehicle, unclip the gear lever gaiter from the facia panel, and slide it up the gear lever **(see illustration 2.2)**.

8 With the gear lever in the neutral position press down on the securing clamp to lock the gear lever in the neutral position.

9 Working under the vehicle, release the securing clips from the gearchange cables, then make sure the transmission is in the neutral position.

10 With the gear lever in the neutral position and the transmission in neutral, secure the cables in position by pressing the securing

3.3a Disconnect the cables from the transmission...

clips back in position on the gear change cables.

11 When completed, release the locking clamp from the base of the gear lever, before refitting the gear lever gaiter.

4 Vehicle speed sensor –
removal and refitting

1 The speed of the vehicle is monitored by the wheel speed sensors, which give information to the ECM. Their removal is covered in Chapter 10.

5 Transmission –
removal and refitting

Note: *The transmission can be removed as a unit with the engine as described in Chapter 2B, then separated from the engine on the bench. However, if work is only necessary on the transmission or clutch unit, it is better to remove the transmission on its own from underneath the vehicle. The latter method is described in this Section. The aid of an assistant will be required during the removal and refitting procedures.*

Note: *New propeller shaft universal joint/ rubber coupling retaining bolts will be required for refitting.*

3.3b ...then unclip them from the side of the transmission

Removal

1 Open the bonnet and disconnect the battery as described in Chapter 5 Section 3.

2 Firmly apply the handbrake, and then jack up the front of the vehicle and support it securely on axle stands (see *Jacking and vehicle support*). **Note:** *There must be sufficient clearance below the vehicle for the transmission to be lowered and removed from under the vehicle.*

3 If any work is to be carried out on the transmission after removal, it is advisable, at this stage, to drain the transmission oil as described in Section 7.

4 Mark the relative positions of the propeller shaft universal joint flange and transmission output shaft flange, as described in Chapter 8 Section 2.

5 Undo the two retaining bolts and remove the safety bracket from around the propeller shaft.

6 Remove the propshaft, as described in Chapter 8 Section 2.

7 Working on the right-hand side of the transmission tunnel, disconnect the wiring plug for the reversing light switch **(see illustration)**.

8 Working on the left-hand side of the gearbox, lever the shift cables from the shift levers, taking note of their positions for refitting (the white cable is the lower of the two) **(see illustration)**.

9 Pull down the retaining collars and detach the shift cable from the gearbox, then cable tie them out of the way **(see illustration)**.

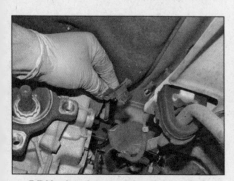

5.7 Unplug the reversing light switch

5.8 Separate the shift cables from the transmission

5.9 Pull down the collar to release each cable

5.10 Undo the bolts and remove the exhaust bracket

5.11 Support the crossmember and remove the outer mounting bolts

5.13 Undo the rear 2 mounting bolts

10 Undo the 4 retaining bolts and remove the exhaust support bracket from place **(see illustration)**.

11 Place a trolley jack under the gearbox to support it, then undo the mounting bolts for the gearbox support crossmember **(see illustration)**.

12 Place a block of wood between the bottom of the engine and crossmember to stop the engine and gearbox moving when the gearbox support crossmember is removed.

13 Slacken the mounting bolts at the rear of the gearbox where it is attached to the crossmember **(see illustration)**.

14 With the crossmember removed, place a transmission jack under the gearbox **(see illustration)**.

15 Unscrew the cap of the brake/clutch fluid reservoir and place a piece of polythene over the opening, then screw the cap back on.

16 Working at the left side of the gearbox, clamp the flexible hose, and place a suitable container underneath it, then release the retaining clip and detach the hose from the gearbox housing **(see illustration)**. Plug the end of the hose and the opening on the gearbox to prevent any ingress of dirt.

17 Lower the jack and transmission slightly, until the engine is supported with the piece of wood put between the engine sump and crossmember.

18 With the aid of an assistant to help steady the transmission, work around the outer edge of the transmission casing and slacken and remove the transmission-to-engine securing bolts. Note the fitted position of any earth cables or mounting brackets for refitting.

19 Check that all fixings are fully disconnected and positioned out of the way, then pull the transmission rearwards and detach it from the engine. Where applicable, it may be necessary to initially prise free the clutch housing from the engine location dowels. At no time during its removal (and subsequent refitting), allow the weight of the transmission to rest on the input shaft.

20 When the unit is fully clear of the engine, lower it, and withdraw it from underneath the vehicle **(see illustration)**.

21 The clutch components can now be inspected with reference to Chapter, and renewed if necessary. Unless they are virtually new, it is worth renewing the clutch components as a matter of course, even if the transmission has been removed for some other reason.

Refitting

22 Before lifting the unit into position, check that the clutch release bearing is correctly positioned, and apply a thin smear of high melting-point grease to the transmission input shaft.

23 With the aid of an assistant, lift the transmission into position, and then carefully slide it onto the rear of the engine, at the same time engaging the input shaft with the clutch friction disc splines. Do not use excessive force to refit the transmission – if the input shaft does not slide into place easily, turn the input shaft so that the splines engage properly with the disc. If problems are still experienced, check that the clutch friction disc is correctly centred (Chapter 6).

24 Once the transmission is fully engaged with the engine, insert the retaining bolts and tighten them to the specified torque.

25 Raise the trolley jack and refit the rear crossmember back into position on the rear of the transmission and tighten the rear mounting retaining nut. Refit the retaining nuts at each side of the crossmember and tighten to the specified torque. With the transmission in position, remove the trolley jack and the wooden block positioned under the sump.

26 Refit the two retaining bolts on the right-hand side of the transmission casing securing the exhaust mounting bracket to the transmission.

27 Refit the starter motor as described in Chapter 5.

28 Refit the hydraulic clutch fluid hose to the transmission, making sure the retaining clip is secure and the pipe securing bracket bolt is tight. Remove the clamp from the flexible hose.

29 Refit the propeller shaft to the output shaft flange on the rear of the transmission, noting the marks made on removal. Fit new retaining bolts.

30 Refit the gear selector cables to the transmission, with reference to Section 2 of this Chapter.

31 If removed, refit the exhaust heat shield under the vehicle.

32 Refill/top-up the transmission oil with reference to Section 7, then lower the vehicle to the ground and reconnect the battery negative terminal.

5.14 Support the gearbox on a transmission jack

5.16 Detach the clutch hose from the gearbox housing

5.20 Support the transmission on the trolley jack and remove

7.1 Transmission model number is on the right side of the casing

7.3 Transmission oil drain plug

7.6 Transmission oil filler/level plug

6 Transmission overhaul – general information

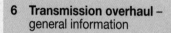

1 Overhauling a manual transmission unit is a difficult and involved job for the DIY home mechanic. In addition to dismantling and reassembling many small parts, clearances must be precisely measured and, if necessary, changed by selecting shims and spacers. Internal transmission components are also often difficult to obtain, and in many instances, extremely expensive. Because of this, if the transmission develops a fault or becomes noisy, the best course of action is to have the unit overhauled by a specialist repairer, or to obtain an exchange reconditioned unit.

2 Nevertheless, it is not impossible for the more experienced mechanic to overhaul the transmission, provided the special tools are available, and the job is done in a deliberate step-by-step manner, so that nothing is overlooked.

3 The tools necessary for an overhaul include internal and external circlip pliers, bearing pullers, slide hammer, set of pin punches, dial test indicator, and possibly a hydraulic press. In addition, a large, sturdy workbench and a vice will be required.

4 During dismantling of the transmission,

make careful notes of how each component is fitted, to make reassembly easier and more accurate.

5 Before dismantling the transmission, it will help if you have some idea what area is malfunctioning. Certain problems can be closely related to specific areas in the transmission, which can make component examination and renewal easier. Refer to the *Fault finding* Section of this manual for more information.

7 Transmission oil – draining and refilling

Caution: If this procedure is to be carried out on a hot transmission unit, take care not to burn yourself on the hot exhaust or the transmission/engine unit.

1 The transmission's oil capacity depends on its model number. This number will be found on the right-hand side next to the raised grid area of the casting **(see illustration)**.

2 Firmly apply the handbrake, and then jack up the front and rear of the vehicle and support it securely on axle stands (see *Jacking and vehicle support*). Make sure the vehicle is kept level to get the correct oil level. Where fitted, remove the undershields from under the transmission.

3 Wipe clean the area around the drain and filler plugs and position a suitable container underneath the transmission **(see illustration)**.

4 Unscrew the drain plug and allow the transmission oil to drain completely into the container. If the oil is hot, take precautions against scalding.

5 Once the oil has finished draining, ensure the drain plug is clean and that its internal magnet is free of debris then refit it to the transmission. Tighten the drain plug to the specified torque. Lower the vehicle to the ground.

6 The transmission is refilled through the filler/level plug hole on the side of the transmission casing **(see illustration)**. Wipe clean the area around the filler/level plug and unscrew it from the casing. Refill the transmission with the specified type and amount of oil given in the specifications, until the oil begins to trickle out of the level hole. Refit the plug and tighten it to the specified torque.

7 When completed. Lower the vehicle to the ground and take the vehicle on a short journey, so that the new oil is distributed fully around the transmission components.

8 On your return, park on level ground and check the transmission oil level as described in Chapter 1 Section 27.

Chapter 8
Propeller shaft and rear axle

Contents

Degrees of difficulty

Easy, suitable for novice with little experience 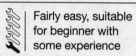	Fairly easy, suitable for beginner with some experience	Fairly difficult, suitable for competent DIY mechanic	Difficult, suitable for experienced DIY mechanic	Very difficult, suitable for expert DIY or professional

Specifications

Propeller shaft

Type .... One-piece with centre support bearing(s), and universal joints at each end

Rear axle

Type .... Semi-floating axle supported on semi-elliptic leaf spring(s)
Gear backlash .... 0.10 to 0.15 mm
Lubricant type .... See *Lubricants and fluids* on page 0•16
Lubricant capacity .... See Chapter 1 Section 1

Torque wrench settings

	Nm	lbf ft
Anti-roll bar clamp-to-rear axle bolts	160	118
Anti-roll bar link arm-to-chassis securing bolts	106	78
Brake actuator rod to axle	34	25
Brake caliper mounting bracket-to-axle bolts (M14 bolts):		
Stage 1	80	59
Stage 2	Angle-tighten a further 40°	
Differential housing cover bolts	65	48
Halfshaft bearing cover retaining bolts:*		
Stage 1	30	22
Stage 2	100	74
Stage 3	Loosen	
Stage 4	30	22
Stage 5	Angle-tighten a further 45°	
Oil drain plug	90	71
Oil filler plug	90	71
Propeller shaft centre bearing housing-to-underbody bolts*	135	100
Propeller shaft safety bracket-to-underbody bolts	70	52
Propeller shaft-to-rear axle final drive coupling flange bolts:*		
Stage 1	40	30
Stage 2	Angle-tighten a further 60°	
Propeller shaft-to-transmission output shaft flange bolts:*		
Stage 1	40	30
Stage 2	Angle-tighten a further 60°	
Rear spring-to-axle U-bolt nuts*	160	118
Roadwheel nuts:		
Steel rims	240	177
Aluminium rims	180	133
Shock absorber lower mounting bolt/nuts M12 x 1.5 (8.8 bolts):		
Stage 1	90	71
Stage 2	Angle-tighten a further 90°	81

* Use new nuts/bolts

2.2 Remove the safety bracket

2.4 ...and the position of the rear prop shaft flange

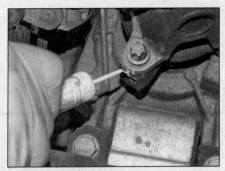

2.3 Mark the position of the front prop shaft flange...

2.7 Undo the mounting bolts to release the centre bearing from the vehicle's underside

1 General Information

Propeller shaft

1 The drive is transmitted from the transmission to the rear axle by a finely balanced tubular propeller shaft, supported at the centre by one or two rubber-mounted bearings.
2 Fitted at the front, centre and rear of the propeller shaft assembly are universal joints, which cater for movement of the rear axle with suspension travel, and slight movement of the power unit on its mountings.

Rear axle

3 The rear axle is a live axle suspended on semi-elliptic leaf spring(s) and utilising

3.2 Undo the two retaining clips

telescopic shock absorbers to provide the damping for the axle assembly. Drive to the wheels is by two solid steel halfshafts, which are secured in the rear axle housing by a retaining plate. This plate also supports the rear wheel bearing on the inside of the axle housing, which is held in place on the shaft by a large 'slotted' retaining nut. The brake backplate and discs are then fitted to the outer flange of the halfshaft.
4 The oil filler plug is located on the rear differential cover, and the drain plug in the lower right-hand side of the differential housing. The internal final drive and differential components are supported on taper-roller bearings and are housed within the axle casing itself. Access to the differential is by means of a removable cover bolted to the rear of the axle.

2 Propeller shaft – removal and refitting

Note: *New propeller shaft retaining bolts will be required for refitting.*

Removal

1 Chock the front wheels then jack up the rear of the vehicle and securely support it on axle stands, as described in *Jacking and vehicle support*. Where applicable, undo the retaining bolts and remove the undershields.
2 Undo the two retaining bolts and remove the safety bracket from around the propeller shaft **(see illustration)**.

3 Mark the front universal joint and transmission flanges in relation to each other **(see illustration)**.
4 Also mark the rear universal joint and final drive coupling flanges in relation to each other **(see illustration)**.
5 Unscrew the four bolts securing the propeller shaft to the final drive coupling flange. If required, hold the shaft stationary with a long lever inserted inside the universal joint. Support the rear of the propeller shaft on an axle stand after disconnecting the flanges. Note that new flange retaining bolts will be required for refitting.
6 Undo the four bolts securing the universal joint flange to the transmission output flange, then separate the flanges and support the front of the propeller shaft on an axle stand. Note that new flange retaining bolts will be required for refitting.
7 With the aid of an assistant to support the propeller shaft, undo the two bolts securing the propeller shaft centre bearing to the underbody **(see illustration)**.
8 Lower the propeller shaft assembly to the ground and remove it from under the vehicle. Noting its fitted position for refitting. New centre bearing retaining bolts will be required for refitting.

Refitting

9 Slide the propeller shaft into position under the vehicle making sure it the correct way around as noted on removal.
10 Align the front flange mark (made on removal) with the mark made on the transmission flange and fit the new retaining bolts. Do not fully tighten the bolts at this stage.
11 Raise the propeller shaft centre section, and fit the new retaining bolts to the centre bearing. Do not fully tighten the bolts at this stage.
12 Raise the propeller shaft rear section, align the coupling flange marks made on removal, and fit the new flange retaining bolts. Do not fully tighten the bolts at this stage.
13 With the propeller shaft in position, tighten all the retaining bolts to the specified torque in the following sequence:
a) Front universal joint flange bolts.
b) Front centre bearing retaining bolts.
c) Final drive coupling flange bolts.
14 Lower the vehicle to the ground and road test to check for any noise or vibration.

3 Propeller shaft centre bearing(s) – renewal

Note: *New propeller shaft retaining bolts will be required for refitting.*

Centre bearing (2-piece shaft)

Removal

1 Remove the propeller shaft, as described in Section 2 of this Chapter.
2 Release the retaining clips and pull back the rubber gaiter **(see illustration)**.

3 Check the shaft for alignment marks, if no marks are found, mark the shafts in relation with each other.

4 Pull the two shafts apart, leaving the centre bearing fitted to the front part of the propeller shaft. The gaiter and retaining clips can now be removed from over the rear shaft splines. Discard the gaiter, as new one will be required for refitting.

5 Using circlip pliers remove the circlip from the end of the front propeller shaft.

6 The centre bearing can now be removed from the front propeller shaft, complete with protective caps and washer. If required use a suitable puller to withdraw the centre bearing from the shaft, noting its fitted position.

Refitting

7 Locate the new centre bearing (including washers and protective caps) on the propeller shaft and drive it fully into position. Make sure it is fitted in the position noted on removal.

8 Refit the new circlip to the end of the front shaft, to secure the bearing in place.

9 Refit the new gaiter complete with securing clips to the rear propeller shaft, and coat the splines with multipurpose grease.

10 Slide the two parts of the propeller shaft together and secure the gaiter in position using the retaining clips. Make sure the marks on the shaft are aligned as noted on removal.

11 Refit the propeller shaft, as described in Section 2 of this Chapter.

4 Rear axle – removal and refitting

Note: *The rear axle removal/refitting details described below are for the removal of the unit on its own. If required, it can be removed together with the roadwheels and rear leaf springs as a combined unit, although this method requires the vehicle to be raised and supported at a greater height (to allow the roadwheels to clear the body during withdrawal of the unit). If the latter method is used, follow the instructions given, but ignore the references to removal of the roadwheels and detaching the springs from the axle. Refer to Chapter 10 for details on detaching the springs from the underbody.*

Note: *New spring-to-axle U-bolt retaining nuts, and new propeller shaft final drive coupling flange retaining bolts will be required for refitting.*

Removal

1 Chock the front wheels then jack up the rear of the vehicle and securely support it on axle stands positioned beneath the underframe sidemembers in front of the rear springs (see *Jacking and vehicle support*). Remove the rear roadwheels on both sides.

2 Mark the propeller shaft rear universal joint and final drive coupling flanges in relation to each other, to make sure the shaft is fitted in the correct position on refitting.

3 Unscrew the four bolts securing the propeller

4.4 Slacken bolts and detach wiring harnesses

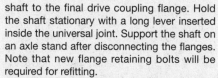

shaft to the final drive coupling flange. Hold the shaft stationary with a long lever inserted inside the universal joint. Support the shaft on an axle stand after disconnecting the flanges. Note that new flange retaining bolts will be required for refitting.

4 Unscrew the bolts and remove the electrical wiring harnesses from both rear brake calipers **(see illustration)**.

5 Undo the retaining bolts and remove the rear brake calipers **(see illustration)**. Using a piece of wire, fasten them to the underbody of the vehicle.

6 Disconnect the handbrake cables from the handbrake shoes, with reference to Chapter 9 Section 15. Trace the handbrake cables back across the axle housing, and then disconnect it from any brackets or cable-ties.

7 Remove the ABS sensors (wheel speed sensors), from the rear axle housing; refer to Chapter 9 Section 20.

4.9 Undo the rear anti-roll bar clamp bolts

4.12a Undo the retaining nuts...

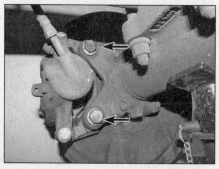

4.5 Remove the rear brake caliper

8 Support the weight of the rear axle, using two trolley jacks, positioned beneath the axle at each side.

9 Undo the two bolts each side and release the anti-roll bar clamps from the axle **(see illustration)**. Note the lower bolt also secures the handbrake cable bracket.

10 Undo the retaining nuts and bolts, and detach the rear shock absorbers from the axle **(see illustration)**.

11 Where fitted, disconnect the vent hose from the top of the differential casing.

12 With the axle still supported, undo the retaining nuts, and remove the spring-to-axle U-bolts and upper mounting plate **(see illustrations)**.

13 Check around the axle to make sure all various fittings and attachments are disconnected, and tied up out of the way.

14 Check that the axle unit is securely supported, by the two trolley jacks. Have an

4.10 Undo the lower shock absorber mounting bolts

4.12b ...and remove the U-bolts and mounting plates

assistant available to steady the axle each side as it is lowered from the vehicle.

Refitting

15 Refitting is a reversal of the removal procedure, noting the following points:
a) *Tighten all retaining nuts and bolts to the specified torque (where given).*
b) *Use new retaining nuts on the spring-to-axle U-bolts.*
c) *If the propeller shaft rear section was separated from the centre section, align the marks made on removal and re-engage the sliding spline connection.*
d) *Align the marks made on removal when refitting the propeller shaft flange, and use new retaining bolts.*
e) *Final tightening of the rear axle U-bolt nuts, and shock absorber mounting nuts should be carried out with the weight of the vehicle resting on the roadwheels.*
f) *Refer to the procedures contained in Chapter 9 for the brake-related procedures, then adjust the handbrake as described in Chapter 1 Section 21.*
g) *If the axle has been dismantled during removal, top-up the oil level as described in Chapter 1.*
h) *When all is completed, refit the roadwheels, and then tighten the wheel nuts to the specified torque. Lower the vehicle to the ground and check the brake operation.*

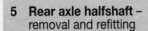

5 Rear axle halfshaft – removal and refitting

Removal

1 Chock the front wheels then jack up the rear of the vehicle and securely support it on axle stands (see *Jacking and vehicle support*). Remove the appropriate rear wheel.
2 Remove the rear brake caliper, brake disc and handbrake shoes, as described in Chapter 9.
3 Working at the rear of the brake backing plate, undo the 4 halfshaft retaining bolts **(see illustration)**.
4 Withdraw the halfshaft from the axle housing **(see illustration)**. Be prepared for some oil spillage.
5 At the time of writing Mercedes only offers

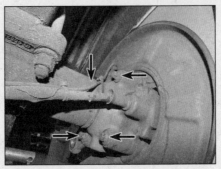

5.3 Undo the 4 retaining bolts

the halfshaft and wheel bearing as one complete unit. However, the wheel bearing is available separately from aftermarket suppliers. Unfortunately, removing the halfshaft from the bearing necessitates the use of a workshop hydraulic press.

Refitting

6 Carefully insert into the axle housing.
7 Insert the halfshaft into the axle housing and tighten the bearing cover mounting bolts to the specified torque setting.
8 Refer to the procedures contained in Chapter 9 for the brake-related procedures, then adjust the handbrake.
9 If the axle has lost some oil during this procedure, top-up the oil level as described in Chapter 1, Section 27.
10 When all is completed, refit the roadwheel, and then tighten the wheel nuts to the specified torque. Lower the vehicle to the ground and check the brake operation.

Rear wheel bearings

Note: *At the time of writing Mercedes only offers the halfshaft and wheel bearing as one complete unit. However, the wheel bearing is available separately from aftermarket suppliers. Unfortunately, removing the halfshaft from the bearing necessitates the use of a workshop hydraulic press.*

6 Differential unit – overhaul

1 The design and layout of the axle is such that any attempt to remove the differential unit

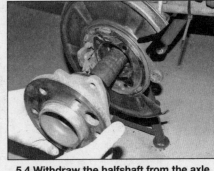

5.4 Withdraw the halfshaft from the axle

or pinion assembly from the axle housing will upset their preset meshing.
2 Since special tools and skills are required to set up the crownwheel and pinion mesh, the removal, overhaul and assembly of these differential types is not recommended, and should be entrusted to a dealer.
3 If the drive pinion radial seal is leaking, it will need to be carried out by a specialist, as there is a compression washer fitted on the pinion shaft. If the flange is removed from the shaft to access the oil seal a new compression washer will need to be fitted, so that the retaining nut can be tightened to the correct friction torque.
4 If required, an inspection inside the differential unit can be made to assess for excessive wear or damage to any component parts. To do this, place a large container beneath the differential to catch the oil, and then remove the differential drain plug. Unbolt and remove the differential housing cover, and check inside for wear.
5 Before refitting the rear cover, clean the cover and axle case mating surfaces, and remove the remains of the old gasket. Also clean the threads of the retaining bolts with a wire brush, and the threaded holes in the casing with a suitable cleaning solvent.
6 Locate the new gasket and the cover, smear the retaining bolt threads with sealant, and fit them. Tighten the bolts in an alternate and progressive sequence to the specified torque setting. Refit the differential drain plug.
7 Referring to Chapter 1 Section 28, refill the rear axle with the correct grade of oil, then refit and tighten the filler plug.

Chapter 9
Braking system

Contents

Degrees of difficulty

Easy, suitable for novice with little experience	Fairly easy, suitable for beginner with some experience	Fairly difficult, suitable for competent DIY mechanic	Difficult, suitable for experienced DIY mechanic	Very difficult, suitable for expert DIY or professional

Specifications

Front brakes

Type	Ventilated disc, with single-piston sliding caliper
Disc thickness:	
New	28.0 mm
Minimum	25.0 mm
Maximum disc run-out	0.03 mm
Maximum disc thickness variation	0.04 mm
Brake pad friction material minimum thickness	2.0 mm

Rear brakes

Type	Solid disc with single-piston sliding caliper. Handbrake shoes incorporated inside the disc centre hub
Disc thickness:	
New	16.0 mm
Minimum	14.0 mm
Maximum disc run-out	0.05 mm
Maximum disc thickness variation	0.03 mm
Brake pad friction material minimum thickness	3.0 mm
Handbrake shoe minimum thickness	4.5 mm

Torque wrench settings	Nm	lb ft
ABS pressure sensor to hydraulic unit	20	15
Brake fluid pipe connections to ABS unit	14	10
Brake fluid pipe unions	14	10
Caliper guide pins/bolts (M8 bolt)	34	25
Caliper mounting bracket bolts (M14 bolts): *		
Stage 1	80	59
Stage 2	Angle-tighten a further 40°	
Handbrake compensator-to-underbody retaining bolts	42	31
Handbrake lever-to-seat frame retaining bolts	62	46
Master cylinder retaining nuts	20	15
Pedal mounting bracket bolts/nuts	23	17
Roadwheel nuts:		
Steel rims	240	177
Aluminium rims	180	133
Vacuum pump-to-cylinder head bolts	14	10
Vacuum servo unit mounting nuts	23	17

* Use new nuts/bolts

1 General Information

1 The braking system is of servo-assisted, dual-circuit hydraulic type split diagonally. The arrangement of the hydraulic system is such that each circuit operates one front and one rear brake from a tandem master cylinder. Under normal circumstances, both circuits operate in unison. However, in the event of hydraulic failure in one circuit, full braking force will still be available at two wheels.

2 All models are fitted with front and rear disc brakes. An Anti-lock Braking System (ABS) is fitted as standard to all vehicles covered in this manual. Refer to Section 19 for further information on ABS operation.

3 The front brake discs are of the ventilated type and the rear brake discs are of the solid type. Both front and rear brakes are fitted with single-piston sliding pin type brake calipers.

4 The rear brake discs incorporate handbrake shoes, which are actuated by a cable through the inside of the axle housing. The cable-operated handbrake provides an independent mechanical means of rear brake application. A self-adjust mechanism is incorporated to automatically compensate for brake shoe wear. As the brake shoe linings wear, the handbrake operation automatically operates the adjuster mechanism, which effectively lengthens the shoe strut, and repositions the brake shoes to maintain the lining-to-drum clearance.

5 A vacuum servo unit is fitted between the master cylinder and the bulkhead, its function being to reduce the amount of pedal pressure required to operate the brakes. Since there is no throttling as such of the inlet manifold on diesel engines, the manifold is not a suitable source of vacuum to operate the vacuum servo unit. The servo unit is therefore connected to a separate engine-mounted vacuum pump. The pump is bolted to the front of the cylinder head and is driven by the end of the camshaft.

⚠ **Warning: When servicing any part of the system, work carefully and methodically; also observe scrupulous cleanliness when overhauling any part of the hydraulic system. Always renew components (in axle sets, where applicable) if in doubt about their condition, and use only genuine parts, or at least those of known good quality. Note the warnings given in Safety first! and at relevant points in this Chapter concerning the dangers of asbestos dust and hydraulic fluid.**

2 Hydraulic system – bleeding

⚠ **Warning: Hydraulic fluid is poisonous. Wash off immediately and thoroughly in the case of skin contact, and seek immediate medical advice if any fluid is swallowed or gets into the eyes. Certain types of hydraulic fluid are inflammable, and may ignite when allowed into contact with hot components. When servicing any hydraulic system, it is safest to assume that the fluid is inflammable, and to take precautions against the risk of fire as though it is petrol that is being handled. Hydraulic fluid is also an effective paint stripper, and will attack plastics; if any is spilt, it should be washed off immediately, using copious quantities of fresh water. Finally, it is hygroscopic (it absorbs moisture from the air) therefore old fluid may be contaminated and unfit for further use. When topping-up or renewing the fluid, always use the recommended type, and ensure that it comes from a freshly opened sealed container.**

General

1 The correct operation of any hydraulic system is only possible after removing all air from the components and circuit; this is achieved by bleeding the system.

2 During the bleeding procedure, add only clean, unused hydraulic fluid of the recommended type; never re-use fluid that has already been bled from the system. Ensure that sufficient fluid is available before starting work.

3 If there is any possibility of incorrect fluid being already in the system, the brake components and circuit must be flushed completely with uncontaminated, correct fluid, and new seals should be fitted to the various components.

4 If hydraulic fluid has been lost from the system, or air has entered because of a leak, ensure that the fault is cured before proceeding further.

5 When bleeding the brakes on vehicles with a load-apportioning valve in the rear brake hydraulic circuit, it is important to note that the vehicle must be standing on its wheels. If the rear of the vehicle is jacked up and the axle is in a 'wheel free' state, the load-apportioning valve will prevent complete bleeding of the system.

6 Check that all pipes and hoses are secure, unions tight and bleed screws closed. Clean any dirt from around the bleed screws.

7 Unscrew the master cylinder reservoir cap, and top-up the master cylinder reservoir to the MAX level line. Refit the cap loosely, and remember to maintain the fluid level at least above the MIN level line throughout the procedure, otherwise there is a risk of further air entering the system.

8 There are a number of one-man, do-it-yourself brake bleeding kits currently available from motor accessory shops. It is recommended that one of these kits is used whenever possible, as they greatly simplify the bleeding operation, and also reduce the risk of expelled air and fluid being drawn back into the system. If such a kit is not available,

the basic (two-man) method must be used, which is described in detail below.

9 If a kit is to be used, prepare the vehicle as described previously, and follow the kit manufacturer's instructions, as the procedure may vary slightly according to the type being used, Generally, they are as outlined below in the relevant sub-Section.

10 If the system has been only partially disconnected, and suitable precautions were taken to minimise fluid loss, it should only be necessary to bleed that part of the system (ie, the primary or secondary circuit). If the master cylinder or main brake lines have been disconnected, then the complete system must be bled.

Bleeding

Basic (two-man) method

11 Collect together a clean glass jar, a suitable length of plastic or rubber tubing, which is a tight fit over the bleed screw, and a ring spanner to fit the screw. The help of an assistant will also be required.

12 Remove the dust cap from the bleed screw at the wheel to be bled. Fit the spanner and tube to the screw, place the other end of the tube in the jar, and pour in sufficient fluid to cover the end of the tube.

13 Ensure that the master cylinder reservoir fluid level is maintained at least above the MIN level line throughout the procedure.

14 Have the assistant fully depress the brake pedal several times to build-up pressure, and then maintain it on the final downstroke.

15 While pedal pressure is maintained, unscrew the bleed screw (approximately one turn) and allow the compressed fluid and air to flow into the jar. The assistant should maintain pedal pressure, following it down to the floor if necessary, and should not release it until instructed to do so. When the flow stops, tighten the bleed screw again, have the assistant release the pedal slowly, and recheck the reservoir fluid level.

16 Repeat the steps given in paragraphs 14 and 15 until the fluid emerging from the bleed screw is free from air bubbles. If the master cylinder has been drained and refilled, and air is being bled from the first bleed screw, allow approximately five seconds between cycles for the master cylinder passages to refill.

17 When no more air bubbles appear, securely tighten the bleed screw, remove the tube and spanner, and refit the dust cap. Do not overtighten the bleed screw.

18 Repeat the procedure on the remaining bleed screws, until all air is removed from the system and the brake pedal feels firm again.

Using a one-way valve kit

19 As the name implies, these kits consist of a length of tubing with a one-way valve fitted, to prevent expelled air and fluid being drawn back into the system. Some kits include a translucent container, which can be positioned so that the air bubbles can be

more easily seen flowing from the end of the tube **(see illustration)**.

20 The kit is connected to the bleed screw, which is then opened. The user returns to the driver's seat, depresses the brake pedal with a smooth, steady stroke, and slowly releases it; this is repeated until the expelled fluid is clear of air bubbles.

21 Note that these kits simplify work so much that it is easy to forget the master cylinder reservoir fluid level, therefore ensure that this is maintained at least above the MIN level line at all times.

Using a pressure-bleeding kit

22 These kits are usually operated by a reservoir of pressurised air contained in the spare tyre. However, note that it will probably be necessary to reduce the pressure to a lower level than normal. Refer to the instructions supplied with the kit.

23 By connecting a pressurised, fluid-filled container to the master cylinder reservoir, bleeding can be carried out simply by opening each bleed screw in turn, and allowing the fluid to flow out until no more air bubbles can be seen in the expelled fluid.

24 This method has the advantage that the large reservoir of fluid provides an additional safeguard against air being drawn into the system during bleeding.

25 Pressure-bleeding is particularly effective when bleeding 'difficult' systems, or when bleeding the complete system at the time of routine fluid renewal.

All methods

26 When bleeding is complete, and firm pedal feel is restored, wash off any spilt fluid, securely tighten the bleed screws, and refit the dust caps.

27 Check the hydraulic fluid level in the master cylinder reservoir, and top-up if necessary (see *Weekly checks*).

28 Discard any hydraulic fluid that has been bled from the system as it will not be fit for re-use.

29 Check the feel of the brake pedal. If it feels at all spongy, air must still be present in the system, and further bleeding is required. Failure to bleed satisfactorily after a reasonable repetition of the bleeding procedure may be due to worn master cylinder seals.

3 Hydraulic pipes and hoses – renewal

Note: *Before starting work, refer to the note at the beginning of Section 2 concerning the dangers of hydraulic fluid.*

1 If any pipe or hose is to be renewed, minimise fluid loss by first removing the master cylinder reservoir cap and screwing it down onto a piece of polythene. Alternatively, flexible hoses can be sealed, if required, using a proprietary brake hose clamp. Metal brake pipe unions can be plugged (if care is taken

2.19 Bleeding a front brake caliper

not to allow dirt into the system) or capped immediately they are disconnected. Place a wad of rag under any union that is to be disconnected, to catch any spilt fluid.

2 If a flexible hose is to be disconnected, unscrew the brake pipe union nut(s) before removing the spring clip (or retaining bolt) which secures the hose to its mounting bracket. Where applicable, unscrew the banjo union bolt securing the hose to the caliper and recover the copper washers. When removing the front flexible hose, undo the retaining bolt and release the hose support bracket from the suspension strut.

3 To unscrew union nuts, it is preferable to obtain a brake pipe spanner of the correct size; these are available from most motor accessory shops. Failing this, a close-fitting open-ended spanner will be required, though if the nuts are tight or corroded, their flats may be rounded-off if the spanner slips. In such a case, a self-locking wrench is often the only way to unscrew a stubborn union, but it follows that the pipe and the damaged nuts must be renewed on reassembly. Always clean a union and surrounding area before disconnecting it. If disconnecting a component with more than one union, make a careful note of the connections before disturbing any of them.

4 If a brake pipe is to be renewed, it can be obtained, cut to length and with the union nuts and end flares in place, from dealers. All that is then necessary is to bend it to shape, following the line of the original, before fitting it to the vehicle. Alternatively, most motor accessory shops can make up brake

pipes from kits, but this requires very careful measurement of the original, to ensure that the new one is of the correct length. The safest answer is usually to take the original to the shop as a pattern.

5 On refitting, do not overtighten the union nuts.

6 When refitting hoses to the front calipers, always use new copper washers and tighten the banjo union bolts to the specified torque. Make sure that the hoses are positioned so that they will not touch surrounding bodywork or the roadwheels.

7 Ensure that the pipes and hoses are correctly routed, with no kinks, and that they are secured in the clips or brackets provided. After fitting, remove the polythene from the reservoir, and bleed the hydraulic system as described in Section 2. On completion, wash off any spilt fluid, and check carefully for fluid leaks.

4 Front brake pads – renewal

⚠️ **Warning: Renew BOTH sets of front brake pads at the same time – NEVER renew the pads on only one wheel, as uneven braking may result. Note that the dust created by wear of the pads may contain asbestos, which is a health hazard. Never blow it out with compressed air, and do not inhale any of it. An approved filtering mask should be worn when working on the brakes. DO NOT use petroleum-based solvents to clean brake parts – use brake cleaner or methylated spirit only.**

1 Apply the handbrake, then jack up the front of the vehicle and support it on axle stands, as described in *Jacking and vehicle support*. Remove the front roadwheels.

2 Follow the accompanying photos **(see illustrations)** for the actual pad renewal procedure, bearing in mind the additional points given in the following paragraphs. Be sure to stay in order and read the caption under each illustration. Note that if the old pads are to be refitted, ensure that they are identified so that they can be returned to their original positions.

4.2a Disconnect the brake pad warning light wiring

4.2b Unscrew the lid from the brake fluid reservoir

4.2c Remove the rubber cap and undo the lower caliper guide pin bolt

4.2d Lever out the bottom edge, swivel the caliper up...

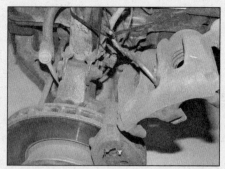

4.2e ...and secure using a cable tie or a hook.

4.2f Remove the brake pads from the caliper

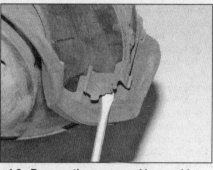

4.2g Remove the upper and lower shims

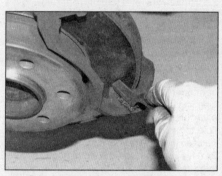

4.3 Remove any dirt or dust from the pad mounting surfaces

3 If the original brake pads are still serviceable, carefully clean them using a clean, fine wire brush or similar, paying particular attention to the sides and back of the metal backing plate. Clean out the grooves in the friction material, and pick out any large embedded particles of dirt or debris. Carefully clean the pad locations in the caliper mounting bracket **(see illustration)**.

4 Prior to fitting the pads (reversal of the removal procedure), check that the guide pins are a snug fit in the caliper. Inspect the dust seals around the pistons for damage, and the pistons for evidence of fluid leaks, corrosion or damage.

5 Refit the upper and lower shims **(see illustrations)**.

6 If new brake pads are to be fitted, the caliper pistons must be pushed back into the cylinder to allow for the extra pad thickness **(see illustration)**. When doing this, keep an eye on the brake fluid reservoir, to make sure it doesn't overflow as the pads are pushed back. Place a rag around the neck of the reservoir to stop drips.

7 Fit the brake pads. Ensure the friction material is against the disc face **(see illustrations)**.

8 Lower the caliper into place **(see illustration)**.

4.5a Fit the upper shim...

4.5b ...and lower shim

4.6 Using a special tool for pushing the piston back into the caliper

4.7a Fit the inner pad to the caliper mounting bracket...

4.7b ...followed by the outer pad

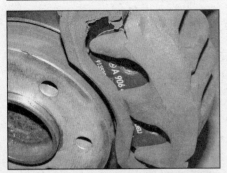

4.8 Pivot the caliper back down into place

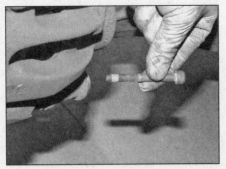

4.9a Insert the guide pin bolt...

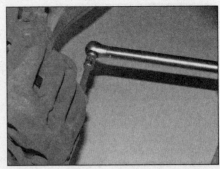

4.9b ...and tighten it to the specified torque

9 Install the guide pin bolt, and tighten it to the specified torque **(see illustrations)**. Don't forget to refit the rubber cap.

10 With the brake pads installed, depress the brake pedal repeatedly, until normal (non-assisted) pedal pressure is restored, and the pads are pressed into firm contact with the brake disc.

11 Repeat the above procedure on the remaining front brake caliper.

12 Refit the roadwheels, then lower the vehicle to the ground and tighten the roadwheel nuts to the specified torque setting.

13 Check the hydraulic fluid level as described in *Weekly checks*.

Caution: New pads will not give full braking efficiency until they have bedded-in. Be prepared for this, and avoid hard braking as far as possible for the first hundred miles or so after pad renewal.

---

5   Front brake disc –
inspection, removal
and refitting

Note: *Before starting work, refer to the warning at the beginning of Section 4 concerning the dangers of asbestos dust. If either disc requires renewal, both should be renewed at the same time together with new pads, to ensure even and consistent braking.*

Inspection

1 Firmly apply the handbrake, and then jack up the front of the vehicle and support it securely on axle stands, as described in

Jacking and vehicle support. Remove the roadwheel.

2 Rotate the brake disc, and examine it for deep scoring or grooving. Light scoring is normal, but if excessive, the disc should be removed and either renewed or machined (within the specified limits) by an engineering works. The minimum thickness is given in the Specifications at the start of this Chapter.

3 Using a dial gauge, or a flat metal block and feeler blades, check that the disc run-out does not exceed the figure given in the Specifications **(see illustration)**. Measure the run-out 10.0 mm in from the outer edge of the disc.

4 If the disc run-out is excessive, remove the disc as described later, and check that the disc-to-hub surfaces are perfectly clean. Refit the disc and check the run-out again.

5 If the run-out is still excessive, the disc should be renewed.

6 To remove a disc, proceed as follows.

5.3 Using a dial gauge to check the run-out of the disc

5.8b Hang the caliper assembly out of the way

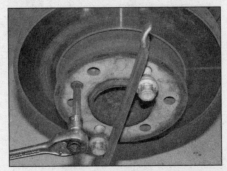

5.10a Undo the retaining screw...

Removal

7 Firmly apply the handbrake, and then jack up the front of the vehicle and support it securely on axle stands, as described in *Jacking and vehicle support*. Remove the relevant front roadwheel.

8 Undo the two bolts securing the brake caliper mounting bracket to the steering knuckle **(see illustrations)**. Slide the caliper and mounting bracket, complete with brake pads, off the disc and suspend the assembly to avoid straining the brake hose.

9 If necessary, place a screwdriver between the caliper and disc, and use it to slightly dislodge the caliper, to ease its removal.

10 Undo the retaining screw and withdraw the brake disc from the hub assembly **(see illustrations)**. If necessary, replace to two wheel bolts and use a lever to stop the brake disc rotating.

11 If necessary, tap the rear of the brake disc

5.8a Caliper mounting bracket bolts

5.10b ...and remove the brake disc

with a soft-faced mallet to free it from the hub assembly.

Refitting

12 Thoroughly clean the mating surfaces of the brake disc and hub flange ensuring that all traces of dirt and corrosion are removed.
13 Place the disc in position on the hub flange, aligning the holes in the centre part of the brake disc. Then fit the retaining screw to secure the brake disc to the hub and tighten.
14 Slide the brake caliper assembly over the disc and into position on the steering knuckle. Refit the two mounting bracket retaining bolts and tighten them to the specified torque.
15 Refit the roadwheel, tighten the wheel nuts to the specified torque, and then lower the vehicle to the ground.

6 Front brake caliper – removal and refitting

Note: *Before starting work, refer to the note at the beginning of Section 2 concerning the dangers of hydraulic fluid, and to the warning at the beginning of Section 4 concerning the dangers of asbestos dust.*

Removal

1 Apply the handbrake, then jack up the front of the vehicle and support it on axle stands, as described in *Jacking and vehicle support*. Remove the roadwheel.
2 Minimise fluid loss by first removing the master cylinder reservoir cap and screwing it down onto a piece of polythene. Alternatively, use a brake hose clamp to clamp the flexible hose leading to the brake caliper.
3 Clean the area around the caliper brake hose union. Unscrew and remove the union, where fitted, recover the sealing washers from the hose union. Discard the washers, as new ones must be used on refitting. Plug the hose end and caliper hole, to minimise fluid loss and prevent the ingress of dust and dirt into the hydraulic system.
4 Undo the retaining bolt and disconnect the brake pad low warning light wire from the caliper. Remove the brake pads as described in Section 4, and withdraw the caliper from the vehicle.

Refitting

5 Refit the brake pads and caliper to the mounting bracket as described in Section 4.
6 Reconnect the brake hose to the caliper and where applicable fit a new sealing washer to the hose union. Ensure that the hose is correctly positioned, and not fouling any components and then tighten it to the specified torque.
7 Remove the brake hose clamp or polythene, and bleed the hydraulic system as described in Section 2. Note that, providing the precautions described were taken to minimise brake fluid loss, it should only be necessary to bleed the relevant front brake circuit.
8 Refit the roadwheel, then lower the vehicle to the ground and tighten the roadwheel nuts to the specified torque.

7 Rear brake pads – renewal

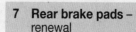

> **Warning:** *Renew BOTH sets of rear brake pads at the same time – NEVER renew the pads on only one wheel, as uneven braking may result. Note that the dust created by wear of the pads may contain asbestos, which is a health hazard. Never blow it out with compressed air, and do not inhale any of it. An approved filtering mask should be worn when working on the brakes. DO NOT use petroleum-based solvents to clean brake parts – use brake cleaner or methylated spirit only.*

1 Apply the handbrake, and then jack up the rear of the vehicle and support it on axle stands (see *Jacking and vehicle support*). Remove the rear roadwheels.
2 Follow the accompanying photos **(illustrations 7.2a to 7.2g)** for the actual pad renewal procedure, bearing in mind the additional points given in the following paragraphs. Be sure to stay in order and read the caption under each illustration. Note that if the old pads are to be refitted, ensure that they are identified so that they can be returned to their original positions.
3 If the original brake pads are still serviceable, carefully clean them using a clean, fine wire brush or similar, paying particular attention to the sides and back

7.2a Disconnect the brake pad warning light wiring

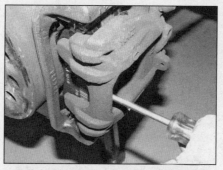

7.2b Loosen the caliper from the pads using a screwdriver...

7.2c ...then undo the upper caliper guide pin bolt

7.2d Swivel the caliper down and secure using a hook. Do NOT let it hang by the brake line

7.2e Remove the inner brake pad from the caliper first...

7.2f ...followed by the outer pad

7.2g Remove the retaining shims from the caliper

7.3 Clean the pad and shim locations

7.4 Using a special tool for pushing the piston back into the caliper

7.5 Fit new pad retaining shims

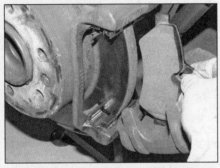

7.6 The inside pad should be fitted first

7.7 Remove the sticky backing

of the metal backing plate. Clean out the grooves in the friction material, and pick out any large embedded particles of dirt or debris. Carefully clean the pad locations in the caliper mounting bracket **(see illustration)**.

4 If new brake pads are to be fitted, the caliper pistons must be pushed back into the cylinder to allow for the extra pad thickness **(see illustration)**.

5 Fit new shims **(see illustration)**, then the pads.

6 Install the inner pad first **(see illustration)**.

7 Install the outer pad and peel off the sticky backing **(see illustration)**.

8 Swivel the caliper back upwards, then grease and install a new upper guide pin bolt and tighten it to the specified torque **(see illustration)**.

9 Insert a 1mm feeler gauge between the flat edge of the guide pin and the caliper **(see illustration)** before finally tightening the bolt to the correct torque. Failure to set this gap will cause extra noise during braking.

10 With the brake pads installed, depress the brake pedal repeatedly, until normal (non-assisted) pedal pressure is restored, and the pads are pressed into firm contact with the brake disc.

11 Repeat the above procedure on the remaining rear brake caliper.

12 Refit the roadwheels, then lower the vehicle to the ground and tighten the roadwheel nuts to the specified torque setting.

13 Check the hydraulic fluid level as described in *Weekly checks*.
Caution: New pads will not give full braking

efficiency until they have bedded-in. Be prepared for this, and avoid hard braking as far as possible for the first hundred miles or so after pad renewal.

---

8   Rear brake disc –
       inspection, removal
       and refitting

Note: *Before starting work, refer to the warning at the beginning of Section 4 concerning the dangers of asbestos dust. If either disc requires renewal, both should be renewed at the same time together with new pads, to ensure even and consistent braking.*

Inspection

1 With the vehicle on level ground, chock the front wheels, and then jack up the rear of the vehicle and support it securely on axle stands,

7.8 Install a freshly greased guide pin bolt

as described in *Jacking and vehicle support*. Remove the roadwheel.

2 Rotate the brake disc, and examine it for deep scoring or grooving. Light scoring is normal, but if excessive, the disc should be removed and either renewed or machined (within the specified limits) by an engineering works. The minimum thickness is given in the Specifications at the start of this Chapter.

3 Using a dial gauge **(see illustration 5.3)**, or a flat metal block and feeler blades, check that the disc run-out does not exceed the figure given in the Specifications. Measure the run-out 10.0 mm in from the outer edge of the disc.

4 If the disc run-out is excessive, remove the disc as described later, and check that the disc-to-hub surfaces are perfectly clean. Refit the disc and check the run-out again.

5 If the run-out is still excessive, the disc should be renewed.

6 To remove a disc, proceed as follows.

7.9 Insert a feeler gauge before tightening the bolt

8.11a Undo the retaining screw...

8.11b ...and remove the brake disc

8.12 Apply a small amount of copper grease to the disc flange

Removal

7 With the vehicle on level ground, chock the front wheels, and then jack up the rear of the vehicle and support it securely on axle stands, as described in *Jacking and vehicle support*. Remove the roadwheel.

8 Remove the rear brake pads and caliper as described in Section 7.

9 If the model has twin rear wheels, counterhold the outer wheel flange by placing a bar between two of the wheel studs.

10 Loosen the retaining bolts and remove the flange for the outer wheel.

11 Undo the retaining screw and withdraw the brake disc from the hub assembly **(see illustrations)**. If necessary, tap the rear of the brake disc with a soft-faced mallet to free it from the hub assembly. **Note:** *Make sure the handbrake is in the full off position, if required, slacken the handbrake adjustment as described in Chapter 1.*

Refitting

12 Thoroughly clean the mating surfaces of the brake disc and hub flange ensuring that all traces of dirt and corrosion are removed **(see illustration)**.

13 Place the disc in position on the hub flange, aligning the holes in the centre part of the brake disc. Then fit the retaining screw to secure the brake disc to the hub and tighten.

14 Slide the brake caliper mounting bracket over the disc and into position on the hub assembly. Refit the two retaining bolts and tighten them to the specified torque.

15 Refit the brake pads and caliper to the mounting bracket as described in Section 7.

16 Refit the roadwheel, tighten the wheel nuts to the specified torque, and then lower the vehicle to the ground.

9 Rear brake caliper – removal and refitting

Note: *Before starting work, refer to the note at the beginning of Section 2 concerning the dangers of hydraulic fluid, and to the warning at the beginning of Section 4 concerning the dangers of asbestos dust.*

Removal

1 Apply the handbrake, then jack up the rear of the vehicle and support it on axle stands (see *Jacking and vehicle support*). Remove the roadwheel.

2 Minimise fluid loss by first removing the master cylinder reservoir cap and screwing it down onto a piece of polythene. Alternatively, use a brake hose clamp to clamp the flexible hose leading to the brake caliper.

3 Clean the area around the caliper brake hose union. Unscrew and remove the union, where fitted, recover the sealing washers from the hose union. Discard the washers, as new ones must be used on refitting. Plug the hose end and caliper hole, to minimise fluid loss and prevent the ingress of dust and dirt into the hydraulic system.

4 On the left-hand caliper, disconnect the brake pad low warning light wire **(see illustration)**. Remove the brake pads as described in Section 7.

5 Undo the caliper carrier retaining bolts **(see illustration)** and withdraw the caliper from place.

Refitting

6 Check the rubber seals on the caliper guide pins are not split and the sleeves are free to slide in the caliper body. If required renew the sleeves and seals, before refitting the caliper.

7 Thereafter, refitting is a reversal of removal.

8 Remove the brake hose clamp or polythene, and bleed the hydraulic system as described in Section 2. Note that, providing the precautions described were taken to minimise brake fluid loss, it should only be necessary to bleed the relevant front brake circuit.

9 Refit the roadwheel, then lower the vehicle to the ground and tighten the roadwheel nuts to the specified torque.

10 Master cylinder – removal, overhaul and refitting

Note: *Before starting work, refer to the warning at the beginning of Section 2 concerning the dangers of hydraulic fluid.*

Removal

1 Remove the master cylinder reservoir cap, and siphon the hydraulic fluid from the reservoir. **Note:** *Do not siphon the fluid by mouth, as it is poisonous therefore use a syringe or an old hydrometer. Alternatively, open the front brake caliper bleed screws, one at a time, and gently pump the brake pedal to expel the fluid through a plastic tube connected to the screw (see Section 2).*

2 Place cloth rags beneath the master cylinder to collect escaping brake fluid. Identify the brake pipes for position, then unscrew the union nuts and move the pipes to one side. Plug or tape over the pipe ends to prevent dirt entry.

3 Unscrew the two mounting nuts and withdraw the master cylinder from the vacuum servo unit. Take care not to spill fluid on the vehicle paintwork. Recover the master cylinder-to-servo unit sealing ring and discard; a new one will be required for refitting.

4 If required, the fluid reservoir can be removed from the master cylinder by releasing the retaining tabs and pulling the reservoir up and off the mounting seals.

9.4 Unplug the brake pad warning connector

9.5 Remove the caliper mounting bolts

Overhaul

5 At the time of writing, master cylinder overhaul is not possible as no spares are available.

6 The only parts available individually are the fluid reservoir and its mounting seals, and the filler cap.

7 If the master cylinder is worn excessively, it must be renewed.

8 If new reservoir seals are to be fitted, extract the old seals from the cylinder body, lubricate the new seals with clean brake hydraulic fluid and push the seals into position.

Refitting

9 Where applicable, refit the fluid reservoir to the master cylinder body, ensuring that the retaining tabs lock into position.

10 Place the master cylinder-to-servo unit sealing ring into position, and then fit the master cylinder to the servo unit. Ensure that the servo unit pushrod enters the master cylinder piston centrally. Fit the retaining nuts and tighten them to the specified torque.

11 Refit the brake pipes and tighten the union nuts securely.

12 Reconnect the clutch hydraulic hose to the fluid reservoir.

13 Reconnect the wiring connector to the brake fluid level sensor.

14 Remove the reservoir filler cap and polythene, then top-up the reservoir with fresh hydraulic fluid to the MAX mark (see *Weekly checks*).

15 Bleed the brake and clutch hydraulic systems as described in Section 2 and Chapter 6 Section 4 then refit the filler cap. Thoroughly check the operation of the brakes and clutch before using the vehicle on the road.

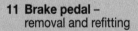

11 Brake pedal – removal and refitting

Removal

1 Open the bonnet and disconnect the battery negative as described in Chapter 5 Section 3.

2 Move the driver's seat fully rearward and, if required, remove the lower facia trim panel from under the steering column for easier access to the pedal assembly, with reference to Chapter 11.

3 If replacing the brake pedal bracket, remove the brake light switch **(see illustration)**.

4 Unclip and remove the brake pedal return spring from the top of the brake pedal**(see illustration)**.

5 Extract the retaining clip and clevis pin and detach the brake master cylinder pushrod from the brake pedal **(see illustrations)**.

6 Using a thin screwdriver, release the securing clip and withdraw the pivot bolt from the top of the brake pedal.

7 The brake pedal can now be withdrawn

11.3 Depress the tabs and unclip the brake light switch

11.5a Remove the securing clip...

from the pedal assembly, check the pedal bushes and renew if required.

Refitting

8 Check the clevis pin and pivot bolt for wear, renew if worn.

9 Manoeuvre the brake pedal into position in the pedal assembly, and slide the pivot pin into position. Fit the securing clip into position, making sure the pivot pin is securely fitted. Make sure the pivot pin and bushes are lubricated with some multipurpose grease before assembly.

10 Engage the brake master cylinder pushrod with the brake pedal, and then insert the clevis pin and secure it in position with the retaining clip. Make sure the clevis pin is lubricated with some multipurpose grease before assembly.

11 Refit the return spring to the brake pedal, and make sure the pedal operates without sticking.

12.5 Remove the clip to release the pushrod

11.4 Unclip the return spring from the pedal

11.5b ...and withdraw the clevis pin

12 Where applicable, refit any facia trim panels, with reference to Chapter 11.

13 Reconnect the battery negative terminal on completion.

12 Vacuum servo unit – testing, removal and refitting

Testing

1 To test the operation of the servo unit, with the engine off, depress the footbrake pedal several times to exhaust the vacuum. Now start the engine, keeping the pedal firmly depressed. As the engine starts, there should be a noticeable 'give' in the brake pedal as the vacuum builds-up. Allow the engine to run for at least two minutes, and then switch it off. The brake pedal should now feel normal, but further applications should result in the pedal feeling firmer, the pedal stroke decreasing with each application.

2 If the servo does not operate as described, first inspect the servo unit check valve as described in.

3 If the servo unit still fails to operate satisfactorily, the fault lies within the unit itself. Repairs to the unit are not possible; if faulty, the servo unit must be renewed.

Removal

4 Remove the brake master cylinder as described in Section 10.

5 Extract the retaining clip and clevis pin and detach the brake master cylinder pushrod from the brake pedal **(see illustration)**.

14.2a Unclip the plastic cover...

14.2b ...and release the central clip

As a guide, a minimum of approximately 500 mm Hg should be recorded. If the vacuum registered is significantly less than this, it is likely that the pump is faulty. However, seek the advice of a Mercedes-Benz dealer before condemning the pump.

Removal

4 Release the retaining clips and disconnect the vacuum hose from the top of the pump, which is mounted on the front of the cylinder head.

5 Unclip the wiring from across the front of the pump and move it to one side. If required remove the oil level dipstick, to access the pump retaining bolts.

6 Undo the retaining bolts and withdraw the vacuum pump from the front of the cylinder head.

Refitting

7 Refitting is the reverse of removal, using new O-ring seals/gasket, and making sure the pump drive flange is correctly engaged.

8 Tighten the vacuum pump mounting bolts to the specified torque.

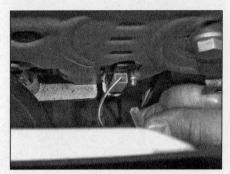

14.3 Unplug the handbrake switch connectors

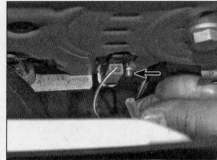

14.4 Remove the bolt and disconnect the switch

| 14 Handbrake lever – removal and refitting | 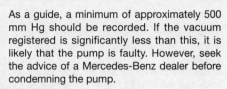 |

6 Carefully ease the vacuum hose out of the servo unit, taking care not to displace the sealing grommet.

7 Undo the four nuts securing the servo unit to the pedal mounting bracket and bulkhead.

8 Return to the engine compartment, and lift the servo unit out of position. Where applicable, recover the servo unit-to-bulkhead gasket.

Refitting

9 Where fitted, refit the gasket, and then locate the vacuum servo unit in position on the bulkhead. Refit the four nuts and tighten them to the specified torque.

10 Engage the servo unit pushrod with the brake pedal, and then insert the clevis pin and secure it in position with the retaining clip. Make sure the clevis pin is lubricated with some multipurpose grease before assembly.

11 Refit the vacuum hose to the servo grommet, ensuring that the hose is correctly seated.

12 Refit the brake master cylinder as described in Section 10.

| 13 Vacuum pump – testing, removal and refitting | 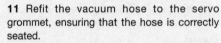 |

Testing

1 The operation of the braking system vacuum pump can be checked using a vacuum gauge.

2 Disconnect the vacuum pipe from the pump, and connect the gauge to the pump union using a suitable length of hose.

3 Start the engine and allow it to idle, and then measure the vacuum created by the pump.

Removal

1 Chock the wheels, to prevent the vehicle from moving and ensure that the handbrake lever is released (off).

2 Lift the plastic cover from the rear of the lever, and prise off the central clip **(see illustrations)**.

3 Disconnect the wiring plugs for the handbrake warning light switch **(see illustration)**.

4 Undo the mounting bolt and remove the handbrake light switch **(see illustration)**.

5 Remove the retaining clip and withdraw the clevis pin to disconnect the front handbrake cable **(see illustrations)**.

6 Depress the tabs to release the handbrake cable from the handbrake mounting **(see illustration)**.

7 Undo the two main mounting bolts and

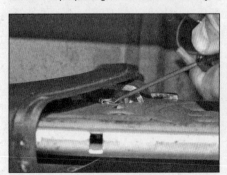

14.5a Release the retaining clip...

14.5b ...and withdraw the clevis pin

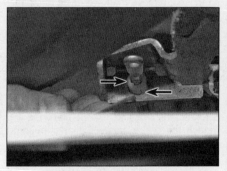

14.6 Depress the tabs and separate the cable from the handbrake

manoeuvre the handbrake lever from place **(see illustration)**.

Refitting

8 Refitting is the reverse of removal, bearing in mind the following points:
a) *Lubricate the end of the handbrake cable and the cable attachment on the lever with grease.*
b) *Tighten the mounting bolts to the specified torque.*
c) *Adjust the handbrake as described in Chapter 1 Section 21.*

15 Handbrake cables and compensator – removal and refitting

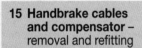

Removal

1 The handbrake cable consists of three sections, a front cable, which connects the handbrake lever to the compensator unit under the centre of the vehicle cable, and two rear cables that link the compensator plate to the rear brake shoes on both sides of the vehicle. Each cable can be removed individually as follows.
2 Chock the front wheels then jack up the rear of the vehicle and securely support it on axle stands (see *Jacking and vehicle support*). Ensure that the handbrake lever is released (off).

Front cable

3 From under the vehicle, slacken the handbrake cable adjuster mechanism by slackening the securing bolts in the compensator plate **(see illustration)**.
4 Release the handbrake cable from the lever on the compensator plate **(see illustration)**.
5 Working inside the vehicle, detach the handbrake inner cable from the lever, as described in Section 14
6 Detach the front cable from the underbody by releasing the securing clip and then withdraw the cable from the vehicle. **Note:** *Check along the length of the cable and release it from any retaining clips/ties.*

Rear cables

7 Remove the handbrake shoes on the relevant side as described in Section 16.
8 Using a pair of long-nose pliers, withdraw the inner cable from the brake shoe linkage.
9 At the rear of the brake backplate, undo the retaining bolt and withdraw the cable from the axle housing **(see illustration)**.
10 Undo the retaining bolt and release the cable support bracket from the rear axle housing.
11 Release the relevant rear cable from the operating lever, and then unclip the outer cable from the mounting bracket. Withdraw the cable from under the vehicle. Check along the length of the cable and release it from any retaining clips/ties.

Refitting

12 Refitting is the reverse of removal, bearing in mind the following points:

14.7 Slacken the bolts and remove the handbrake lever

15.4 Unhook the front handbrake cable from the lever

a) *Lubricate the handbrake cables and compensator mechanism with grease.*
b) *Tighten the mounting bolts to the specified torque.*
c) *Adjust the handbrake as described in Chapter 1 Section 21 on completion.*

16 Handbrake shoes – renewal

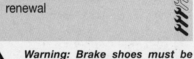

> ⚠ *Warning: Brake shoes must be renewed on BOTH rear wheels at the same time – NEVER renew the shoes on only one wheel, as uneven braking may result. The dust created as the shoes wear may contain asbestos, which is a health hazard. Never blow it out with compressed air, and don't inhale any of it. An approved filtering mask should be worn when working*

16.3 Using long-nose pliers to remove the retaining springs

15.3 Handbrake compensator mounting bolts

15.9 Remove the handbrake cable securing bolt

on the brakes. DO NOT use petroleum-based solvents to clean brake parts – use brake cleaner or methylated spirit only.

Removal

1 Remove the rear brake disc as described in Section 8, making a note of the correct fitted position of all components.
2 Clean off the handbrake shoe assembly using brake cleaner, place rags below the brake assembly to catch any spillage. DO NOT use compressed air to blow out brake dust.
3 Using a pair of long-nose pliers, compress the shoe retaining springs then rotate them through 90° and remove them from the backplate. Access to the springs can be gained through the hub flange holes **(see illustration)**.
4 Prise apart the brake shoes and ease the adjuster from place **(see illustration)**.

16.4 Remove the adjuster from place

16.5 Using long-nose pliers to remove the brake shoe front spring

16.7a Release the ends from the linkage...

16.7b ...and then remove the handbrake shoes

5 Carefully unhook and the handbrake shoe front spring, noting which way round the spring is fitted **(see illustration)**.

6 Working behind the upper brake shoe, prise the spring from place.

7 Free the ends of the shoes from the handbrake linkage plates, and remove the shoes from the vehicle **(see illustrations)**.

8 Inspect the handbrake shoes for signs of wear or contamination, and renew if necessary. It is recommended that the return springs be renewed as a matter of course. Check the shoe friction material thickness; shoes with anything less than the minimum friction material given in this Chapter's Specifications should be renewed.

9 With the shoes removed, clean and inspect the condition of the shoe adjuster and expander mechanisms, and renew them if they show signs of wear or damage. If all is well, apply a fresh coat of brake grease (Mercedes-Benz recommend Molykote Paste U or G-Rapid) to the threads of the adjuster and sliding surfaces of the handbrake linkage plates. Do not allow the grease to contact the shoe friction material.

Refitting

10 Prior to installation, clean the backplate, and apply a thin smear of high-temperature brake grease or anti-seize compound to all those surfaces of the backplate which bear on the shoes. Do not allow the lubricant to foul the friction material.

11 Assemble the shoes and the adjuster mechanism, noting the correct fitted position

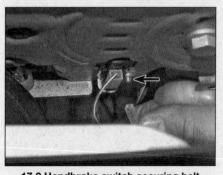

17.2 Handbrake switch securing bolt

as noted on removal. Fully retract the adjuster and fit the return springs.

12 Manoeuvre the assembly into position and fit the shoe return spring, making sure it locates in the shoes securely.

13 Ensure that the shoes are correctly positioned, and secure them with the retaining springs.

14 Check all components are correctly fitted, and centralise the handbrake shoes.

15 Refit the brake disc as described in Section 8. Prior to refitting the roadwheel, check the handbrake adjustment as described in Chapter 1 Section 21.

17 Handbrake warning light switch – removal and refitting

1 Remove the handbrake lever as described in Section 14.

2 Undo the retaining bolt and remove the switch from the handbrake lever bracket **(see illustration)**.

3 Refitting is a reversal of removal.

18 Stop-light switch – removal, refitting and adjustment

Removal

1 The stop-light switch is located above the brake pedal on the mounting bracket in the driver's footwell**(see illustration)**.

18.1 Stop-light switch location

2 Move the driver's seat fully rearward, and if required, remove the lower facia trim panel from under the steering column for easier access to the pedal assembly, with reference to Chapter 11.

3 Turn the switch and remove it from the rear of the pedal mounting bracket.

4 Disconnect the wiring plug from the stop-light switch as it is removed.

Refitting and adjustment

5 Pull the plunger of the switch out to adjust.

6 Reconnect the wiring connector to the switch.

7 Press the brake pedal down, and then insert the stop-light switch into the hole in the pedal mounting bracket, turn the switch to lock it in position.

8 The pedal can now be released, this will settle against the switch at its preset adjustment.

9 Where applicable, refit any facia trim panels, with reference to Chapter 11.

19 Anti-lock Braking and Traction Control systems – general information

⚠ **Warning: Diagnosis of the faults within ABS/ASR/ESP systems requires access to dedicated test equipment. For safety reasons, owners are strongly advised against attempting to investigate complex problems with these systems using standard workshop equipment.**

Note: *On models equipped with traction control, the ABS unit is a dual-function unit, and performs both the anti-lock braking system (ABS) and traction control (ASR) system functions. On models with the Electronic Stability Program (ESP), the ABS unit is also used to modulate the brakes as required.*

Models without traction control (ASR) or ESP

1 The ABS system comprises the following components:

a) *A hydraulic unit, which contains four hydraulic solenoid valves (one for each front brake, and one for each rear brake) and the electrically driven return pump.*

b) *Four road wheel sensors (one for each front wheel, and one for each rear wheel). The sensors for each front wheel are fitted to the hubs, as are the sensors for each rear wheel.*

c) *The electronic control unit (ECU), located in the module box at the right-hand rear of the engine compartment (right as seen from the driver's seat).*

2 The purpose of the system is to prevent the wheel(s) locking during heavy braking and/or slippery road conditions. This is achieved by automatic release of the brake on the relevant wheel, followed by re-application of the brake.

3 The solenoids are controlled by the ECU, which itself receives signals from the wheel sensors, which monitor the speed of rotation of each wheel and can determine the speed at which the vehicle is travelling. It can then use this speed to determine when a wheel is decelerating at an abnormal rate compared to the speed of the vehicle, and therefore predicts when a wheel is about to lock.

4 During normal operation, the system functions in the same way as a non-ABS braking system.

5 If the ECU senses that a wheel is about to lock, it operates the relevant solenoid valve in the hydraulic unit, which then isolates from the master cylinder the relevant brake caliper(s) on the wheel(s) which is/are about to lock – effectively sealing-in the hydraulic pressure.

6 If the speed of rotation of the wheel continues to decrease at an abnormal rate, the ECU switches on the electrically-driven return pump which pumps the hydraulic fluid back into the master cylinder, releasing pressure on the brake caliper(s) so that the brake is released. Once the speed of rotation of the wheel returns to an acceptable rate, the pump stops; the solenoid valve opens, allowing the hydraulic master cylinder pressure to return to the caliper, which then re-applies the brake. This cycle can be carried out at up to 10 times a second.

7 The action of the solenoid valves and return pump creates pulses in the hydraulic circuit. When the ABS system is functioning, these pulses can be felt through the brake pedal.

8 The operation of the ABS system is entirely dependent on electrical signals. To prevent the system responding to any inaccurate signals, a built-in safety circuit monitors all signals received by the ECU. If an inaccurate signal or low battery voltage is detected, the ABS system is automatically shut down, and the warning light on the instrument panel is illuminated to inform the driver that the ABS system is not operational. Normal braking should still be available, however.

9 If a fault does develop in the ABS system, the vehicle must be taken to a Mercedes-Benz dealer for fault diagnosis and repair.

Models with traction control (ASR) and/or ESP

10 On models with traction control (ASR) and/

or the stability program (ESP), the hydraulic unit performs the traction control and stability program functions as well as the anti-lock braking.

11 On models with ASR and/or ESP, a modified hydraulic unit and electronic control unit is fitted. The ABS electronic control unit (ECU) is linked to the engine management ECU, to operate the throttle valve position actuator.

12 The braking side of the system works as described above, and the rear axle speed is monitored solely by the rear wheel ABS sensor(s).

13 The traction control system prevents the rear wheels from losing traction by either gently applying the brake or by closing the throttle valve, depending on the speed of the vehicle. In extreme cases, a combination of both may be used.

14 On the braking side of the system, if a wheel is about to lose traction, the hydraulic unit uses the hydraulic pressure stored in the accumulator to gently apply the brake on the relevant wheel. Once the risk of wheel spin has passed, the hydraulic unit allows the fluid to return to the accumulator and releases the brake, allowing the wheel to rotate freely again.

15 On the throttle side of the system, if traction is about to be lost, the engine management ECM operates the throttle valve actuator and closes the throttle valve, decreasing the engine power output. Once the risk of wheel spin has passed, the actuator returns the throttle valve to its normal position and returns control of the throttle to the driver.

16 On models with the stability program (ESP), the traction control system is further refined to help retain control of the car during cornering. An accelerometer is fitted, which monitors the lateral (cornering) forces on the vehicle. If the vehicle starts to slide sideways, the system reacts by gently applying one of the brakes to help steer the vehicle – if appropriate, the throttle valve is also closed.

17 In the same way as for the ABS, the vehicle must be taken to a Mercedes-Benz dealer for testing if a fault develops in the traction control (ASR) or ESP systems.

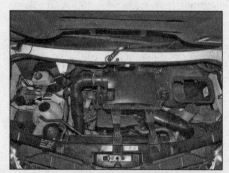

20.3 ABS hydraulic unit location

20 Anti-lock Braking and Traction Control components – removal and refitting

⚠️ *Warning: If any of the ABS system components have been disturbed or renewed, the operation of the system must be verified before the vehicle is brought back into service. This procedure must be carried out using dedicated test equipment, and as such should be entrusted to a Mercedes-Benz dealer.*

Note: *Before starting work, refer to the note at the beginning of Section 2 concerning the dangers of hydraulic fluid.*

Hydraulic unit and ECU

Removal

1 Disconnect the battery negative terminal as described in Chapter 5 Section 3.

2 Remove the master cylinder reservoir cap, and siphon the hydraulic fluid from the reservoir. Alternatively, open the front brake caliper bleed screws, one at a time, and gently pump the brake pedal to expel the fluid through a plastic tube connected to the screw (see Section 2).

Caution: Do not siphon the fluid by mouth, as it is poisonous. Use a syringe or an old hydrometer.

3 The hydraulic unit and ECU located on the right-hand side of the engine compartment, on top of the chassis leg at the front **(see illustration)**.

4 Note and record the fitted position of the brake pipes at the hydraulic unit, and then unscrew the union nuts and release the pipes. As a precaution, place absorbent rags beneath the brake pipe unions when unscrewing them. Suitably plug or cap the disconnected unions to prevent dirt entry and fluid loss.

5 Where fitted, unclip the plastic cover from the ECU and wiring connector. Release the locking lever and disconnect the wiring harness plug from the ECU on the front of the hydraulic unit.

6 Disconnect the wiring connector from the pressure sensor on the rear of the hydraulic unit.

7 Carefully pull the hydraulic unit upwards to release it from the three rubber mountings in the mounting bracket, and then manoeuvre the assembly out from its location in the engine compartment.

Refitting

8 Refitting is the reverse of the removal procedure, noting the following points:

a) *Refit the brake pipes to their respective locations, and tighten the union nuts securely.*

b) *Ensure that the wiring is correctly routed, and that the ECU wiring harness plug is firmly pressed into position and secured locked.*

c) *On completion, reconnect the battery negative terminal, and then bleed the complete hydraulic system as described in Section 2.*

20.24 Front wheel speed sensor

20.29 Unplug the connector for the ABS sensor

20.31 Insert the new speed sensor

Electronic control unit (ECU)

Removal

9 The electronic control unit (ECU) is located on the back of the ABS hydraulic unit.
10 Disconnect the battery negative terminal (refer to *Disconnecting the battery* in the Reference chapter).
11 Where fitted, unclip the plastic cover from the ECU and wiring connector. Release the locking lever and disconnect the wiring harness plug from the ECU on the back of the hydraulic unit.
12 Thoroughly clean the area around the ECU and hydraulic modulator and exercise extreme cleanliness during the following operations.
13 Undo the six securing screws and carefully withdraw the ECU from the ABS hydraulic unit.

Refitting

14 Ensure that the mating faces of the modulator and ECU are clean and dry, do not use any sharp-edged tools for this as damage may occur.
15 Carefully position the ECU on the ABS hydraulic unit; making sure that it is sitting flat. **Note:** *The seal on the rear of the ECU must not be removed, and is part of the control unit.*
16 Refit the securing screws and tighten them progressively.
17 Reconnect the ECU wiring harness plug ensuring it is securely locked in position, taking great care not to damage the contact pins.
18 Refit the plastic cover to the ECU wiring connector (where applicable), and then reconnect the battery negative terminal.

Hydraulic unit pressure sensor

Removal

19 The pressure sensor is located on the rear of the ABS hydraulic unit.
20 Disconnect the battery as described in Chapter 5 Section 3).
21 Disconnect the wiring connector from the pressure sensor.
22 Unscrew the pressure sensor from the hydraulic unit. As a precaution, place absorbent rags beneath the brake pipe unions when unscrewing them. Suitably plug or cap

the hydraulic unit to prevent dirt entry and fluid loss.

Refitting

23 Refitting is the reverse of the removal procedure, noting the following points:
a) *Make sure all threads are clean and undamaged.*
b) *Tighten the sensor to the specified torque setting.*
c) *Ensure that the wiring connector is firmly pressed into position on the sensor.*
d) *Reconnect the battery negative terminal.*
e) *On completion, bleed the hydraulic system as described in Section 2.*

Wheel speed sensors

Removal

24 The front wheel speed sensor is located in the hub assembly at the front of the lower strut mounting **(see illustration)**.
25 The rear wheel speed sensor is located in the halfshaft bearing cover at the top of the rear axle.
26 Apply the handbrake, then jack up the front/rear of the vehicle (depending on which sensor is to be removed) and support it on axle stands (see *Jacking and vehicle support*). Remove the relevant roadwheel.
27 Release the sensor wiring from the retaining brackets on the suspension/rear axle and unclip it from under the wheel arch.
28 Withdraw the sensor from the front hub/axle, this will be a tight fit, so carefully tap the sensor out of position using a puller or drift.
29 Disconnect the wiring plug on the side of the front chassis rail, behind the wheelarch liner **(see illustration)**.
30 Once the sensor has been removed, withdraw the clamping bush from the hub. Discard, as a new sensor and clamping bush will be required for refitting.

Refitting

31 Apply a small amount of acid-free grease (Mercedes-Benz part No A 000 989 62 51 10) to the sides of the speed sensor, and then slide it into the new clamping bush in the hub **(see illustration)**. Press it firmly into position, until it is seated all the way in. **Note:** *The clearance between the sensor and the*

target ring on the hub/halfshaft adjusts itself automatically while driving.
32 The speed sensor wiring can now be reconnected, solder the new sensor wiring to the loom wiring on the vehicle, and cover the soldered joint using a heat-shrink sleeve.
33 Clip the sensor wiring back in position on the suspension strut/rear axle and support brackets under the wheel arch.
34 Refit the roadwheel, then lower the vehicle to the ground and tighten the roadwheel nuts to the specified torque.

Wheel speed sensors target rings

Note: *The speed sensor target rings are a tight fit on the front hub and rear axle halfshafts. They can be removed by using a chisel, but will need to be heated up to approx 180ºc for refitting. Check on the availability of parts before removal.*
35 The front wheel speed sensor target ring is located on the rear of the hub assembly. Remove the front hub assembly, as described in Chapter 10.
36 The rear wheel speed sensor target ring is located in the rear axle halfshaft. Remove the rear axle halfshaft and wheel bearing, as described in Chapter 8.

Lateral acceleration (Yaw rate) sensor

Note: *On models with traction control (ASR) and/or the stability program (ESP), the sensor is located under the driver's front seat.*

Removal

37 Disconnect the battery negative terminal as described in *Disconnecting the battery* Chapter 5 Section 3.
38 Remove the driver's seat, as described in Chapter 11 Section 24.
39 Working inside the rear of the seat base, undo the retaining bolts and move the relay mounting bracket and move it to one side.
40 Note the direction arrow on the sensor for refitting. Undo the two retaining bolts from the sensor, disconnect the wiring connector, and then remove it from the vehicle.

Refitting

41 Refitting is a reversal of removal.

Chapter 10
Suspension and steering

Contents

Degrees of difficulty

Easy, suitable for novice with little experience	Fairly easy, suitable for beginner with some experience 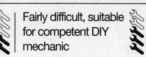	Fairly difficult, suitable for competent DIY mechanic	Difficult, suitable for experienced DIY mechanic	Very difficult, suitable for expert DIY or professional

Specifications

Front suspension

Type . . . . Transverse leaf spring inside the front subframe, telescopic shock absorbers and anti-roll bar connected to lower suspension arms by connecting links

Front spring (depending on model):
  Spring length . . . . 1350 mm
  Number of leaves . . . . 1 or 2
  Leaf thickness (measured at centre):
    GRP spring x 1 . . . . 29.0 mm
  Spring travel (per 1000N load):
    GRP spring x 1 . . . . 3.6 mm

Rear suspension

Type . . . . Semi-floating hypoid axle supported on semi-elliptic springs, telescopic shock absorbers and anti-roll bar connected to chassis by connecting links

Rear spring length (installed dimension – including shackle). . . . . 1469 mm

Steering

Type . . . . Hydraulic power-assisted steering with rack-and-pinion, with adjustable tie rods
Filling capacity . . . . 1.0 litre
Fluid type . . . . See *Lubricants and fluids* on page 0•16

Torque wrench settings

	Nm	lbf ft
Front suspension		
Anti-roll bar clamp bolts....................................	30	22
Anti-roll bar link arm retaining nuts*............................	106	78
Brake caliper mounting bracket bolts (M14 x 1.5):		
Stage 1..	80	60
Stage 2..	Angle-tighten a further 40°	
Spring lower clamp plate to front subframe (M12 bolt):		
Stage 1..	106	78
Stage 2..	Angle-tighten a further 90°	
Spring upper stop-plate to lower arm:		
M10 bolt...	58	43
M12 x 1.5 bolt		
Stage 1..	106	78
Stage 2..	Angle-tighten a further 90°	
Steering knuckle balljoint-to-lower suspension arm nut *..........	170	125
Subframe mounting bolts...................................	125	92
Suspension lower arm mounting bolt/nuts:		
Stage 1..	172	126
Stage 2..	Angle-tighten a further 90°	
Suspension strut flange upper retaining bolts: *		
Stage 1..	28	21
Stage 2..	Angle-tighten a further 60°	
Suspension strut-to-steering knuckle bolts/nuts: *		
Stage 1..	140	103
Stage 2..	Angle-tighten a further 120°	
Rear suspension		
Anti-roll bar clamp-to-rear axle bolts:		
Stage 1..	100	74
Stage 2..	Angle-tighten a further 60°	
Anti-roll bar link arm-to-chassis securing bolts..................	106	74
Leaf spring centre (M10) bolt...............................	42	31
Leaf spring-to-spring shackle at front:		
M12 x 1.5 bolt		
Stage 1..	60	44
Stage 2..	Angle-tighten a further 180°	
M16 x 1.5 bolt..	240	177
Leaf spring-to-spring shackle at rear:		
M12 x 1.5 bolt..	85	63
M16 x 1.5 bolt..	240	177
Leaf spring shackle-to-spring bracket at rear:		
M12 x 1.5 bolt:		
Stage 1..	70	52
Stage 2..	Angle-tighten a further 180°	
M16 x 1.5 bolt..	240	177
Shock absorber lower mounting nut/bolts:		
M12 x 1.5 (10.9) nut/bolt:		
Stage 1..	90	66
Stage 2..	Angle-tighten a further 90°	
M14 x 1.5 bolt..	135	100
Shock absorber upper mounting nut/bolts....................	135	100
Spring-to-axle U-bolt nuts.................................	160	118
Steering		
Power steering fluid pipes to steering gear...................	42	31
Power steering pump attachments:		
High-pressure pipe union................................	38	28
Mounting bolts.......................................	20	14
Pulley retaining bolts.................................	25	18
Steering column retaining bolts.............................	25	18
Steering column UJ-to-steering gear pinion shaft pinch-bolt*.......	28	20
Steering gear-to-front subframe bolts*:		
Stage 1..	25	18
Stage 2..	80	59
Stage 3..	Angle-tighten a further 90°	
Steering wheel retaining bolt*..............................	80	59
Track rod end balljoint nut:		
Stage 1..	50	37
Stage 2..	Angle-tighten a further 60°	

Torque wrench settings (continued)

	Nm	lbf ft
Roadwheels		
Roadwheel nuts:		
Steel rims	240	177
Aluminium rims	180	133

* Use new nuts/bolts

---

1 General Information

1 The independent front suspension is of the transverse leaf spring type, which is fitted across the inside of the front subframe. Telescopic shock absorbers are bolted to the top of the steering knuckle and are mounted under the wheel arch to the vehicle body by an upper rubber mounting point. Lower suspension arms are connected to the front subframe by rubber mounting bushes, and to the steering knuckle by a balljoint. The front steering knuckles, which carry the hub bearings, brake calipers and disc assemblies, are bolted to the front shock absorbers, and connected to the lower arms via the balljoints. A front anti-roll bar is fitted, which has link arms at each end to connect to the lower suspension arms.

2 The rear axle is a live axle suspended on semi-elliptic leaf springs and utilising telescopic shock absorbers to provide the damping for the axle assembly. Further information and procedures relating to the rear axle assembly are contained in Chapter 8.

3 The steering column incorporates a universal joint at the lower end, which is connected to the steering gear pinion shaft. The steering gear is mounted on the front subframe, and is connected by two tie rods and track rod ends to the steering arms, which project forwards from the steering knuckles. The track rod ends are threaded to enable wheel alignment adjustment.

4 Power steering is fitted to all models and is driven by the auxiliary drivebelt on the front of the engine. The system has a fluid cooler, which is a loop of metal pipe that is located in front of the cooling system radiator.

2 Steering knuckle and bearing – removal and refitting

Removal

Note: *At the time of writing Mercedes offers the steering knuckle and wheel bearing as one complete unit only. However, the wheel bearing is available separately from aftermarket suppliers, which may prove more cost-effective for those running a fleet of such vehicles. Unfortunately, replacing the bearing on its own necessitates the use of expensive specialist equipment, rendering it uneconomical for the home mechanic.*

1 Remove the front brake disc as described in Chapter 9 Section 5.

2 On vehicles with ABS, remove the wheel speed sensor as described in Chapter 9, Section 20.

3 Slacken the track rod end balljoint nut several turns, then use a balljoint separator tool to release the balljoint shank from the steering arm. With the balljoint released, unscrew the nut and disconnect the balljoint from the steering arm **(see illustrations)**. Discard the nut, as a new one must be used for refitting.

4 Slacken the nut securing the steering knuckle balljoint to the lower suspension arm **(see illustrations)**. Strike the end of the lower suspension arm with a hammer a few times to see if you can shock-free the balljoint shank taper. If this is unsuccessful, attach a suitable puller to the lower suspension arm and tighten the puller to apply tension to the balljoint shank. Once more, strike the end of the lower suspension arm with a hammer a few times to shock-free the balljoint shank taper.

2.3a Undo the retaining nut...

2.3b ...then unscrew the retaining bolt and remove the shield

2.3c Using a separator tool, release the balljoint taper

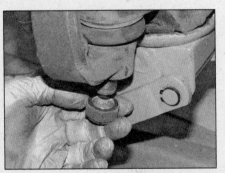

2.4a Undo the lower arm balljoint nut...

2.4b ...then use a separator to release the joint

2.4c Mark the position of the bolts

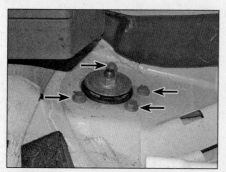

2.5 Suspension strut lower mounting bolts/ nuts

5 Unscrew and remove the bolts/nuts securing the steering knuckle assembly to the front suspension strut **(see illustration)**. Note that new bolts and nuts will be required upon reassembly.

6 The steering knuckle can now be moved downwards, to disengage it from the lower arm balljoint. Remove the knuckle from the vehicle.

Refitting

7 Thoroughly clean the bottom end of the suspension strut and its location to the steering knuckle. Locate the knuckle onto the lower arm balljoint and fit the securing nut a couple of threads.

8 Locate the knuckle onto the strut, and then insert the new mounting bolts from the front, ensuring that the new nuts are on the brake caliper side. Tighten the nuts (the replacement

bolts are eccentric to allow camber adjustment and should not be moved), but not yet to the specified torque. The final tightening should be performed after the vehicle is on its wheels and an alignment check is carried out. There are a number of cost-effective tools available from online suppliers to allow you to do this. Alternatively, sit a metal bar across the wheel center flange and mark where the bar meets the floor, the camber can then be adjusted (using the new replacement bolt with the cam) back to that position. **Note:** *In order to access the nuts, the brake caliper must be moved to one side as described in Chapter 9 Section 6. There's no need to disconnect the brake pipes.*

9 Push down on the lower suspension arm and engage the steering knuckle balljoint with the arm. The new balljoint retaining nut can now be tightened to the specified torque.

10 Locate the track rod end balljoint on the steering arm. Screw on a new nut and tighten it to the specified torque. If the balljoint shank is hollow, an Allen key can be used to prevent the balljoint from rotating as the nut is tightened. If the shank is solid, use a stout bar to lever up on the underside of the track rod end. This will lock the balljoint shank taper in the steering arm and prevent rotation as the nut is tightened.

11 On vehicles with ABS, refit the wheel speed sensor as described in Chapter 9, Section 20.

12 The remainder of refitting is a reversal of removal. Have the front wheel alignment checked at the earliest opportunity.

3 Front suspension strut – removal and refitting

Removal

1 Firmly apply the handbrake, and then jack up the front of the vehicle and support it securely on axle stands as described in *Jacking and vehicle support*. Remove the roadwheel.

2 Undo the nuts and clips and remove both parts of the wheelarch liner.

3 Working inside the vehicle the passenger compartment, remove the floor mat and plastic trim to access the 4 upper mounting bolts **(see illustration)**. **Note:** *On the passenger side, remove the cover from the vehicle jack and tools to access the retaining nut. On the driver's side, it may be necessary to undo the retaining screws and remove the accelerator pedal.*

4 Slacken the suspension strut upper mounting bolts, but do not remove them completely at this stage.

5 Unclip the wiring from the bracket on the lower part of the suspension strut **(see illustration)**.

6 Prior to undoing the strut lower mounting bolts/nuts, position a straight edge across the hub face, and make an alignment mark on the floor **(see illustration)**. This will greatly assist restoring the camber angle to the pre-dismantled position.

7 Undo the suspension strut lower mounting bolts from the steering knuckle. Note that new bolts and nuts will be required upon reassembly.

8 When the bolts are removed, support the steering knuckle and tie it using a strong cable or wire, to prevent damage to the brake hose **(see illustration)**.

9 The upper suspension bolts can now be completely removed, and then have an assistant lower the strut to remove it from under the vehicle **(see illustration)**. Discard the bolts – new ones must be fitted during reassembly.

Refitting

10 Lift the suspension strut into position and

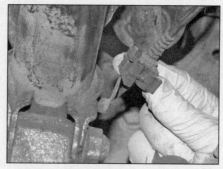

3.3 Suspension strut upper retaining bolts

3.5 Unclip the wiring from the bottom of the strut

3.6 With a straight-edge in position, make an alignment mark on the floor

3.8 Tie the steering knuckle to avoid brake hose damage

3.9 Withdraw the strut from under the wheel arch

insert the upper mounting through the hole in the body. Then with the aid of an assistant, screw on the upper mounting bolts and tighten them to the specified torque.

11 Thoroughly clean the bottom end of the suspension strut and its location to the steering knuckle. Locate the strut onto the steering knuckle and insert the retaining bolts.

12 If a camber angle alignment mark was made during removal, use the straight-edge again to position the hub. If no mark was made, inexpensive camber angle gauges are available **(see illustration)**.

13 Holding the strut-to-steering knuckle bolt to prevent rotation, fit the new nuts and tighten them to the specified torque.

14 Clip the wiring back into the bracket on the lower part of the suspension strut.

15 Working inside the passenger compartment, refit the plastic trims and floor mat. **Note:** *On the passenger side, refit the cover to the vehicle jack and tools. On the driver's side, refit the accelerator pedal, where removed.*

16 Refit the roadwheel, and then lower the vehicle to the ground. Tighten the roadwheel bolts to the specified torque. Have the front wheel alignment checked at the earliest opportunity

4 Front suspension lower arm – removal and refitting

Removal

1 Firmly apply the handbrake, and then jack up the front of the vehicle and support it securely on axle stands as described in *Jacking and vehicle support*. Remove the roadwheel.

2 Remove the steering knuckle as described in Section 2. If the lower balljoint is a tight fit in the steering knuckle, it can be removed with the lower arm.

3 With the jack still in position under the lower arm, undo the 4 retaining bolts and remove the spring stop-plate from the top of the lower suspension arm **(see illustrations)**.

4 Lower the jack from under the lower arm, and then remove the bush from the end of the spring **(see illustration)**.

5 Slacken the front and rear mounting bolts/ nuts and withdraw the lower arm from the subframe **(see illustration)**.

6 If the steering knuckle is still attached to the lower arm, slacken the nut securing the steering knuckle balljoint to the lower suspension arm, until it is at the end of the threads. Attach a two-legged puller to the lower part of the steering knuckle, and tighten the puller to apply tension to the balljoint shank. If a puller is not available, strike the end of the balljoint with a hammer a few times to shock-free the balljoint shank taper. Fit the nut to the end of the balljoint to prevent the threads getting damaged.

3.12 This type of camber angle gauge attaches to the disc face with a magnet

Refitting

7 Locate the lower arm in position in the subframe and fit new retaining nuts/bolts. Do not tighten fully at this point.

8 Place a jack under the lower arm, and lift it into position under the end of the spring, refitting the bush at the end of the spring.

9 Refit the upper spring stop-plate to the top of the lower suspension arm and fit new retaining bolts. Tighten to the specified torque setting.

10 Refit the steering knuckle as described in Section 2.

11 Refit the roadwheel, and then lower the vehicle to the ground and tighten the roadwheel nuts to the specified torque.

12 Finally, with the weight of the vehicle back on its wheels, tighten the lower arm-to-subframe mounting bolts to the specified torque.

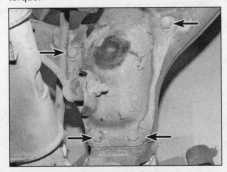

4.3a Undo the retaining bolts...

4.4 When free, remove the bush from the end of the spring

5 Lower suspension arm balljoint – renewal

1 Remove the lower suspension arm as described in Section 4.

2 Place the lower arm over a strong bench vice, with the sides resting on the top of the vice jaws.

3 Using a hammer, firmly tap the top of the balljoint and drift it out of the lower suspension arm.

4 Clean the balljoint locating area in the lower arm and remove any burrs that might hinder refitting.

5 Lubricate the balljoint locating area in the arm with multipurpose grease

6 Place the new balljoint in the jaws of the vice, taking care not to damage the balljoint rubber boot.

7 Fit the lower arm squarely onto the ball-joint and tap the lower arm onto the balljoint. Use a large socket to fit the new balljoint back into position in the lower arm.

8 Refit the lower suspension arm as described in Section 4.

6 Front anti-roll bar and link arms – removal, overhaul and refitting

Removal

1 Firmly apply the handbrake, and then jack up the front of the vehicle and support

4.3b ...and remove the spring stop-plate

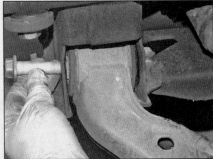

4.5 Remove the lower suspension arm

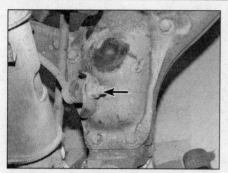

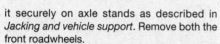

6.2 Undo the nut to disconnect the anti-roll bar link

6.5 Anti-roll bar clamp retaining bolt

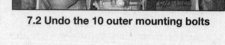

7.2 Undo the 10 outer mounting bolts

it securely on axle stands as described in *Jacking and vehicle support*. Remove both the front roadwheels.

2 Undo the retaining nuts and disconnect the anti-roll bar link from the lower suspension stop-plates on both sides of the vehicle **(see illustration)**. Apply a small amount of penetrating oil onto the bush to aid removal.

3 Remove the left-hand lower control arm, as described in Section 4.

4 Gradually undo the 10 retaining bolts for the subframe clamp plates, as described in Section 7.

5 Undo the two bolts (one at each side) securing the anti-roll bar clamps to the subframe **(see illustration)**.

6 Unclip the upper part of the clamps from the subframe and then remove the anti-roll bar out from the bottom of the vehicle.

Overhaul

7 With the anti-roll bar removed, check the condition of the mounting bushes and renew as necessary.

8 To remove the link arms from the end of the anti-roll bar, use a balljoint splitter (or similar). Tighten the tool and withdraw the link arms from the end of the anti-roll bar.

9 If new bushes are required, remove the old bushes from the link arms by using a screwdriver to release them. To fit new bushes, lubricate the bushes with oil, and then press them firmly into position in the link arms.

10 To fit new clamp bushes to the anti-roll bar, remove the clamps from the rubber bush

and then remove the bush from the anti-roll bar. Clean the rubber bush locating area on the anti-roll bar and remove any burrs. Fit the new bush in place around the anti-roll bar, and fit the clamp back in position.

Refitting

11 Refitting is a reversal of removal, tightening all fastenings to the specified torque.

7   Front transverse leaf spring
    – removal and refitting

Removal

1 Firmly apply the handbrake, and then jack up the front of the vehicle and support it securely on axle stands as described in *Jacking and vehicle support*). Remove both the front roadwheels.

2 Partially undo the 10 front and rear retaining bolts for the two spring clamp plates under the front subframe **(see illustration)**. Do this gradually because the subframe will be under tension and removing the bolts one at a time could damage the threads.

3 Fully remove the 10 bolts.

4 Slacken the top retaining bolt and detach the torsion link bar from the anti-roll bar.

5 Detach the stop plate from the left and right lower control arms as described in Section 4.

6 Remove the left-hand lower control arm as described in Section 4.

7 With the aid of an assistant, lower the

spring from under the subframe and withdraw it through the front-left wheel opening.

8 It is possible to perform this procedure without removing the steering knuckle. Slacken the spring clamp plates, remove the stop plates and remove the lower arm's pivot bolts, but we advise caution because there is a chance the spring could still be under slight tension at this point.

Refitting

9 Refitting is a reversal of removal, using new nuts/bolts where applicable, and tightening all fastenings to the specified torque.

8   Rear axle leaf spring –
    removal, overhaul and refitting

Removal

1 Chock the front wheels then jack up the rear of the vehicle and securely support it on axle stands, as described in *Jacking and vehicle support*.

2 Support the rear axle with a trolley jack and remove the rear roadwheels.

3 Undo the retaining nuts, and remove the spring-to-axle U-bolts and fittings each side **(see illustration)**. Discard the nuts, as new ones must be used for refitting.

4 Unscrew and remove the front mounting and rear mounting retaining nuts, and drive out the mounting bolts with a soft metal drift **(see illustrations)**. Discard the bolts/nuts, as new ones must be used for refitting.

8.3 Remove the U-bolts and upper mounting plate

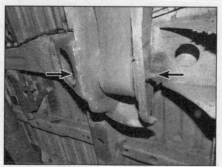

8.4a Remove the front...

8.4b ...and rear spring shackle bolts

5 The rear spring can now be lifted from the rear axle and withdrawn from beneath the vehicle. If necessary, lower the rear axle on the trolley jack to allow the leaf spring to be removed, making sure that the brake hoses and handbrake cables are not damaged.

6 Examine the front and rear mounting bushes/shackle, and check the condition of the U-bolts and spring leaves; renew any faulty components.

Overhaul

7 With the leaf spring removed, check the condition of the mounting bushes and shackle bushes, renew as necessary.

8 If new bushes are required, remove the old bushes from the leaf spring, by using a threaded rod, washers and a length of tube to fit over the end of the eye on the leaf spring. Tighten the nuts on the threaded rod to push the bush out from the leaf spring.

9 To fit new bushes, lubricate the bushes with oil, and then press them firmly into position using the threaded rod, nuts and washers, as used on removal.

Refitting

10 Refitting is a reversal of removal, but note the following additional points:
Before refitting the leaf spring, check the dimension of the rear spring including shackle as specified in the specifications **(see illustration)**.

a) *Make sure the locating peg on the underside of the leaf spring is located in the axle when fitting.*

b) *Use new retaining nuts on the spring-to-axle U-bolts and the spring mounting bolts.*

c) *Tighten all nuts and bolts to the specified torque, noting that the mounting bolt nuts must not be fully tightened until after the vehicle is lowered to the ground.*

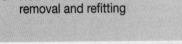

9 Rear shock absorber –
removal and refitting

Note: *The upper mounting bolts can become seized in the chassis and may break, it is recommended that new bolts/nuts be used on refitting.*

Removal

1 Chock the front wheels then jack up the rear of the vehicle and securely support it on axle stands as described in *Jacking and vehicle support*.

2 Support the rear axle with a trolley jack.

3 Undo the retaining nut, and withdraw the shock absorber lower mounting bolt **(see illustration)**.

4 On the right-hand unit, unscrew the upper mounting bolt and remove the shock absorber **(see illustration)**.

5 On the left-hand rear shock absorber, release the securing clip, unhook the return

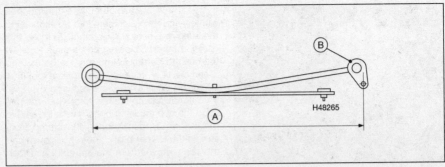

8.10 Before fitting the rear spring, set shackle (B) to installed dimension of spring (A)

spring and remove the load sensing lever from the shock absorber upper mounting bolt. Then unscrew the upper mounting bolt and remove the shock absorber.

6 To test the shock absorber for efficiency, grip the upper or lower mounting eye in a vice, and then pump the piston repeatedly through its full stroke. If the resistance is weak or is felt to be uneven, the shock absorber is defective and must be renewed. It must also be renewed if it is leaking fluid. It is advisable to renew both rear shock absorbers at the same time, or the handling characteristics of the vehicle could be adversely affected.

Refitting

7 Refitting is a reversal of removal. Ensure that the mounting bolts are tightened to the specified torque.

10 Rear anti-roll bar
and link arms –
removal, overhaul and refitting

Note: *Mercedes-Benz special tool (601 589 04 43 00) is required, or a tapered sleeve manufactured to aid refitting.*

Removal

1 Firmly apply the handbrake, and then jack up the rear of the vehicle and support it securely on axle stands, as described in *Jacking and vehicle support*. Remove both the rear roadwheels.

2 Unscrew the nut and bolt from each side and detach the anti-roll bar connecting links from the vehicle chassis **(see illustration)**.

3 Undo the mounting bolts (two bolts each side) and release the anti-roll bar clamps from the rear axle **(see illustration)**. Note the

9.3 Undo the lower mounting bolt...

9.4 ...and upper mounting bolt

10.2 Disconnect the anti-roll bar connecting links from the chassis

10.3 Rear anti-roll bar clamp retaining bolts

10.6 Disconnect the connecting links from the anti-roll bar

fitted position of the handbrake cable support brackets on the lower bolts for refitting.
4 Manoeuvre the anti-roll bar out from under the rear of the vehicle, releasing it from the handbrake cables. Take care not to stretch or damage the cables as the anti-roll bar is withdrawn.

Overhaul

5 With the anti-roll bar removed, check the condition of the mounting bushes and renew as necessary.
6 To remove the link arms from the end of the anti-roll bar, undo the nut and bolt at each end of the anti-roll bar **(see illustration)**.
7 If new bushes are required, remove the old bushes by using a threaded rod, washers and a length of tube (large socket) to fit over the end of the eye. Tighten the nuts on the threaded rod to push the bush out from the anti-roll bar/link arms.

11.3 Unscrew the retaining bolt securing the steering wheel to the column

12.2 Remove the trim ring from the switch

8 To fit new bushes, lubricate the bushes with oil, and then pull them into position using threaded rod, nuts and washers. To make this easier, a tapered sleeve can be used to allow the bush to be drawn into the eye on the end of the bar. A Mercedes-Benz special tool (601 589 04 43 00) is available, if required.
9 To fit new clamp bushes to the anti-roll bar, undo the two retaining bolts/nuts and remove the flat plate, then remove the clamp from around the rubber bush. The rubber bush can then be removed from the anti-roll bar. Clean the rubber bush locating area on the anti-roll bar and remove any burrs. Fit the new bush in place around the anti-roll bar, and fit the clamp back in position.

Refitting

10 Refitting is a reversal of removal, tightening all fastenings to the specified torque.

---

11 Steering wheel – removal and refitting

⚠️ *Warning: Make sure that the airbag safety recommendations given in Chapter 12 are followed, to prevent personal injury.*

Removal

1 Remove the drivers airbag as described in Chapter 12 Section 22.
2 Set the front wheels in the straight-ahead position, and then remove the ignition key to lock the column in position.

11.4 Align the alignment marks. If no such marks are visible, mark wheel and column shaft with quick-drying paint

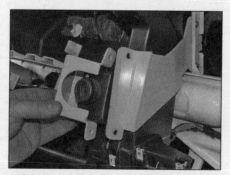

12.4 Use a saw and molegrips to remove the security bracket

3 Unscrew the Allen bolt securing the steering wheel to the column **(see illustration)**.
4 Check that there are alignment marks between the steering column shaft and steering wheel. If no marks are visible, suitably mark the wheel and column shaft with quick-drying paint to ensure correct alignment when refitting **(see illustration)**.
5 Refit the Allen bolt a couple of threads and then grip the steering wheel with both hands and carefully rock it from side-to-side to release it from the splines on the steering column. When released from the splines, remove the Allen bolt fully. As the steering wheel is being removed, guide any wiring (where applicable) through the aperture in the wheel, taking care not to damage the wiring connectors.

Refitting

6 Refit the steering wheel, aligning the marks made prior to removal. Where applicable, route the wiring connectors through the steering wheel aperture. **Note:** *Make sure the airbag/horn wiring is routed correctly. If necessary, refer to the procedures contained in Chapter 12.*
7 Clean the threads in the steering column, then fit the new Allen bolt, and tighten to the specified torque.
8 Release the steering lock, and refit the airbag as described in Chapter 12 Section 22.

---

12 Ignition switch/ steering column lock – removal and refitting

Removal

1 Disconnect the battery negative lead as described in Chapter 5 Section 3.
2 Unscrew the trim ring from around the ignition switch in the facia **(see illustration)**.
3 Remove the instrument cluster panel as described in Chapter 12 Section 5.
4 If your vehicle's ignition has an aftermarket security bracket, as ours did, use a hacksaw and molegrips to remove the shear bolts **(see illustration)**.
5 Manoeuvre the ignition switch from place and disconnect the wiring plug **(see illustration)**.

12.5 Remove the switch and unplug the wiring connector

Refitting

6 Refitting is a reversal of removal.

13 Steering column – removal and refitting

Removal

1 Remove the steering wheel, as described in Section 11.

2 Remove the steering column shrouds and trim panels, as described in Chapter 11.

3 Remove the clock spring/angle sensor and combination switches, as described in Chapter 12.

4 Remove the driver's side central airvent cover, as described in Chapter 11 Section 26.

5 Remove the instrument cluster and surround, as described in Chapter 11 Section 26.

6 Disconnect the wiring plugs from the steering column.

7 Slacken the retaining bolts at the steering column bracket **(see illustration)** and lower the column out of the way.

8 Working inside the engine compartment, undo the pinch-bolt securing the steering column to the steering rack. Note the fitted position, by marking the universal joint and steering rack pinion, and then slide the universal joint from the steering rack pinion. Note that a new pinch-bolt will be required for refitting.

9 Working inside the vehicle, remove the column from vehicle, withdrawing the rubber gaiter from the floor panel.

Refitting

10 Refitting is a reversal of removal, but note the following additional points:

a) *Ensure that both the steering column and roadwheels are centralised when refitting the universal joint to the rack pinion in the position noted on removal secure with a new pinch-bolt.*

b) *Tighten all fastenings to the specified torque.*

c) *Refit the steering wheel as described in Section 12.*

d) *Refit the steering column shrouds and trim panels as described in Chapter 11.*

e) *Refit the fusebox, clock spring/angle sensor and switches as described in Chapter 12.*

f) *Ensure that all wiring is securely connected and correctly routed.*

14 Steering gear – removal and refitting

Removal

1 Disconnect the battery negative lead as described in Chapter 5 Section 3.

2 Set the front wheels in the straight-ahead

13.7 Undo the bolts holding the column to the facia support

position, and then remove the ignition key to lock the column in position.

3 Firmly apply the handbrake, and then jack up the front of the vehicle and support it securely on axle stands, as described in *Jacking and vehicle support*. Remove both front roadwheels.

4 Slacken the track rod end balljoint nut several turns, then use a balljoint separator tool to release the balljoint shank from the steering arm. With the balljoint released, unscrew the nut and disconnect the balljoint from the steering arm on both sides **(see illustration)**. Discard the nut, as a new one must be used for refitting. Note the position of the track rod end locknut by counting the number of threads from the nut face to the end of the track rod. Record this figure, then unscrew and remove the locknut.

5 Unlock the steering and turn it all the way to the right.

14.4 Using the separator tool to release the balljoint taper

14.8 Disconnect the fluid pipes from the steering rack

6 Undo the pinch bolt and separate the steering rack from the steering column. Note the fitted position by marking the universal joint and steering rack pinion, and then slide the universal joint from the steering rack pinion. Note that a new pinch-bolt will be required for refitting.

7 Undo the retaining bolts and detach the high-pressure pipe clamp **(see illustration)**.

8 Thoroughly clean the area around the fluid pipe connections on the steering gear **(see illustration)**. Place a suitable container beneath the steering gear, then unscrew the retaining nuts and withdraw the pipes from the pinion housing. Allow the fluid to drain into the container as the pipes are released. Cover the pipe ends and steering gear orifices after disconnection, to prevent the ingress of foreign matter.

9 Undo the 10 retaining bolts and remove both front spring clamp plates from the bottom of the subframe.

10 Undo the four bolts securing the steering gear to the front subframe **(see illustration)**, noting the position of the hose retaining bracket on the upper left-hand mounting bolt. Discard the mounting bolts, as a new ones must be used for refitting.

11 Manoeuvre the steering gear from place.

Refitting

12 Refitting is a reversal of removal, but note the following additional points:

a) *Ensure that both the steering wheel and steering gear are centralised when refitting the intermediate shaft flexible coupling to the steering gear pinion.*

14.7 Slacken the bolts and remove the clamp

14.10 Undo the power steering rack mounting bolts

b) If a new steering gear unit is being fitted, the straight-ahead position can be ascertained by halving the number of turns necessary to move the rack from lock-to-lock.

c) Use new bolts for the steering gear, universal joint pinch-bolt and track rod end balljoints.

d) Tighten all fastenings to the specified torque.

e) Fill and bleed the power steering hydraulic system as described in Section 19.

f) Have the front wheel alignment checked and adjusted at the earliest opportunity.

15 Steering gear rubber gaiters – renewal

1 Remove the track rod end as described in Section 16.

2 Note the position of the track rod end locknut by counting the number of threads from the nut face to the end of the track rod. Record this figure, then unscrew and remove the locknut.

3 Remove the clips, and slide the gaiter from the track rod and steering gear housing.

4 Slide the new gaiter over the track rod, and onto the steering gear. Where applicable, make sure that the gaiter locates in the cut-outs provided in the track rod and steering gear housing.

5 Fit and tighten the clips, ensuring that the gaiter is not twisted.

6 Screw the track rod end locknut onto the

16.3 Use the separator tool to release the balljoint taper

track rod, and position it with the exact number of threads exposed as noted during removal.

7 Refit the track rod end as described in Section 16.

16 Track rod end – removal and refitting

Removal

1 Firmly apply the handbrake, and then jack up the front of the vehicle and support it securely on axle stands, as described in *Jacking and vehicle support*. Remove the relevant front roadwheel.

2 Loosen the track rod end securing locknut on the track rod a quarter turn, while holding the track rod stationary with a second spanner

on the flats provided. If necessary, use a wire brush to remove rust from the nut and threads and lubricate the threads with penetrating oil before unscrewing the nut. As an additional check, measure the visible amount of threads on the track rod using vernier calipers. This will ensure the track rod end is refitted in the same position.

3 Slacken the track rod end balljoint nut several turns, then use a balljoint separator tool to release the balljoint shank from the steering arm **(see illustration)**. With the balljoint released, unscrew the nut and disconnect the balljoint from the steering arm. Discard the nut, as a new one must be used for refitting.

4 Unscrew the track rod end from the track rod, counting the number of turns necessary to remove it and taking care not to disturb the locknut.

Refitting

5 Screw the new track rod end onto the track rod the exact number of turns as noted during removal.

6 Engage the track rod end balljoint shank in the steering arm, and screw on the new retaining nut. Tighten the nut to the specified torque. If the shank of the balljoint turns, use an Allen key to hold it still while tightening the securing nut.

7 Tighten the track rod end locknut.

8 Refit the roadwheel, then lower the vehicle to the ground, and tighten the roadwheel nuts to the specified torque.

9 Have the front wheel alignment checked and adjusted at the earliest opportunity.

17 Power steering pump – removal and refitting

Removal

1 Open the bonnet and siphon off as much of the power steering fluid from the reservoir as possible, taking care not to introduce dirt into the system **(see illustration)**.

2 Remove the air filter housing, as described in Chapter 4A Section 2, and lift off the engine trim panel.

3 Remove the auxiliary drivebelt as described in Chapter 1 Section 8.

4 Unclip the vacuum lines from around the edge of the power steering fluid tank **(see illustration)**.

5 Wipe clean the area around the pump union, undo the securing nut and disconnect the high-pressure pipe from the pump **(see illustration)**. Discard the sealing ring from the high-pressure pipe, as new one will be required for refitting.

6 Slacken the retaining clip and disconnect the return hose from the bottom of the fluid reservoir **(see illustration)**.

7 Slacken and remove the two front power steering pump mounting bolts, and the one

17.1 Siphon out as much fluid as you can

17.4 Unclip the vacuum lines from the reservoir

17.5 Disconnect the high-pressure pipe from the pump

17.6 Unscrew the clip from the return hose

behind the pump, then remove the pump assembly from the engine compartment **(see illustrations)**.

Refitting

8 If the power steering pump is faulty, seek the advice of your Mercedes-Benz dealer as to the availability of spare parts. If spares are available, it may be possible to have the pump overhauled by a suitable specialist or alternately obtain an exchange unit. If not, the pump must be renewed.

9 Refit the pump and tighten the mounting bolts to the specified torque.

10 Reconnect the high-pressure pipe and return hose/pipe, tightening the union nuts to the specified torque. Use new sealing rings, where applicable.

11 If removed, refit the pulley to the power steering pump, making sure it is fitted the correct way round and tighten the retaining bolts to the specified torque.

12 Fit the drivebelt and tension as described in Chapter 1 Section 8.

13 On completion, refill the reservoir and bleed the hydraulic system as described in Section 19.

18 Power steering fluid cooler – removal and refitting

Removal

1 The power steering fluid cooler is a loop of metal pipe that is located above the intercooler, in front of the radiator **(see illustration)**.

2 Undo the retaining screws and remove the front grille, with reference to Chapter 11.

3 Position a suitable container beneath the fluid cooler, and then detach the two fluid hoses from the left-hand side of the cooler.

4 Release the retaining clips and disconnect the fluid hoses from the cooler pipe. Allow the surplus fluid to drain into the container. Cover the hose ends and fluid cooler orifices after disconnection to prevent the ingress of foreign matter.

5 Undo the fluid cooler pipe retaining clamp screws and manoeuvre the cooler pipe out from its location **(see illustrations)**.

17.7a Undo the two front power steering pump mounting bolts...

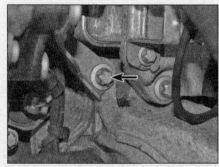

17.7b ...and the rearmost bolt (arrowed)

Refitting

6 Refitting is a reversal of removal. On completion, fill and bleed the power steering hydraulic system as described in Section 19.

19 Power steering hydraulic system – bleeding

1 This will normally only be required if any part of the hydraulic system has been disconnected.

2 Referring to *Weekly checks*, remove the fluid reservoir filler cap, and top-up with the specified fluid to the maximum level mark.

3 Firmly apply the handbrake, and then jack up the front of the vehicle and support it securely on axle stands (see *Jacking and vehicle support*).

4 With the engine switched off, slowly turn the steering wheel from lock-to-lock several times, adding fluid to the reservoir as necessary. Continue turning the steering wheel from lock-to-lock until the fluid level in the reservoir stops dropping. Do not hold the wheel on either lock, as this imposes strain on the hydraulic system.

5 Start the engine and allow it to idle, then slowly turn the steering wheel from lock-to-lock several times, adding fluid to the reservoir as necessary. Continue turning the steering wheel from lock-to-lock until the fluid level in the reservoir stops dropping. Do not hold the wheel on either lock, as this imposes strain on the hydraulic system.

6 Stop the engine, lower the vehicle to the ground and recheck the fluid level. Top-up the fluid if necessary.

20 Wheel alignment and steering angles – general information

Definitions

1 A vehicle's steering and suspension geometry is defined in four basic settings **(see illustration)** – all angles are expressed in degrees (toe settings are also expressed as a measurement); the steering axis is defined as an imaginary line drawn through the axis of the suspension strut, extended where necessary to contact the ground.

2 Camber is the angle between each roadwheel and a vertical line drawn through its centre and tyre contact patch, when viewed from the front or rear of the vehicle. Positive camber is when the roadwheels are tilted outwards from the vertical at the top; negative camber is when they are tilted inwards. The camber angle is not adjustable.

3 Castor is the angle between the steering axis and a vertical line drawn through each roadwheel's centre and tyre contact patch, when viewed from the side of the vehicle. Positive castor is when the steering axis is tilted so that it contacts the ground ahead of the vertical; negative castor is when it contacts the ground behind the vertical. The castor angle is not adjustable.

4 Toe is the difference, viewed from above,

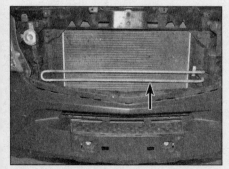

18.1 Power steering fluid cooler, in front of radiator

18.5a Undo the cooler mounting screw...

18.5b ...and release from the mounting clips

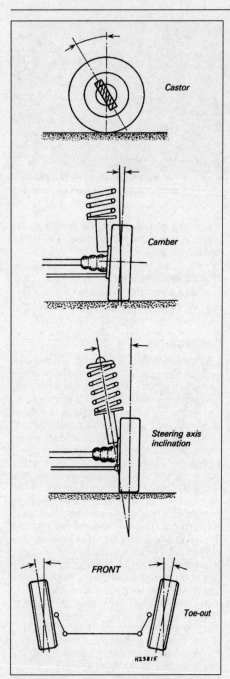

20.1 Wheel alignment and steering angles

between lines drawn through the roadwheel centres and the vehicle's centre-line. 'Toe-in' is when the roadwheels point inwards, towards each other at the front, while 'toe-out' is when they splay outwards from each other at the front.

5 The front wheel toe setting is adjusted by screwing the track rod in or out of its track rod ends, to alter the effective length of the track rod assembly.

6 Rear wheel toe setting is not adjustable.

Checking and adjustment

7 Due to the special measuring equipment necessary to check the wheel alignment and steering angles, and the skill required to use it properly, the checking and adjustment of these settings is best left to a Mercedes-Benz dealer or similar expert. Note that most tyre-fitting shops now possess sophisticated checking equipment.

Chapter 11
Bodywork and fittings

Contents

Degrees of difficulty

Easy, suitable for novice with little experience	Fairly easy, suitable for beginner with some experience	Fairly difficult, suitable for competent DIY mechanic	Difficult, suitable for experienced DIY mechanic	Very difficult, suitable for expert DIY or professional

Specifications

Torque wrench settings	Nm	lbf ft
Bonnet hinge retaining nuts	20	14
Door check strap to A-pillar	30	22
Door check strap to door	14	10
Door lock securing Torx screws*	10	7
Facia support crossmember bolts/screws	20	14
Rear bumper retaining bolts	9	6
Seat belt height adjuster:		
Upper bolt	37	27
Lower bolt	25	18
Seat belt/inertia reel mounting bolts	37	27
Seat retaining bolts	37	27

* Use new nuts/bolts

1 General Information

1 The body and chassis on all versions of the Sprinter is of all-steel construction. Three basic chassis types are available: short-wheelbase, medium-wheelbase and long-wheelbase models.

2 The three main body types are Van, Bus and Chassis Cab. Twin opening rear doors and side opening door(s) are available. The bodyshell is as aerodynamic in shape as possible, to promote economy and reduce wind noise levels.

3 Extensive use is made of plastic materials, mainly on the interior, but also in exterior components. The front and rear bumpers are injection-moulded from a synthetic material, which is very strong and yet light. Plastic components such as wheel arch liners are fitted to the underside of the vehicle, to improve the body's resistance to corrosion.

4 Due to the large number of specialist applications of this vehicle range, information contained in this Chapter is given on parts found to be common on the popular factory-produced versions. No information is provided on special body versions.

2 Maintenance – bodywork and underframe

1 The general condition of a vehicle's bodywork is the one thing that significantly affects its value. Maintenance is easy, but needs to be regular. Neglect, particularly after minor damage, can lead quickly to further deterioration and costly repair bills. It is important also to keep watch on those parts of the vehicle not immediately visible, for instance the underside, inside all the wheel arches, and the lower part of the engine compartment.

2 The basic maintenance routine for the bodywork is washing – preferably with a lot of water, from a hose. This will remove all the loose solids, which may have stuck to the vehicle. It is important to flush these off in such a way as to prevent grit from scratching the finish. The wheel arches and underframe need washing in the same way, to remove any accumulated mud, which will retain moisture and tend to encourage rust. Paradoxically enough, the best time to clean the underframe and wheel arches is in wet weather, when the mud is thoroughly wet and soft. In very wet weather, the underframe is usually cleaned of large accumulations automatically, and this is a good time for inspection.

3 Periodically, except on vehicles with a wax-based underbody protective coating, it is a good idea to have the whole of the underframe of the vehicle steam-cleaned, engine compartment included, so that a thorough inspection can be carried out to see what minor repairs and renovations are necessary. Steam cleaning is available at many garages, and is necessary for the removal of the accumulation of oily grime, which sometimes is allowed to become thick in certain areas. If steam-cleaning facilities are not available, there are some excellent grease solvents available which can be brush-applied; the dirt can then be simply hosed off. Note that these methods should not be used on vehicles with wax-based underbody protective coating, or the coating will be removed. Such vehicles should be inspected annually, preferably just prior to winter, when the underbody should be washed down, and any damage to the wax coating repaired. Ideally, a completely fresh coat should be applied. It would also be worth considering the use of such wax-based protection for injection into door panels, sills, box sections, etc, as an additional safeguard against rust damage, where such protection is not provided by the vehicle manufacturer.

4 After washing paintwork, wipe off with a chamois leather to give an unspotted clear finish. A coat of clear protective wax polish will give added protection against chemical pollutants in the air. If the paintwork sheen has dulled or oxidised, use a cleaner/polisher combination to restore the brilliance of the shine. This requires a little effort, but such dulling is usually caused because regular washing has been neglected. Care needs to be taken with metallic paintwork, as special non-abrasive cleaner/polisher is required to avoid damage to the finish. Always check that the door and ventilator opening drain holes and pipes are completely clear, so that water can be drained out. Brightwork should be treated in the same way as paintwork. Windscreens and windows can be kept clear of the smeary film, which often appears, by the use of proprietary glass cleaner. Never use any form of wax or other body or chromium polish on glass.

3 Maintenance – upholstery and carpets

1 Mats and carpets should be brushed or vacuum-cleaned regularly, to keep them free of grit. If they are badly stained, remove them from the vehicle for scrubbing or sponging, and make quite sure they are dry before refitting. Seats and interior trim panels can be kept clean by wiping with a damp cloth. If they do become stained (which can be more apparent on light-coloured upholstery), use a little liquid detergent and a soft nail brush to scour the grime out of the grain of the

material. Do not forget to keep the headlining clean in the same way as the upholstery. When using liquid cleaners inside the vehicle, do not over-wet the surfaces being cleaned. Excessive damp could get into the seams and padded interior, causing stains, offensive odours or even rot.

4 Minor body damage – repair

Minor scratches

1 If the scratch is very superficial, and does not penetrate to the metal of the bodywork, repair is very simple. Lightly rub the area of the scratch with a paintwork renovator, or a very fine cutting paste, to remove loose paint from the scratch, and to clear the surrounding bodywork of wax polish. Rinse the area with clean water.

2 Apply touch-up paint to the scratch using a fine paintbrush; continue to apply fine layers of paint until the surface of the paint in the scratch is level with the surrounding paintwork. Allow the new paint at least two weeks to harden, and then blend it into the surrounding paintwork by rubbing the scratch area with a paintwork renovator or a very fine cutting paste. Finally, apply wax polish.

3 Where the scratch has penetrated right through to the metal of the bodywork, causing the metal to rust, a different repair technique is required. Remove any loose rust from the bottom of the scratch with a penknife, and then apply rust-inhibiting paint to prevent the formation of rust in the future. Using a rubber or nylon applicator, fill the scratch with bodystopper paste. If required, this paste can be mixed with cellulose thinners to provide a very thin paste that is ideal for filling narrow scratches. Before the stopper-paste in the scratch hardens, wrap a piece of smooth cotton rag around the top of a finger. Dip the finger in cellulose thinners, and quickly sweep it across the surface of the stopper-paste in the scratch; this will ensure that the surface of the stopper-paste is slightly hollowed. The scratch can now be painted over as described earlier in this Section.

Dents

4 When deep denting of the vehicle's bodywork has taken place, the first task is to pull the dent out, until the affected bodywork almost attains its original shape. There is little point in trying to restore the original shape completely, as the metal in the damaged area will have stretched on impact, and cannot be reshaped fully to its original contour. It is better to bring the level of the dent up to a point, which is about 3 mm below the level of the surrounding bodywork. In cases where the dent is very shallow anyway, it is not worth trying to pull it out at all. If the underside of

the dent is accessible, it can be hammered out gently from behind, using a mallet with a wooden or plastic head. Whilst doing this, hold a suitable block of wood firmly against the outside of the panel, to absorb the impact from the hammer blows and thus prevent a large area of the bodywork from being 'belled-out'.

5 Should the dent be in a section of the bodywork that has a double skin, or some other factor making it inaccessible from behind, a different technique is called for. Drill several small holes through the metal inside the area – particularly in the deeper section. Then screw long self-tapping screws into the holes, just sufficiently for them to gain a good purchase in the metal. Now the dent can be pulled out by pulling on the protruding heads of the screws with a pair of pliers.

6 The next stage of the repair is the removal of the paint from the damaged area, and from an inch or so of the surrounding 'sound' bodywork. This is accomplished most easily by using a wire brush or abrasive pad on a power drill, although it can be done just as effectively by hand, using sheets of abrasive paper. To complete the preparation for filling, score the surface of the bare metal with a screwdriver or the tang of a file, or alternatively, drill small holes in the affected area. This will provide a really good 'key' for the filler paste.

7 To complete the repair, see the Section on filling and respraying.

Rust holes or gashes

8 Remove all paint from the affected area, and from an inch or so of the surrounding 'sound' bodywork, using an abrasive pad or a wire brush on a power drill. If these are not available, a few sheets of abrasive paper will do the job most effectively. With the paint removed, you will be able to judge the severity of the corrosion, and therefore decide whether to renew the whole panel (if this is possible) or to repair the affected area. New body panels are not as expensive as most people think, and it is often quicker and more satisfactory to fit a new panel than to attempt to repair large areas of corrosion.

9 Remove all fittings from the affected area, except those, which will act as a guide to the original shape of the damaged bodywork (e.g. headlight shells etc). Then, using tin snips or a hacksaw blade, remove all loose metal and any other metal badly affected by corrosion. Hammer the edges of the hole inwards, in order to create a slight depression for the filler paste.

10 Wire-brush the affected area to remove the powdery rust from the surface of the remaining metal. Paint the affected area with rust-inhibiting paint, if the back of the rusted area is accessible, treat this also.

11 Before filling can take place, it will be necessary to block the hole in some way. This can be achieved by the use of aluminium or plastic mesh, or aluminium tape.

12 Aluminium or plastic mesh, or glass-fibre matting, is probably the best material to use for a large hole. Cut a piece to the approximate size and shape of the hole to be filled, then position it in the hole so that its edges are below the level of the surrounding bodywork. It can be retained in position by several blobs of filler paste around its periphery.

13 Aluminium tape should be used for small or very narrow holes. Pull a piece off the roll, trim it to the approximate size and shape required, then pull off the backing paper (if used) and stick the tape over the hole; it can be overlapped if the thickness of one piece is insufficient. Burnish down the edges of the tape with the handle of a screwdriver or similar, to ensure that the tape is securely attached to the metal underneath.

Filling and respraying

14 Before using this Section, see the Sections on dent, deep scratch, rust holes and gash repairs.

15 Many types of bodyfiller are available, but generally speaking, those proprietary kits, which contain a tin of filler paste and a tube of resin hardener, are best for this type of repair. A wide, flexible plastic or nylon applicator will be found invaluable for imparting a smooth and well-contoured finish to the surface of the filler.

16 Mix up a little filler on a clean piece of card or board – measure the hardener carefully (follow the maker's instructions on the pack), otherwise the filler will set too rapidly or too slowly. Using the applicator, apply the filler paste to the prepared area; draw the applicator across the surface of the filler to achieve the correct contour and to level the surface. As soon as a contour that approximates to the correct one is achieved, stop working the paste – if you carry on too long, the paste will become sticky and begin to 'pick-up' on the applicator. Continue to add thin layers of filler paste at 20-minute intervals, until the level of the filler is just proud of the surrounding bodywork.

17 Once the filler has hardened, the excess can be removed using a metal plane or file. From then on, progressively finer grades of abrasive paper should be used, starting with a 40-grade production paper, and finishing with a 400-grade wet-and-dry paper. Always wrap the abrasive paper around a flat rubber, cork, or wooden block – otherwise the surface of the filler will not be completely flat. During the smoothing of the filler surface, the wet-and-dry paper should be periodically rinsed in water. This will ensure that a very smooth finish is imparted to the filler at the final stage.

18 At this stage, the 'dent' should be surrounded by a ring of bare metal, which in turn should be encircled by the finely 'feathered' edge of the good paintwork. Rinse the repair area with clean water, until all of the dust produced by the rubbing-down operation has gone.

19 Spray the whole area with a light coat of primer – this will show up any imperfections in the surface of the filler. Repair these imperfections with fresh filler paste or bodystopper, and once more smooth the surface with abrasive paper. Repeat this spray-and-repair procedure until you are satisfied that the surface of the filler, and the feathered edge of the paintwork, are perfect. Clean the repair area with clean water, and allow to dry fully.

20 The repair area is now ready for final spraying. Paint spraying must be carried out in a warm, dry, windless and dust-free atmosphere. This condition can be created artificially if you have access to a large indoor working area, but if you are forced to work in the open, you will have to pick your day very carefully. If you are working indoors, dousing the floor in the work area with water will help to settle the dust that would otherwise be in the atmosphere. If the repair area is confined to one body panel, mask off the surrounding panels; this will help to minimise the effects of a slight mis-match in paint colours. Bodywork fittings (e.g. chrome strips, door handles etc) will also need to be masked off. Use genuine masking tape, and several thicknesses of newspaper, for the masking operations.

21 Before commencing to spray, agitate the aerosol can thoroughly, and then spray a test area (an old tin, or similar) until the technique is mastered. Cover the repair area with a thick coat of primer; the thickness should be built up using several thin layers of paint, rather than one thick one. Using 400-grade wet-and-dry paper, rub down the surface of the primer until it is really smooth. While doing this, the work area should be thoroughly doused with water, and the wet-and-dry paper periodically rinsed in water. Allow to dry before spraying on more paint.

22 Spray on the topcoat, again building up the thickness by using several thin layers of paint. Start spraying at one edge of the repair area, and then, using a side-to-side motion, work until the whole repair area and about 2 inches of the surrounding original paintwork is covered. Remove all masking material 10 to 15 minutes after spraying on the final coat of paint.

23 Allow the new paint at least two weeks to harden, then, using a paintwork renovator, or a very fine cutting paste, blend the edges of the paint into the existing paintwork. Finally, apply wax polish.

Plastic components

24 With the use of more and more plastic body components by the vehicle manufacturers (e.g. bumpers. spoilers, and in some cases major body panels), rectification of more serious damage to such items has become a matter of either entrusting repair work to a specialist in this field, or renewing complete components. Repair of such damage by the DIY owner is not really feasible, owing to the cost of the equipment and materials required for effecting such repairs. The basic technique involves making a groove along the line of the crack in the plastic, using a rotary burr in a power drill. The damaged part is then welded back together, using a hot-air gun to heat up and fuse a plastic filler rod into the groove. Any excess plastic is then removed, and the area rubbed down to a smooth finish. It is important that a filler rod of the correct plastic is used, as body components can be made of a variety of different types (e.g. polycarbonate, ABS, polypropylene).

25 Damage of a less serious nature (abrasions, minor cracks etc) can be repaired by the DIY owner using a two-part epoxy filler repair material. Once mixed in equal proportions, this is used in similar fashion to the bodywork filler used on metal panels. The filler is usually cured in twenty to thirty minutes, ready for sanding and painting.

26 If the owner is renewing a complete component himself, or if he has repaired it with epoxy filler, he will be left with the problem of finding a suitable paint for finishing which is compatible with the type of plastic used. At one time, the use of a universal paint was not possible, owing to the complex range of plastics encountered in body component applications. Standard paints, generally speaking, will not bond to plastic or rubber satisfactorily. However, it is now possible to obtain a plastic body parts finishing kit, which consists of a pre-primer treatment, a primer and coloured topcoat. Full instructions are normally supplied with a kit, but basically, the method of use is to first apply the pre-primer to the component concerned, and allow it to dry for up to 30 minutes. Then the primer is applied, and left to dry for about an hour before finally applying the special-coloured topcoat. The result is a correctly coloured component, where the paint will flex with the plastic or rubber, a property that standard paint does not normally possess.

---

5 Major body damage – repair

1 With the exception of Chassis Cab versions, the chassis members are spot-welded to the underbody, and in this respect can be termed of being monocoque or unit construction. Major damage repairs to this type of body combination must of necessity be carried out by body shops with welding and hydraulic straightening facilities.

2 Extensive damage to the body may distort the chassis, and result in unstable and dangerous handling, as well as excessive wear to tyres and suspension or steering components. It is recommended that checking of the chassis alignment be entrusted to a Mercedes-Benz agent or accident repair specialist with special checking jigs.

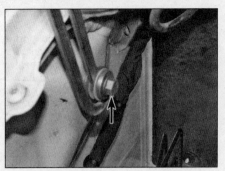

6.2 Bonnet stay securing nut/bolt

6.4 Slacken the retaining nuts and remove the bonnet

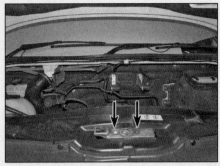

7.2 Bonnet lock retaining bolts

6 Bonnet – removal, refitting and adjustment

Removal

1 Open the bonnet, and have an assistant support the bonnet.
2 Undo the securing nut and disconnect the bonnet stay bracket from the inner wing panel **(see illustration)**.
3 Mark around the bonnet hinges, to show the outline of their fitted positions for correct realignment on assembly.
4 With the assistant still supporting the bonnet, unscrew and remove the hinge retaining nuts, and then lift the bonnet clear of the vehicle **(see illustration)**.

Refitting

5 Refitting is a reversal of removal. Tighten the hinge nuts fully when bonnet alignment is satisfactory. Apply a small amount of grease to the hinges.

Adjustment

6 Adjustment of the bonnet fit is available by loosening the hinges and moving it to the correct position required. Further adjustment can be made by slackening the locknut on the bonnet upper catch, and then realigning it. Also there are rubber bump stops on the bonnet, which can be adjusted. The bonnet requires adjustment to give an even clearance between its outer edges and the surrounding panels. Adjust the front bump stops to align the edges of the bonnet with the front wing panels and grille. When aligned, retighten all the relevant retaining nuts securely.

7 Bonnet lock – removal and refitting

Removal

1 Open the bonnet.
2 Undo the two bolts and withdraw the bonnet lock from the front crossmember **(see illustration)**.
3 Turn the bonnet lock over and disconnect the bonnet release cable from the lock assembly.

Refitting

4 Refitting is a reversal of removal.

8 Door trim panels – removal and refitting

Front doors

Removal

1 Prise out the two circular trim covers at the top of the door panel, and remove the screws behind **(see illustrations)**.
2 Rotate the two locking clips and remove the lower door panel **(see illustrations)**.
3 On models with manual window regulators, release the securing ring at the rear of the handle by pushing it to one side, and then release the handle from the regulator shaft splines.

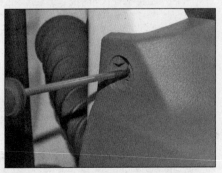

8.1a Remove the circular cover at the trailing edge of the door panel...

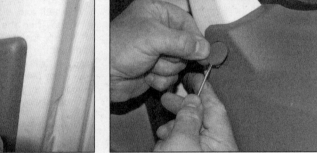

8.1b ...then the leading edge...

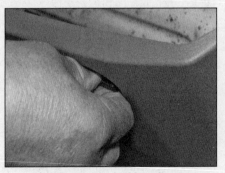

8.1c ...and remove the screws behind

8.2a Rotate the locking clips...

8.2b ...and remove the lower trim panel

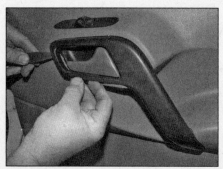

8.4 Unclip the grab handle trim cover

8.5 Undo the retaining screws

8.6a Prise the trim panel away from the door...

8.6b ...then lift from the door frame

8.7a Unclip the door operating cable

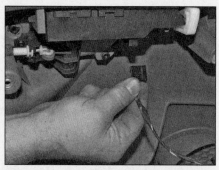

8.7b Unplug the electric window connector

4 Carefully unclip the plastic cover from the inner panel grab handle **(see illustration)**.
5 Undo the two lower screws securing the trim panel to the door **(see illustration)**.
6 Lift the door trim panel upwards and then carefully withdraw the trim panel from the door. Use a trim removal tool and prise the panel around its outer and lower edges to release it from the door **(see illustrations)**.
7 Unclip the outer cable from the release lever housing and then unhook the inner cable from the release lever **(see illustration)**. On models with electric windows, disconnect the wiring connectors from the switches **(see illustration)**.The panel can now be completely withdrawn from the door.

Refitting

8 Refitting is a reversal of removal. On models with manual window regulators, refit the locking ring to the regulator handle, and then push the handle onto the regulator shaft in the position noted on removal.

Rear and sliding doors

Removal

9 Remove the interior handle (where applicable) by lifting up the trim covers and undoing the retaining screws.
10 Where fitted, the trim panels are secured by plastic retaining clips, the removal of which requires the use of a suitable forked tool. These clips are easily broken, so take care when prising them free. Remove the trim panel.

Refitting

11 Refitting is a reversal of removal. Align the panel, and press the clips into position.

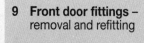

9 Front door fittings –
removal and refitting

Exterior handle

Removal

1 Open the door and prise the rubber grommet out of the door **(see illustration)**.
2 Undo the securing screw from the end of the door panel, then manoeuvre the lock barrel from place **(see illustrations)**.
3 Prise out the plastic trim, then pull the rear of the handle out from the door and then unhook the front edge of the handle **(see illustration)**.

Refitting

4 Refitting is a reversal of removal.

9.1 Remove the grommet

9.2a Undo the retaining screw...

9.2b ...then pull out the lock barrel

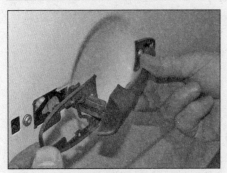

9.3 Pull the handle outwards and unhook it from the door

9.6 Prise off lock release and remove

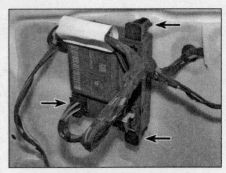

9.9a Depress the retaining clips...

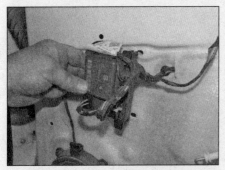

9.9b ...and remove the door lock unit

Door lock cylinder

Removal

5 Remove the exterior handle as described earlier in this Section.

9.16a Remove the two exterior bolts...

9.14 Prise away the weather sealing membrane

6 Prise off the lock cable and remove the door lock cylinder **(see illustration)**.

Refitting

7 Refitting is a reversal of removal. Note the lock cylinder will only fit in one position.

9.16b ...then the three on the door edge

Door control unit

Removal

8 Remove the front door trim panel as described in Section 8.

9 Depress the three retaining clips and remove the door lock unit **(see illustrations)**. Disconnect the wiring plugs.

10 Where applicable, extract the retaining clips and cut off the cable-ties securing the release cable/wiring harness to the doorframe.

Refitting

11 Refitting is a reversal of removal.

Door lock unit

12 Remove the door trim panel as described in Section 8.

13 Remove the door control unit as described earlier in this Section.

14 Gently prise away the inner door sealing membrane **(see illustration)**.

15 Remove the door handle as described earlier in this Section.

16 Remove the two exterior Torx bolts and the three on the edge of the door **(see illustrations)**.

17 Unclip the door sealing gasket from the door handle carrier **(see illustration)**.

18 Manoeuvre the door lock unit and handle carrier from place, unplugging the wiring connector as it becomes available **(see illustration)**.

Refitting

19 Refitting is a reversal of removal, ensuring that the lock cable clips into the door where needed **(see illustration)**.

9.17 Detach the handle gasket from the handle carrier

9.18 Remove the door lock from place and disconnect the wiring plug

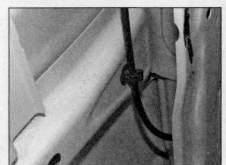

9.19 Remember to clip the lock cable back in place

10.3 Door check strap retaining bolt

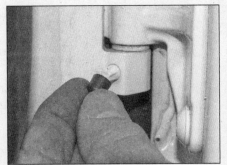

10.5a Remove the caps...

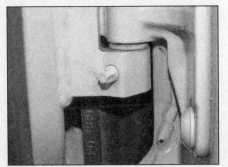

10.5b ...and loosen the retaining screws
from the door hinge pins

10 Front door – removal, refitting and adjustment

Removal

1 On models with central locking/ electric windows, disconnect the battery negative lead as described in Chapter 5 Section 3.

2 Open the door, and position a suitable padded jack or support blocks underneath the lower part of the door; don't lift the door, just take its weight.

3 Undo the screw and remove the door check strap bracket from the body pillar **(see illustration)**.

4 On models with central locking/electric windows, pull back the rubber grommet between the door and the A-pillar and disconnect the wiring connectors. Note the routing of the wiring and the connections for refitting.

5 Prise off the caps covering the retaining screws from the upper and lower door hinge pins and unscrew **(see illustrations)**.

6 With the aid of an assistant, lift the door to release the hinge pins from the hinge bracket, and then remove the door.

Refitting and adjustment

7 Refitting is a reversal of removal. Use thread-lock on the check strap securing bolts. Open and shut the door to ensure that it does not bind with the body aperture at any point. Adjust the door striker plate if necessary.

11 Sliding side door fittings – removal and refitting

Exterior handle

Removal

1 Slide the door open, remove the rubber grommet and undo the securing screw from the end of the door panel **(see illustration)**.

2 Pull the front of the handle out from the door and then unhook the rear edge of the handle **(see illustrations)**.

3 If necessary, remove the 2 outer and one inner mounting screw and manoeuvre the inner handle carriage from place, disconnecting the cables as they become accessible **(see illustrations)**, taking note of their position for refitting.

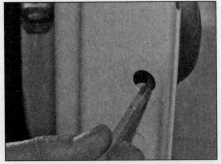

11.1 Undo the door handle retaining screw

11.2a Remove the front cover...

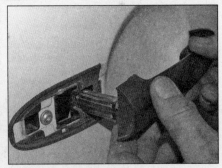

11.2b ...then pull the handle outwards to
unclip it from the door panel

11.3a Undo the 2 outside screws...

11.3b ...and the single inside screw...

11.3c ...then manoeuvre the carriage from
the door...

11.3d ...disconnectiing the cables as they become available, and taking note of the positions in which they must be refitted

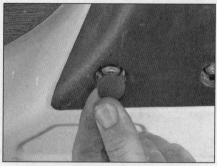

11.5a Remove each plastic cover...

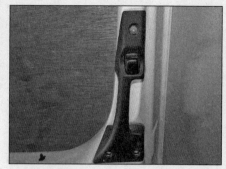

11.5b ...and remove each retaining screw

11.6 Remove the interior handle from the door and note the location of the operating cables when removing

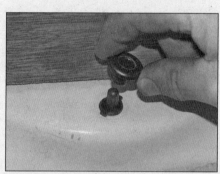

11.9 Lift the button collar from place

11.10 Squeeze the tabs and raise the door lock button

Refitting

4 Refitting is a reversal of removal.

Interior release handle and mechanism

Removal

5 Remove the 3 plastic plugs from the handle and undo the securing screws **(see illustrations)**.
6 Withdraw the interior handle from the door, noting the fitted position of the operating cables **(see illustration)**. If required unclip the release cable from the release mechanism.

Refitting

7 Refitting is a reversal of removal.

Door lock button

8 Remove the door interior panel.
9 Prise up the collar from around the button **(see illustration)** and remove.
10 Working inside the door, depress the tabs on either side of the lock button shaft then push it up from place **(see illustration)**.
11 Release the locking cables from the lock at the rear of the door and remove the lock button from place.

Door lock unit

Removal

12 Where fitted release the retaining clips and remove the door trim panel from the inside of the door.
13 Slide the door open and unscrew the two

retaining bolts from the catch at the top of the door and pull from place then detach the locking cable. Attach a long wire or string to the end of the locking cable, to make pulling

it back up through the door easier **(see illustrations)**.
14 Undo the three Torx screws from the rear end of the door **(see illustration)**.

11.13a Undo the bolts and remove the catch...

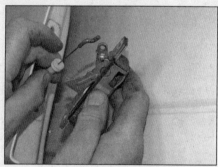

11.13b ...then detach the locking cable

11.13c Attaching a wire to the cable makes it easier to pull it up through the door

11.14 Door lock retaining screws

11.15a Manoeuvre the door lock out...

11.15b ...the unplug the central locking wiring connector...

11.15c ...and detach the locking cables, taking note of their locations for refitting

15 Working from inside the rear of the vehicle, slide the door forwards, so that it is possible to remove the door lock unit, complete with release cable from the interior release handle, from inside the door aperture **(see illustrations)**.

Refitting

16 Refitting is a reversal of removal.

12 Sliding side door –
removal, refitting and adjustment

Note: *Before slackening any retaining bolts, make alignment marks on the guide supports to aid alignment when refitting. An assistant will be required to support the weight of the door when removing the sliding brackets, and also to help with removal.*

Removal

1 Depress the tabs top and bottom, and remove the plastic end stop from the centre rail **(see illustration)**.
2 Slide the door open, and then mark the position of the lower mounting bracket on the door. Unscrew the bolts securing the door lower guide support **(see illustration)**.
3 Unplug the wiring connector for the central locking **(see illustration)**.
4 Mark the position of the upper mounting bracket on the door. With the aid of an assistant to support the weight of the door on the centre rail, remove the bolts securing the upper guide support **(see illustration)**.
5 Support the door at each end, slide it to the rear of the centre rail, and then carefully remove it from the vehicle.
6 To remove the upper carriage from the rail,

slide it to the rear of the track and withdraw it from the vehicle.
7 To remove the lower carriage from the rail, withdraw the plastic covers from the side step and undo the retaining screws. Remove the plastic end trim at the end of the step,m then unclip the plastic cover from the step and unhook the carriage from the lower track **(see illustrations)**.

Refitting

8 Refitting is a reversal of removal. Align the door and engage it onto the centre track, then reconnect the fittings. Fit new self-locking screw to the end stop on the centre rail. Clean the rails and sliding carriages, and then apply grease to lubricate the rails.

Adjustment

9 To adjust the height, slacken the lower and upper support bolts to reposition the door as

12.1 Remove the centre rail end cap

12.2 Lower mounting bracket retaining bolts

12.3 Disconnect the central locking wiring plug

12.4 Upper mounting bracket retaining bolts

12.7a Remove the plastic covers...

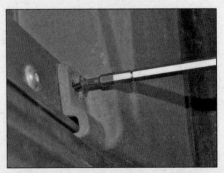

12.7b ...remove the retaining screws...

12.7c ...remove the plastic end trim from the step...

12.7d ...lift up the plastic step cover...

12.7e ...and slide the lower carriage from the bottom rail

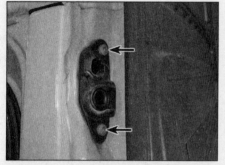

12.10 Door guide wedge securing bolts

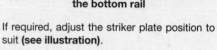

12.11 Door striker plate securing bolts

required, then tighten them and recheck the fitting.
10 Check the door for satisfactory flush-fitting adjustment. To adjust, slacken the screws on the guide wedge on the front edge of the

sliding door, adjust the guide as required, then retighten to secure **(see illustration)**.
11 When fitted, and in the closed position, the door should be aligned flush to the surrounding body, and should close securely.

If required, adjust the striker plate position to suit **(see illustration)**.

13 Fuel flap –
removal and refitting

1 Open the fuel flap and unclip the fuel cap retaining strap from the flap **(see illustration)**.
2 Undo the two retaining bolts and remove the fuel flap from place **(see illustration)**.

Refitting

3 Refitting is a reversal of removal.

14 Rear door fittings –
removal and refitting

13.1 Detach the fuel cap strap

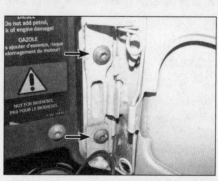

13.2 Unscrew the bolts and detach the flap

Exterior handle (right-hand door)

Removal

1 Open the door and remove the grommet from the end of the door panel, then undo the lock retaining screw **(see illustrations)**.
2 Remove the lock barrel from place, then pull the rear of the handle out from the door and unhook the front edge of the handle.

Refitting

3 Refitting is a reversal of removal.

Door lock cylinder

Removal

4 Remove the grommet from the edge of the rear door, as described in the previous Section.
5 Undo the Torx screw in the edge of the door.
6 Remove the large grommet on the rear door to allow access to the lock actuation rod **(see illustration)**.
7 Working through the circular aperture, detach the lock actuation rod from the rear of the lock barrel **(see illustration)**.
8 Pull out the rear door handle and pull the lock barrel from place **(see illustration)**.

14.1a Prise out the grommet...

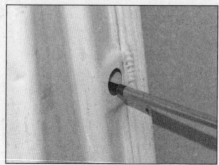

14.1b ...then undo the exterior handle retaining screw

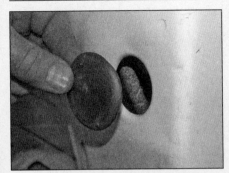

14.6 Prise out the large grommet

14.7 Separate the lock rod from the barrel

14.8 Pull the lock barrel out

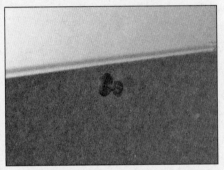

14.14 Undo the clips to release the panel

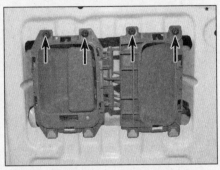

14.16a Undo the four retaining screws...

14.16b ...and remove it from the door

Refitting

9 Refitting is a reversal of removal. Note the lock cylinder will only fit in one position.

Door lock unit

Removal

10 Where fitted, release the retaining clips and remove the door inner trim panel.
11 On models with central locking, trace the wiring from the lock and then disconnect the wiring block connector. Note the routing of the wiring and the connections for refitting.
12 Undo the three Torx screws and remove the door lock unit from inside the door aperture. Disconnect the inner door handle release cable from the lever on the lock unit.

Refitting

13 Refitting is a reversal of removal. Fit new self-locking screws to the door lock and tighten to the specified torque setting.

Interior release handle (right-hand door)

Removal

14 Where fitted, release the clips and remove the inner door trim panel **(see illustration)**.
15 Using a suitable trim removal tool, prise off the interior handle surround.
16 Undo the four securing screws and remove the release handle housing from the door **(see illustrations)**.
17 Unclip the release cable from the rear of the handle assembly.

Refitting

18 Refitting is a reversal of removal.

Latch assembly (right-hand rear door)

Before removing the latch, draw a line around the edge of it, so you can relocate it in the right place during reassembly.

19 Undo the three Torx bolts **(see illustration)**.
20 Remove the latch mechanism from place.
21 Disconnect the locking cable from the latch.
22 Refitting is a reversal of removal.

Locking cable assembly (right-hand door)

23 Remove the door lock mechanism as described earlier in this Section.
24 Remove the latch at the top of the door, as described earlier in this Section.
25 Unhook the locking cable from the top latch.
26 Using a screwdriver, unfasten the clip and detach the locking cable from the door lock mechanism **(see illustrations)**.
27 Refitting is a reversal of removal, taking care to feed the cable up from the bottom of the door to the latch.

14.19 Remove the three Torx bolts

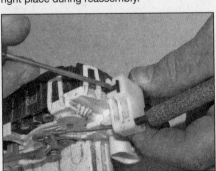

14.26a Use screwdriver to unfasten the clip...

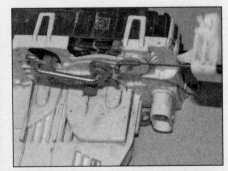

14.26b ...and detach the locking cable

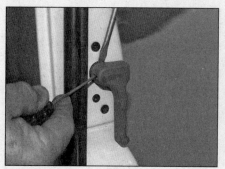

14.28 Use two screwdrivers to lever off the handle

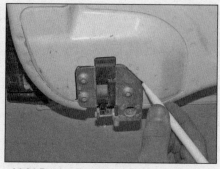

14.31 Draw a line around the latches and remove

14.33a Remove the bolts...

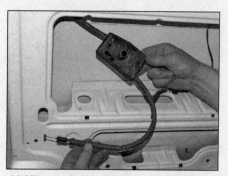

14.33b ...and take out the lock mechanism

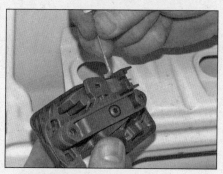

14.34 Unhook the upper cable from the mechanism

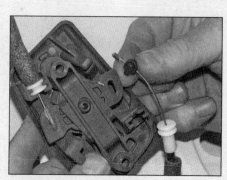

14.35 Rotate the cable until the mount can be pulled free

Door release handle (left-hand door)

28 Insert a small screwdriver into the slot in the doorhandle and use a trim removal too to lever the handle off the spline (**see illustration**).
29 Refitting is a reversal of removal.

Locking cables (left-hand door)

30 Remove the release handle as described in this Section.
31 Slacken the three Torx screws in the top and bottom latches and remove, taking care to draw a line around each for ease of reassembly (**see illustration**).
32 Remove the latches and detach the locking cables from each one.
33 Undo the three bolts and manoeuvre the door release mechanism from place (**see illustrations**).

34 Detach the upper locking cable from the mechanism by unhooking it (**see illustration**).
35 Detach the lower cable by rotating it until the circular mount comes free (**see illustration**).
36 Refitting is a reversal of removal

---

15 Rear doors – removal, refitting and adjustment

Removal

1 Open the rear doors, and then detach the safety check strap from the body on the side which the door is being removed (**see illustration**).
2 Gently tease the wiring bellow from the van body (**see illustration**).

3 Disconnect the wiring plug.
4 Mark around the periphery of each door hinge with a suitable marker pen to show the fitted position of the hinges when refitting the door.
5 Have an assistant support the door, undo the three retaining bolts from each hinge, and withdraw the door (**see illustration**).

Refitting and adjustment

6 Refitting is a reversal of removal. Align the hinges with the previously-made marks, and then tighten the bolts. Ensure that the check strap is central with the door when reconnected.
7 Open and shut the doors, and ensure that they don't bind with the body aperture at any point.
8 Adjust the door hinges by slackening the hinge mounting bolts and then with the door

15.1 Detach the safety check strap from the body

15.2 Gently prise the bellows from the van body

15.5 Hinge-to-door retaining bolts

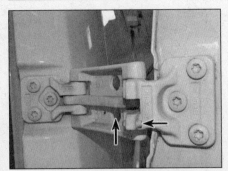

15.8 Slacken the hinge mounting bolts and then adjust through the hole in the hinge

15.9 Door striker plate adjusting nut

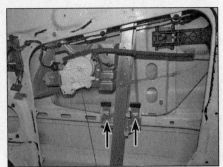

16.2 Slacken the bolts holding the glass to the regulator

closed, adjust the Allen screw from outside of the rear hinge through the access hole **(see illustration)**. When adjusted to the correct position, open the door and tighten the hinge mounting bolts.

9 To align the rear doors so that they are flush, slacken the securing nut and adjust the striker plate on the locking rod mounting plate **(see illustration)**.

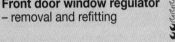

16 Front door window regulator – removal and refitting

Removal

1 Remove the door inner trim panel as described in Section 8.

2 Position the window so that it is halfway down the doorframe, and then undo the

two bolts attaching it to the regulator **(see illustration)**.

3 On vehicles with electric windows, disconnect the wiring connector from the window regulator motor **(see illustration)**.

4 Slide the glass up and attach it to the top of the doorframe using strong tape **(see illustration)**.

5 Unclip the wiring harness from the window regulator **(see illustration)**.

6 Undo the four retaining screws and slide the window regulator and mounting bracket forwards out of the door **(see illustrations)**.

7 Depending on model, either drill out the rivets or undo the retaining bolts to remove the window regulator from the mounting bracket.

Refitting

8 Refitting is a reversal of removal. Before refitting the door trim panel, raise and lower

the window to ensure that it operates in a satisfactory manner.

17 Front door window glass – removal and refitting

Removal

1 Remove the window regulator (see Section 16).

2 Support the window glass and then remove the masking tape. Carefully lower the window glass out through the lower part of the door **(see illustration)**.

Refitting

3 Refitting is a reversal of removal. Before refitting the door trim panel, raise and lower the window to ensure that it operates in a satisfactory manner.

16.3 Unplug the wiring connector from the regulator

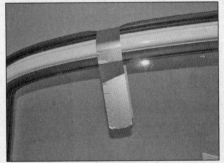

16.4 Hold the glass up with strong tape

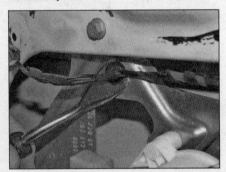

16.5 Detach the harness from the regulator

16.6a Undo the retaining bolts...

16.6b ...and remove the window regulator assembly

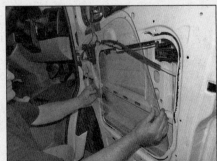

17.2 Slide the window glass out through the bottom of the door

19.1 Remove the rubber bellows at either end

19.2 Unclip the clamping rings from the A-pillar and door

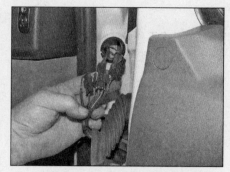

19.3 Disconnect the wiring plug

18 Windscreen and fixed/sliding windows – removal and refitting

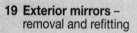

1 The windscreen and fixed/sliding side window assemblies are direct-glazed to the body, using special adhesive. Purpose-made tools are required to remove the old glass and fit the new, and therefore this work is best entrusted to a specialist.

19 Exterior mirrors – removal and refitting

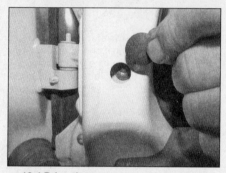

19.4 Prise the screw cover from place

19.9 Prise out the mirror glass from the housing

Complete mirror

Removal

1 Carefully prise out the rubber bellows joining the door and the doorframe **(see illustration)**.
2 Carefully unclip the clamping rings from the A-pillar and door **(see illustration)**.
3 Disconnect the wiring plug **(see illustration)**.
4 Remove the screw cover from the door **(see illustration)**.
5 Undo the three retaining bolts, taking care not to let the bolts fall into the door.
6 Carefully manoeuvre the exterior mirror from place, taking care to guide the wiring harness through the aperture.

Refitting

7 Refitting is a reversal of removal. On electric mirrors, make sure the wiring is routed and

connected correctly before refitting the door trim panel.

Main mirror glass

Removal

Note: *It is worth covering the glass with strong tape, to lessen the possibility of it breaking during removal*
8 Carefully press the left edge of the mirror glass inwards.
9 Use a trim removal tool to prise the right edge from the guides in the mirror housing **(see illustration)**.
10 On models with heated mirrors, disconnect the wiring connectors from the rear of the mirror glass.

Refitting

11 Refitting is a reversal of removal. On heated mirrors, make sure the wiring is connected securely before refitting the glass.

Lower mirror glass

12 Using a trim removal tool, gently prise the mirror glass from place.

Refitting

13 Gently press the mirror glass into place.

20 Front bumper – removal and refitting

Removal

1 Remove the number plate from the bumper.
2 Unplug the exterior temperature sensor from behind the bumper **(see illustration)**.
3 Remove the radiator grille as described in Section 22.
4 Undo the three expanding plastic rivets securing the bumper to each front wheelarch liner **(see illustration)**.
5 Remove the four plastic rivets securing the bottom edge of the bumper **(see illustration)**.
6 Undo the four screws holding on the bumper **(see illustration)**.
7 Slacken the two retaining bolts for the front step above the front numberplate **(see illustration)** and remove.
8 With the aid of an assistant, unclip the bumper from place at each end **(see illustrations)** and remove.
9 Check the rear of the bumper cover for and other wiring connections, disconnect any wiring plugs and remove the bumper cover from the vehicle.

20.2 Detach the exterior temperature sensor

20.4 Remove the three rivets (one side shown)

20.5 Remove the two bottom rivets (one side shown)

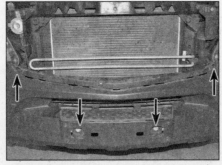

20.6 Remove the four retaining bolts

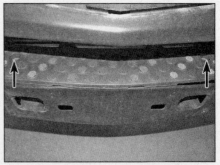

20.7 Undo the front step bolts

Refitting

10 Refitting is a reversal of removal. Align the bumper correctly before fully-tightening the retaining bolts.

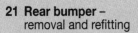

21 Rear bumper – removal and refitting

Removal

1 Unscrew the mounting screw in the rear wheelarch to release the side moulding.
2 Release the securing clips from the left and right edges of the bumper.
3 Using a long trim removal tool, prise out each bumper corner in the area of each lower door hinge.
4 Remove the two clips along the underside edge of the rear bumper.
5 Where fitted, disconnect the wiring plug for the rear parking sensors.
6 Unscrew the bolts around the upper inside edge of the rear bumper.
7 Manoeuvre the bumper from place.

Refitting

8 Refitting is a reversal of removal. Align the bumper correctly before fully tightening the retaining bolts. Make sure any wiring connectors have been refitted, where applicable.

22 Radiator grille – removal and refitting

Removal

1 Open the bonnet.
2 Remove the two retaining screws and four retaining clips from the top of the grille panel. If securing clips are used, remove them by pressing the centre pin inwards, and then releasing the clip from the grille **(see illustrations)**.
3 Pull the top of the radiator grille forward until the front catch hooks along the lower edge are accessible **(see illustration)**.

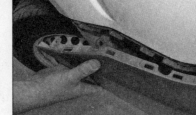

20.8a Unclip each edge of the bumper...

4 Press the four lower clips downwards to release, and pull the grille forward to remove **(see illustration)**.

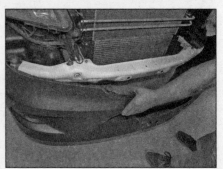

20.8b ...then slide the bumper cover forwards to remove

Refitting

5 Refitting is a reversal of removal. Check the alignment of the grille with the surrounding panels.

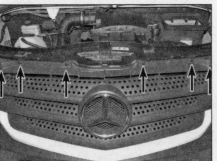

22.2a Release the clips and screws along the top of the grille

22.2b Pull out the centre of the clips to release

22.3 Pull forward the grille until the clips are accessible

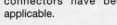

22.4 Withdraw the grille forward

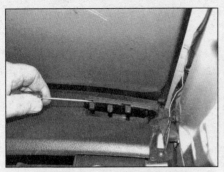

23.2 Remove the speaker cover

23.4 Unclip the A-pillar trim panel

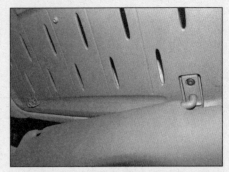

23.12 Remove the four mounting screws to move the sunvisor

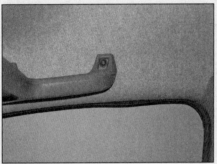

23.13 Remove the screws and detach the mounts

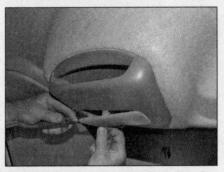
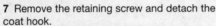

23.14 Detach the courtesy light and unplug

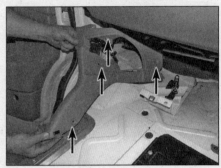

23.18 Slacken the screws and remove the panel

23 Interior trim – removal and refitting

Door trim panels

1 See Section 8.

A-pillar trim

Removal

2 Using a screwdriver, lift up the speaker cover and remove **(see illustration)**.
3 Remove the weather seal from around the edge of the A-pillar trim.
4 Unclip the upper edge of the trim away from the pillar to disengage the retaining clips, then lift the trim up to disengage the lower lugs from the facia **(see illustration)**.
5 If fitted, unbolt the check strap and remove the panel.

Refitting

6 Refitting is a reversal of removal.

B-pillar trim

7 Remove the retaining screw and detach the coat hook.
8 Detach the seatbelt from the seat, as described in Section 25.
9 Slacken the seatbelt retaining bolt from the seatbelt height adjuster.
10 Unclip the B-pillar trim from top to bottom.

Refitting

11 Refitting is a reversal of removal.

Headlining

12 Undo the mounting screws and remove the two sunvisors **(see illustration)**.
13 Undo the mounting screws and remove the sunvisor mounts **(see illustration)**.
14 Unclip the courtesy light from place and unplug the wiring connector **(see illustration)**.

15 Gently pull down the headlining at the front to release, and manoeuvre it from place.
16 Refitting is a reversal of removal.

Lower kick panels

17 Lift the footwell mat.
18 Undo the four mounting screws and manoeuvre the panel from place **(see illustration)**.

Load space trim

Removal

19 The load space trim panels are secured by a combination of screws and plastic retaining clips, the removal of which requires the use of a suitable forked tool. These clips are easily broken, so take care when prising them free.
20 Remove the rear seats, where applicable, for access to the panel attachments.
21 Release the panel retaining clips and screws, and withdraw the panel.

Refitting

22 Refitting is a reversal of removal.

24 Seats – removal and refitting

Driver's seat

Removal

1 Using a small screwdriver, prise out the small cap covering the seatbelt lower mounting **(see illustrations)** and remove the bolt.

24.1a Ease out the cap covering the mounting bolt

24.1b Remove the seatbelt lower mounting bolt

24.2 Slide the seat back to reveal the mounting bolts

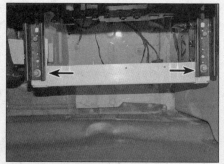

24.3 Slide the seat forward to expose the rear two mounting bolts

24.12 Undo the seatbelt retaining bolt

2 Move the seat fully to the rear, and then undo the two front seat rail retaining bolts **(see illustration)**.

3 Then move the seat fully to the front and undo the two rear seat rail retaining bolts **(see illustration)**.

4 Check for any wiring to the underside of the seat and disconnect any wiring connectors (where applicable), then remove the seat from the vehicle.

Refitting

5 Refitting is a reversal of removal. Tighten the mountings to the specified torque.

Front passenger's seat (single)

Removal

6 Unclip the plastic cover off the seat belt lower mounting, then unscrew the mounting bolt and disconnect it from the seat frame **(see illustrations 24.2 and 24.3)**. Ensure that the spacer and washer remain in place on the mounting bolt when it is removed.

7 Undo the four seat base mounting bolts (two at each side).

8 Check for any wiring to the underside of the seat and disconnect any wiring connectors (where applicable), then remove the seat from the vehicle.

Refitting

9 Refitting is a reversal of removal. Tighten the mountings to the specified torque.

Front passenger's seat (bench)

10 Disconnect the battery negative lead as described in Chapter 5 Section 3.

11 Where fitted, remove the headrests from the back of the bench seat.

12 Unclip the plastic cover off the seat belt lower mounting, then unscrew the mounting bolt and disconnect it from the side of the seat frame **(see illustration)**. Ensure that the spacer and washer remain in place on the mounting bolt when it is removed.

13 Fold forward the front seat cushion then disconnect the seatbelt tensioner wiring plug and detach the wire from the seat frame **(see illustration)**.

14 Undo the mounting bolts from the base of the seat and remove the seat from place **(see illustration)**.

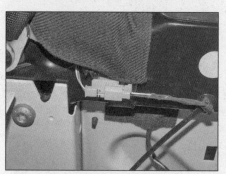

24.13 Fold forward the cushion and disconnect the seatbelt wiring plug

Refitting

15 Refitting is a reversal of removal. Tighten the mounting bolts to the specified torque.

Rear seats

16 Depending on model, various combinations of rear seats may be fitted, according to vehicle type and specification. The removal and refitting procedures are essentially the same as those described previously for the front seats.

25 Seat belt components – removal and refitting

Note: *On models equipped with seat belt pretensioners, disconnect the battery negative lead as described in Chapter 5 Section 3.*

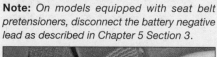

25.4 Detach the seatbelt from the seat

24.14 Remove the bolts, then the seat

Front seat belt

Removal

1 Disconnect the battery negative lead as described in Chapter 5 Section 3.

2 Remove the B-pillar trim panel as described in Section 23, then undo the two retaining bolts and remove the height adjuster from the B-pillar.

3 Undo the retaining bolt and remove the inertia reel from the B-pillar. Disconnect the wiring plug as the unit is withdrawn.

4 Undo the retaining bolt and remove the seatbelt from the seat frame **(see illustration)**.

Refitting

5 Refitting is a reversal of removal, ensuring that the height adjuster engages correctly in the B-pillar. Tighten the retaining bolts to the specified torque.

Front centre seat belt

Removal

6 On vehicles equipped with a double front passenger's bench seat, the seat belt inertia reel is fitted internally within a mounting post.

7 To access the seat belt mounting post, remove the bench seat, as described in Section 24.

8 With the seat removed, undo the inertia reel retaining bolt.

9 Remove the inertia reel from place.

Refitting

10 Refitting is a reversal of removal. Tighten the retaining bolts to the specified torque.

25.13 Centre seat belt stalk mounted to lower seat frame

Seat belt stalks

Removal

11 On the driver's side, the front seat belt stalk is mounted on the side of the seat base. Unclip the plastic cover (where fitted) off the seat stalk mounting bolt, and then unscrew the mounting bolt and remove the stalk from the side of the seat frame. Ensure that any spacers or washers remain with mounting bolt when it is removed.

12 On the passenger side with a single seat, follow the procedures as described in paragraph 15.

13 On the passenger side with a bench seat, the front seat belt stalk is mounted at the centre of the seat base. To access the seat belt stalk mounting point, undo the mounting bolts on the rear of the bench seat and tilt it forwards, with reference to Section 24.

With the seat tilted forwards, undo the seat belt stalk mounting bolt and then remove the seat belt stalk from the seat frame **(see illustration)**.

14 For the centre belt with a bench seat, follow the procedures as described in paragraph 15.

Refitting

15 Refitting is a reversal of removal. Tighten the mounting bolts to the specified torque.

---

26 Facia panel components – removal and refitting

1 Disconnect the battery negative lead as described in Chapter 5 Section 3.

Steering column shroud

Removal

2 Remove the steering wheel, as described in Chapter 10 Section 11.

3 Undo the retaining screws from the top and bottom shrouds and remove the shrouds from place.

Refitting

4 Refitting is a reversal of removal.

Instrument panel surround

Removal

5 Remove the steering wheel, as described in Chapter 10 Section 11.

6 Remove the airbag rotary controller, as described in Chapter 12 Section 22.

7 Remove the ignition switch surround, as described in Chapter 10 Section 12.

8 Remove the side air vent panel, as described in Chapter 3 Section 8.

9 Remove the central vent panel, as described in Section 26.

10 Undo the retaining screws and remove the instrument panel surround **(see illustration)**.

Refitting

11 Refitting is a reversal of removal.

Glove compartment

Removal

12 Remove the mounting screw under the passenger-side lower facia panel and detach the panel **(see illustration)**.

13 Open the glove compartment lid and depress the tabs at the top to allow the door to swivel fully downwards **(see illustration)**.

14 Undo the six retaining screws from inside the glove compartment **(see illustration)**.

15 Withdraw the glove compartment from the facia panel and disconnect the wiring connector from the light unit (where fitted) as it is removed **(see illustration)**.

Refitting

16 Refitting is a reversal of removal.

Bonnet release lever

17 Slacken the two mounting screws and remove the lever from place **(see illustration)**.

18 Disconnect the bonnet release cable.

26.10 Undo the screws and remove the instrument panel surround

26.12 Undo the screw and remove the panel

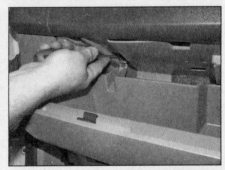

26.13 Press the tabs to let the glovebox lid swing down

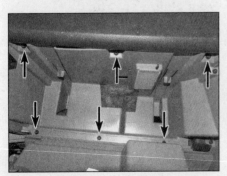

26.14 Undo the six retaining screws

26.15 Disconnect the wiring connector

26.17 Undo the two mounting screws and remove the lever

26.19 Prise the panel from place

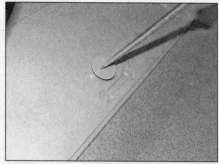

26.23 Undo the fastenings to release the toolkit cover

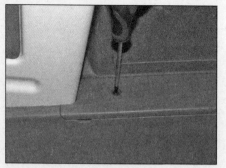

26.24a Undo the mounting screws for the step trim...

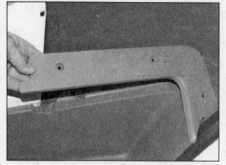

26.24b ...and remove the trim from place

26.25 Lift the floor mat from place

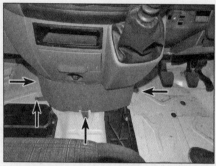

26.26 Remove the four mounting bolts

Central instrument surround panel

19 Working from the top, use a trim removal tool to prise the central instrument surround panel from place **(see illustration)**.
20 Refitting is a reversal of removal.

Heater control panel

21 This procedure is described in Chapter 3 Section 8.

Centre console lower panel

Removal

22 Remove the passenger-side floor covering, as described in Chapter 5 Section 3.
23 Remove the toolkit cover **(see illustration)** and take out the toolkit.
24 Undo the screws on the driver's-side step and remove the trim **(see illustrations)**.
25 Remove the floor covering from the driver's footwell **(see illustration)**.
26 Slacken the four mounting bolts holding the panel to the floor **(see illustration)**.
27 Pull the panel rearwards to unclip it from place **(see illustration)**.

Gearlever surround panel

28 Remove the lower centre console panel as described earlier in this Section.
29 Remove the glovebox as described earlier in this Section.
30 Using a suitable trim removal tool, prise out the central storage compartment **(see illustration)**.
31 Remove the central instrument surround panel as described earlier in this Section.

32 Unclip the gearlever boot and slide the gearlever upwards **(see illustration)**.
33 Loosen the retaining screws for the gearlever surround panel.

34 Pull the panel rearwards and disconnect the wiring plug for the 12V socket **(see illustrations)**.

26.27 Pull the panel towards the rear and remove

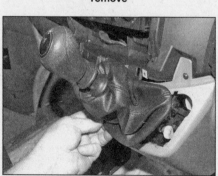

26.32 Unclip the gearlever boot and slide it up the gearlever

26.30 Use a trim removal tool to ease the storage area from place

26.34a Pull the panel rearwards...

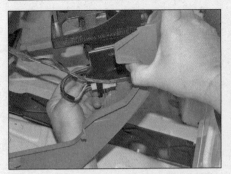

26.34b ...and unplug the connector for the 12V socket

26.38a Remove the screws on the left of the panel...

26.38b ...then the two on the front of the panel...

26.38c ...and slide the panel left to release it

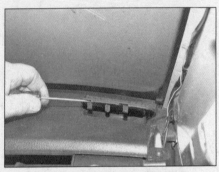

26.41 Prise up the speaker grille

air vent, as described in Chapter 3 Section 8.

38 Slacken the four mounting screws and tug the panel towards the passenger door to unhook it from its mounting clips (**see illustrations**).

39 Refitting is a reversal of removal.

Outer facia top panels

40 Remove the outer side vent and central vents as described in Chapter 3 Section 8.

41 Unclip the speaker grille (**see illustration**).

42 Remove the four mounting screws and remove the facia top panel, and unplug the speaker wiring plug when it becomes available (**see illustrations**).

Central facia top panel

43 Remove the left and right central vent panels as described in Section 26.

44 Slacken the mounting screws on each side of the central top panel and remove (**see illustration**).

45 Refitting is a reversal of removal.

Central dashboard top tray

46 Remove all dashboard top panels as described earlier in this Section.

47 Undo the two front mounting screws and withdraw the tray (**see illustrations**).

48 Refitting is a reversal of removal.

Complete facia panel

Removal

49 Remove the A-pillar trim panels on both sides as described in Section 23.

Refitting

35 Refitting is a reversal of removal ensuring that all wiring is correctly reconnected and all mountings securely tightened.

Passenger-side facia panel

36 Remove the outer air vent as described earlier in this Section.

37 Remove the passenger-side central

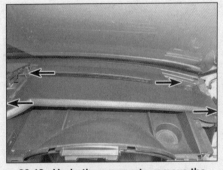

26.42a Undo the screws to remove the panel...

26.42b ...and unplug the speaker

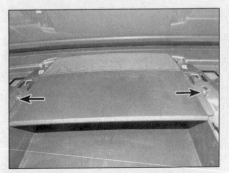

26.44 Undo the screws to remove the panel

26.47a Remove the two mounting screws at the front...

26.47b ...and manoeuvre the tray from place

50 Remove the following facia panels as described previously in this Section:
a) *Steering column shrouds.*
b) *Instrument panel surround.*
c) *Facia centre panel.*
d) *Outer vent panels.*

51 Remove the following components as described in Chapter 12 :
a) *Instrument panel.*
b) *Tachograph (where fitted).*

c) *Facia speakers*

52 Remove the heater control panel as described in Chapter 3 Section 8.

53 Undo the retaining screws from under the speaker grille at each end of the facia panel.

54 Remove the ashtray, and disconnect the wiring connector from the cigarette lighter.

55 Remove the centre console from the lower part of the facia panel.

56 Detach the ventilation ducts from the heater housing, and then check that all wiring has been disconnected.

57 Working along the facia panel, undo the retaining screws and then maneuver the facia panel out from inside of the vehicle.

Refitting

58 Refitting is a reversal of removal ensuring that all wiring is correctly reconnected and all mountings securely tightened.

Chapter 12
Body electrical systems

Contents

Degrees of difficulty

Easy, suitable for novice with little experience	Fairly easy, suitable for beginner with some experience	Fairly difficult, suitable for competent DIY mechanic	Difficult, suitable for experienced DIY mechanic	Very difficult, suitable for expert DIY or professional

Specifications

Fuses and relays

Refer to the wiring diagrams at the end of this Chapter.

Bulbs

	Wattage
Direction indicator lights:	
Front	21 (PY21W amber glass)
Rear	21 (P21W)
Direction indicator side repeater lights.	5 (W5W)
Foglights:	
Front	55 (H1 type)
Rear (driver's side only)	21 (P21W)
Headlights:	
Dipped beam	55 (H1 type)
Main beam	55 (H1 type)
Interior lights in passenger and load compartments	18 (K type)
Interior lights with reading light	10 (K type)
Number plate light:	
Pick-up models	5 (R5W)
All other models	5 (C5W)
Perimeter lights (Pick-up models)	5 (R5W)
Reversing lights	21 (P21W)
Sidelights	5 (W5W)
Side marker lights/outline lights	5 (W5W)
Stop-light (additional)	LED
Stop/tail lights	21/5 (P21/5W)
Tail lights (Pick-up models)	5 (R5W)

Torque wrench settings

	Nm	lbf ft
Passenger airbag retaining bolts*	8	6
Airbag control unit mounting bolts	10	7
Windscreen wiper arm-to-spindle nuts	30	22
Windscreen wiper motor bracket-to-body bolts	12	8
Windscreen wiper spindle nuts	10	7

* Use new nuts/bolts

1 General information and precautions

⚠️ **Warning: Before carrying out any work on the electrical system, read through the precautions given in Safety first! at the beginning of this manual, and in Chapter 5.**

1 The electrical system is of the 12-volt negative earth type. Power for the lights and all electrical accessories is supplied by a lead-calcium type battery, which is charged by the engine-driven alternator.

2 This Chapter covers repair and service procedures for the various electrical components not associated with the engine. Information on the battery, alternator and starter motor can be found in Chapter 5.

3 It should be noted that, prior to working on any component in the electrical system, the battery negative terminal should first be disconnected, to prevent the possibility of electrical short-circuits and/or fires.

Caution: Before proceeding, disconnect the battery as described in Chapter 5 Section 3.

2 Electrical fault finding – general information

Note: *Refer to the precautions given in 'Safety first!' and in Section 1 of this Chapter before starting work. The following tests relate to testing of the main electrical circuits, and should not be used to test delicate electronic circuits, particularly where an electronic control module is used.*

General

1 A typical electrical circuit consists of an electrical component; any switches, relays, motors, fuses, fusible links or circuit breakers related to that component, and the wiring and connectors which link the component to both the battery and the chassis. To help to pinpoint a problem in an electrical circuit, wiring diagrams are included at the end of this Chapter.

2 Before attempting to diagnose an electrical fault, first study the appropriate wiring diagram, to obtain a complete understanding of the components included in the particular circuit concerned. The possible sources of a fault can be narrowed down by noting if other components related to the circuit are operating properly. If several components or circuits fail at one time, the problem is likely to be related to a shared fuse or earth connection.

3 Electrical problems usually stem from simple causes, such as loose or corroded connections, a faulty earth connection, a blown fuse, a melted fusible link, or a faulty relay (refer to Section 3 for details of testing relays). Visually inspect the condition of all fuses, wires and connections in a problem circuit before testing the components. Use the wiring diagrams to determine which terminal connections will need to be checked in order to pinpoint the trouble spot.

4 The basic tools required for electrical fault-finding include a circuit tester or voltmeter (a 12 volt bulb with a set of test leads can also be used for certain tests); an ohmmeter (to measure resistance and check for continuity); a battery and set of test leads; and a jumper wire, preferably with a circuit breaker or fuse incorporated, which can be used to bypass suspect wires or electrical components. Before attempting to locate a problem with test instruments, use the wiring diagram to determine where to make the connections.

5 To find the source of an intermittent wiring fault (usually due to a poor or dirty connection, or damaged wiring insulation), a 'wiggle' test can be performed on the wiring. This involves wiggling the wiring by hand to see if the fault occurs as the wiring is moved. It should be possible to narrow down the source of the fault to a particular section of wiring. This method of testing can be used in conjunction with any of the tests described in the following sub-Sections.

6 Apart from problems due to poor connections, two basic types of fault can occur in an electrical circuit – open-circuit, or short-circuit.

7 Open-circuit faults are caused by a break somewhere in the circuit, which prevents current from flowing. An open-circuit fault will prevent a component from working.

8 Short-circuit faults are caused by a 'short' somewhere in the circuit, which allows the current flowing in the circuit to 'escape' along an alternative route, usually to earth. Short-circuit faults are normally caused by a breakdown in wiring insulation, which allows a feed wire to touch either another wire, or an earthed component such as the bodyshell. A short-circuit fault will normally cause the relevant circuit fuse to blow.

Finding an open-circuit

9 To check for an open-circuit, connect one lead of a circuit tester or the negative lead of a voltmeter either to the battery negative terminal or to a known good earth.

10 Connect the other lead to a connector in the circuit being tested, preferably nearest to the battery or fuse. At this point, battery voltage should be present, unless the lead from the battery or the fuse itself is faulty (bearing in mind that some circuits are live only when the ignition switch is moved to a particular position).

11 Switch on the circuit, then connect the tester lead to the connector nearest the circuit switch on the component side.

12 If voltage is present (indicated either by the tester bulb lighting or a voltmeter reading, as applicable), this means that the section of the circuit between the relevant connector and the switch is problem-free.

13 Continue to check the remainder of the circuit in the same fashion.

14 When a point is reached at which no voltage is present, the problem must lie between that point and the previous test point with voltage. Most problems can be traced to a broken, corroded or loose connection.

Finding a short-circuit

15 To check for a short-circuit; first disconnect the load(s) from the circuit (loads are the components which draw current from a circuit, such as bulbs, motors, heating elements, etc).

16 Remove the relevant fuse from the circuit, and connect a circuit tester or voltmeter to the fuse connections.

17 Switch on the circuit, bearing in mind that some circuits are live only when the ignition switch is moved to a particular position.

18 If voltage is present (indicated either by the tester bulb lighting or a voltmeter reading, as applicable), this means that there is a short-circuit.

19 If no voltage is present during this test, but the fuse still blows with the load(s) reconnected, this indicates an internal fault in the load(s).

Finding an earth fault

20 The battery negative terminal is connected to 'earth' – the metal of the engine/transmission and the vehicle body – and many systems are wired so that they only receive a positive feed, the current returning via the metal of the vehicle body. This means that the component mounting and the body form part of that circuit. Loose or corroded mountings can therefore cause a range of electrical faults, ranging from total failure of a circuit, to a puzzling partial failure. In particular, lights may shine dimly (especially when another circuit sharing the same earth point is in operation), motors (eg, wiper motors or the heater blower motor) may run slowly, and the operation of one circuit may have an apparently unrelated effect on another. Note that on many vehicles, earth straps are used between certain components, such as the engine/transmission and the body, usually where there is no metal-to-metal contact between components, due to flexible rubber mountings, etc.

21 To check whether a component is properly earthed, disconnect the battery and connect one lead of an ohmmeter to a known good earth point. Connect the other lead to the wire or earth connection being tested. The resistance reading should be zero; if not, check the connection as follows.

22 If an earth connection is thought to be faulty, dismantle the connection, and clean both the bodyshell and the wire terminal (or the component earth connection mating surface) back to bare metal. Be careful to remove all traces of dirt and corrosion, and then use a knife to trim away any paint, so that a clean metal-to-metal joint is made.

On reassembly, tighten the joint fasteners securely; if a wire terminal is being refitted, use serrated washers between the terminal and the bodyshell, to ensure a clean and secure connection. When the connection is remade, prevent the onset of corrosion in the future by applying a coat of petroleum jelly or silicone-based grease, or by spraying on (at regular intervals) a proprietary water-dispersant lubricant.

3 Fuses and relays – general information

3.1 Fusebox located under dashboard facia

3.2 Fusebox located under driver's seat

Fuses

1 The main fuses and relays are located in the fuse/relay box situated at the left-hand underside of the facia in the passenger footwell. To gain access, turn the locking screw anti-clockwise a quarter of a turn and fold the cover downwards **(see illustration)**.

2 Additional fuses and relays are located in the fuse/relay box under the driver's seat. To gain access, release the catches at the top of the cover and then unclip the cover from the bottom **(see illustration)**.

3 The fuses and relays are identified on the diagram on the inside surface of the fuse/relay box cover or lid. Each fuse is also marked with its rating. Plastic tweezers are attached to the inside face of the lid to remove and fit the fuses.

4 To remove a fuse, pull it out of the holder, preferably using the tweezers, then slide the fuse sideways from the tweezers. The wire within the fuse is clearly visible, and it will be broken if the fuse is blown.

5 Always renew a fuse with one of an identical rating. Never renew a fuse more than once without tracing the source of the trouble. The fuse rating is stamped on top of the fuse.

6 Fusible links are incorporated in the positive feed from the battery, their function being to protect the main wiring loom in the event of a short-circuit. When the links blow, all of the wiring circuits are disconnected, and will remain so until the cause of the malfunction is repaired and the link renewed.

Relays

7 A relay is an electrically operated switch, which is used for the following reasons:
a) *A relay can switch a heavy current remotely from the circuit in which the current is flowing, allowing the use of lighter-gauge wiring and switch contacts.*
b) *A relay can receive more than one control input, unlike a mechanical switch.*
c) *A relay can have a timer function – for example an intermittent wiper delay.*

8 The relays and timers are located in the two fuse/relay boxes. The various relays can be removed from their locations by carefully pulling them from the sockets.

9 If a system controlled by a relay becomes inoperative and the relay is suspect, listen to the relay as the circuit is operated. If the relay is functioning, it should be possible to hear it click as it is energised. If the relay proves satisfactory, the fault lies with the components or wiring of the system. If the relay is not being energised, then it is not receiving a main supply voltage or a switching voltage, or the relay is faulty.

4 Switches – removal and refitting

Note: *Disconnect the battery negative terminal, as described in Chapter 5 Section 3 before removing any switch, and reconnect the terminal after refitting.*

4.1 Remove the bottom right-hand panel

4.3 Unscrew the trim ring from place

Ignition switch/ steering column lock

1 Remove the mounting screw and remove the lower right-hand facia panel **(see illustration)**.

2 Remove the two mounting screws on the driver's-side lower facia panel **(see illustration)** and manoeuvre panel from place.

3 Using a suitable tool, unscrew the trim ring from around the ignition switch **(see illustration)**.

4 Remove the instrument panel surround, as described in Chapter 11 Section 26.

5 Manoeuvre the ignition switch backwards from place, and disconnect the spacer ring behind the facia and the wiring plugs **(see illustration)**.

6 Our van was fitted with an additional aftermarket ignition security protector, which we removed using a hacksaw and screwdriver.

7 Refitting is a reversal of removal.

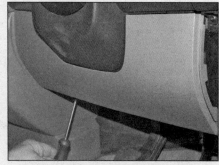

4.2 Unscrew the two mounting screws

4.5 Pull the switch backwards and disconnect

4.10 Remove the rotary connector from the column

4.11 Remove the retaining screws and manoeuvre the switch from place

4.12 Undo the retaining screw for the bracket holding the indicator stalk

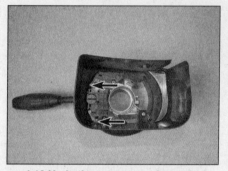

4.13 Undo the screws to release the combination stalk

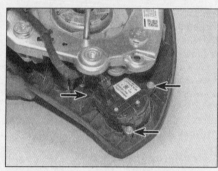

4.16 Undo the screws and remove the switch

Steering column combination switch

8 Remove the steering wheel as described in Chapter 10, Section 11.

9 Remove the steering column shroud as described in Chapter 11, Section 26.

10 On models with airbags fitted, remove the rotary 'clock spring' contact unit, as described in Section 22. Disconnect the wiring connectors to the rotary unit, and then withdraw it from the the steering column (see illustration). Note the fitted position of the rotary connector unit for refitting.

11 Remove the switch for the cruise control (see illustration).

12 Remove the retaining screw from the bracket holding the combination switch, then lift the switch upwards and off the top of the steering column (see illustration).

13 Working at the rear of the unit, remove the retaining screws and manoeuvre the combination switch from place (see illustration).

14 Refitting is a reversal of removal.

Steering wheel switches

15 Remove the airbag unit as described in Section 22.

16 On the rear of the airbag unit, undo the three mounting screws for each steering wheel switch and manoeuvre from place (see illustration).

17 Disconnect the wiring plug as it becomes available.

18 Refitting is a reversal of removal.

Headlight switch

19 Remove the A-pillar trim as described in Chapter 11 Section 23.

20 Slacken the mounting screws for the bottom panel by the driver's outer-side knee (see illustration 4.1) and manoeuvre the panel from place.

21 Remove the two mounting screws at the bottom of the headlight switch panel, and the screw at the top, then manoeuvre the panel from place (see illustration).

22 Manoeuvre the panel from place, disconnecting the wiring plugs as they become available (see illustration).

23 Undo the two mounting screws and manoeuvre the headlight switch from place (see illustration).

24 Refitting is a reversal of removal

Headlight height adjuster switch

25 Remove the lower panel as described previously in this Section.

26 Working at the rear of the panel, depress the two tabs and manoeuvre the switch from place (see illustration).

27 Refitting is a reversal of removal

4.21 Undo the screws and remove the panel

4.22 Disconnect the wiring plugs

4.23 Remove the screws to release the switch

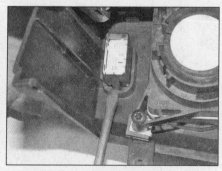

4.26 Squeeze the tabs to release the switch

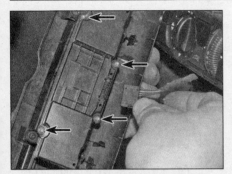

4.29 Undo the screws to remove the switches from the panel

4.34 Slide the retaining clip from the switch

4.35 Remove the switch from place

Facia centre panel switches

28 Remove the facia centre panel as described in Chapter 11, Section 26.
29 Undo the four retaining screws and remove the switches from the panel **(see illustration)**.
30 Refitting is a reversal of removal.

Stop-light switch

31 Refer to Chapter 9, Section 18.

Handbrake warning light switch

32 Refer to Chapter 9, Section 17.

Electric window switch

33 Remove the door trim panel as described in Chapter 11 Section 8.
34 Slide off the plastic retaining clip on the rear of the switch panel **(see illustration)**.
35 Withdraw the switch from the panel **(see illustration)**.

5.3a Insert a tool between the instrument panel and it's surround...

5.4 Disconnect the wiring plug

36 Refitting is a reversal of removal.

Heating/ventilation/ air conditioning system switches

37 The switches are all an integral part of the heating/ventilation control unit. Refer to Chapter 3 Section 8 to remove the heater control panel.

5 Instrument panel – removal and refitting

Removal

1 Disconnect the battery negative terminal, as described in Chapter 5 Section 3.
2 Activate the steering lock and adjust the steering wheel as low as it will go.
3 Insert a suitable trim removal tool between

5.3b ...and swivel the panel forward (steering wheel removed for clarity)

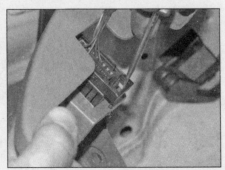

6.2 Slide out the retaining clip (panel removed for clarity)

the top of the instrument panel and the inner surface of the instrument binnacle and swivel the top of the instruments forward **(see illustrations)**.
4 Disconnect the wiring plug and remove the instrument panel **(see illustration)**.

Refitting

5 Refitting is a reversal of removal.

6 On-Board Diagnostic (OBD) plug – removal and refitting

1 Remove the glovebox as described in Chapter 11 Section 26.
2 Slide out the retaining clip for the OBD port **(see illustration)**.
3 Manoeuvre the port from place and unplug the wiring connector **(see illustration)**.
4 Refitting is a reversal of removal.

7 Body control module – removal and refitting

Removal

1 Remove the glovebox and lower trim panels, as described in Chapter 11 Section 23.
2 Depress the tabs along the top and separate the lower fusebox panel from the main fusebox **(see illustration)**.

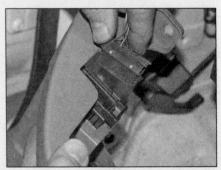

6.3 Remove the port and unplug the connector

7.2 Unclip the lower fusebox from the main section

7.3 Use a screwdriver to open the tabs and move the main fusebox

7.4 Loosen the module mounting screw

7.5 Pull the body control module out

3 Press the main fusebox tabs to manoeuvre it from place **(see illustration)**.
4 Undo the body control module mounting screw at its bottom edge **(see illustration)**.
5 Pull the body control module backwards and downwards to manoeuvre it from place **(see illustration)**.
6 Disconnect the wiring plugs as the unit is withdrawn.

Refitting

7 Refitting is a reversal of removal.

8 Tachograph – removal and refitting

Note: *Where fitted, there are a number of different types of tachograph available for these vehicles. Some are fitted with anti-tamper seals, check with your local*

dealer or specialist to obtain new seals before removal.
Note: *Mercedes-Benz use a special tool (part No 000 545 0744) to remove the tachograph from the facia. Alternatively, a suitable tool can be fabricated from 3 mm diameter wire, such as welding rod.*

Removal

1 Turn the ignition key to position 0.
2 Insert the special tools into the holes on the front of the unit at each end, and then push them until they snap into place. The tachograph can then be slid out of the facia.
3 Remove the anti-tamper seal from the wiring connection cover, and then the cover can be removed. Discard the anti-tamper seal, as a new one will be required for refitting.
4 Disconnect the wiring connections at the rear of the unit, and remove the unit from the vehicle.
5 Remove the special tools.

Refitting

6 To refit the tachograph, reconnect the wiring connector and secure the cover in place by using a new anti-tamper seal. Push the unit firmly into the facia until the retaining lugs snap into place.

9 Headlight beam alignment – general information

1 Accurate adjustment of the headlight beam is only possible using optical beam-setting equipment, and this work should therefore be carried out by a Mercedes-Benz dealer or suitably equipped workshop.
2 All models have an electric headlight beam adjustment system, controlled via a switch in the facia. With the vehicle unladen, the switch should be set in position 0. With the vehicle partially or fully loaded, set the switch position to provide adequate illumination without dazzling oncoming drivers.
3 All models have manual adjusters on the rear of the headlight unit for initial setting. This should be set when the vehicle is unladen and the switch on the facia is set to 0. The outer adjuster on the rear of the light unit is for the horizontal adjustment and the inner one for vertical adjustment.

10 Bulbs (exterior lights) – renewal

General

1 Whenever a bulb is renewed, note the following points:
a) *Make sure the switch is in the OFF position for the bulb you are working on.*
b) *Remember that if the light has just been in use, the bulb may be extremely hot.*
c) *Always check the bulb contacts and holder, ensuring that there is clean metal-to-metal contact between the bulb and its live(s) and earth. Clean off any corrosion or dirt before fitting a new bulb.*
d) *Wherever bayonet-type bulbs are fitted, ensure that the live contact(s) bear firmly against the bulb contact.*
e) *Always ensure that the new bulb is of the correct rating, and that it is completely clean before fitting it; this applies particularly to headlight/foglight bulbs.*

Headlight

2 Rotate the cover at the rear of the headlight unit to remove it **(see illustration)**.

Dipped beam/main beam

Note: *These are two separate bulbs – the dipped beam is the higher of the two, with the main beam bulb below, but they are removed in the same way.*
3 Rotate the bulbholder anti-clockwise and remove from the unit. Pull the bulb out of the

10.2 Rotate the cover anti-clockwise

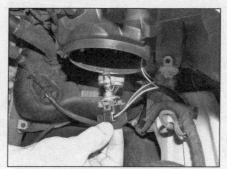

10.3a Twist and remove the bulbholder from place...

10.3b ...and remove the headlight bulb

10.7 Remove the bulbholder

10.8 Pull the capless type bulb to remove

10.10 Unscrew the rear cover

10.11 Squeeze the tabs to remove the bulbholder

10.12 Pull the bulb from the bulbholder

light unit **(see illustrations)**. When handling the new bulb, use a tissue or clean cloth to avoid touching the glass with the fingers; moisture and grease from the skin can cause blackening and rapid failure of this type of bulb. If the glass is accidentally touched, wipe it clean using methylated spirit.

4 Fit the new bulb to the headlight unit and reconnect the wiring connector.

5 Refit the plastic cover to the rear of the headlight unit. Check for satisfactory operation on completion.

Front sidelight

6 Rotate the cover at the rear of the headlight unit to remove **(see illustration 10.2)**.

7 Pull the sidelight bulbholder from the rear of the headlight **(see illustration)**.

8 Remove the bulb from the bulbholder **(see illustration)**.

9 Fit the new bulb using a reversal of the removal procedure. Check for satisfactory operation on completion.

Daytime running light

10 Rotate the cover anti-clockwise to remove it **(see illustration)**.

11 Depress the two tabs and withdraw the bulbholder from the unit **(see illustration)**.

12 Pull the bulb from the bulbholder.**(see illustration)**

13 Refitting is a reversal of removal.

Side marker lights

14 There are LED marker light units on each side of the van. Use a screwdriver or trim removal tool to prise them from place **(see illustration)**.

15 Disconnect the wiring plug **(see illustration)**.

16 Refitting is reversal of removal.

Direction indicator

17 Twist the indicator bulbholder anti-

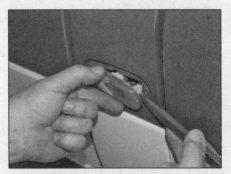

10.14 Prise the running lights from the panels they're mounted in

10.17 Twist the bulbholder to remove it

clockwise, and remove it from the rear of the headlight unit **(see illustration)**.

18 The bulb is a bayonet-fit in the holder, and can be removed by pressing it and twisting in an anti-clockwise direction **(see illustration)**.

10.15 Disconnect the light's wiring plug

10.18 Push the bulb in and twist to remove it

10.21 Rotate the bulbholder anti-clockwise

10.24 Unclip the bulbholder

10.25 Push the bulb in and twist to remove it

19 Fit the new bulb using a reversal of the removal procedure. Check for satisfactory operation on completion.

Direction indicator in mirror housing

20 Remove the mirror glass as described in Chapter 11 Section 19.
21 Rotate the bulb holder and remove from place (see illustration).
22 Fit the new bulb and refit using a reversal of this procedure.

Rear light cluster

23 Remove the light cluster as described in Section 12.
24 Unclip the tabs to release the bulbholder (see illustration).
25 The bulbs are a bayonet-fit in the holder, and can be removed by pressing the relevant bulb in and twisting it in an anti-clockwise direction (see illustration).
26 Fit the new bulb(s) using a reversal of the removal procedure. Check for satisfactory operation on completion.

High-level brake light

27 This is an LED unit, and the procedure is covered in the exterior light unit removal procedure in Section 12.

Number plate light

28 Prise free the light unit using a small screwdriver, and then remove the festoon type bulb from the contacts.
29 Fit the new bulb using a reversal of the

removal procedure. Check for satisfactory operation on completion.

11 Bulbs (interior lights) – renewal

General

1 Refer to Section 12, paragraph 1.

Courtesy lights

2 Insert a small screwdriver blade into the indent in the light unit, and carefully prise it free.
3 The courtesy lights have festoon-type bulbs, and this type is simply prised free from its holder.
4 Fit the new bulb using a reversal of the removal procedure. Check for satisfactory operation on completion.

Instrument panel illumination and warning lights

5 Procedures for the removal and refitting of the instrument panel and warning light bulbs are contained in Section 5.

Stepwell light

6 Carefully prise the light unit from its location and twist the bulbholder to remove it from the light unit. Pull the bulb from the bulbholder.
7 Fit the new bulb using a reversal of the removal procedure. Check for satisfactory operation on completion.

Heater control illumination

8 Remove the heater/air conditioning control panel as described in Chapter 3 Section 8. At the time of writing there was no information on the stripdown of the heater control panel to renew any bulbs. See your local Mercedes-Benz dealer for availability of any spares for the illumination of the heater control panel.

12 Exterior light units – removal and refitting

Note: *Disconnect the battery, as described in Chapter 5 Section 3 before removing any light unit. Reconnect the battery after refitting.*

Headlight/direction indicator

1 Remove the front grille as described in Chapter 11, Section 22.
2 Remove the front bumper, as described in Chapter 11 Section 20.
3 Undo the four screws (arrowed) securing the headlight unit to the vehicle (see illustration).
4 Disconnect the wiring plug, and then remove the unit from the vehicle (see illustrations).
5 Refit in the reverse order of removal. Refer to Section 9 for details on headlight beam alignment. Check the headlights and indicators for satisfactory operation on completion.

12.3 Headlight retaining screws

12.4a Disconnect the wiring plug...

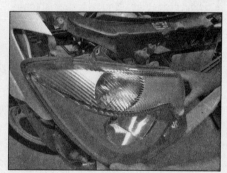

12.4b ...and remove the headlight

12.7 Undo the four screws to separate the mirror surround

12.8 Manoeuvre the indicator from place

12.10 Remove the three Torx screws

Direction indicator in mirror housing

6 Remove the mirror glass as described in Chapter 11 Section 19.

7 Remove the four mounting screws and remove the rear mirror surround **(see illustration)**.

8 Slide the indicator surround from place **(see illustration)**.

9 Refitting is a reversal of removal.

Rear light cluster

10 Unscrew the three Torx mounting screws from the light unit **(see illustration)**.

11 Push the light cluster assembly towards the outer edge of the vehicle to release it from it mounting clips **(see illustration)**.

12 Depress the tabs to release the wiring plug **(see illustration)**.

13 Refit in the reverse order of removal. Check the lights for satisfactory operation on completion.

High-level brake light

14 Remove the two mounting screws **(see illustrations)** and gently prise the unit from place. **Note:** *The unit may have sealant around it, so gently scrape this away while teasing the LED unit from place.*

15 Clean up the area around the light unit.

16 Peel off the protective covering of a new unit (or apply a bead of sealant around the edge of the old unit if it's being refitted) and refit the light unit **(see illustration)**.

17 Tighten the mounting screws

Number plate light

18 Unscrew the door interior trim to expose the numberplate light's wiring plug.

19 Disconnect the wiring plug and prise the numberplate light unit from place.

20 Gently pull through the wiring to remove.

21 Refitting is reversal of removal.

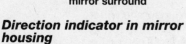

13 Headlight levelling actuator/motor – removal and refitting

Note: *Read the information on headlight beam alignment in Section 9 before removing the levelling actuator/motor.*

12.11 Nudge the assembly towards the outer edge of the vehicle (right-hand side shown)

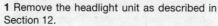

1 Remove the headlight unit as described in Section 12.

2 Release the two clips at each side of the headlight unit and remove the cover at the rear of the headlight unit.

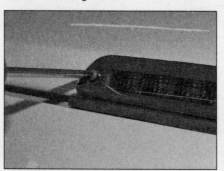

12.14a Undo the screws...

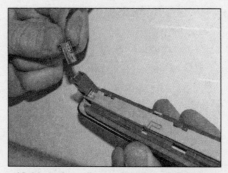

12.14c ...then disconnect the wiring plug

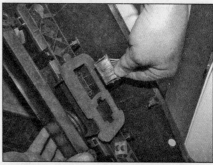

12.12 Squeeze the tabs and remove the wiring plug

3 Disconnect the wiring connector from the levelling motor.

4 Rotate the levelling motor and withdraw it from the rear of headlight, while disconnecting the pullrod balljoint from the rear of the reflector.

12.14b ...and prise out the LED unit...

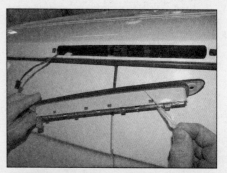

12.16 Apply sealant before reinstalling

14.1 Horn location – beside the O/S headlight unit

5 Refit in the reverse order of removal. Make sure the balljoint is connected securely in the socket on the back of the headlight reflector. Check for satisfactory operation of the levelling motor on completion.

14 Horn – removal and refitting

Removal

1 The horn is located beside the right-hand headlight unit inside the engine compartment (**see illustration**).
2 Remove the front grille as described in Chapter 11 Section 22.
3 Detach the wiring plug from the horn, then unscrew the horn mounting bracket bolt and withdraw the horn (**see illustration**).

14.3 Disconnect the wiring plug

4 If required, the horn can be separated from the mounting bracket by undoing the retaining nut.

Refitting

5 Refit in the reverse order of removal. Check for satisfactory operation on completion.

15 Wiper arms – removal and refitting

Removal

1 Ensure the wipers are 'parked' (ie, in the normal at-rest position). There are small horizontal marks on the windscreen to allow you to verify this.
2 Disconnect the nozzle from the end of the

washer pipe and withdraw the pipe from the wiper arm (**see illustration**).
3 Lift up the plastic cap from the bottom of the wiper arm, and remove the nut (**see illustrations**).
4 Wiggle the wiper arm to loosen it, and release it from the spindle (**see illustration**). If necessary, use a puller to release it.

Refitting

5 Refitting is a reversal of removal. Make sure the arm is fitted in its previously noted position, and take care to feed the washer hose up through the centre of the wiper spring.

16 Windscreen wiper motor and linkage – removal and refitting

Removal

1 Disconnect the battery negative terminal as described in Chapter 5 Section 3.
2 Remove the air filter assembly, as described in Chapter 4A Section 2.
3 Remove the wiper arms as described in Section 15.
4 Slacken and remove the securing nuts and washers from the wiper arm spindles (**see illustration**).
5 Disconnect the wiper motor wiring plug (**see illustration**).
6 Undo the bolt securing the wiper motor to the bracket, and remove the complete motor and linkage assembly from the vehicle (**see illustration**).

15.2 Disconnect the washer nozzle

15.3a Unclip the plastic cover...

15.3b ...and undo the securing nut

15.4 Release the wiper arm from the spindle

16.4 Remove the spindle securing nut and washer

16.5 Disconnect the wiring plug

Refitting

7 Refitting is a reversal of removal, noting the following points:

a) *Refit the air filter assembly with reference to Chapter 4A Section 2.*

b) *Refit the wiper arms with reference to Section 15.*

c) *On completion, reconnect the battery and check the wipers for satisfactory operation.*

17 Windscreen washer reservoir – removal and refitting

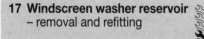

Removal

1 Open the bonnet and undo the two retaining screws from the reservoir **(see illustration)**.

2 Disconnect all washer hoses from the reservoir.

3 Lift the reservoir up to disengage the locating lug with the grommet in the inner wing panel **(see illustration)**.

4 Disconnect the wiring connector. Fit blanking plug over the end of the outlet pipe on the pump to prevent washer fluid loss.

5 Remove the windscreen washer reservoir out from the engine bay, taking care not to spill any fluid.

6 If required, the pump can be removed from the reservoir by prising it from its location. Recover the seal after removal of the pump. **Note:** *If the pump is to be removed from the reservoir, make sure the reservoir is empty or a container is available to catch the washer fluid.*

17.1 Slacken the two retaining screws

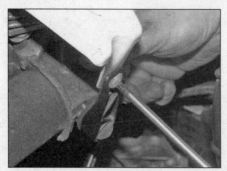

16.6 Undo the mounting screw and remove the wiper motor and linkage

Refitting

7 Refitting is a reversal of removal. Lubricate the pump seal (if removed) with a little washing-up liquid, to ease fitting.

8 On completion, top-up the reservoir with the required water/washer solution mix, and check for leaks and satisfactory operation.

18 Radio/media unit – removal and refitting

Removal

1 Disconnect the battery, as described in Chapter 5 Section 3.

2 Remove the central instrument surround panel, as described in Chapter 11 Section 26.

3 Remove the four retaining screws (see

17.3 Pull up to disengage the locating lug

18.4 Disconnect the wiring plugs and aerial lead

illustrations) and the radio/media unit can then be slid out of the facia.

4 Disconnect the aerial and wiring plugs at the rear of the unit, and remove the unit from the vehicle **(see illustration)**.

Refitting

5 Refitting is a reversal of removal bearing in mind the following points:

a) *When the leads are reconnected to the rear of the unit, press it into position to the point where the retaining clips are felt to engage.*

b) *On units with a security code, reactivate the unit in accordance with the code and the instructions given in the Mercedes-Benz Audio Operating Manual, usually supplied with the vehicle.*

USB/line-in socket

6 The socket is located in the left edge of the dash-top tray behind the instrument binnacle. Using a trim removel tool, prise it from place, disconnecting the wiring plugs as they become available **(see illustration)**.

19 Loudspeakers – removal and refitting

Facia panel

Removal

1 Prise up the speaker grille in the top of the dashboard **(see illustration)**.

18.3a Remove the four mounting bolts...

18.6 Prise out the socket and disconnect the wiring plugs

18.3b ...and withdraw the audio unit from place

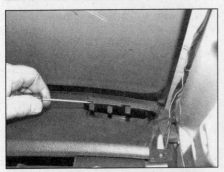

19.1 Unclip the speaker grille from the facia

2 Slacken the four mounting screws and remove the dashboard top panel, as described in Chapter 11 Section 26.

3 Withdraw the speaker from the panel and disconnect the wiring plugs **(see illustration)**.

Refitting

4 Refitting is a reversal of removal.

Front doors

Removal

5 Remove the door trim panel, as described in Chapter 11 Section 8.

6 Disconnect the wiring plug for the speaker **(see illustration)**.

7 Remove the four mounting screws and withdraw the speaker from place **(see illustration)**.

Refitting

8 Refitting is a reversal of removal.

20 Anti-theft alarm system – general information

1 Most models in the range are fitted with an anti-theft alarm system, incorporating an engine immobiliser, as standard equipment. The system is activated when the vehicle is locked, and has both active and passive capabilities. The active section includes the front, side and rear door lock actuators, bonnet lock, audio unit security and the alarm horn. The passive section includes the ignition

19.6 Disconnect the wiring plug

19.3 Disconnect the wiring plug and loosen the retainign screw to remove the speaker

key transponder, passive anti-theft system (PATS) transceiver and LED, starter relay, and fuel injection pump.

2 When activating the anti-theft alarm system, there is a 20 second delay during which time it is still possible to open the vehicle without triggering the alarm. After the 20 second delay, the system monitors all doors and bonnet, provided they are closed. If one of these items is closed later, the system will monitor it after the 20-second delay.

3 If the alarm is triggered, the alarm horn will sound for a period of 30 seconds, and the hazard lights will flash for a period of 5 minutes. An attempt to start the engine or remove the audio unit automatically triggers the alarm horn.

4 To deactivate the system, one of the front doors must be unlocked with the ignition key or remote control. The rear doors may be unlocked with the ignition key or remote control with the alarm still activated, however the alarm is again reactivated when the rear doors are locked.

5 The PATS includes a starter inhibitor circuit, which makes it impossible to start the engine with the system armed. The immobiliser is deactivated by a transponder chip built into the ignition key.

6 The PATS transceiver unit is fitted around the ignition switch, and it 'reads' the code from a microchip in the ignition key. This means that any keys must be obtained through a Mercedes-Benz dealer – any keys cut locally will not contain the microchip, and will therefore not disarm the immobiliser.

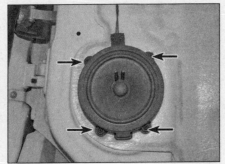

19.7 Undo the screws and remove the speaker

7 If any attempt is made to remove the audio unit while the alarm is active the alarm will sound.

21 Airbag system – general information and precautions

General information

1 Depending on model, a driver's airbag and passenger airbag in the facia are fitted as standard equipment.

2 The system is armed only when the ignition is switched on, however, a reserve power source maintains a power supply to the system in the event of a break in the main electrical supply. The steering wheel and facia airbags are activated by a 'g' sensor (deceleration sensor), and controlled by an electronic control unit located under the facia.

3 The airbags are inflated by a gas generator, which forces the bag out from its location in the steering wheel or facia.

Precautions

⚠️ **Warning: The following precautions must be observed when working on vehicles equipped with an airbag system, to prevent the possibility of personal injury.**

General precautions

a) Do not disconnect the battery with the engine running.

b) Before carrying out any work in the vicinity of the airbag, removal of any of the airbag components, or any welding work on the vehicle, de-activate the system as described in the following sub-Section.

c) Do not attempt to test any of the airbag system circuits using test meters or any other test equipment.

d) If the airbag warning light comes on, or any fault in the system is suspected, consult a Mercedes-Benz dealer without delay. Do not attempt to carry out fault diagnosis, or any dismantling of the components.

Precautions when handling an airbag

a) Transport the airbag by itself, bag upward

b) Do not put your arms around the airbag.

c) Carry the airbag close to the body, bag outward.

d) Do not drop the airbag or expose it to impacts.

e) Do not attempt to dismantle the airbag unit.

f) Do not connect any form of electrical equipment to any part of the airbag circuit.

Precautions when storing an airbag

a) Store the unit in a cupboard with the airbag upward.

b) Do not expose the airbag to temperatures above 80ºC.

c) Do not expose the airbag to flames.

d) *Do not attempt to dispose of the airbag – consult a Mercedes-Benz dealer.*

e) *Never refit an airbag, which is known to be faulty or damaged.*

De-activation of airbag system

4 The system must be de-activated before carrying out any work on the airbag components or surrounding area:

a) *Switch on the ignition and check the operation of the airbag warning light on the instrument panel. The light should illuminate when the ignition is switched on, then extinguish.*

b) *Switch off the ignition.*

c) *Remove the ignition key.*

d) *Switch off all electrical equipment.*

e) *Disconnect the battery negative terminal, as described in Chapter 5 Section 3.*

f) *Insulate the battery negative terminal and the end of the battery negative lead to prevent any possibility of contact.*

g) *Wait for at least two minutes before carrying out any further work. Wait at least ten minutes if the airbag warning light did not operate correctly.*

Activation of airbag system

5 To activate the system on completion of any work, proceed as follows:

a) *Ensure that there are no occupants in the vehicle, and that there are no loose objects around the vicinity of the steering wheel.*

b) *Ensure that the ignition is switched off then reconnect the battery negative terminal.*

c) *Open the driver's door and switch on the ignition, without reaching in front of the steering wheel. Check that the airbag warning light illuminates briefly then extinguishes.*

d) *Switch off the ignition.*

e) *If the airbag warning light does not operate as described in paragraph c), consult a Mercedes-Benz dealer before driving the vehicle.*

22 Airbag system components
  – removal and refitting

⚠ **Warning: Refer to the precautions given in Section 21 before attempting to carry out work on any of the airbag components.**

1 Deactivate the airbag system as described in the previous Section, then proceed as described under the relevant heading.

Driver's airbag

2 Turn the steering wheel as necessary, so that one of the airbag unit retaining bolts becomes accessible from the rear of the steering wheel and undo the retaining bolt. Turn the steering wheel back again then remove the remaining bolt **(see illustration)**.

3 Withdraw the airbag unit from the steering wheel, far enough to access the wiring plugs.

4 Disconnect the airbag wiring connector, and the horn wiring connectors, from the rear of the unit, and remove it from the vehicle.

5 Refitting is a reversal of the removal procedure, with reference to Section 21.

Passenger's airbag

6 Remove the glovebox, as described in Chapter 11 Section 26.

7 Remove the passenger side airvent and central airvent on the passenger side, as described in Chapter 11 Section 26.

8 Undo the two retaining screws and remove the retaining brackets, noting their fitted position for refitting.

9 Undo the three retaining bolts along the rear of the airbag unit and discard, as new ones will be required for refitting.

10 Carefully withdraw the airbag forward until the wiring plug is in view on the side of the unit.

11 Release the locking clip and disconnect the wiring plug from the right-hand side of the airbag unit.

12 Refitting is a reversal of the removal procedure, with reference to Section 21.

Airbag control unit

13 The airbag control unit is located behind the bottom of the facia, inside the metal base.

14 Remove the facia base panel, as described in Chapter 11 Section 26.

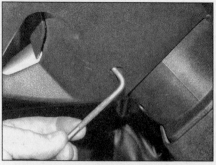
22.2 Undo the airbag retaining screws using a T30 Torx bit/key

15 Unlock and disconnect the wiring plugs **(see illustration)**.

16 Undo the two bolts securing bolts from the control unit retaining bracket and remove from place **(see illustration)**.

17 Remove the control unit. Note the fitted position of the control unit, check for a direction arrow, which must face forwards **(see illustration)**.

18 Refitting is a reversal of the removal procedure, with reference to Section 21.

Airbag rotary connector

19 Remove the steering wheel as described in Chapter 10, Section 11.

20 Place a small pin in the bottom left-hand aperture to lock the position of the clockspring **(see illustration)**.

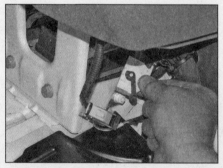
22.15 Unlock and disconnect the wiring plugs

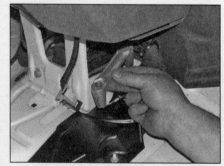
22.16 Undo the screws for the retaining bracket

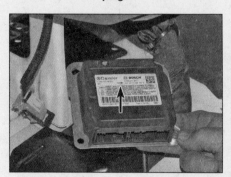
22.17 Manoeuvre the control unit from place, noting the direction arrow

22.20 Pin the clockspring to hold it in place

22.21 Undo the three retaining screws

22.22 Prise out the small panel from the shroud

21 Slacken the three securing screws in the rotary 'clock spring' connector unit **(see illustration)**.
22 Prise off the small panel in the steering column shroud at the 10 o'clock position of the clockspring **(see illustration)**.
23 Pull the clockspring from place **(see illustration)**.
24 Take care to keep hold of the small brass collar that goes around the mount at the bottom of the clockspring **(see illustration)**.
25 Refitting is a reversal of the removal procedure, with reference to Section 21.

22.23 Gently manoeuvre out the clockspring

22.24 Make sure to retain the small brass collar

FUSE AND RELAY BOX IN PASSENGER COMPARTMENT (F55/1; F55/2; K40/9)

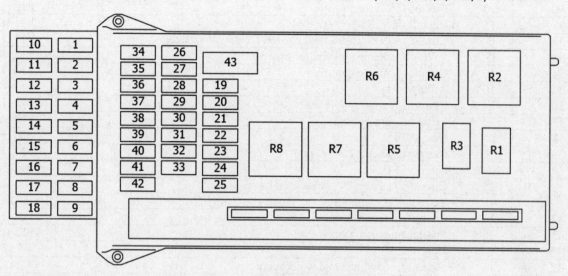

FUSE/RELAY	VALUE	DESCRIPTION	OEM NAME
1	25 A	Driver door control unit	F1 (F55/1)
2	10 A	Diagnostic socket	F2 (F55/1)
3	25 A	Brake system (valves)	F3 (F55/1)
4	40 A	Brake system (delivery pump)	F4 (F55/1)
5	10 A	Motors circuit 87, 7.5 A also used	F5 (F55/1)
6	10 A	Motors circuit 87, 7.5 A also used	F6 (F55/1)
7	30 A	Headlamp cleaning system	F7 (F55/1)
8	15 A	EDW, Rotating beacon/tone sequence	F8 (F55/1)
9	10 A	Additional turn signal module or not used	F9; F9/1 (F55/1)
10	20A	Radio, 15 A also used	F1 (F55/2)
11	7.5 A	Mobile phone, tachograph	F2 (F55/2)
12	30 A	Front blower	F3 (F55/2)
13	7.5 A	Warm air heater timer, FleetBoard (if fitted)	F4 (F55/2)
14	30 A	Heated seats	F5 (F55/2)
15	10 A	Non-MB body electrical system (up to June 2013)	F6 (F55/2)
	5 A	Brake system (from July 2013)	F6/1 (F55/2)
16	10 A	Front climate control, CD changer	F7 (F55/2)
17	10 A	Motion detector/comfort illumination	F8 (F55/2)
18	7.5 A	Rear climate control	F9 (F55/2)
19	15 A	Signaling horn	F1 (K40/9)
20	25 A	ELV/EZS (electronic ignition lock)	F2 (K40/9)
21	10 A	EZS (electronic ignition lock), Instrument cluster	F3 (K40/9)
22	5 A	Circuit 30 LDS, OBF (upper control panel)	F4 (K40/9)
23	30 A	Front windshield wiper	F5 (K40/9)
24	15 A	Fuel pump (up to June 2013)	F6 (K40/9)
	10 A	Circuit 87 engine control system (from July 2013)	F6/1 (K40/9)
25	5 A	MRM	F7 (K40/9)
26	20 A	Circuit 87 engine control	F8 (K40/9)
27	25 A	Circuit 87 engine control, 20 A also used	F9 (K40/9)
28	10 A	Circuit 87 engine control	F10 (K40/9)

29	15 A	Circuit 15R	F11 (K40/9)
30	10 A	Circuit 15R airbag	F12 (K40/9)
31	15 A	Cigar lighter, Radio	F13 (K40/9)
32	5 A	Circuit 15 LDS, Instrument cluster, Diagnostic socket	F14 (K40/9)
33	5 A	LWR (Headlamp range adjustment)	F15 (K40/9)
34	10 A	Circuit 87 engine control	F16 (K40/9)
35	10 A	Airbag	F17 (K40/9)
36	7.5 A	Circuit 15	F18 (K40/9)
37	7.5 A	Circuit 30 interior lights	F19 (K40/9)
38	25 A	Circuit 30	F20 (K40/9)
39	5 A	Circuit 15 engine control unit	F21 (K40/9)
40	5 A	Circuit 15 ESP	F22 (K40/9)
41	25 A	Circuit 50 starter, 20 A also used (up to June 2013)	F23 (K40/9)
	10 A	Terminal 87 engine control system (from July 2013)	F23/1 (K40/9)
42	10 A	Engine components circuit 15	F24 (K40/9)
43	25 A	Instrument panel socket	F25 (K40/9)
R1	-	Horn relay	K1 (K40/9)
R2	-	Stage 2 front windshield wiper relay	K2 (K40/9)
R3	-	Fuel pump relay	K3 (K40/9)
R4	-	Stage 1 front windshield wiper relay	K4 (K40/9)
R5	-	Circuit 50 starter relay	K5 (K40/9)
R6	-	Circuit 15R relay	K6 (K40/9)
R7	-	Circuit 87 engine control relay	K7 (K40/9)
R8	-	Circuit 15 relay	K8 (K40/9)

FUSE AND RELAY BOX IN PASSENGER COMPARTMENT (F55/3; F55/4; F55/5; F55/6)

| R7 | R6 | R8 | R1 | R4 | R3 | | R2 | R5 |

| 1 | 2 | 3 | 4 | 5 | 6 | 7 | 8 | 9 | | 10 | 11 | 12 | 13 | 14 | 15 | 16 | 17 | 18 |

| 19 | 20 | 21 | 22 | 23 | 24 | 25 | 26 | 27 | | 28 | 29 | 30 | 31 | 32 | 33 | 34 | 35 | 36 |

FUSE/RELAY	VALUE	DESCRIPTION	OEM NAME
1	5 A	Mirror adjustment, Heated rear window relay	F1 (F55/3)
2	30 A	Rear wiper	F2 (F55/3)
3	5 A	Start-off assist, Heater timer, Backup camera, Telephone	F3 (F55/3)
4	7.5 A	AAG, Tachograph, ADR	F4 (F55/3)
5	10 A	EGS circuit 87, 5A also used	F5 (F55/3)
6	10 A	All-wheel drive , Automatic transmission auxiliary oil pump (if fitted), 5A also used	F6 (F55/3)
7	10 A	ESM (EWM) (Electronic selector lever module)	F7 (F55/3)
8	10 A	Three-way dump truck, Cargo lift gate circuit 15, Parktronic (if fitted)	F8 (F55/3)
9	15 A	Multitone horn, Roof fan (up to June 2013)	F9 (F55/3)
	7.5 A	Refrigerant compressor magnetic clutch (from July 2013)	F9/3 (F55/3)
10	25 A	Body manufacturer circuit 30	F1 (F55/4)
11	15 A	Body manufacturer circuit 15	F2 (F55/4)
12	10 A	Body manufacturer circuit D+	F3 (F55/4)
13	10 A	Additional flasher module (up to March 2007)	F4 (F55/4)
	30 A	Rear air conditioning (from April 2007 to June 2013)	F4/1 (F55/4)
	20 A	Fuel pump (from July 2013)	F4/2 (F55/4)
14	20 A	Trailer socket	F5 (F55/4)
15	25 A	AAG	F6 (F55/4)
16	7.5 A	TPM [RDK] (Tire pressure monitor), Parktronic	F7 (F55/4)
17	25 A	PSM (Parametrizable special module)	F8 (F55/4)
18	25 A	PSM (Parametrizable special module)	F9 (F55/4)
19	25 A	OCP [DBE] (Overhead control panel), Tilting/Sliding roof (if fitted), 10 A, 5 A also used	F1 (F55/5)

20	7.5 A	Clearance lamps or not used	F2; F2/1 (F55/5)
21	30 A	Rear window heater, 15 A also used	F3 (F55/5)
22	15 A	Rear window heater, electric step (if fitted)	F4 (F55/5)
23	10 A	Electrical components, other make body, Left rear socket, 15 A also used	F5 (F55/5)
24	15 A	Driver seat frame socket	F6 (F55/5)
25	15 A	Right rear socket	F7 (F55/5)
26	25 A	Warm water auxiliary heater	F8 (F55/5)
27	25 A	Heater booster, Warm air auxiliary heater, 20 A also used	F9 (F55/5)
28	30 A	Rear A/C system (up to June 2013)	F1 (F55/6)
	25 A	Starter relay (from July 2013)	F1/3 (F55/6)
29	30 A	All-wheel drive	F2 (F55/6)
30	15 A	Additional heat exchanger fan or not used	F3; F3/2 (F55/6)
31	15 A	Closing assist, Left sliding door, Rear blower, 30 A also used	F4 (F55/6)
32	10 A	Keyless entry	F5 (F55/6)
33	15 A	Closing assist, Right sliding door, Electronic level control, 30 A also used	F6 (F55/6)
34	30 A	Left sliding door or not used	F7; F7/1 (F55/6)
35	-	Not used	F8 (F55/6)
36	-	Not used	F9 (F55/6)
R1	-	Headlamp cleaning system relay	K2
R2	-	Tone sequence relay	K39/1
R3	-	EDW (Anti-theft alarm system) horn relay	K39/3
R4	-	Rotating beacon relay	K51/10
R5	-	Circulation pump relay	K60
R6	-	Body manufacturer circuit 15 relay	K88
R7	-	Body manufacturer circuit D+ relay	K88/1
R8	-	Illumination relay or Cargo lift gate relay	K93 or K95

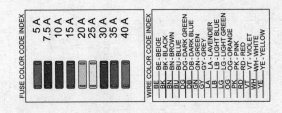

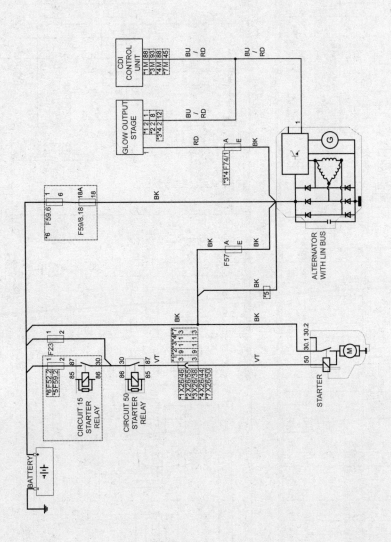

Diagram 1 – Starting and charging

*1 Engine code: 651 up to 08.2010
*2 Engine code: 651 up to 09.2010–06.2013
*3 Engine code: 646 up to 08.2011
*4 Engine code: 646 from 09.2011 up to 04.2012
*5 Engine code: 651 up to 06.2013
*6 Engine code: 651 from 07.2013
*7 Engine code: 646 from 05.2012 up to 04.2013

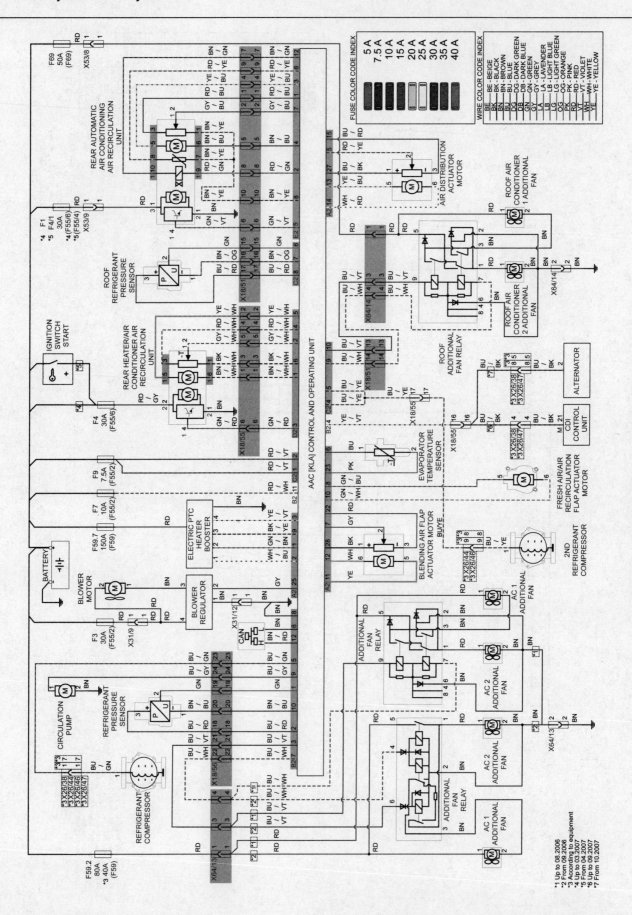

2Diagram 2 – AC Heating & Cooling – up to 31.08.2009

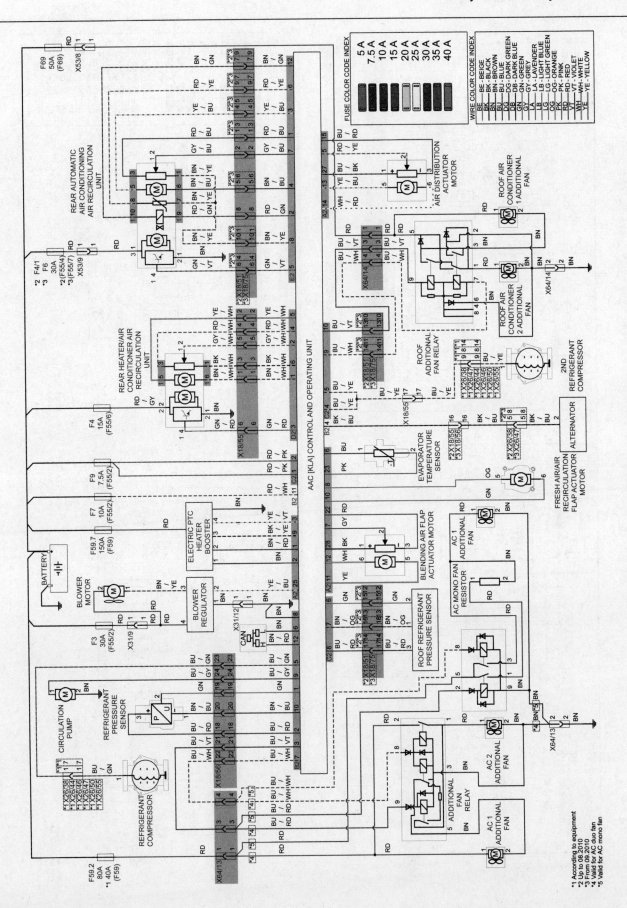

Diagram 3 – AC Heating & Cooling – from 01.09.2009 to 30.06.2013

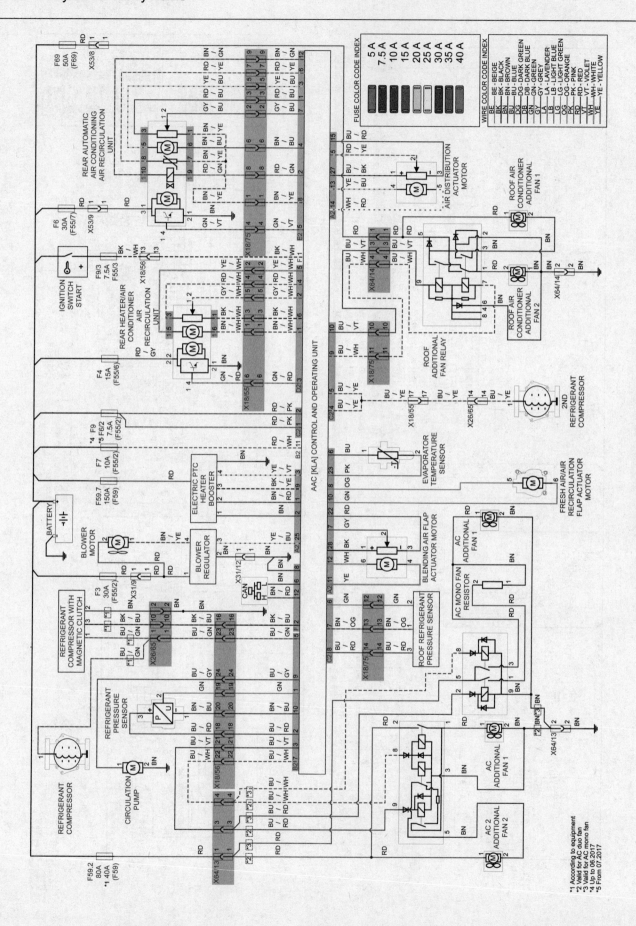

Diagram 4 – AC Heating & Cooling – from 01.07.2013

*1 According to equipment
*2 Valid for AC duo fan
*3 Valid for AC mono fan
*4 Up to 06.2017
*5 From 07.2017

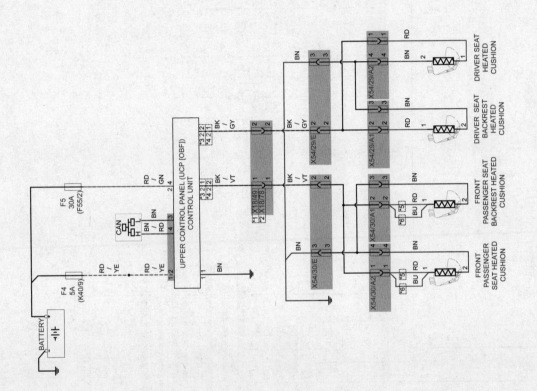

Diagram 5 – Heated seats

FUSE COLOR CODE INDEX

5 A
7.5 A
10 A
15 A
20 A
25 A
30 A
35 A
40 A

WIRE COLOR CODE INDEX

BE - BEIGE
BK - BLACK
BN - BROWN
BU - BLUE
DG - DARK GREEN
DB - DARK BLUE
GN - GREEN
GY - GREY
LA - LAVENDER
LB - LIGHT BLUE
LG - LIGHT GREEN
OG - ORANGE
PK - PINK
RD - RED
VT - VIOLET
WH - WHITE
YE - YELLOW

*1 Up to 08.2010
*2 From 09.2010
*3 Left-hand drive
*4 Right-hand drive
*5 Up to 06.2013
*6 From 07.2013

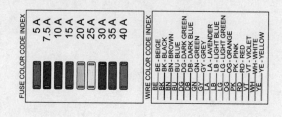

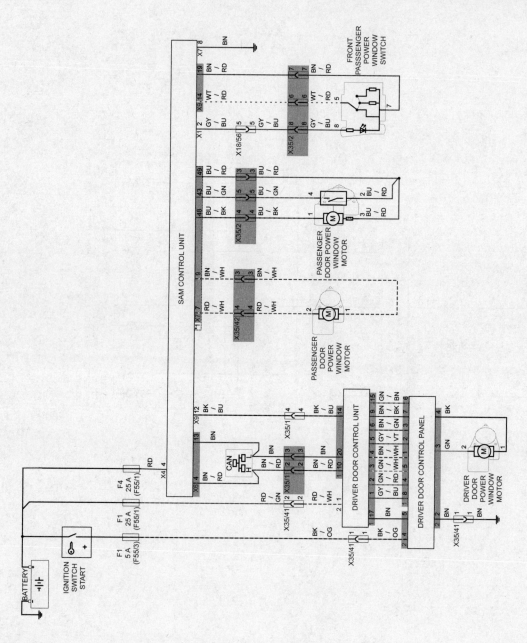

Diagram 6 – Electric windows

*1 According to equipment

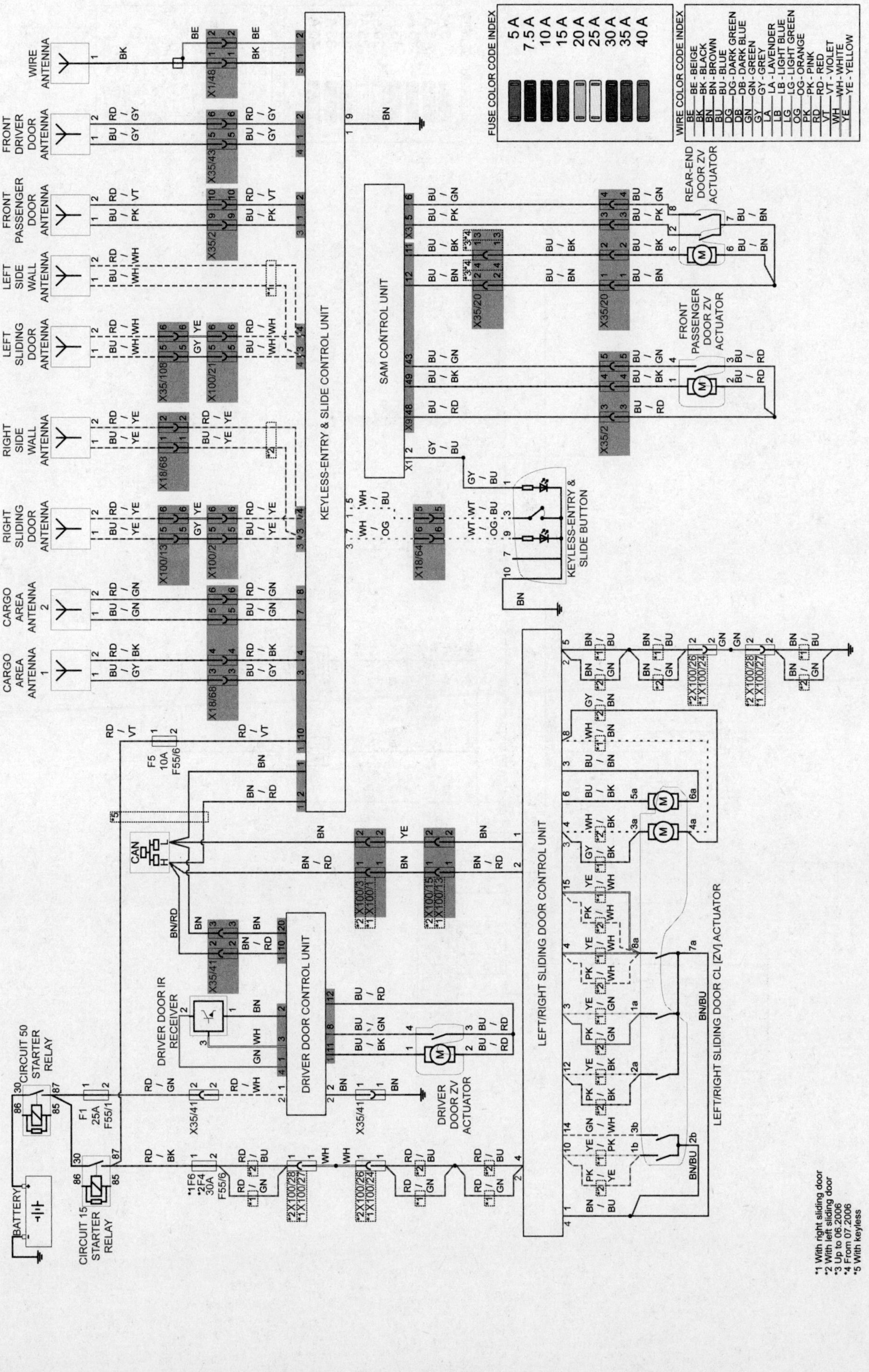

FUSE COLOR CODE INDEX

5 A	
7.5 A	
10 A	
15 A	
20 A	
25 A	
30 A	
35 A	
40 A	

WIRE COLOR CODE INDEX

BE - BEIGE
BK - BLACK
BN - BROWN
BU - BLUE
DG - DARK GREEN
DB - DARK BLUE
GN - GREEN
GY - GREY
LA - LAVENDER
LB - LIGHT BLUE
LG - LIGHT GREEN
OG - ORANGE
PK - PINK
RD - RED
VT - VIOLET
WH - WHITE
YE - YELLOW

WIRE ANTENNA

FRONT DRIVER DOOR ANTENNA

FRONT PASSENGER DOOR ANTENNA

LEFT SIDE WALL ANTENNA

LEFT SLIDING DOOR ANTENNA

RIGHT SIDE WALL ANTENNA

RIGHT SLIDING DOOR ANTENNA

CARGO AREA ANTENNA

CARGO AREA ANTENNA

KEYLESS-ENTRY & SLIDE CONTROL UNIT

SAM CONTROL UNIT

KEYLESS-ENTRY & SLIDE BUTTON

REAR-END DOOR ZV ACTUATOR

FRONT PASSENGER DOOR ZV ACTUATOR

CAN

DRIVER DOOR IR RECEIVER

DRIVER DOOR CONTROL UNIT

DRIVER DOOR ZV ACTUATOR

LEFT/RIGHT SLIDING DOOR CONTROL UNIT

LEFT/RIGHT SLIDING DOOR CL (ZV) ACTUATOR

BATTERY

CIRCUIT 50 STARTER RELAY

CIRCUIT 15 STARTER RELAY

F1 25A F55/1

F5 10A F55/6

Diagram 7 – Central locking

*1 With right sliding door
*2 With left sliding door
*3 Up to 06.2006
*4 From 07.2006
*5 With keyless

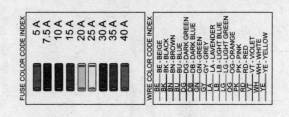

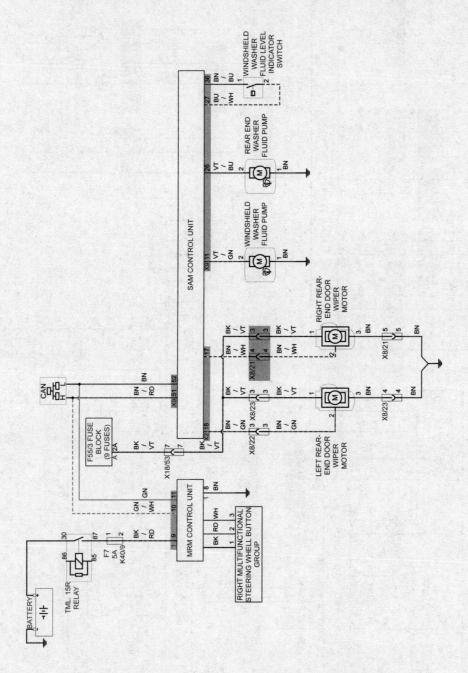

Diagram 8 – Wipers and washers

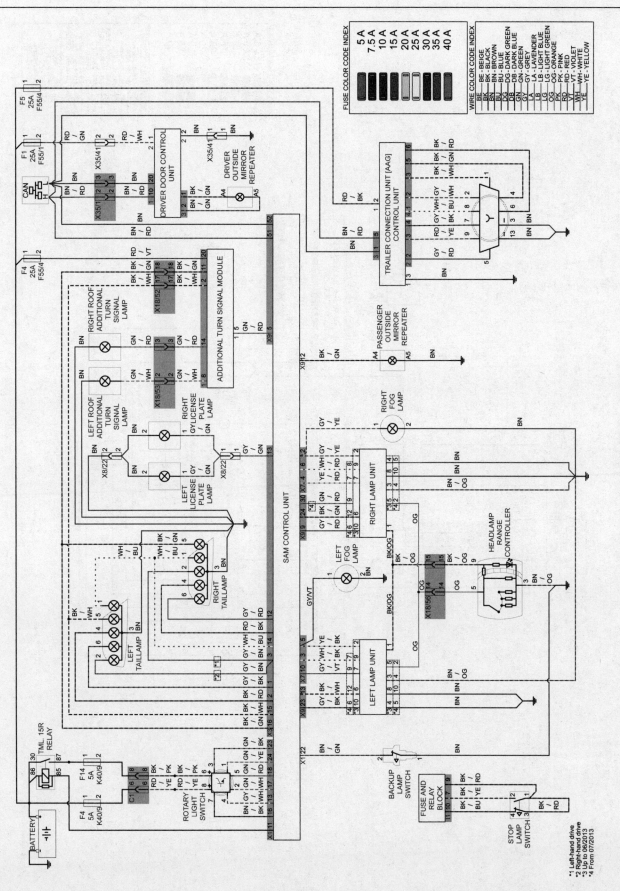

Diagram 9 – Exterior lights – Halogen

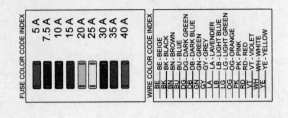

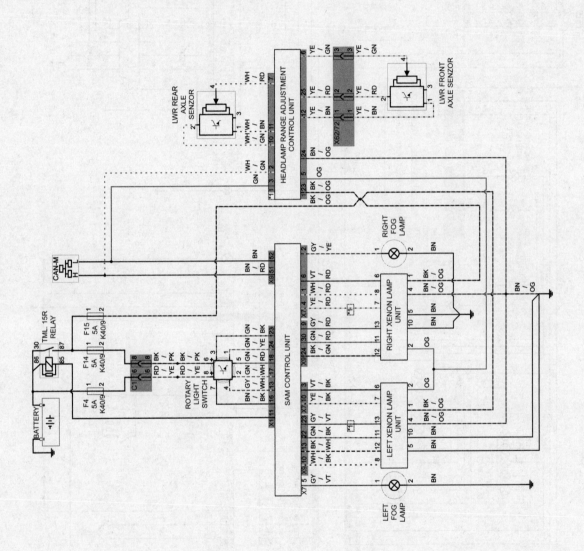

Diagram 10 – Exterior lights – Xenon

*1According to equipment

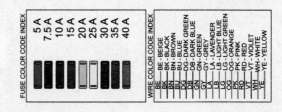

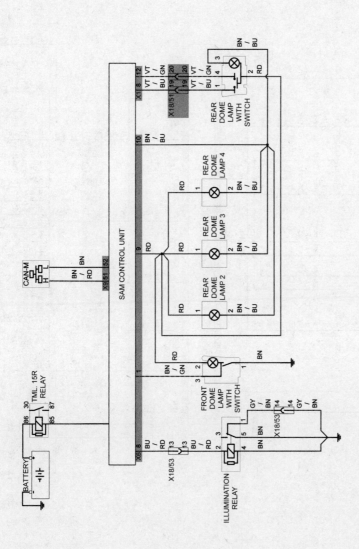

Diagram 11 – Interior lights

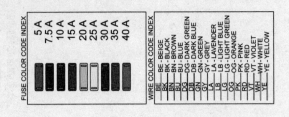

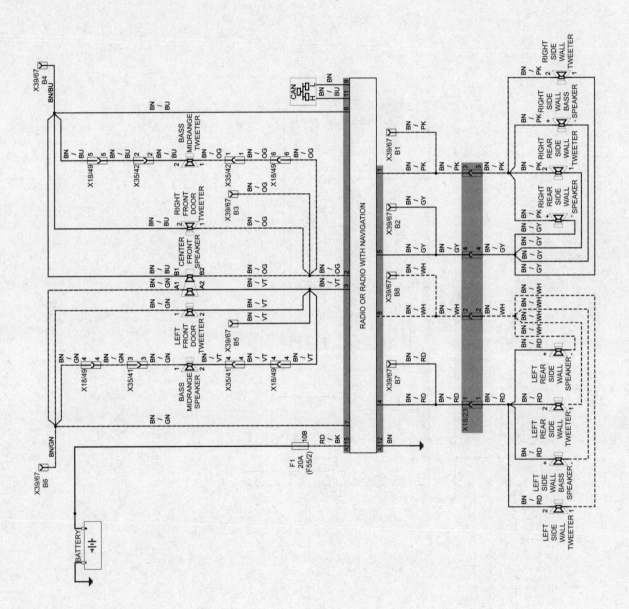

Diagram 12 – Audio system

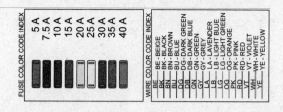

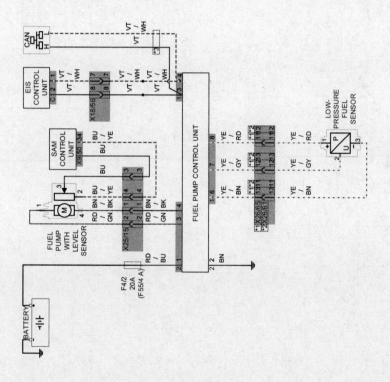

Diagram 13 – Fuel pump

*1 For model engine OM651
*2 For model engine OM642
*3 From 01.2013

Notes

Dimensions and weights

Note: *All figures are approximate and may vary according to model. Refer to manufacturer's data for exact figures.*

Dimensions

Overall length:
- Short wheelbase . . . . 5245 mm
- Medium wheelbase . . . . 5910 mm
- Long wheelbase . . . . 6945 mm
- Extra-long wheelbase. . . . . 7345 mm

Turning circle:
- Short wheelbase. . . . . 14.6 metres
- Medium wheelbase . . . . 14.6 metres
- Long wheelbase . . . . 16.6 metres
- Extra-long wheelbase. . . . . 16.6 metres

Max loading length:
Van:
- Short wheelbase. . . . . 2600 mm
- Medium wheelbase. . . . . 3265 mm
- Long wheelbase . . . . 4300 mm
- Extra-long wheelbase. . . . . 4700 mm

Cargo area:
Van:
- Short wheelbase. 7.5/8.5 m3
- Medium wheelbase. 9.0/10.5 m3
- Long wheelbase 14.0/15.5 m3
- Extra-long wheelbase. 15.5/17.0 m3

Weights

Kerbweight:
- Short wheelbase. . . . . 2285 kg
- Medium wheelbase . . . . 2315 kg
- Long wheelbase . . . . 2465 kg
- Extra-long wheelbase. . . . . 2520 kg

Fuel economy

Although depreciation is still the biggest part of the cost of motoring for most car owners, the cost of fuel is more immediately noticeable. These pages give some tips on how to get the best fuel economy.

Working it out

Manufacturer's figures

Car manufacturers are required by law to provide fuel consumption information on all new vehicles sold. These 'official' figures are obtained by simulating various driving conditions on a rolling road or a test track. Real life conditions are different, so the fuel consumption actually achieved may not bear much resemblance to the quoted figures.

How to calculate it

Many cars now have trip computers which will

display fuel consumption, both instantaneous and average. Refer to the owner's handbook for details of how to use these.

To calculate consumption yourself (and maybe to check that the trip computer is accurate), proceed as follows.

1. Fill up with fuel and note the mileage, or zero the trip recorder.
2. Drive as usual until you need to fill up again.
3. Note the amount of fuel required to refill the tank, and the mileage covered since the previous fill-up.
4. Divide the mileage by the amount of fuel used to obtain the consumption figure.

For example:

Mileage at first fill-up (a) = 27,903
Mileage at second fill-up (b) = 28,346
Mileage covered (b - a) = 443
Fuel required at second fill-up = 48.6 litres

The half-completed changeover to metric units in the UK means that we buy our fuel

in litres, measure distances in miles and talk about fuel consumption in miles per gallon. There are two ways round this: the first is to convert the litres to gallons before doing the calculation (by dividing by 4.546, or see Table 1). So in the example:

48.6 litres ÷ 4.546 = 10.69 gallons
443 miles ÷ 10.69 gallons = 41.4 mpg

The second way is to calculate the consumption in miles per litre, then multiply that figure by 4.546 (or see Table 2).

So in the example, fuel consumption is:

443 miles ÷ 48.6 litres = 9.1 mpl
9.1 mpl x 4.546 = 41.4 mpg

The rest of Europe expresses fuel consumption in litres of fuel required to travel 100 km (l/100 km). For interest, the conversions are given in Table 3. In practice it doesn't matter what units you use, provided you know what your normal consumption is and can spot if it's getting better or worse.

Table 1: conversion of litres to Imperial gallons

litres	1	2	3	4	5	10	20	30	40	50	60	70
gallons	0.22	0.44	0.66	0.88	1.10	2.24	4.49	6.73	8.98	11.22	13.47	15.71

Table 2: conversion of miles per litre to miles per gallon

miles per litre	5	6	7	8	9	10	11	12	13	14
miles per gallon	23	27	32	36	41	46	50	55	59	64

Table 3: conversion of litres per 100 km to miles per gallon

litres per 100 km	4	4.5	5	5.5	6	6.5	7	8	9	10
miles per gallon	71	63	56	51	47	43	40	35	31	28

Maintenance

A well-maintained car uses less fuel and creates less pollution. In particular:

Filters

Change air and fuel filters at the specified intervals.

Oil

Use a good quality oil of the lowest viscosity specified by the vehicle manufacturer (see *Lubricants and fluids*). Check the level often and be careful not to overfill.

Spark plugs

When applicable, renew at the specified intervals.

Tyres

Check tyre pressures regularly. Under-inflated tyres have an increased rolling resistance. It is generally safe to use the higher pressures specified for full load conditions even when not fully laden, but keep an eye on the centre band of tread for signs of wear due to over-inflation.

When buying new tyres, consider the 'fuel saving' models which most manufacturers include in their ranges.

Driving style

Acceleration

Acceleration uses more fuel than driving at a steady speed. The best technique with modern cars is to accelerate reasonably briskly to the desired speed, changing up through the gears as soon as possible without making the engine labour.

Air conditioning

Air conditioning absorbs quite a bit of energy from the engine – typically 3 kW (4 hp) or so. The effect on fuel consumption is at its worst in slow traffic. Switch it off when not required.

Anticipation

Drive smoothly and try to read the traffic flow so as to avoid unnecessary acceleration and braking.

Automatic transmission

When accelerating in an automatic, avoid depressing the throttle so far as to make the transmission hold onto lower gears at higher speeds. Don't use the 'Sport' setting, if applicable.

When stationary with the engine running, select 'N' or 'P'. When moving, keep your left foot away from the brake.

Braking

Braking converts the car's energy of motion into heat – essentially, it is wasted. Obviously some braking is always going to be necessary, but with good anticipation it is surprising how much can be avoided, especially on routes that you know well.

Carshare

Consider sharing lifts to work or to the shops. Even once a week will make a difference.

Electrical loads

Electricity is 'fuel' too; the alternator which charges the battery does so by converting some of the engine's energy of motion into electrical energy. The more electrical accessories are in use, the greater the load on the alternator. Switch off big consumers like the heated rear window when not required.

Freewheeling

Freewheeling (coasting) in neutral with the engine switched off is dangerous. The effort required to operate power-assisted brakes and steering increases when the engine is not running, with a potential lack of control in emergency situations.

In any case, modern fuel injection systems automatically cut off the engine's fuel supply on the overrun (moving and in gear, but with the accelerator pedal released).

Gadgets

Bolt-on devices claiming to save fuel have been around for nearly as long as the motor car itself. Those which worked were rapidly adopted as standard equipment by the vehicle manufacturers. Others worked only in certain situations, or saved fuel only at the expense of unacceptable effects on performance, driveability or the life of engine components.

The most effective fuel saving gadget is the driver's right foot.

Journey planning

Combine (eg) a trip to the supermarket with a visit to the recycling centre and the DIY store, rather than making separate journeys.

When possible choose a travelling time outside rush hours.

Load

The more heavily a car is laden, the greater the energy required to accelerate it to a given speed. Remove heavy items which you don't need to carry.

One load which is often overlooked is the contents of the fuel tank. A tankful of fuel (55 litres / 12 gallons) weighs 45 kg (100 lb) or so. Just half filling it may be worthwhile.

Lost?

At the risk of stating the obvious, if you're going somewhere new, have details of the route to hand. There's not much point in achieving record mpg if you also go miles out of your way.

Parking

If possible, carry out any reversing or turning manoeuvres when you arrive at a parking space so that you can drive straight out when you leave. Manoeuvering when the engine is cold uses a lot more fuel.

Driving around looking for free on-street parking may cost more in fuel than buying a car park ticket.

Premium fuel

Most major oil companies (and some supermarkets) have premium grades of fuel which are several pence a litre dearer than the standard grades. Reports vary, but the consensus seems to be that if these fuels improve economy at all, they do not do so by enough to justify their extra cost.

Roof rack

When loading a roof rack, try to produce a wedge shape with the narrow end at the front. Any cover should be securely fastened – if it flaps it's creating turbulence and absorbing energy.

Remove roof racks and boxes when not in use – they increase air resistance and can create a surprising amount of noise.

Short journeys

The engine is at its least efficient, and wear is highest, during the first few miles after a cold start. Consider walking, cycling or using public transport.

Speed

The engine is at its most efficient when running at a steady speed and load at the rpm where it develops maximum torque. (You can find this figure in the car's handbook.) For most cars this corresponds to between 55 and 65 mph in top gear.

Above the optimum cruising speed, fuel consumption starts to rise quite sharply. A car travelling at 80 mph will typically be using 30% more fuel than at 60 mph.

Supermarket fuel

It may be cheap but is it any good? In the UK all supermarket fuel must meet the relevant British Standard. The major oil companies will say that their branded fuels have better additive packages which may stop carbon and other deposits building up. A reasonable compromise might be to use one tank of branded fuel to three or four from the supermarket.

Switch off when stationary

Switch off the engine if you look like being stationary for more than 30 seconds or so. This is good for the environment as well as for your pocket. Be aware though that frequent restarts are hard on the battery and the starter motor.

Windows

Driving with the windows open increases air turbulence around the vehicle. Closing the windows promotes smooth airflow and

reduced resistance. The faster you go, the more significant this is.

And finally . . .

Driving techniques associated with good fuel economy tend to involve moderate acceleration and low top speeds. Be considerate to the needs of other road users who may need to make brisker progress; even if you do not agree with them this is not an excuse to be obstructive.

Safety must always take precedence over economy, whether it is a question of accelerating hard to complete an overtaking manoeuvre, killing your speed when confronted with a potential hazard or switching the lights on when it starts to get dark.

Conversion factors

Length (distance)

Inches (in)	x 25.4	= Millimetres (mm)	x 0.0394	=	Inches (in)
Feet (ft)	x 0.305	= Metres (m)	x 3.281	=	Feet (ft)
Miles	x 1.609	= Kilometres (km)	x 0.621	=	Miles

Volume (capacity)

Cubic inches (cu in; in³)	x 16.387	= Cubic centimetres (cc; cm³)	x 0.061	=	Cubic inches (cu in; in³)
Imperial pints (Imp pt)	x 0.568	= Litres (l)	x 1.76	=	Imperial pints (Imp pt)
Imperial quarts (Imp qt)	x 1.137	= Litres (l)	x 0.88	=	Imperial quarts (Imp qt)
Imperial quarts (Imp qt)	x 1.201	= US quarts (US qt)	x 0.833	=	Imperial quarts (Imp qt)
US quarts (US qt)	x 0.946	= Litres (l)	x 1.057	=	US quarts (US qt)
Imperial gallons (Imp gal)	x 4.546	= Litres (l)	x 0.22	=	Imperial gallons (Imp gal)
Imperial gallons (Imp gal)	x 1.201	= US gallons (US gal)	x 0.833	=	Imperial gallons (Imp gal)
US gallons (US gal)	x 3.785	= Litres (l)	x 0.264	=	US gallons (US gal)

Mass (weight)

Ounces (oz)	x 28.35	= Grams (g)	x 0.035	=	Ounces (oz)
Pounds (lb)	x 0.454	= Kilograms (kg)	x 2.205	=	Pounds (lb)

Force

Ounces-force (ozf; oz)	x 0.278	= Newtons (N)	x 3.6	=	Ounces-force (ozf; oz)
Pounds-force (lbf; lb)	x 4.448	= Newtons (N)	x 0.225	=	Pounds-force (lbf; lb)
Newtons (N)	x 0.1	= Kilograms-force (kgf; kg)	x 9.81	=	Newtons (N)

Pressure

Pounds-force per square inch (psi; lbf/in²; lb/in²)	x 0.070	= Kilograms-force per square centimetre (kgf/cm²; kg/cm²)	x 14.223	=	Pounds-force per square inch (psi; lbf/in²; lb/in²)
Pounds-force per square inch (psi; lbf/in²; lb/in²)	x 0.068	= Atmospheres (atm)	x 14.696	=	Pounds-force per square inch (psi; lbf/in²; lb/in²)
Pounds-force per square inch (psi; lbf/in²; lb/in²)	x 0.069	= Bars	x 14.5	=	Pounds-force per square inch (psi; lbf/in²; lb/in²)
Pounds-force per square inch (psi; lbf/in²; lb/in²)	x 6.895	= Kilopascals (kPa)	x 0.145	=	Pounds-force per square inch (psi; lbf/in²; lb/in²)
Kilopascals (kPa)	x 0.01	= Kilograms-force per square centimetre (kgf/cm²; kg/cm²)	x 98.1	=	Kilopascals (kPa)
Millibar (mbar)	x 100	= Pascals (Pa)	x 0.01	=	Millibar (mbar)
Millibar (mbar)	x 0.0145	= Pounds-force per square inch (psi; lbf/in²; lb/in²)	x 68.947	=	Millibar (mbar)
Millibar (mbar)	x 0.75	= Millimetres of mercury (mmHg)	x 1.333	=	Millibar (mbar)
Millibar (mbar)	x 0.401	= Inches of water (inH₂O)	x 2.491	=	Millibar (mbar)
Millimetres of mercury (mmHg)	x 0.535	= Inches of water (inH₂O)	x 1.868	=	Millimetres of mercury (mmHg)
Inches of water (inH₂O)	x 0.036	= Pounds-force per square inch (psi; lbf/in²; lb/in²)	x 27.68	=	Inches of water (inH₂O)

Torque (moment of force)

Pounds-force inches (lbf in; lb in)	x 1.152	= Kilograms-force centimetre (kgf cm; kg cm)	x 0.868	=	Pounds-force inches (lbf in; lb in)
Pounds-force inches (lbf in; lb in)	x 0.113	= Newton metres (Nm)	x 8.85	=	Pounds-force inches (lbf in; lb in)
Pounds-force inches (lbf in; lb in)	x 0.083	= Pounds-force feet (lbf ft; lb ft)	x 12	=	Pounds-force inches (lbf in; lb in)
Pounds-force feet (lbf ft; lb ft)	x 0.138	= Kilograms-force metres (kgf m; kg m)	x 7.233	=	Pounds-force feet (lbf ft; lb ft)
Pounds-force feet (lbf ft; lb ft)	x 1.356	= Newton metres (Nm)	x 0.738	=	Pounds-force feet (lbf ft; lb ft)
Newton metres (Nm)	x 0.102	= Kilograms-force metres (kgf m; kg m)	x 9.804	=	Newton metres (Nm)

Power

Horsepower (hp)	x 745.7	= Watts (W)	x 0.0013	=	Horsepower (hp)

Velocity (speed)

Miles per hour (miles/hr; mph)	x 1.609	= Kilometres per hour (km/hr; kph)	x 0.621	=	Miles per hour (miles/hr; mph)

Fuel consumption*

Miles per gallon, Imperial (mpg)	x 0.354	= Kilometres per litre (km/l)	x 2.825	=	Miles per gallon, Imperial (mpg)
Miles per gallon, US (mpg)	x 0.425	= Kilometres per litre (km/l)	x 2.352	=	Miles per gallon, US (mpg)

Temperature

Degrees Fahrenheit = (°C x 1.8) + 32   Degrees Celsius (Degrees Centigrade; °C) = (°F - 32) x 0.56

It is common practice to convert from miles per gallon (mpg) to litres/100 kilometres (l/100km), where mpg x l/100 km = 282

Spare parts are available from many sources, including maker's appointed garages, accessory shops, and motor factors. To be sure of obtaining the correct parts, it will sometimes be necessary to quote the vehicle identification number. If possible, it can also be useful to take the old parts along for positive identification. Items such as starter motors and alternators may be available under a service exchange scheme – any parts returned should be clean.

Our advice regarding spare parts is as follows.

Officially appointed garages

This is the best source of parts which are peculiar to your vehicle, and which are not otherwise generally available (eg, badges, interior trim, certain body panels, etc). It is also the only place at which you should buy parts if the vehicle is still under warranty.

Accessory shops

These are very good places to buy materials and components needed for the maintenance of your vehicle (oil, air and fuel filters, light bulbs, drivebelts, greases, brake pads, touch-up paint, etc). Components of this nature sold by a reputable shop are usually of the same standard as those used by the vehicle manufacturer.

Besides components, these shops also sell tools and general accessories, usually have convenient opening hours, charge lower prices, and can often be found close to home. Some accessory shops have parts counters where components needed for almost any repair job can be purchased or ordered.

Motor factors

Good factors will stock all the more important components which wear out comparatively quickly, and can sometimes supply individual components needed for the overhaul of a larger assembly (eg, brake seals and hydraulic parts, bearing shells, pistons, valves). They may also handle work such as cylinder block reboring, crankshaft regrinding, etc.

Engine reconditioners

These specialise in engine overhaul and can also supply components. It is recommended that the establishment is a member of the Federation of Engine Re-Manufacturers, or a similar society.

Tyre and exhaust specialists

These outlets may be independent, or members of a local or national chain. They frequently offer competitive prices when compared with a main dealer or local garage, but it will pay to obtain several quotes before making a decision. When researching prices, also ask what extras may be added – for instance fitting a new valve, balancing the wheel and tyre disposal all both commonly charged on top of the price of a new tyre.

Other sources

Beware of parts or materials obtained from market stalls, car boot sales, on-line auctions or similar outlets. Such items are not invariably sub-standard, but there is little chance of compensation if they do prove unsatisfactory. In the case of safety-critical components such as brake pads, there is the risk not only of financial loss, but also of an accident causing injury or death.

Second-hand components or assemblies obtained from a vehicle breaker can be a good buy in some circumstances, but this sort of purchase is best made by the experienced DIY mechanic.

Vehicle identification

Modifications are a continuing and unpublished process in vehicle manufacture, quite apart from major model changes. Spare parts manuals and lists are compiled upon a numerical basis, the individual vehicle numbers being essential to correct identification of the component required.

When ordering spare parts, always give as much information as possible. Quote the vehicle type, year of manufacture and vehicle identification and/or engine numbers as appropriate.

The *vehicle identification plate* is attached to the driver's seat base (see illustration) and includes the Vehicle Identification Number (VIN),

vehicle weight information and paint and trim colour codes. On some models it may also be on a sticker attached to the front crossmember, under the bonnet.

The *transmission number* is stamped on the right-hand side of the transmission housing (see illustration).

The *engine number* is either stamped on to the rear of the cylinder block, near the transmission mounting face, or on to the front left-hand face of the cylinder block, depending on engine type. The engine number can also be found on the vehicle's registration document (V5C or log book). The engine code is the first part of the engine number.

Vehicle identification plate attached to the driver's seat base

Transmission identification plate

Whenever servicing, repair or overhaul work is carried out on the car or its components, observe the following procedures and instructions. This will assist in carrying out the operation efficiently and to a professional standard of workmanship.

Joint mating faces and gaskets

When separating components at their mating faces, never insert screwdrivers or similar implements into the joint between the faces in order to prise them apart. This can cause severe damage which results in oil leaks, coolant leaks, etc upon reassembly. Separation is usually achieved by tapping along the joint with a soft-faced hammer in order to break the seal. However, note that this method may not be suitable where dowels are used for component location.

Where a gasket is used between the mating faces of two components, a new one must be fitted on reassembly; fit it dry unless otherwise stated in the repair procedure. Make sure that the mating faces are clean and dry, with all traces of old gasket removed. When cleaning a joint face, use a tool which is unlikely to score or damage the face, and remove any burrs or nicks with an oilstone or fine file.

Make sure that tapped holes are cleaned with a pipe cleaner, and keep them free of jointing compound, if this is being used, unless specifically instructed otherwise.

Ensure that all orifices, channels or pipes are clear, and blow through them, preferably using compressed air.

Oil seals

Oil seals can be removed by levering them out with a wide flat-bladed screwdriver or similar implement. Alternatively, a number of self-tapping screws may be screwed into the seal, and these used as a purchase for pliers or some similar device in order to pull the seal free.

Whenever an oil seal is removed from its working location, either individually or as part of an assembly, it should be renewed.

The very fine sealing lip of the seal is easily damaged, and will not seal if the surface it contacts is not completely clean and free from scratches, nicks or grooves. If the original sealing surface of the component cannot be restored, and the manufacturer has not made provision for slight relocation of the seal relative to the sealing surface, the component should be renewed.

Protect the lips of the seal from any surface which may damage them in the course of fitting. Use tape or a conical sleeve where possible. Where indicated, lubricate the seal lips with oil before fitting and, on dual-lipped seals, fill the space between the lips with grease.

Unless otherwise stated, oil seals must be fitted with their sealing lips toward the lubricant to be sealed.

Use a tubular drift or block of wood of the appropriate size to install the seal and, if the seal housing is shouldered, drive the seal down to the shoulder. If the seal housing is unshouldered, the seal should be fitted with its face flush with the housing top face (unless otherwise instructed).

Screw threads and fastenings

Seized nuts, bolts and screws are quite a common occurrence where corrosion has set in, and the use of penetrating oil or releasing fluid will often overcome this problem if the offending item is soaked for a while before attempting to release it. The use of an impact driver may also provide a means of releasing such stubborn fastening devices, when used in conjunction with the appropriate screwdriver bit or socket. If none of these methods works, it may be necessary to resort to the careful application of heat, or the use of a hacksaw or nut splitter device. Before resorting to extreme methods, check that you are not dealing with a left-hand thread!

Studs are usually removed by locking two nuts together on the threaded part, and then using a spanner on the lower nut to unscrew the stud. Studs or bolts which have broken off below the surface of the component in which they are mounted can sometimes be removed using a stud extractor.

Always ensure that a blind tapped hole is completely free from oil, grease, water or other fluid before installing the bolt or stud. Failure to do this could cause the housing to crack due to the hydraulic action of the bolt or stud as it is screwed in.

For some screw fastenings, notably cylinder head bolts or nuts, torque wrench settings are no longer specified for the latter stages of tightening, "angle-tightening" being called up instead. Typically, a fairly low torque wrench setting will be applied to the bolts/nuts in the correct sequence, followed by one or more stages of tightening through specified angles.

When checking or retightening a nut or bolt to a specified torque setting, slacken the nut or bolt by a quarter of a turn, and then retighten to the specified setting. However, this should not be attempted where angular tightening has been used.

Locknuts, locktabs and washers

Any fastening which will rotate against a component or housing during tightening should always have a washer between it and the relevant component or housing.

Spring or split washers should always be renewed when they are used to lock a critical component such as a big-end bearing retaining bolt or nut. Locktabs which are folded over to retain a nut or bolt should always be renewed.

Self-locking nuts can be re-used in non-critical areas, providing resistance can be felt when the locking portion passes over the bolt or stud thread. However, it should be noted that self-locking stiffnuts tend to lose their effectiveness after long periods of use, and should then be renewed as a matter of course.

Split pins must always be replaced with new ones of the correct size for the hole.

When thread-locking compound is found on the threads of a fastener which is to be re-used, it should be cleaned off with a wire brush and solvent, and fresh compound applied on reassembly.

Special tools

Some repair procedures in this manual entail the use of special tools such as a press, two or three-legged pullers, spring compressors, etc. Wherever possible, suitable readily-available alternatives to the manufacturer's special tools are described, and are shown in use. In some instances, where no alternative is possible, it has been necessary to resort to the use of a manufacturer's tool, and this has been done for reasons of safety as well as the efficient completion of the repair operation. Unless you are highly-skilled and have a thorough understanding of the procedures described, never attempt to bypass the use of any special tool when the procedure described specifies its use. Not only is there a very great risk of personal injury, but expensive damage could be caused to the components involved.

Environmental considerations

When disposing of used engine oil, brake fluid, antifreeze, etc, give due consideration to any detrimental environmental effects. Do not, for instance, pour any of the above liquids down drains into the general sewage system, or onto the ground to soak away, as this is likely to pollute your local environment. Many local council refuse tips provide a facility for waste oil disposal, as do some garages. You can find your nearest disposal point by calling the Environment Agency on 03708 506 506 or by visiting www.oilbankline.org.uk.

Note: It is illegal and anti-social to dump oil down the drain. To find the location of your local oil recycling bank, call 03708 506 506 or visit www.oilbankline.org.uk.

The jack supplied with the vehicle tool kit should only be used for changing roadwheels – see *Wheel changing* at the front of this manual. Ensure the jack head is correctly engaged before attempting to raise the vehicle. When carrying out any other kind of work, raise the vehicle using a hydraulic jack, and always supplement the jack with axle stands positioned under the vehicle jacking points.

When jacking up the vehicle with a trolley jack, position the jack head under one of the relevant jacking points **(see illustration)**. Do not jack the vehicle under the sump or any of the steering or suspension components. Supplement the jack using axle stands.

 Warning: Never work under, around, or near a raised vehicle, unless it is adequately supported in at least two places.

Jacking points are provided at the front and rear of the vehicle

Disconnecting the battery

Numerous systems fitted to the vehicle require battery power to be available at all times, either to ensure their continued operation (such as the clock) or to maintain control unit memories which would be erased if the battery were to be disconnected. Whenever the battery is to be disconnected therefore, first note the following, to ensure that there are no unforeseen consequences of this action:

a) *First, on any vehicle with central locking, it is a wise precaution to remove the key from the ignition, and to keep it with you, so that it does not get locked in if the central locking should engage accidentally when the battery is reconnected.*

b) *Depending on vehicle and specification, the Mercedes-Benz anti-theft alarm system may be of the type which is automatically activated when the vehicle battery is disconnected and/ or reconnected. To prevent the alarm sounding on models so equipped, switch* the ignition on, then off, and disconnect the battery within 15 seconds. If the alarm is activated when the battery is reconnected, deactivate the alarm by locking and unlocking one of the front doors.

c) *If a security-coded audio unit is fitted, and the unit and/or the battery is disconnected, the unit will not function again on reconnection until the correct security code is entered. Details of this procedure, which varies according to the unit fitted, are given in the vehicle audio system operating instructions. Ensure you have the correct code before you disconnect the battery. If you do not have the code or details of the correct procedure, but can supply proof of ownership and a legitimate reason for wanting this information, a Mercedes-Benz dealer may be able to help.*

d) *The engine management ECU is* of the 'self-learning' type, meaning that as it operates, it also monitors and stores the settings which give optimum engine performance under all operating conditions. When the battery is disconnected, these settings are lost and the ECU reverts to the base settings programmed into its memory at the factory. On restarting, this may lead to the engine running/idling roughly for a short while, until the ECU has relearned the optimum settings. This process is best accomplished by taking the vehicle on a road test (for approximately 15 minutes), covering all engine speeds and loads, concentrating mainly in the 2500 to 3500 rpm region.

e) *On all models, when reconnecting the battery after disconnection, switch on the ignition and wait 10 seconds to allow the electronic vehicle systems to stabilise and re-initialise.*

Introduction

A selection of good tools is a fundamental requirement for anyone contemplating the maintenance and repair of a motor vehicle. For the owner who does not possess any, their purchase will prove a considerable expense, offsetting some of the savings made by doing-it-yourself. However, provided that the tools purchased meet the relevant national safety standards and are of good quality, they will last for many years and prove an extremely worthwhile investment.

To help the average owner to decide which tools are needed to carry out the various tasks detailed in this manual, we have compiled three lists of tools under the following headings: *Maintenance and minor repair*, *Repair and overhaul*, and *Special*. Newcomers to practical mechanics should start off with the *Maintenance and minor repair* tool kit, and confine themselves to the simpler jobs around the vehicle. Then, as confidence and experience grow, more difficult tasks can be undertaken, with extra tools being purchased as, and when, they are needed. In this way, a *Maintenance and minor repair* tool kit can be built up into a *Repair and overhaul* tool kit over a considerable period of time, without any major cash outlays. The experienced do-it-yourselfer will have a tool kit good enough for most repair and overhaul procedures, and will add tools from the *Special* category when it is felt that the expense is justified by the amount of use to which these tools will be put.

Maintenance and minor repair tool kit

The tools given in this list should be considered as a minimum requirement if routine maintenance, servicing and minor repair operations are to be undertaken. We recommend the purchase of combination spanners (ring one end, open-ended the other); although more expensive than open-ended ones, they do give the advantages of both types of spanner.

☐ *Combination spanners:*
  Metric - 8 to 19 mm inclusive
☐ *Adjustable spanner - 35 mm jaw (approx.)*
☐ *Spark plug spanner (with rubber insert) - petrol models*
☐ *Spark plug gap adjustment tool - petrol models*
☐ *Set of feeler gauges*
☐ *Brake bleed nipple spanner*
☐ *Screwdrivers:*
  Flat blade - 100 mm long x 6 mm dia
  Cross blade - 100 mm long x 6 mm dia
  Torx - various sizes (not all vehicles)
☐ *Combination pliers*
☐ *Hacksaw (junior)*
☐ *Tyre pump*
☐ *Tyre pressure gauge*
☐ *Oil can*
☐ *Oil filter removal tool (if applicable)*
☐ *Fine emery cloth*
☐ *Wire brush (small)*
☐ *Funnel (medium size)*
☐ *Sump drain plug key (not all vehicles)*

Repair and overhaul tool kit

These tools are virtually essential for anyone undertaking any major repairs to a motor vehicle, and are additional to those given in the *Maintenance and minor repair* list. Included in this list is a comprehensive set of sockets. Although these are expensive, they will be found invaluable as they are so versatile - particularly if various drives are included in the set. We recommend the half-inch square-drive type, as this can be used with most proprietary torque wrenches.

The tools in this list will sometimes need to be supplemented by tools from the *Special* list:

☐ *Sockets to cover range in previous list (including Torx sockets)*
☐ *Reversible ratchet drive (for use with sockets)*
☐ *Extension piece, 250 mm (for use with sockets)*
☐ *Universal joint (for use with sockets)*
☐ *Flexible handle or sliding T "breaker bar" (for use with sockets)*
☐ *Torque wrench (for use with sockets)*
☐ *Self-locking grips*
☐ *Ball pein hammer*
☐ *Soft-faced mallet (plastic or rubber)*
☐ *Screwdrivers:*
  Flat blade - long & sturdy, short (chubby), and narrow (electrician's) types
  Cross blade – long & sturdy, and short (chubby) types
☐ *Pliers:*
  Long-nosed
  Side cutters (electrician's)
  Circlip (internal and external)
☐ *Cold chisel - 25 mm*
☐ *Scriber*
☐ *Scraper*
☐ *Centre-punch*
☐ *Pin punch*
☐ *Hacksaw*
☐ *Brake hose clamp*
☐ *Brake/clutch bleeding kit*
☐ *Selection of twist drills*
☐ *Steel rule/straight-edge*
☐ *Allen keys (inc. splined/Torx type)*
☐ *Selection of files*
☐ *Wire brush*
☐ *Axle stands*
☐ *Jack (strong trolley or hydraulic type)*
☐ *Light with extension lead*
☐ *Universal electrical multi-meter*

Sockets and reversible ratchet drive

Brake bleeding kit

Torx key, socket and bit

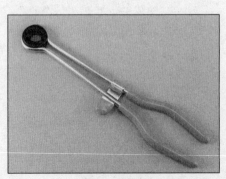

Hose clamp

Angular-tightening gauge

Special tools

The tools in this list are those which are not used regularly, are expensive to buy, or which need to be used in accordance with their manufacturers' instructions. Unless relatively difficult mechanical jobs are undertaken frequently, it will not be economic to buy many of these tools. Where this is the case, you could consider clubbing together with friends (or joining a motorists' club) to make a joint purchase, or borrowing the tools against a deposit from a local garage or tool hire specialist.

The following list contains only those tools and instruments freely available to the public, and not those special tools produced by the vehicle manufacturer specifically for its dealer network. You will find occasional references to these manufacturers' special tools in the text of this manual. Generally, an alternative method of doing the job without the vehicle manufacturers' special tool is given. However, sometimes there is no alternative to using them. Where this is the case and the relevant tool cannot be bought or borrowed, you will have to entrust the work to a dealer.

- [ ] Angular-tightening gauge
- [ ] Valve spring compressor
- [ ] Valve grinding tool
- [ ] Piston ring compressor
- [ ] Piston ring removal/installation tool
- [ ] Cylinder bore hone
- [ ] Balljoint separator
- [ ] Coil spring compressors (where applicable)
- [ ] Two/three-legged hub and bearing puller
- [ ] Impact screwdriver
- [ ] Micrometer and/or vernier calipers
- [ ] Dial gauge
- [ ] Tachometer
- [ ] Fault code reader
- [ ] Cylinder compression gauge
- [ ] Hand-operated vacuum pump and gauge
- [ ] Clutch plate alignment set
- [ ] Brake shoe steady spring cup removal tool
- [ ] Bush and bearing removal/installation set
- [ ] Stud extractors
- [ ] Tap and die set
- [ ] Lifting tackle

Buying tools

Reputable motor accessory shops and superstores often offer excellent quality tools at discount prices, so it pays to shop around.

Remember, you don't have to buy the most expensive items on the shelf, but it is always advisable to steer clear of the very cheap tools. Beware of 'bargains' offered on market stalls, on-line or at car boot sales. There are plenty of good tools around at reasonable prices, but always aim to purchase items which meet the relevant national safety standards. If in doubt, ask the proprietor or manager of the shop for advice before making a purchase.

Care and maintenance of tools

Having purchased a reasonable tool kit, it is necessary to keep the tools in a clean and serviceable condition. After use, always wipe off any dirt, grease and metal particles using a clean, dry cloth, before putting the tools away. Never leave them lying around after they have been used. A simple tool rack on the garage or workshop wall for items such as screwdrivers and pliers is a good idea. Store all normal spanners and sockets in a metal box. Any measuring instruments, gauges, meters, etc, must be carefully stored where they cannot be damaged or become rusty.

Take a little care when tools are used. Hammer heads inevitably become marked, and screwdrivers lose the keen edge on their blades from time to time. A little timely attention with emery cloth or a file will soon restore items like this to a good finish.

Working facilities

Not to be forgotten when discussing tools is the workshop itself. If anything more than routine maintenance is to be carried out, a suitable working area becomes essential.

It is appreciated that many an owner-mechanic is forced by circumstances to remove an engine or similar item without the benefit of a garage or workshop. Having done this, any repairs should always be done under the cover of a roof.

Wherever possible, any dismantling should be done on a clean, flat workbench or table at a suitable working height.

Any workbench needs a vice; one with a jaw opening of 100 mm is suitable for most jobs. As mentioned previously, some clean dry storage space is also required for tools, as well as for any lubricants, cleaning fluids, touch-up paints etc, which become necessary.

Another item which may be required, and which has a much more general usage, is an electric drill with a chuck capacity of at least 8 mm. This, together with a good range of twist drills, is virtually essential for fitting accessories.

Last, but not least, always keep a supply of old newspapers and clean, lint-free rags available, and try to keep any working area as clean as possible.

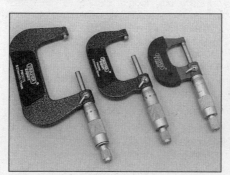

Micrometers

Dial test indicator ("dial gauge")

Oil filter removal tool (strap wrench type)

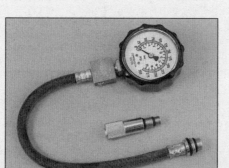

Compression tester

Bearing puller

This is a guide to getting your vehicle through the MOT test. Obviously it will not be possible to examine the vehicle to the same standard as the professional MOT tester. However, working through the following checks will enable you to identify any problem areas before submitting the vehicle for the test.

It has only been possible to summarise the test requirements here, based on the regulations in force at the time of printing. Test standards are becoming increasingly stringent, although there are some exemptions for older vehicles.

An assistant will be needed to help carry out some of these checks.

The checks have been sub-divided into four categories, as follows:

1 Checks carried out **FROM THE VEHICLE INTERIOR**

2 Checks carried out **WITH THE VEHICLE ON THE GROUND**

3 Checks carried out **WITH THE VEHICLE RAISED AND THE WHEELS FREE TO TURN**

4 Checks carried out on **YOUR VEHICLE'S EXHAUST EMISSION SYSTEM**

1 Checks carried out **FROM THE VEHICLE INTERIOR**

Handbrake (parking brake)

☐ Test the operation of the handbrake. Excessive travel (too many clicks) indicates incorrect brake or cable adjustment.
☐ Check that the handbrake cannot be released by tapping the lever sideways. Check the security of the lever mountings.

☐ If the parking brake is foot-operated, check that the pedal is secure and without excessive travel, and that the release mechanism operates correctly.
☐ Where applicable, test the operation of the electronic handbrake. The brake should engage and disengage without excessive delay. If the warning light does not extinguish, or a warning message is displayed when the brake is disengaged, this could indicate a fault which will need further investigation.

Footbrake

☐ Depress the brake pedal and check that it does not creep down to the floor, indicating a master cylinder fault. Release the pedal, wait a few seconds, then depress it again. If the pedal travels nearly to the floor before firm resistance is felt, brake adjustment or repair is necessary. If the pedal feels spongy, there is air in the hydraulic system which must be removed by bleeding.

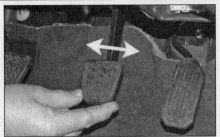

☐ Check that the brake pedal is secure and in good condition. Check also for signs of fluid leaks on the pedal, floor or carpets, which would indicate failed seals in the brake master cylinder.
☐ Check the servo unit (when applicable) by operating the brake pedal several times, then keeping the pedal depressed and starting the engine. As the engine starts, the pedal will move down. If not, the vacuum hose or the servo itself may be faulty.

Steering wheel and column

☐ Examine the steering wheel for fractures or looseness of the hub, spokes or rim.
☐ Move the steering wheel from side to side and then up and down. Check that the steering wheel is not loose on the column, indicating wear or a loose retaining nut. Continue moving the steering wheel as before, but also turn it slightly from left to right.
☐ Check that the steering wheel is not loose on the column, and that there is no abnormal movement of the steering wheel, indicating wear in the column support bearings or couplings.

☐ Check that the ignition lock (where fitted) engages and disengages correctly.
☐ Steering column adjustment mechanisms (where fitted) must be able to lock the column securely in place with no play evident.

Windscreen, mirrors and sunvisor

☐ The windscreen must be free of cracks or other significant damage within the 'swept area' of the windscreen. This is the area swept by the windscreen wipers. A second test area, known as 'Zone A', is the part of the swept area 290 mm wide, centred on the steering wheel centre line. Any damage in Zone A that cannot be contained in a 10 mm diameter circle, or any damage in the remainder of the swept area that cannot be contained in a 40 mm diameter circle, may cause the vehicle to fail the test.

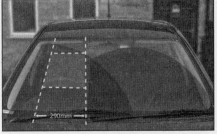

☐ Any items that may obscure the drivers view, such as stickers, sat-navs, anything hanging from the interior mirror, should be removed prior to the test.
☐ Vehicles registered after 1st August 1978 must have a drivers side mirror, and either an interior mirror, or a passenger's side mirror. Cameras (or indirect vision devices) may replace the mirrors, but they must function correctly.
☐ The driver's sunvisor must be capable of being stored in the "up" position.

Seat belts, seats and supplementary restraint systems (SRS)

Note: *The following checks are applicable to all seat belts, front and rear.*

Examine the webbing of all the belts (including rear belts if fitted) for cuts, serious fraying or deterioration. Fasten and unfasten each belt to check the buckles. If applicable, check the retracting mechanism. Check the security of all seat belt mountings accessible from inside the vehicle, ensuring any height adjustable mountings lock securely in place.

Where the seat belt is attached to a seat, the frame and mountings of the seat form part of the belt mountings, and are to be inspected as such.

Any airbag, or SRS warning light must extinguish a few seconds after the ignition is switched on. Failure to do so indicates a fault which must be investigated.

Seat belts with pre-tensioners, once activated, have a "flag" or similar showing on the seat belt stalk. This, in itself, is a reason for test failure.

Check that the original airbag(s) is/are present, and not obviously defective.

The seats themselves must be securely attached and the backrests must lock in the upright position. The driver's seat must also be able to slide forwards/rearwards, and lock in several positions.

Doors

Both front doors must be able to be opened and closed from outside and inside, and must latch securely when closed.

The rear doors must open from the outside.

Examine all door hinges, catches and striker plates for missing, deteriorated, or insecure parts that could effect the opening and closing of the doors.

Speedometer

The vehicle speedometer must be present, and appear operative. The figures on the speedometer must be legible, and illuminated when the lights are switched on.

2 Checks carried out WITH THE VEHICLE ON THE GROUND

Vehicle identification

Number plates must be in good condition, secure and legible, with letters and numbers correctly spaced – spacing at (A) should be 33 mm and at (B) 11 mm. At the front, digits must be black on a white background and at the rear

black on a yellow background. Other background designs (such as honeycomb) are not permitted.

The VIN plate and/or homologation plate must be permanently displayed and legible.

Electrical equipment

Switch on the ignition and check the operation of the horn.

Check the windscreen washers and wipers, examining the wiper blades; renew damaged or perished blades. The wiper blades must clear a large enough area of the windscreen to provide an 'adequate' view of the road, and be able to be parked in a position where they will not affect the drivers' view.

On vehicles first used from 1st September 2009, the headlight washers (where fitted) must operate correctly.

Check the operation of the stop-lights. This includes any lights that appear to be connected – Eg. high-level lights.

Check the operation of the sidelights and number plate lights. The lenses and reflectors must be secure, clean and undamaged.

Check the operation and alignment of the headlights. The headlight reflectors must not be tarnished and the lenses must be undamaged. Where plastic lenses are fitted, check they haven't deteriorated to the extent where they affect the light ouput or beam image. It's often possible to restore the plastic lens using a suitable polish or aftermarket treatment.

Where HID or LED headlights are fitted, check the operation of the cleaning and self-levelling functions.

The headlight main beam warning lamp must be functional.

On vehicles first used from 1st March 2018, the daytime running lights (where fitted) must operate correctly.

Switch on the ignition and check the operation of the direction indicators (including the instrument panel tell-tale) and the hazard warning lights. Operation of the sidelights and stop-lights must not affect the indicators – if it does, the cause is usually a bad earth at the rear light cluster. Indicators should flash at a rate of between 60 and 120 times per minute – faster or slower than this could indicate a fault with the flasher unit or a bad earth at one of the light units.

The hazard warning lights must operate with the ignition on and off.

Check the operation of the rear foglight(s), including the warning light on the instrument panel or in the switch. Note that the foglight

must be positioned in the centre or driver's side of the vehicle. If only the passenger's side illuminates, the test will fail.

The warning lights must illuminate in accordance with the manufacturers' design (this includes any warning messages). For most vehicles, the ABS and other warning lights should illuminate when the ignition is switched on, and (if the system is operating properly) extinguish after a few seconds. Refer to the owner's handbook.

On vehicles first used from 1st September 2009, the reversing lights must operate correctly when reverse gear is selected.

Check the vehicle battery for security and leakage.

Check the visible/accessible vehicle wiring is adequately supported, with no evidence of damage or deterioration that could result in a short-circuit.

Footbrake

Examine the master cylinder, brake pipes and servo unit for leaks, loose mountings, corrosion or other damage. If ABS is fitted, this unit should also be examined for signs of leaks or corrosion.

The fluid reservoir must be secure and the fluid level must be between the upper (**A**) and lower (**B**) markings.

Check the fluid in the reservoir for signs of contamination.

Inspect both front brake flexible hoses for cracks or deterioration of the rubber. Turn the steering from lock to lock, and ensure that the hoses do not contact the wheel, tyre, or any part of the steering or suspension mechanism. With the brake pedal firmly depressed, check the hoses for bulges or leaks under pressure.

Steering and suspension

Have your assistant turn the steering wheel from side to side slightly, up to the point where the steering gear just begins to transmit this movement to the roadwheels. Check for excessive free play between the steering wheel and the steering gear, indicating wear or insecurity of the steering column joints, the column-to-steering gear coupling, or the steering gear itself. With a standard (380 mm diameter) steering wheel, there should be no more than 13 mm of free play for rack-and-pinion systems, and no more than 75 mm for non-rack-and-pinion designs.

Have your assistant turn the steering

wheel more vigorously in each direction, so that the roadwheels just begin to turn. As this is done, examine all the steering joints, linkages, fittings and attachments. Renew any component that shows signs of wear or damage. On vehicles with hydraulic power steering, check the security and condition of the steering pump, drivebelt and hoses.

☐ Note that all movement checks on power steering systems are carried out with the engine running.

☐ Check that the vehicle is standing level, and at approximately the correct ride height.

Exhaust system

☐ Start the engine. With your assistant holding a rag over the tailpipe, check the entire system for leaks. Repair or renew leaking sections.

3 Checks carried out **WITH THE VEHICLE RAISED AND THE WHEELS FREE TO TURN**

Jack up the front and rear of the vehicle, and securely support it on axle stands. Position the stands clear of the suspension assemblies. Ensure that the wheels are clear of the ground and that the steering can be turned from lock to lock.

Steering mechanism

☐ Have your assistant turn the steering from lock to lock. Check that the steering turns smoothly, and that no part of the steering mechanism, including a wheel or tyre, fouls any brake hose or pipe or any part of the body structure.

☐ Examine the steering rack rubber gaiters for damage or insecurity of the retaining clips. If power steering is fitted, check for signs of damage or leakage of the fluid hoses, pipes or connections. Also check for excessive stiffness or binding of the steering, a missing split pin or locking device, or severe corrosion of the body structure within 30 cm of any steering component attachment point.

☐ Check the track rod end ball joint dust covers. Any covers that are missing, seriously damaged, deteriorated or insecure, may fail inspection.

Front and rear suspension and wheel bearings

☐ Starting at the front right-hand side, grasp the roadwheel at the 3 o'clock and 9 o'clock positions and rock gently but firmly. Check for free play or insecurity at the wheel bearings, suspension balljoints, or suspension mountings, pivots and attachments.

☐ Now grasp the wheel at the 12 o'clock and 6 o'clock positions and repeat the previous inspection. Spin the wheel, and check for roughness or tightness of the front wheel bearing.

☐ If excess free play is suspected at a component pivot point, this can be confirmed by using a large screwdriver or similar tool and levering between the mounting and the component attachment. This will confirm whether the wear is in the pivot bush, its retaining bolt, or in the mounting itself (the bolt holes can often become elongated).

☐ Carry out all the above checks at the other front wheel, and then at both rear wheels.

Springs and shock absorbers

☐ Examine the suspension struts (when applicable) for serious fluid leakage, corrosion, or damage to the casing. Also check the security of the mounting points.

☐ If coil springs are fitted, check that the spring ends locate in their seats, and that the spring is not corroded, cracked or broken.

☐ If leaf springs are fitted, check that all leaves are intact, that the axle is securely attached to each spring, and that there is no deterioration of the spring eye mountings, bushes, and shackles.

☐ The same general checks apply to vehicles fitted with other suspension types, such as torsion bars, hydraulic displacer units, etc. Ensure that all mountings and attachments are secure, that there are no signs of excessive wear, corrosion or damage, and (on hydraulic types) that there are no fluid leaks or damaged pipes.

☐ Check any suspension and anti-roll bar link ball joint dust covers. Any covers that are missing, seriously damaged, deteriorated or insecure, may fail inspection.

☐ Examine each shock absorber for signs of leakage, corrosion of the casing, missing, detached or worn pivots and/or rubber bushes.

Driveshafts (fwd vehicles only)

☐ Rotate each front wheel in turn and inspect the inner and outer joint gaiters for splits or damage. Also check that each driveshaft is straight and undamaged.

Braking system

☐ If possible without dismantling, check brake pad wear and disc condition. Ensure that the friction lining material has not worn excessively, (A) and that the discs are not fractured, pitted, scored or badly worn (B). As a general rule, if the friction material is less than 1.5 mm thick, the inspection will fail.

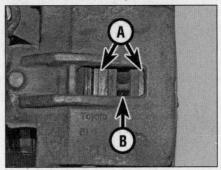

☐ Examine all the rigid brake pipes underneath the vehicle, and the flexible hose(s) at the rear. Look for corrosion, chafing or insecurity of the pipes, and for signs of bulging under pressure, chafing, splits or deterioration of the flexible hoses.

☐ Look for signs of fluid leaks at the brake calipers or on the brake backplates. Repair or renew leaking components.

☐ Slowly spin each wheel, while your assistant depresses and releases the footbrake. Ensure that each brake is operating and does not bind when the pedal is released.

☐ Examine the handbrake mechanism, checking for frayed or broken cables, excessive corrosion, or wear or insecurity of the linkage. Check that the mechanism works on each relevant wheel, and releases fully, without binding.

☐ Check the ABS sensors' wiring for signs of damage, deterioration or insecurity.

☐ It is not possible to test brake efficiency without special equipment, but a road test can be carried out later to check that the vehicle pulls up in a straight line.

Fuel and exhaust systems

☐ Inspect the fuel tank (including the filler cap), fuel pipes, hoses and unions. All components must be secure and free from leaks. Locking fuel caps must lock securely and the key must be provided for the MOT test.

☐ Examine the exhaust system over its entire length, checking for any damaged, broken or missing mountings, security of the retaining clamps and rust or corrosion.

☐ If the vehicle was originally equipped with a catalytic converter or particulate filter, one must be fitted.

Wheels and tyres

☐ Examine the sidewalls and tread area of each tyre in turn. Check for cuts, tears, lumps, bulges, separation of the tread, and exposure of the ply or cord due to wear or damage. Check that the tyre bead is correctly seated on the wheel rim, that the valve is sound and properly seated, and that the wheel is not distorted or damaged.

☐ Check that the tyres are of the correct size for the vehicle, that they are of the same size and type on each axle, and that the pressures are correct. The vehicle will fail the test if the tyres are obviously under-inflated.

☐ Check the tyre tread depth. The legal minimum at the time of writing is 1.6 mm over the central three-quarters of the tread width. Abnormal tread wear may indicate incorrect front wheel alignment or wear in steering or suspension components.

☐ Check that all wheel bolts/nuts are present.

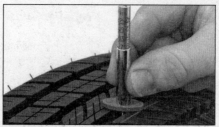

☐ If the spare wheel is fitted externally or in a separate carrier beneath the vehicle, check that mountings are secure and free of excessive corrosion.

Body corrosion

☐ Check the condition of the entire vehicle structure for signs of corrosion in load-bearing areas. (These include chassis box sections, side sills, cross-members, pillars, and all suspension, steering, braking system and seat belt mountings and anchorages.) Any corrosion which has seriously reduced the thickness of a load-bearing area (or is within 30 cm of safety-related components such as steering or suspension) is likely to cause the vehicle to fail. In this case professional repairs are likely to be needed.

☐ Damage or corrosion which causes sharp or otherwise dangerous edges to be exposed will also cause the vehicle to fail.

Towbars

☐ Check the condition of mounting points (both beneath the vehicle and within boot/hatchback areas) for signs of corrosion, ensuring that all fixings are secure and not worn or damaged. There must be no excessive play in detachable tow ball arms or quick-release mechanisms.

☐ Examine the security and condition of the towbar electrics socket. If the later 13-pin socket is fitted, the MOT tester will check its' wiring functions/connections are correct.

General leaks

☐ The vehicle will fail the test if there is a fluid leak of any kind that poses an environmental risk.

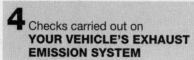

4 Checks carried out on
YOUR VEHICLE'S EXHAUST EMISSION SYSTEM

Petrol models

☐ The engine should be warmed up, and running well (ignition system in good order, air filter element clean, etc).

☐ Before testing, run the engine at around 2500 rpm for 20 seconds. Let the engine drop to idle, and watch for smoke from the exhaust. If the idle speed is too high, or if dense blue or black smoke emerges for more than 5 seconds, the vehicle will fail. Typically, blue smoke signifies oil burning (engine wear); black smoke means unburnt fuel (dirty air cleaner element, or other fuel system fault).

☐ An exhaust gas analyser for measuring carbon monoxide (CO) and hydrocarbons (HC) is now needed. If one cannot be hired or borrowed, have a local garage perform the check.

CO emissions (mixture)

☐ The MOT tester has access to the CO limits for all vehicles from 1st August 1992. The CO level is measured at idle speed, and at 'fast idle' (2500 to 3000 rpm). The following limits are given as a general guide:
  At idle speed – Less than 0.3% CO
  At 'fast idle' – Less than 0.2% CO
  Lambda reading – 0.97 to 1.03

☐ If the CO level is too high, this may point to poor maintenance, a fuel injection system problem, faulty lambda (oxygen) sensor or catalytic converter. Try an injector cleaning treatment, and check the vehicle's ECU for fault codes.

HC emissions

☐ The MOT tester has access to HC limits for all vehicles. The HC level is measured at 'fast idle' (2500 to 3000 rpm). The following limits are given as a general guide:
  At 'fast idle' – Less than 200 ppm

☐ Excessive HC emissions are typically caused by oil being burnt (worn engine), or by a blocked crankcase ventilation system ('breather'). If the engine oil is old and thin, an oil change may help. If the engine is running badly, check the vehicle's ECU for fault codes.

Diesel models

☐ If the vehicle was fitted with a DPF (Diesel Particulate Filter) when it left the factory, it will fail the test if the MOT tester can see smoke of any colour emitting from the exhaust, or finds evidence that the filter has been tampered with.

☐ The only emission test for diesel engines is measuring exhaust smoke density, using a calibrated smoke meter.

☐ This test involves accelerating the engine to its maximum unloaded speed a minimum of once, and a maximum of 6 times. With the smoke meter connected, the engine is accelerated quickly to its maximum speed. If the smoke level is at or below the limit specified, the vehicle will pass. If the level is more than the specified limit then two further accelerations are carried out, and an average of the readings calculated. If the vehicle is still over the limit, a further three accelerations are carried out, with the average of the last three calculated after each check.

Note: *On engines with a timing belt, it is VITAL that the belt is in good condition before the test is carried out.*

Vehicles registered after 1st July 2008
Smoke level must not exceed 1.5m-1 – Turbo-charged and non-Turbocharged engines

Vehicles registered before 1st July 2008
Smoke level must not exceed 2.5m-1 – Non-turbo vehicles
Smoke level must not exceed 3.0m-1 – Turbocharged vehicles:

☐ If excess smoke is produced, try fitting a new air cleaner element, or using an injector cleaning treatment. If the engine is running badly, where applicable, check the vehicle's ECU for fault codes. Also check the vehicle's EGR system, where applicable. At high mileages, the injectors may require professional attention.

Engine

- [ ] Engine fails to rotate when attempting to start
- [ ] Engine rotates, but will not start
- [ ] Engine difficult to start when cold
- [ ] Engine difficult to start when hot
- [ ] Starter motor noisy or excessively-rough in engagement
- [ ] Engine starts, but stops immediately
- [ ] Engine idles erratically
- [ ] Engine misfires at idle speed
- [ ] Engine misfires throughout the driving speed range
- [ ] Engine hesitates on acceleration
- [ ] Engine stalls
- [ ] Engine lacks power
- [ ] Engine backfires
- [ ] Oil pressure warning light illuminated with engine running
- [ ] Engine runs-on after switching off
- [ ] Engine noises

Cooling system

- [ ] Overheating
- [ ] Overcooling
- [ ] External coolant leakage
- [ ] Internal coolant leakage
- [ ] Corrosion

Fuel and exhaust systems

- [ ] Excessive fuel consumption
- [ ] Fuel leakage and/or fuel odour
- [ ] Excessive noise or fumes from exhaust system

Clutch

- [ ] Pedal travels to floor – no pressure or very little resistance
- [ ] Clutch fails to disengage (unable to select gears)
- [ ] Clutch slips (engine speed increases, with no increase in vehicle speed)
- [ ] Judder as clutch is engaged
- [ ] Noise when depressing or releasing clutch pedal

Transmission

- [ ] Noisy in neutral with engine running
- [ ] Noisy in one particular gear
- [ ] Difficulty engaging gears
- [ ] Jumps out of gear
- [ ] Vibration
- [ ] Lubricant leaks

Propeller shaft

- [ ] Vibration when accelerating or decelerating
- [ ] Noise (grinding or high-pitched squeak) when moving slowly
- [ ] Noise (knocking or clicking) when accelerating or decelerating

Rear axle

- [ ] Roughness or rumble from the rear of the vehicle (perhaps less with the handbrake slightly applied)
- [ ] Noise (high-pitched whine) increasing with road speed
- [ ] Noise (knocking or clicking) when accelerating or decelerating
- [ ] Lubricant leaks

Braking system

- [ ] Vehicle pulls to one side under braking
- [ ] Noise (grinding or high-pitched squeal) when brakes applied
- [ ] Excessive brake pedal travel
- [ ] Brake pedal feels spongy when depressed
- [ ] Excessive brake pedal effort required to stop vehicle
- [ ] Judder felt through brake pedal or steering wheel when braking
- [ ] Brakes binding
- [ ] Rear wheels locking under normal braking

Suspension and steering

- [ ] Vehicle pulls to one side
- [ ] Wheel wobble and vibration
- [ ] Excessive pitching and/or rolling around corners, or during braking
- [ ] Wandering or general instability
- [ ] Excessively-stiff steering
- [ ] Excessive play in steering
- [ ] Lack of power assistance
- [ ] Tyre wear excessive

Electrical system

- [ ] Battery will not hold a charge for more than a few days
- [ ] Ignition/no-charge warning light remains illuminated with engine running
- [ ] Ignition/no-charge warning light fails to come on
- [ ] Lights inoperative
- [ ] Instrument readings inaccurate or erratic
- [ ] Horn inoperative, or unsatisfactory in operation
- [ ] Windscreen wipers inoperative, or unsatisfactory in operation
- [ ] Windscreen washers inoperative, or unsatisfactory in operation
- [ ] Electric windows inoperative, or unsatisfactory in operation
- [ ] Central locking system inoperative, or unsatisfactory in operation

Introduction

The vehicle owner who does his or her own maintenance according to the recommended service schedules should not have to use this section of the manual very often. Modern component reliability is such that, provided those items subject to wear or deterioration are inspected or renewed at the specified intervals, sudden failure is comparatively rare. Faults do not usually just happen as a result of sudden failure, but develop over a period of time. Major mechanical failures in particular are usually preceded by characteristic symptoms over hundreds or even thousands of miles. Those components that do occasionally fail without warning are often small and easily carried in the vehicle.

With any fault-finding, the first step is to decide where to begin investigations. Sometimes this is obvious, but on other occasions, a little detective work will be necessary. The owner who makes half a dozen haphazard adjustments or replacements may be successful in curing a fault (or its symptoms), but will be none the wiser if the fault recurs, and ultimately may have spent more time and money than was necessary. A calm and logical approach will be found to be more satisfactory in the long run. Always take into account any warning signs or abnormalities that may have been noticed in the period preceding the fault – power loss, high or low gauge readings, unusual smells, etc – and remember that failure of components such as fuses may only be pointers to some underlying fault.

The pages that follow provide an easy-reference guide to the more common problems, which may occur during the operation of the vehicle. These problems and their possible causes are grouped under headings denoting various components or systems, such as Engine, Cooling system, etc. The general Chapter, which deals with the problem, is also shown in brackets; refer to the relevant part of that Chapter for system-specific information. Whatever the fault, certain basic principles apply. These are as follows:

Verify the fault. This is simply a matter of

being sure that you know what the symptoms are before starting work. This is particularly important if you are investigating a fault for someone else, who may not have described it very accurately.

Don't overlook the obvious. For example, if the vehicle won't start, is there fuel in the tank? (Don't take anyone else's word on this particular point, and don't trust the fuel gauge either!) If an electrical fault is indicated, look for loose or broken wires before digging out the test gear.

Cure the disease, not the symptom. Substituting a flat battery with a fully charged one will get you off the hard shoulder, but if the underlying cause is not attended to, the new battery will go the same way.

Don't take anything for granted. Particularly, don't forget that a 'new' component may itself be defective (especially if it's been rattling around in the boot for months), and don't leave components out of a fault diagnosis sequence just because they are new or recently fitted. When you do finally diagnose a difficult fault, you'll probably realise that all the evidence was there from the start.

Consider what work, if any, has recently been carried out. Many faults arise through careless or hurried work. For instance, if any work has been performed under the bonnet, could some of the wiring have been dislodged or incorrectly routed, or a hose trapped? Have all the fasteners been properly tightened? Were new, genuine parts and new gaskets used? There is often a certain amount of detective work to be done in this case, as an apparently unrelated task can have far-reaching consequences.

Diesel fault diagnosis

The majority of starting problems on small diesel engines are electrical in origin. The mechanic who is familiar with petrol engines but less so with diesel may be inclined to view the diesel's injectors and pump in the same light as the spark plugs and distributor, but this is generally a mistake.

When investigating complaints of difficult starting for someone else, make sure that the correct starting procedure is understood and is being followed. Some drivers are unaware of the significance of the preheating warning light – many modern engines are sufficiently forgiving for this not to matter in mild weather, but with the onset of winter, problems begin.

As a rule of thumb, if the engine is difficult to start but runs well when it has finally got going, the problem is electrical (battery, starter motor or preheating system). If poor performance is combined with difficult starting, the problem is likely to be in the fuel system. The low-pressure (supply) side of the fuel system should be checked before suspecting the injectors and high-pressure pump. The most common fuel supply problem is air getting into the system, and any pipe from the fuel tank forwards must be scrutinised if air leakage is suspected. Normally the pump is the last item to suspect, since unless it has been tampered with, there is no reason for it to be at fault.

Engine

Engine fails to rotate when attempting to start

- [ ] Battery terminal connections loose or corroded *(see Weekly checks)*
- [ ] Battery discharged or faulty (Chapter 5)
- [ ] Broken, loose or disconnected wiring in the starting circuit (Chapter 5)
- [ ] Defective starter solenoid or ignition switch (Chapter 5 or 12)
- [ ] Defective starter motor (Chapter 5)
- [ ] Starter pinion or flywheel ring gear teeth loose or broken (Chapter 5)
- [ ] Engine earth strap broken or disconnected (Chapter 5)
- [ ] Engine suffering 'hydraulic lock' (eg, from water drawn into the engine after traversing flooded roads, or from a serious internal coolant leak) – consult a main dealer for advice

Engine rotates, but will not start

- [ ] Fuel tank empty
- [ ] Battery discharged (engine rotates slowly) (Chapter 5)
- [ ] Battery terminal connections loose or corroded *(see Weekly checks)*
- [ ] Immobiliser fault, or 'uncoded' ignition key being used (Chapter 12 or *Roadside repairs*)
- [ ] Preheating system faulty (Chapter 5)
- [ ] Fuel injection/engine management system fault (Chapter 4A)
- [ ] Air in fuel system (Chapter 4A)
- [ ] Major mechanical failure (Chapter 2A)

Engine difficult to start when cold

- [ ] Battery discharged (Chapter 5)
- [ ] Battery terminal connections loose or corroded *(see Weekly checks)*
- [ ] Preheating system faulty (Chapter 5)
- [ ] Fuel injection/engine management system fault (Chapter 4A)
- [ ] Wrong grade of engine oil used (*Weekly checks*, Chapter 1)
- [ ] Low cylinder compression (Chapter 2A)
- [ ] Air in fuel system (Chapter 4A)

Engine difficult to start when hot

- [ ] Air filter element dirty or clogged (Chapter 1)
- [ ] Fuel injection/engine management system fault (Chapter 4A)

- [ ] Low cylinder compression (Chapter 2A)
- [ ] Air in fuel system (Chapter 4A)

Starter motor noisy or excessively-rough in engagement

- [ ] Starter pinion or flywheel ring gear teeth loose or broken (Chapter 5)
- [ ] Starter motor mounting bolts loose or missing (Chapter 5)
- [ ] Starter motor internal components worn or damaged (Chapter 5)

Engine starts, but stops immediately

- [ ] Fuel injection/engine management system fault (Chapter 4A)

Engine idles erratically

- [ ] Air filter element clogged (Chapter 1)
- [ ] Uneven or low cylinder compression (Chapter 2A)
- [ ] Camshaft lobes worn (Chapter 2A)
- [ ] Fuel injection/engine management system fault (Chapter 4A)
- [ ] Air in fuel system (Chapter 4A)

Engine misfires at idle speed

- [ ] Faulty injector(s) (Chapter 4A)
- [ ] Uneven or low cylinder compression (Chapter 2A)
- [ ] Disconnected, leaking, or perished crankcase ventilation hoses (Chapter 4B)
- [ ] Fuel injection/engine management system fault (Chapter 4A)

Engine misfires throughout the driving speed range

- [ ] Fuel filter choked (Chapter 1)
- [ ] Fuel tank vent blocked, or fuel pipes restricted (Chapter 4A)
- [ ] Faulty injector(s) (Chapter 4A)
- [ ] Uneven or low cylinder compression (Chapter 2A)
- [ ] Blocked catalytic converter (Chapter 4B)
- [ ] Fuel injection/engine management system fault (Chapter 4A)
- [ ] Engine overheating (Chapter 3)

Engine hesitates on acceleration

- [ ] Faulty injector(s) (Chapter 4A)
- [ ] Fuel injection/engine management system fault (Chapter 4A)

Engine (continued)

Engine stalls

- [ ] Fuel filter choked (Chapter 1)
- [ ] Fuel tank vent blocked, or fuel pipes restricted (Chapter 4A)
- [ ] Faulty injector(s) (Chapter 4A)
- [ ] Fuel injection/engine management system fault (Chapter 4A)

Engine lacks power

- [ ] Air filter element blocked (Chapter 1)
- [ ] Fuel filter choked (Chapter 1)
- [ ] Fuel pipes blocked or restricted (Chapter 4A)
- [ ] Engine overheating (Chapter 3)
- [ ] Accelerator pedal position sensor faulty (Chapter 4A)
- [ ] Faulty injector(s) (Chapter 4A)
- [ ] Uneven or low cylinder compression (Chapter 2A)
- [ ] Fuel injection/engine management system fault (Chapter 4A)
- [ ] Blocked catalytic converter (Chapter 4B)
- [ ] Brakes binding (Chapter 9)
- [ ] Clutch slipping (Chapter 6)

Engine backfires

- [ ] Fuel injection/engine management system fault (Chapter 4A)
- [ ] Blocked catalytic converter (Chapter 4B)

Oil pressure warning light illuminated with engine running

- [ ] Low oil level, or incorrect oil grade (see Weekly checks)
- [ ] Faulty oil pressure warning light switch, or wiring damaged (Chapter 2A)
- [ ] Worn engine bearings and/or oil pump (Chapter 2A)
- [ ] High engine operating temperature (Chapter 3)
- [ ] Oil pump pressure relief valve defective (Chapter 2A)
- [ ] Oil pump pick-up strainer clogged (Chapter 2A)

Engine runs-on after switching off

- [ ] High engine operating temperature (Chapter 3)
- [ ] Fuel injection/engine management system fault (Chapter 4A)

Engine noises

Pre-ignition (pinking) or knocking during acceleration or under load

- [ ] Excessive carbon build-up in engine (Chapter 2A)
- [ ] Fuel injection/engine management system fault (Chapter 4A)
- [ ] Faulty injector(s) (Chapter 4A)

Whistling or wheezing noises

- [ ] Leaking exhaust manifold gasket or pipe-to-manifold joint (Chapter 4B)
- [ ] Leaking vacuum hose (Chapter 4B)
- [ ] Blowing cylinder head gasket (Chapter 2A)
- [ ] Partially blocked or leaking crankcase ventilation system (Chapter 2B)

Tapping or rattling noises

- [ ] Worn valve gear or camshaft(s) (Chapter 2A)
- [ ] Ancillary component fault (coolant pump, alternator, etc) (Chapter 3, 5, etc)

Knocking or thumping noises

- [ ] Worn big-end bearings (regular heavy knocking, perhaps less under load) (Chapter 2B)
- [ ] Worn main bearings (rumbling and knocking, perhaps worsening under load) (Chapter 2B)
- [ ] Piston slap – most noticeable when cold, caused by piston/bore wear (Chapter 2B)
- [ ] Ancillary component fault (coolant pump, alternator, etc) (Chapter 3, 5, etc)
- [ ] Engine mountings worn or defective (Chapter 2A)
- [ ] Front suspension or steering components worn (Chapter 10)

Cooling system

Overheating

- [ ] Insufficient coolant in system (see Weekly checks)
- [ ] Thermostat faulty (Chapter 3)
- [ ] Radiator core blocked, or grille restricted (Chapter 3)
- [ ] Cooling fan faulty (Chapter 3)
- [ ] Inaccurate cylinder head temperature sensor (Chapter 2A)
- [ ] Airlock in cooling system (Chapter 1)
- [ ] Expansion tank pressure cap faulty (Chapter 1 or 3)
- [ ] Engine management system fault (Chapter 4A)

Overcooling

- [ ] Thermostat faulty (Chapter 3)
- [ ] Inaccurate cylinder head temperature sensor (Chapter 2A)
- [ ] Cooling fan faulty (Chapter 3)
- [ ] Engine management system fault (Chapter 4A)

External coolant leakage

- [ ] Deteriorated or damaged hoses or hose clips (Chapter 1)
- [ ] Radiator core or heater matrix leaking (Chapter 3)
- [ ] Expansion tank pressure cap faulty (Chapter 1 or 3)
- [ ] Coolant pump internal seal leaking (Chapter 3)
- [ ] Coolant pump gasket leaking (Chapter 3)
- [ ] Boiling due to overheating (Chapter 3)
- [ ] Cylinder block core plug leaking (Chapter 2B)

Internal coolant leakage

- [ ] Leaking cylinder head gasket (Chapter 2A)
- [ ] Cracked cylinder head or cylinder block (Chapter 2A or 2B)

Corrosion

- [ ] Infrequent draining and flushing (Chapter 1)
- [ ] Incorrect coolant mixture or inappropriate coolant type (Chapter 1)

Fuel and exhaust systems

Excessive fuel consumption

- ☐ Air filter element dirty or clogged (Chapter 1)
- ☐ Fuel injection system fault (Chapter 4A)
- ☐ Engine management system fault (Chapter 4A)
- ☐ Crankcase ventilation system blocked (Chapter 4B)
- ☐ Tyres underinflated (see Weekly checks)
- ☐ Brakes binding (Chapter 9)
- ☐ Fuel leak, causing apparent high consumption (Chapter 4A)

Fuel leakage and/or fuel odour

- ☐ Damaged or corroded fuel tank, pipes or connections (Chapter 4A)

Excessive noise or fumes from exhaust system

- ☐ Leaking exhaust system or manifold joints (Chapter 4B)
- ☐ Leaking, corroded or damaged silencers or pipe (Chapter 4B)
- ☐ Broken mountings causing body or suspension contact (Chapter 2A)

Clutch

Pedal travels to floor – no pressure or very little resistance

- ☐ Air in hydraulic system/faulty master or slave cylinder (Chapter 6)
- ☐ Faulty hydraulic release system (Chapter 6)
- ☐ Faulty clutch release/slave cylinder (Chapter 6)
- ☐ Broken diaphragm spring in clutch pressure plate (Chapter 6)

Clutch fails to disengage (unable to select gears)

- ☐ Air in hydraulic system/faulty master or release/slave cylinder (Chapter 6)
- ☐ Faulty hydraulic release system (Chapter 6)
- ☐ Clutch disc sticking on transmission input shaft splines (Chapter 6)
- ☐ Clutch disc sticking to flywheel or pressure plate (Chapter 6)
- ☐ Faulty pressure plate assembly (Chapter 6)
- ☐ Clutch release mechanism worn or incorrectly assembled (Chapter 6)

Clutch slips (engine speed increases, with no increase in vehicle speed)

- ☐ Faulty hydraulic release system (Chapter 6)
- ☐ Clutch disc linings excessively worn (Chapter 6)
- ☐ Clutch disc linings contaminated with oil or grease (Chapter 6)
- ☐ Faulty pressure plate or weak diaphragm spring (Chapter 6)

Judder as clutch is engaged

- ☐ Clutch disc linings contaminated with oil or grease (Chapter 6)
- ☐ Clutch disc linings excessively worn (Chapter 6)
- ☐ Faulty or distorted pressure plate or diaphragm spring (Chapter 6).
- ☐ Worn or loose engine or transmission mountings (Chapter 2A)
- ☐ Clutch disc hub or transmission input shaft splines worn (Chapter 6)

Noise when depressing or releasing clutch pedal

- ☐ Faulty clutch release/slave cylinder (Chapter 6)
- ☐ Worn or dry clutch pedal bushes (Chapter 6)
- ☐ Faulty pressure plate assembly (Chapter 6)
- ☐ Pressure plate diaphragm spring broken (Chapter 6)
- ☐ Broken clutch disc cushioning springs (Chapter 6)

Transmission

Noisy in neutral with engine running

- ☐ Lack of oil (Chapter 7)
- ☐ Input shaft bearings worn (noise apparent with clutch pedal released, but not when depressed) (Chapter 7)*
- ☐ Clutch release/slave cylinder faulty (noise apparent with clutch pedal depressed, possibly less when released) (Chapter 6)

Noisy in one particular gear

- ☐ Worn, damaged or chipped gear teeth (Chapter 7)*

Difficulty engaging gears

- ☐ Clutch fault (Chapter 6)
- ☐ Worn, damaged, or poorly-adjusted gearchange (Chapter 7)
- ☐ Lack of oil (Chapter 7)
- ☐ Worn synchroniser units (Chapter 7)*

Jumps out of gear

- ☐ Worn, damaged, or poorly-adjusted gearchange (Chapter 7)
- ☐ Worn synchroniser units (Chapter 7)*
- ☐ Worn selector forks (Chapter 7)*

Vibration

- ☐ Lack of oil (Chapter 7)
- ☐ Worn bearings (Chapter 7)*

Lubricant leaks

- ☐ Leaking driveshaft or selector shaft oil seal (Chapter 7)
- ☐ Leaking housing joint (Chapter 7)*
- ☐ Leaking input shaft oil seal (Chapter 7)*

* Although the corrective action necessary to remedy the symptoms described is beyond the scope of the home mechanic, the above information should be helpful in isolating the cause of the condition, so that the owner can communicate clearly with a professional mechanic.

Propeller shaft

Vibration when accelerating or decelerating

- ☐ Propeller shaft out of balance or incorrectly fitted (Chapter 8)
- ☐ Propeller shaft flange bolts loose (Chapter 8)
- ☐ Excessive wear in universal joints (Chapter 8)
- ☐ Excessive wear in centre bearings (Chapter 8)

Noise (grinding or high-pitched squeak) when moving slowly

- ☐ Excessive wear in universal joints (Chapter 8)
- ☐ Excessive wear in centre bearings (Chapter 8)

Noise (knocking or clicking) when accelerating or decelerating

- ☐ Propeller shaft flange bolts loose (Chapter 8)
- ☐ Excessive wear in universal joints (Chapter 8)
- ☐ Excessive wear in centre bearings (Chapter 8)

Rear axle

Roughness or rumble from the rear of the vehicle (perhaps less with the handbrake slightly applied)

- ☐ Rear hub bearings worn (Chapter 8)
- ☐ Differential pinion flange bolts loose (Chapter 8)
- ☐ Loose rear spring U-bolts (Chapter 10)
- ☐ Roadwheel nuts loose (Chapter 1 and 10)

Lubricant leaks

- ☐ Leaking oil seal (Chapter 8)
- ☐ Leaking differential housing cover joint (Chapter 8)

Braking system

Note: *Before assuming that a brake problem exists, make sure that the tyres are in good condition and correctly inflated, that the front wheel alignment is correct, and that the vehicle is not loaded with weight in an unequal manner. Apart from checking the condition of all pipe and hose connections, any faults occurring on the anti-lock braking system should be referred to a Mercedes-Benz dealer for diagnosis.*

Vehicle pulls to one side under braking

- ☐ Worn, defective, damaged or contaminated brake pads/shoes on one side (Chapter 9)
- ☐ Seized or partially-seized brake caliper/wheel cylinder piston (Chapter 9)
- ☐ A mixture of brake pad/shoe lining materials fitted between sides (Chapter 9)
- ☐ Brake caliper mounting bolts loose (Chapter 9)
- ☐ Worn or damaged steering or suspension components (Chapter 10)

Noise (grinding or high-pitched squeal) when brakes applied

- ☐ Brake pad/shoe friction lining material worn down to wear sensor or metal backing (Chapter 9)
- ☐ Excessive corrosion of brake disc/drum (may be apparent after the vehicle has been standing for some time (Chapter 9)
- ☐ Foreign object (stone chipping, etc) trapped between brake disc and shield

Excessive brake pedal travel

- ☐ Faulty master cylinder (Chapter 9)
- ☐ Air in hydraulic system (Chapter 9)
- ☐ Faulty vacuum servo unit (Chapter 9)
- ☐ Faulty vacuum pump (Chapter 9)
- ☐ Disconnected, damaged or insecure brake servo vacuum hose (Chapter 9)

Brake pedal feels spongy when depressed

- ☐ Air in hydraulic system (Chapter 9)
- ☐ Deteriorated flexible rubber brake hoses (Chapter 1)
- ☐ Master cylinder mounting nuts loose (Chapter 9)
- ☐ Faulty master cylinder (Chapter 9)

Excessive brake pedal effort required stopping vehicle

- ☐ Faulty vacuum servo unit (Chapter 9)
- ☐ Faulty vacuum pump (Chapter 9)
- ☐ Disconnected, damaged or insecure brake servo vacuum hose (Chapter 1)
- ☐ Primary or secondary hydraulic circuit failure (Chapter 9)
- ☐ Seized brake caliper/wheel cylinder piston (Chapter 9)
- ☐ Brake pads/shoes incorrectly fitted (Chapter 9)
- ☐ Incorrect grade of brake pads/shoes fitted (Chapter 9)
- ☐ Brake pad/shoe linings contaminated (Chapter 9)

Judder felt through brake pedal or steering wheel when braking

Note: *Under heavy braking on models equipped with ABS, vibration may be felt through the brake pedal. This is a normal feature of ABS operation, and does not constitute a fault.*

- ☐ Excessive run-out or distortion of discs/drums (Chapter 9)
- ☐ Brake pad/shoe linings worn (Chapter 9)
- ☐ Brake caliper mounting bolts loose (Chapter 9)
- ☐ Wear in suspension or steering components or mountings (Chapter 1)
- ☐ Front wheels out of balance (see *Weekly checks*)

Brakes binding

- ☐ Seized brake caliper/wheel cylinder piston (Chapter 9)
- ☐ Faulty master cylinder (Chapter 9)

Rear wheels locking under normal braking

- ☐ Rear brake pads contaminated or damaged (Chapter 9)
- ☐ Rear brake disc warped (Chapter 9)

Suspension and steering

Note: *Before diagnosing suspension or steering faults, be sure that the trouble is not due to incorrect tyre pressures, mixtures of tyre types, or binding brakes.*

Vehicle pulls to one side

- ☐ Defective tyre *(see Weekly checks)*
- ☐ Excessive wear in suspension or steering components (Chapter 1)
- ☐ Incorrect front wheel alignment (Chapter 10)
- ☐ Accident damage to steering or suspension components

Wheel wobble and vibration

- ☐ Front wheels out of balance (vibration felt mainly through the steering wheel) *(see Weekly checks)*
- ☐ Rear wheels out of balance (vibration felt throughout the vehicle) *(see Weekly checks)*
- ☐ Roadwheels damaged or distorted *(see Weekly checks)*
- ☐ Faulty or damaged tyre *(see Weekly checks)*
- ☐ Worn steering or suspension joints, bushes or components (Chapter 1)
- ☐ Wheel nuts loose (Chapter 1)

Excessive pitching and/or rolling around corners, or during braking

- ☐ Defective shock absorbers (Chapter 10)
- ☐ Broken or weak spring and/or suspension component (Chapter 10)
- ☐ Worn or damaged anti-roll bar or mountings (Chapter 10)

Wandering or general instability

- ☐ Incorrect front wheel alignment (Chapter 1)
- ☐ Worn steering or suspension joints, bushes or components (Chapter 10)
- ☐ Roadwheels out of balance *(see Weekly checks)*
- ☐ Faulty or damaged tyre *(see Weekly checks)*
- ☐ Wheel nuts loose (Chapter 1)
- ☐ Defective shock absorbers (Chapter 10)
- ☐ Power steering system fault (Chapter 10)

Excessively-stiff steering

- ☐ Seized steering linkage balljoint or suspension balljoint (Chapter 1)
- ☐ Incorrect front wheel alignment (Chapter 10)
- ☐ Steering rack damaged (Chapter 10)
- ☐ Power steering system fault (Chapter 10)

Excessive play in steering

- ☐ Worn steering column/intermediate shaft joints (Chapter 1)
- ☐ Worn track rod balljoints (Chapter 10)
- ☐ Worn steering rack (Chapter 10)
- ☐ Worn steering or suspension joints, bushes or components (Chapter 10)

Lack of power assistance

- ☐ Power steering system fault (Chapter 10)
- ☐ Faulty steering rack (Chapter 10)

Tyre wear excessive

Tyres worn on inside or outside edges

- ☐ Tyres underinflated (wear on both edges) *(see Weekly checks)*
- ☐ Incorrect camber or castor angles (wear on one edge only) (Chapter 10)
- ☐ Worn steering or suspension joints, bushes or components (Chapter 10)
- ☐ Excessively-hard cornering or braking
- ☐ Accident damage

Tyre treads exhibit feathered edges

- ☐ Incorrect toe-setting (Chapter 10)

Tyres worn in centre of tread

- ☐ Tyres overinflated *(see Weekly checks)*

Tyres worn on inside and outside edges

- ☐ Tyres underinflated *(see Weekly checks)*

Tyres worn unevenly

- ☐ Tyres/wheels out of balance *(see Weekly checks)*
- ☐ Excessive wheel or tyre run-out
- ☐ Worn shock absorbers (Chapter 10)
- ☐ Faulty tyre *(see Weekly checks)*

Electrical system

Note: *For problems associated with the starting system, refer to the faults listed under 'Engine' earlier in this Section.*

Battery will not hold a charge for more than a few days

- ☐ Battery defective internally (Chapter 5)
- ☐ Battery terminal connections loose or corroded *(see Weekly checks)*
- ☐ Auxiliary drivebelt worn or faulty automatic adjuster (Chapter 1)
- ☐ Alternator not charging at correct output (Chapter 5)
- ☐ Alternator or voltage regulator faulty (Chapter 5)
- ☐ Short-circuit causing continual battery drain

Ignition/no-charge warning light remains illuminated with engine running

- ☐ Auxiliary drivebelt broken, worn, or faulty automatic adjuster (Chapter 1)

- ☐ Internal fault in alternator or voltage regulator (Chapter 5)
- ☐ Broken, disconnected, or loose wiring in charging circuit (Chapter 5)

Ignition/no-charge warning light fails to come on

- ☐ Warning light bulb blown (Chapter 12)
- ☐ Broken, disconnected, or loose wiring in warning light circuit (Chapter 12)
- ☐ Alternator faulty (Chapter 5)

Lights inoperative

- ☐ Bulb blown (Chapter 12)
- ☐ Corrosion of bulb or bulbholder contacts (Chapter 12)
- ☐ Blown fuse (Chapter 12)
- ☐ Faulty relay (Chapter 12)
- ☐ Broken, loose, or disconnected wiring (Chapter 12)
- ☐ Faulty switch (Chapter 12)

Electrical system (continued)

Instrument readings inaccurate or erratic

Fuel or temperature gauges give no reading

- [ ] Faulty gauge sender unit (Chapter 4A)
- [ ] Wiring open-circuit (Chapter 12)
- [ ] Faulty gauge (Chapter 12)

Fuel or temperature gauges give continuous maximum reading

- [ ] Faulty gauge sender unit (Chapter 4A)
- [ ] Wiring short-circuit (Chapter 12)
- [ ] Faulty gauge (Chapter 12)

Horn inoperative, or unsatisfactory in operation

Horn operates all the time

- [ ] Horn push either earthed or stuck down (Chapter 10)
- [ ] Horn cable-to-horn push earthed (Chapter 12)

Horn fails to operate

- [ ] Blown fuse (Chapter 12)
- [ ] Cable or connections loose, broken or disconnected (Chapter 12)
- [ ] Faulty horn (Chapter 12)

Horn emits intermittent or unsatisfactory sound

- [ ] Cable connections loose (Chapter 12)
- [ ] Horn mountings loose (Chapter 12)
- [ ] Faulty horn (Chapter 12)

Windscreen wipers inoperative, or unsatisfactory in operation

Wipers fail to operate, or operate very slowly

- [ ] Wiper blades stuck to screen, or linkage seized or binding (Chapter 12)
- [ ] Blown fuse (Chapter 12)
- [ ] Battery discharged (Chapter 5)
- [ ] Cable or connections loose, broken or disconnected (Chapter 12)
- [ ] Faulty relay (Chapter 12)
- [ ] Faulty wiper motor (Chapter 12)

Wiper blades sweep over too large or too small an area of the glass

- [ ] Wiper blades incorrectly fitted, or wrong size used (see Weekly checks)
- [ ] Wiper arms incorrectly positioned on spindles (Chapter 12)
- [ ] Excessive wear of wiper linkage (Chapter 12)
- [ ] Wiper motor or linkage mountings loose or insecure (Chapter 12)

Wiper blades fail to clean the glass effectively

- [ ] Wiper blade rubbers dirty, worn or perished (see Weekly checks)
- [ ] Wiper blades incorrectly fitted, or wrong size used (see Weekly checks)
- [ ] Wiper arm tension springs broken, or arm pivots seized (Chapter 12)
- [ ] Insufficient windscreen washer additive to adequately remove road film (see Weekly checks)

Windscreen washers inoperative, or unsatisfactory in operation

One or more washer jets inoperative

- [ ] Blocked washer jet
- [ ] Disconnected, kinked or restricted fluid hose (Chapter 12)
- [ ] Insufficient fluid in washer reservoir (see Weekly checks)

Washer pump fails to operate

- [ ] Broken or disconnected wiring or connections (Chapter 12)
- [ ] Blown fuse (Chapter 12)
- [ ] Faulty washer switch (Chapter 12)
- [ ] Faulty washer pump (Chapter 12)

Washer pump runs for some time before fluid is emitted from jets

- [ ] Faulty one-way valve in fluid supply hose (Chapter 12)

Electric windows inoperative, or unsatisfactory in operation

Window glass will only move in one direction

- [ ] Faulty switch (Chapter 12)

Window glass slow to move

- [ ] Battery discharged (Chapter 5)
- [ ] Regulator seized or damaged, or in need of lubrication (Chapter 11)
- [ ] Door internal components or trim fouling regulator (Chapter 11)
- [ ] Faulty motor (Chapter 11)

Window glass fails to move

- [ ] Blown fuse (Chapter 12)
- [ ] Faulty relay (Chapter 12)
- [ ] Broken or disconnected wiring or connections (Chapter 12)
- [ ] Faulty motor (Chapter 11)

Central locking system inoperative, or unsatisfactory in operation

Complete system failure

- [ ] Remote handset battery discharged, where applicable
- [ ] Blown fuse (Chapter 12)
- [ ] Faulty relay (Chapter 12)
- [ ] Broken or disconnected wiring or connections (Chapter 12)
- [ ] Faulty motor (Chapter 11)

Latch locks but will not unlock, or unlocks but will not lock

- [ ] Remote handset battery discharged, where applicable
- [ ] Faulty master switch (Chapter 12)
- [ ] Broken or disconnected latch operating rods or levers (Chapter 11)
- [ ] Faulty relay (Chapter 12)
- [ ] Faulty motor (Chapter 11)

One solenoid/motor fails to operate

- [ ] Broken or disconnected wiring or connections (Chapter 12)
- [ ] Faulty operating assembly (Chapter 11)
- [ ] Broken, binding or disconnected latch operating rods or levers (Chapter 11)
- [ ] Fault in door latch (Chapter 11)

A

ABS (Anti-lock brake system) A system, usually electronically controlled, that senses incipient wheel lockup during braking and relieves hydraulic pressure at wheels that are about to skid.

Air bag An inflatable bag hidden in the steering wheel (driver's side) or the dash or glovebox (passenger side). In a head-on collision, the bags inflate, preventing the driver and front passenger from being thrown forward into the steering wheel or windscreen.

Air cleaner A metal or plastic housing, containing a filter element, which removes dust and dirt from the air being drawn into the engine.

Air filter element The actual filter in an air cleaner system, usually manufactured from pleated paper and requiring renewal at regular intervals.

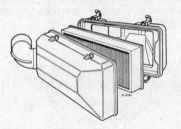

Air filter

Allen key A hexagonal wrench which fits into a recessed hexagonal hole.

Alligator clip A long-nosed spring-loaded metal clip with meshing teeth. Used to make temporary electrical connections.

Alternator A component in the electrical system which converts mechanical energy from a drivebelt into electrical energy to charge the battery and to operate the starting system, ignition system and electrical accessories.

Alternator (exploded view)

Ampere (amp) A unit of measurement for the flow of electric current. One amp is the amount of current produced by one volt acting through a resistance of one ohm.

Anaerobic sealer A substance used to prevent bolts and screws from loosening. Anaerobic means that it does not require oxygen for activation. The Loctite brand is widely used.

Antifreeze A substance (usually ethylene glycol) mixed with water, and added to a vehicle's cooling system, to prevent freezing of the coolant in winter. Antifreeze also contains chemicals to inhibit corrosion and the formation of rust and other deposits that

would tend to clog the radiator and coolant passages and reduce cooling efficiency.

Anti-seize compound A coating that reduces the risk of seizing on fasteners that are subjected to high temperatures, such as exhaust manifold bolts and nuts.

Anti-seize compound

Asbestos A natural fibrous mineral with great heat resistance, commonly used in the composition of brake friction materials. Asbestos is a health hazard and the dust created by brake systems should never be inhaled or ingested.

Axle A shaft on which a wheel revolves, or which revolves with a wheel. Also, a solid beam that connects the two wheels at one end of the vehicle. An axle which also transmits power to the wheels is known as a live axle.

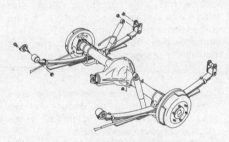

Axle assembly

Axleshaft A single rotating shaft, on either side of the differential, which delivers power from the final drive assembly to the drive wheels. Also called a driveshaft or a halfshaft.

B

Ball bearing An anti-friction bearing consisting of a hardened inner and outer race with hardened steel balls between two races.

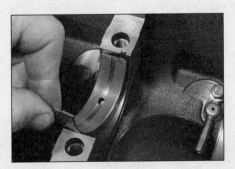

Bearing

Bearing The curved surface on a shaft or in a bore, or the part assembled into either, that permits relative motion between them with minimum wear and friction.

Big-end bearing The bearing in the end of the connecting rod that's attached to the crankshaft.

Bleed nipple A valve on a brake wheel cylinder, caliper or other hydraulic component that is opened to purge the hydraulic system of air. Also called a bleed screw.

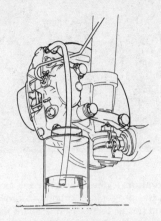

Brake bleeding

Brake bleeding Procedure for removing air from lines of a hydraulic brake system.

Brake disc The component of a disc brake that rotates with the wheels.

Brake drum The component of a drum brake that rotates with the wheels.

Brake linings The friction material which contacts the brake disc or drum to retard the vehicle's speed. The linings are bonded or riveted to the brake pads or shoes.

Brake pads The replaceable friction pads that pinch the brake disc when the brakes are applied. Brake pads consist of a friction material bonded or riveted to a rigid backing plate.

Brake shoe The crescent-shaped carrier to which the brake linings are mounted and which forces the lining against the rotating drum during braking.

Braking systems For more information on braking systems, consult the *Haynes Automotive Brake Manual*.

Breaker bar A long socket wrench handle providing greater leverage.

Bulkhead The insulated partition between the engine and the passenger compartment.

C

Caliper The non-rotating part of a disc-brake assembly that straddles the disc and carries the brake pads. The caliper also contains the hydraulic components that cause the pads to pinch the disc when the brakes are applied. A caliper is also a measuring tool that can be set to measure inside or outside dimensions of an object.

Camshaft A rotating shaft on which a series of cam lobes operate the valve mechanisms. The camshaft may be driven by gears, by sprockets and chain or by sprockets and a belt.

Canister A container in an evaporative emission control system; contains activated charcoal granules to trap vapours from the fuel system.

Canister

Carburettor A device which mixes fuel with air in the proper proportions to provide a desired power output from a spark ignition internal combustion engine.

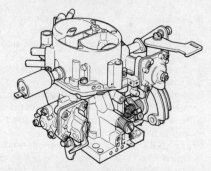

Carburettor

Castellated Resembling the parapets along the top of a castle wall. For example, a castellated balljoint stud nut.

Castellated nut

Castor In wheel alignment, the backward or forward tilt of the steering axis. Castor is positive when the steering axis is inclined rearward at the top.

Catalytic converter A silencer-like device in the exhaust system which converts certain pollutants in the exhaust gases into less harmful substances.

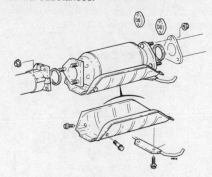

Catalytic converter

Circlip A ring-shaped clip used to prevent endwise movement of cylindrical parts and shafts. An internal circlip is installed in a groove in a housing; an external circlip fits into a groove on the outside of a cylindrical piece such as a shaft.

Clearance The amount of space between two parts. For example, between a piston and a cylinder, between a bearing and a journal, etc.

Coil spring A spiral of elastic steel found in various sizes throughout a vehicle, for example as a springing medium in the suspension and in the valve train.

Compression Reduction in volume, and increase in pressure and temperature, of a gas, caused by squeezing it into a smaller space.

Compression ratio The relationship between cylinder volume when the piston is at top dead centre and cylinder volume when the piston is at bottom dead centre.

Constant velocity (CV) joint A type of universal joint that cancels out vibrations caused by driving power being transmitted through an angle.

Core plug A disc or cup-shaped metal device inserted in a hole in a casting through which core was removed when the casting was formed. Also known as a freeze plug or expansion plug.

Crankcase The lower part of the engine block in which the crankshaft rotates.

Crankshaft The main rotating member, or shaft, running the length of the crankcase, with offset "throws" to which the connecting rods are attached.

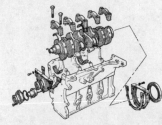

Crankshaft assembly

Crocodile clip See Alligator clip

D

Diagnostic code Code numbers obtained by accessing the diagnostic mode of an engine management computer. This code can be used to determine the area in the system where a malfunction may be located.

Disc brake A brake design incorporating a rotating disc onto which brake pads are squeezed. The resulting friction converts the energy of a moving vehicle into heat.

Double-overhead cam (DOHC) An engine that uses two overhead camshafts, usually one for the intake valves and one for the exhaust valves.

Drivebelt(s) The belt(s) used to drive accessories such as the alternator, water pump, power steering pump, air conditioning compressor, etc. off the crankshaft pulley.

Accessory drivebelts

Driveshaft Any shaft used to transmit motion. Commonly used when referring to the axleshafts on a front wheel drive vehicle.

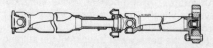

Driveshaft

Drum brake A type of brake using a drum-shaped metal cylinder attached to the inner surface of the wheel. When the brake pedal is pressed, curved brake shoes with friction linings press against the inside of the drum to slow or stop the vehicle.

Drum brake assembly

E

EGR valve A valve used to introduce exhaust gases into the intake air stream.

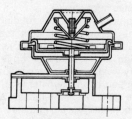

EGR valve

Electronic control unit (ECU) A computer which controls (for instance) ignition and fuel injection systems, or an anti-lock braking system. For more information refer to the *Haynes Automotive Electrical and Electronic Systems Manual.*

Electronic Fuel Injection (EFI) A computer controlled fuel system that distributes fuel through an injector located in each intake port of the engine.

Emergency brake A braking system, independent of the main hydraulic system, that can be used to slow or stop the vehicle if the primary brakes fail, or to hold the vehicle stationary even though the brake pedal isn't depressed. It usually consists of a hand lever that actuates either front or rear brakes mechanically through a series of cables and linkages. Also known as a handbrake or parking brake.

Endfloat The amount of lengthwise movement between two parts. As applied to a crankshaft, the distance that the crankshaft can move forward and back in the cylinder block.

Engine management system (EMS) A computer controlled system which manages the fuel injection and the ignition systems in an integrated fashion.

Exhaust manifold A part with several passages through which exhaust gases leave the engine combustion chambers and enter the exhaust pipe.

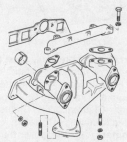

Exhaust manifold

F

Fan clutch A viscous (fluid) drive coupling device which permits variable engine fan speeds in relation to engine speeds.

Feeler blade A thin strip or blade of hardened steel, ground to an exact thickness, used to check or measure clearances between parts.

Feeler blade

Firing order The order in which the engine cylinders fire, or deliver their power strokes, beginning with the number one cylinder.

Flywheel A heavy spinning wheel in which energy is absorbed and stored by means of momentum. On cars, the flywheel is attached to the crankshaft to smooth out firing impulses.

Free play The amount of travel before any action takes place. The "looseness" in a linkage, or an assembly of parts, between the initial application of force and actual movement. For example, the distance the brake pedal moves before the pistons in the master cylinder are actuated.

Fuse An electrical device which protects a circuit against accidental overload. The typical fuse contains a soft piece of metal which is calibrated to melt at a predetermined current flow (expressed as amps) and break the circuit.

Fusible link A circuit protection device consisting of a conductor surrounded by heat-resistant insulation. The conductor is smaller than the wire it protects, so it acts as the weakest link in the circuit. Unlike a blown fuse, a failed fusible link must frequently be cut from the wire for replacement.

G

Gap The distance the spark must travel in jumping from the centre electrode to the side

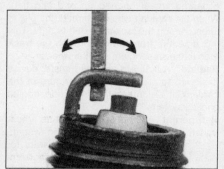

Adjusting spark plug gap

electrode in a spark plug. Also refers to the spacing between the points in a contact breaker assembly in a conventional points-type ignition, or to the distance between the reluctor or rotor and the pickup coil in an electronic ignition.

Gasket Any thin, soft material - usually cork, cardboard, asbestos or soft metal - installed between two metal surfaces to ensure a good seal. For instance, the cylinder head gasket seals the joint between the block and the cylinder head.

Gasket

Gauge An instrument panel display used to monitor engine conditions. A gauge with a movable pointer on a dial or a fixed scale is an analogue gauge. A gauge with a numerical readout is called a digital gauge.

H

Halfshaft A rotating shaft that transmits power from the final drive unit to a drive wheel, usually when referring to a live rear axle.

Harmonic balancer A device designed to reduce torsion or twisting vibration in the crankshaft. May be incorporated in the crankshaft pulley. Also known as a vibration damper.

Hone An abrasive tool for correcting small irregularities or differences in diameter in an engine cylinder, brake cylinder, etc.

Hydraulic tappet A tappet that utilises hydraulic pressure from the engine's lubrication system to maintain zero clearance (constant contact with both camshaft and valve stem). Automatically adjusts to variation in valve stem length. Hydraulic tappets also reduce valve noise.

I

Ignition timing The moment at which the spark plug fires, usually expressed in the number of crankshaft degrees before the piston reaches the top of its stroke.

Inlet manifold A tube or housing with passages through which flows the air-fuel mixture (carburettor vehicles and vehicles with throttle body injection) or air only (port fuel-injected vehicles) to the port openings in the cylinder head.

J

Jump start Starting the engine of a vehicle with a discharged or weak battery by attaching jump leads from the weak battery to a charged or helper battery.

L

Load Sensing Proportioning Valve (LSPV) A brake hydraulic system control valve that works like a proportioning valve, but also takes into consideration the amount of weight carried by the rear axle.

Locknut A nut used to lock an adjustment nut, or other threaded component, in place. For example, a locknut is employed to keep the adjusting nut on the rocker arm in position.

Lockwasher A form of washer designed to prevent an attaching nut from working loose.

M

MacPherson strut A type of front suspension system devised by Earle MacPherson at Ford of England. In its original form, a simple lateral link with the anti-roll bar creates the lower control arm. A long strut - an integral coil spring and shock absorber - is mounted between the body and the steering knuckle. Many modern so-called MacPherson strut systems use a conventional lower A-arm and don't rely on the anti-roll bar for location.

Multimeter An electrical test instrument with the capability to measure voltage, current and resistance.

N

NOx Oxides of Nitrogen. A common toxic pollutant emitted by petrol and diesel engines at higher temperatures.

O

Ohm The unit of electrical resistance. One volt applied to a resistance of one ohm will produce a current of one amp.

Ohmmeter An instrument for measuring electrical resistance.

O-ring A type of sealing ring made of a special rubber-like material; in use, the O-ring is compressed into a groove to provide the sealing action.

O-ring

Overhead cam (ohc) engine An engine with the camshaft(s) located on top of the cylinder head(s).

Overhead valve (ohv) engine An engine with the valves located in the cylinder head, but with the camshaft located in the engine block.

Oxygen sensor A device installed in the engine exhaust manifold, which senses the oxygen content in the exhaust and converts this information into an electric current. Also called a Lambda sensor.

P

Phillips screw A type of screw head having a cross instead of a slot for a corresponding type of screwdriver.

Plastigage A thin strip of plastic thread, available in different sizes, used for measuring clearances. For example, a strip of Plastigage is laid across a bearing journal. The parts are assembled and dismantled; the width of the crushed strip indicates the clearance between journal and bearing.

Plastigage

Propeller shaft The long hollow tube with universal joints at both ends that carries power from the transmission to the differential on front-engined rear wheel drive vehicles.

Proportioning valve A hydraulic control valve which limits the amount of pressure to the rear brakes during panic stops to prevent wheel lock-up.

R

Rack-and-pinion steering A steering system with a pinion gear on the end of the steering shaft that mates with a rack (think of a geared wheel opened up and laid flat). When the steering wheel is turned, the pinion turns, moving the rack to the left or right. This movement is transmitted through the track rods to the steering arms at the wheels.

Radiator A liquid-to-air heat transfer device designed to reduce the temperature of the coolant in an internal combustion engine cooling system.

Refrigerant Any substance used as a heat transfer agent in an air-conditioning system. R-12 has been the principle refrigerant for many years; recently, however, manufacturers have begun using R-134a, a non-CFC substance that is considered less harmful to the ozone in the upper atmosphere.

Rocker arm A lever arm that rocks on a shaft or pivots on a stud. In an overhead valve engine, the rocker arm converts the upward movement of the pushrod into a downward movement to open a valve.

Rotor In a distributor, the rotating device inside the cap that connects the centre electrode and the outer terminals as it turns, distributing the high voltage from the coil secondary winding to the proper spark plug. Also, that part of an alternator which rotates inside the stator. Also, the rotating assembly of a turbocharger, including the compressor wheel, shaft and turbine wheel.

Runout The amount of wobble (in-and-out movement) of a gear or wheel as it's rotated. The amount a shaft rotates "out-of-true." The out-of-round condition of a rotating part.

S

Sealant A liquid or paste used to prevent leakage at a joint. Sometimes used in conjunction with a gasket.

Sealed beam lamp An older headlight design which integrates the reflector, lens and filaments into a hermetically-sealed one-piece unit. When a filament burns out or the lens cracks, the entire unit is simply replaced.

Serpentine drivebelt A single, long, wide accessory drivebelt that's used on some newer vehicles to drive all the accessories, instead of a series of smaller, shorter belts. Serpentine drivebelts are usually tensioned by an automatic tensioner.

Serpentine drivebelt

Shim Thin spacer, commonly used to adjust the clearance or relative positions between two parts. For example, shims inserted into or under bucket tappets control valve clearances. Clearance is adjusted by changing the thickness of the shim.

Slide hammer A special puller that screws into or hooks onto a component such as a shaft or bearing; a heavy sliding handle on the shaft bottoms against the end of the shaft to knock the component free.

Sprocket A tooth or projection on the periphery of a wheel, shaped to engage with a chain or drivebelt. Commonly used to refer to the sprocket wheel itself.

Starter inhibitor switch On vehicles with an automatic transmission, a switch that prevents starting if the vehicle is not in Neutral or Park.

Strut See MacPherson strut.

T

Tappet A cylindrical component which transmits motion from the cam to the valve stem, either directly or via a pushrod and rocker arm. Also called a cam follower.

Thermostat A heat-controlled valve that regulates the flow of coolant between the cylinder block and the radiator, so maintaining optimum engine operating temperature. A thermostat is also used in some air cleaners in which the temperature is regulated.

Thrust bearing The bearing in the clutch assembly that is moved in to the release levers by clutch pedal action to disengage the clutch. Also referred to as a release bearing.

Timing belt A toothed belt which drives the camshaft. Serious engine damage may result if it breaks in service.

Timing chain A chain which drives the camshaft.

Toe-in The amount the front wheels are closer together at the front than at the rear. On rear wheel drive vehicles, a slight amount of toe-in is usually specified to keep the front wheels running parallel on the road by offsetting other forces that tend to spread the wheels apart.

Toe-out The amount the front wheels are closer together at the rear than at the front. On front wheel drive vehicles, a slight amount of toe-out is usually specified.

Tools For full information on choosing and using tools, refer to the *Haynes Automotive Tools Manual*.

Tracer A stripe of a second colour applied to a wire insulator to distinguish that wire from another one with the same colour insulator.

Tune-up A process of accurate and careful adjustments and parts replacement to obtain the best possible engine performance.

Turbocharger A centrifugal device, driven by exhaust gases, that pressurises the intake air. Normally used to increase the power output from a given engine displacement, but can also be used primarily to reduce exhaust emissions (as on VW's "Umwelt" Diesel engine).

U

Universal joint or U-joint A double-pivoted connection for transmitting power from a driving to a driven shaft through an angle. A U-joint consists of two Y-shaped yokes and a cross-shaped member called the spider.

V

Valve A device through which the flow of liquid, gas, vacuum, or loose material in bulk may be started, stopped, or regulated by a movable part that opens, shuts, or partially obstructs one or more ports or passageways. A valve is also the movable part of such a device.

Valve clearance The clearance between the valve tip (the end of the valve stem) and the rocker arm or tappet. The valve clearance is measured when the valve is closed.

Vernier caliper A precision measuring instrument that measures inside and outside dimensions. Not quite as accurate as a micrometer, but more convenient.

Viscosity The thickness of a liquid or its resistance to flow.

Volt A unit for expressing electrical "pressure" in a circuit. One volt that will produce a current of one ampere through a resistance of one ohm.

W

Welding Various processes used to join metal items by heating the areas to be joined to a molten state and fusing them together. For more information refer to the *Haynes Automotive Welding Manual*.

Wiring diagram A drawing portraying the components and wires in a vehicle's electrical system, using standardised symbols. For more information refer to the *Haynes Automotive Electrical and Electronic Systems Manual*.

Note: *References throughout this index are in the form* "**Chapter number**" • "**Page number**". *So, for example, 2C•15 refers to page 15 of Chapter 2C.*

*Note: References throughout this index are in the form "***Chapter number***" • "***Page number***". So, for example, 2C•15 refers to page 15 of Chapter 2C.*

Note: *References throughout this index are in the form* "**Chapter number**" • "**Page number**". *So, for example, 2C•15 refers to page 15 of Chapter 2C.*

Note: *References throughout this index are in the form* **"Chapter number"** • **"Page number"**. *So, for example, 2C•15 refers to page 15 of Chapter 2C.*

Preserving Our Motoring Heritage

The Model J Duesenberg Derham Tourster. Only eight of these magnificent cars were ever built – this is the only example to be found outside the United States of America

Almost every car you've ever loved, loathed or desired is gathered under one roof at the Haynes Motor Museum. Over 300 immaculately presented cars and motorbikes represent every aspect of our motoring heritage, from elegant reminders of bygone days, such as the superb Model J Duesenberg to curiosities like the bug-eyed BMW Isetta. There are also many old friends and flames. Perhaps you remember the 1959 Ford Popular that you did your courting in? The magnificent 'Red Collection' is a spectacle of classic sports cars including AC, Alfa Romeo, Austin Healey, Ferrari, Lamborghini, Maserati, MG, Riley, Porsche and Triumph.

A Perfect Day Out

Each and every vehicle at the Haynes Motor Museum has played its part in the history and culture of Motoring. Today, they make a wonderful spectacle and a great day out for all the family. Bring the kids, bring Mum and Dad, but above all bring your camera to capture those golden memories for ever. You will also find an impressive array of motoring memorabilia, a comfortable 70 seat video cinema and one of the most extensive transport book shops in Britain. The Pit Stop Cafe serves everything from a cup of tea to wholesome, home-made meals or, if you prefer, you can enjoy the large picnic area nestled in the beautiful rural surroundings of Somerset.

John Haynes O.B.E., Founder and Chairman of the museum at the wheel of a Haynes Light 12.

Graham Hill's Lola Cosworth Formula 1 car next to a 1934 Riley Sports.

The Museum is situated on the A359 Yeovil to Frome road at Sparkford, just off the A303 in Somerset. It is about 40 miles south of Bristol, and 25 minutes drive from the M5 intersection at Taunton.

Open 9.30am - 5.30pm (10.00am - 4.00pm Winter) 7 days a week, *except Christmas Day, Boxing Day and New Years Day*

Special rates available for schools, coach parties and outings Charitable Trust No. 292048